Addendum

Acknowledgements

We wanted this text to be a truly valuable and useful teaching tool, and therefore polled our colleagues working in the area of Indigenous literatures to determine which essays they return to again and again in their teaching. We would like to thank the following esteemed scholars for their input: Kim Anderson, Jennifer Andrews, Jesse Archibald-Barber, Kristina (Fagan) Bidwell, Daniel Coleman, Jonathan Dewar, Renate Eigenbrod, Jo-Ann Episkenew, Margery Fee, Maurizio Gatti, Susan Gingell, Sarah Henzi, Kate Higginson, Renée Hulan, Daniel Heath Justice, Michele Lacombe, Emma LaRocque, Keavy Martin, Sophie McCall, Sam McKegney, Rick Monture, Daniel David Moses, Deanna Reder, Niigaan-wewidam Sinclair, and Isabelle St. Amand. We are also grateful to the Ojibway artist Barry Ace for permission to use his art on the cover, and to Broadview Press for their support.

Miigwech to all.

INTRODUCTION TO INDIGENOUS LITERARY CRITICISM IN CANADA

INTRODUCTION TO INDIGENOUS LITERARY CRITICISM IN CANADA

Edited by Heather Macfarlane
and Armand Garnet Ruffo

broadview press

BROADVIEW PRESS – www.broadviewpress.com
Peterborough, Ontario, Canada

Founded in 1985, Broadview Press remains a wholly independent publishing house. Broadview's focus is on academic publishing; our titles are accessible to university and college students as well as scholars and general readers. With over 600 titles in print, Broadview has become a leading international publisher in the humanities, with world-wide distribution. Broadview is committed to environmentally responsible publishing and fair business practices.

The interior of this book is printed on 100% recycled paper.

Library and Archives Canada Cataloguing in Publication

Library and Archives Canada Cataloguing in Publication

        Introduction to indigenous literary criticism in Canada / edited by Heather Macfarlane and Armand Garnet Ruffo.

Includes bibliographical references.
ISBN 978-1-55481-183-0 (paperback)

        1. Canadian literature—Indian authors—History and criticism. I. Macfarlane, Heather, 1968-, editor II. Ruffo, Armand Garnet, 1955-, editor

PS8089.5.I6I58 2015   C810.9'897   C2015-907031-7

Broadview Press handles its own distribution in North America
PO Box 1243, Peterborough, Ontario K9J 7H5, Canada
555 Riverwalk Parkway, Tonawanda, NY 14150, USA
Tel: (705) 743-8990; Fax: (705) 743-8353
email: customerservice@broadviewpress.com

Distribution is handled by Eurospan Group in the UK, Europe, Central Asia, Middle East, Africa, India, Southeast Asia, Central America, South America, and the Caribbean. Distribution is handled by Footprint Books in Australia and New Zealand.

Broadview Press acknowledges the financial support of the Government of Canada through the Canada Book Fund for our publishing activities.

Copy edited by Michel Pharand

Book design by Chris Rowat Design

PRINTED IN CANADA

This anthology is dedicated to the memory of Renate Eigenbrod, whose countless initiatives supporting and promoting Indigenous literatures and literary scholarship have had an enormous impact on the field in Canada. Miigwech Renate.

"...*those word drummers pound away and hurtle words into that english landscape...*"
—Marvin Francis

Contents

xi **Preface**
Opening a Window by Heather Macfarlane and Armand Garnet Ruffo

1 **E. Pauline Johnson, "A Strong Race Opinion: On the Indian Girl in Modern Fiction" (1892)**
gender ~ stereotypes ~ sovereignty/nationhood ~ appropriation of voice

7 **N. Scott Momaday, "The Man Made of Words" (1970)**
imagination ~ language ~ orality ~ spirituality ~ land

21 **Tomson Highway, "On Native Mythology" (1987)**
theatre ~ orality ~ language ~ imagination ~ spirituality/traditional knowledge

25 **Basil Johnston, "One Generation from Extinction" (1990)**
language ~ land ~ spirituality/traditional knowledge ~ orality

33 **Lenore Keeshig [Tobias], "Stop Stealing Native Stories" (1990)**
appropriation of voice ~ stereotypes ~ spirituality/traditional knowledge

37 **Thomas King, "Godzilla vs. Post-Colonial" (1990)**
post-colonialism ~ hybridity ~ stereotypes ~ imagination

47 **Emma LaRocque, "Preface or Here Are Our Voices—Who Will Hear?" (1990)**
colonialism ~ stereotypes ~ language ~ orality ~ appropriation of voice ~ "authenticity" ~ resistance ~ ethical scholarship

61 **Lee Maracle, "Oratory: Coming to Theory" (1992)**
orality ~ traditional knowledge/spirituality ~ ethical scholarship ~ language

67   **Kimberley Blaeser, "Native Literature: Seeking a Critical Centre" (1993)**
imagination ~ stereotypes ~ nationhood ~ colonization ~ ethical scholarship

77   **Bernard Assiniwi, "Je suis ce que je dis que je suis" / "I am what I say I am" (1993)**
imagination ~ "authenticity" ~ hybridity ~ nationhood

87   **Gail G. Valaskakis, "Parallel Voices: Indians and Others, Narratives of Cultural Struggle" (1993)**
stereotypes ~ appropriation of voice ~ gender ~ "authenticity"

101   **Willie Ermine, "Aboriginal Epistemology" (1995)**
land ~ spirituality/traditional knowledge ~ language ~ community ~ ethical scholarship

113   **Margery Fee, "Writing Orality: Interpreting Literature in English by Aboriginal Writers in North America, Australia and New Zealand" (1997)**
orality ~ nationhood ~ "authenticity"/hybridity ~ resistance ~ pan-Indigenous experience

133   **Armand Garnet Ruffo, "Why Native Literature?" (1997)**
appropriation of voice ~ spirituality/traditional knowledge ~ healing ~ land ~ stereotypes ~ community

145   **Jeannette Armstrong, "Land Speaking" (1998)**
land ~ language ~ imagination ~ spirituality/traditional knowledge ~ orality ~ nationhood ~ resistance and empowerment

161   **Kateri Akiwenzie-Damm, "Erotica, Indigenous Style" (2000)**
sexuality ~ gender ~ healing ~ pan-Indigenous experience ~ nationhood

169   **Neal McLeod, "Coming Home through Stories" (2001)**
diaspora ~ language ~ imagination ~ hybridity/"authenticity"

187   **Jo-Ann Episkenew, "Socially Responsible Criticism: Aboriginal Literature, Ideology, and the Literary Canon" (2002)**
stereotypes ~ ethical scholarship ~ nationhood ~ colonization

201 Renée Hulan, "'Everybody likes the Inuit': Inuit Revision and
Representations of the North" (2002)
*stereotypes ~ "authenticity" ~ appropriation of voice ~ gender ~ autobiography ~
nationhood*

221 Qwo-Li Driskill, "Stolen from Our Bodies: First Nations Two-Spirits/
Queers and the Journey to a Sovereign Erotic" (2004)
sexuality ~ two-spirits ~ violence ~ gender ~ erotica ~ healing ~ nationhood

235 Daniel David Moses, "The Trickster's Laugh: My Meeting with Tomson
and Lenore" (2004)
imagination ~ traditional knowledge/spirituality ~ resistance

241 Daniel Heath Justice, "The Necessity of Nationhood: Affirming the
Sovereignty of Indigenous National Literatures" (2005)
*nationhood ~ immigrants and indigenous peoples ~ traditional knowledge/
spirituality ~ hybridity ~ healing*

257 Sam McKegney, "Indigenous Writing and the Residential School Legacy:
A Public Interview with Basil Johnston" (2009)
residential schools ~ violence ~ healing ~ resistance

269 Keavy Martin, "Truth, Reconciliation and Amnesia: *Porcupines and
China Dolls* and the Canadian Conscience" (2009)
*healing ~ reconciliation ~ residential schools ~ colonialism/violence/racism ~
spirituality/traditional knowledge*

287 Kristina (Fagan) Bidwell, "Code-Switching Humour in Aboriginal
Literature" (2009)
language ~ humour ~ "authenticity" ~ resistance

309 Renate Eigenbrod, "A Necessary Inclusion: Native Literature in Native
Studies" (2010)
nationhood ~ ethical scholarship ~ orality/language

325 Permissions Acknowledgements

Preface

Opening a Window

Over the last twenty-five years literature by Indigenous writers has proliferated to such an extent that it is now difficult to imagine writing in Canada without it. Certainly Indigenous literature existed prior to this period, particularly in the form of orature and life writing, but never before have there been as many Indigenous authors writing at any one time in the history of Canada. The reasons for this are varied, and span time and history, but in hindsight we can see a convergence of the social and political that created the conditions necessary for these voices to emerge and claim their rightful place within Canada's literary culture. Along with this proliferation of creative writing has come a deluge of scholarly attention, and, since the early 1990s there has been no less than a steady production of critical work that has served to open the literature to analysis. One might even observe that the creative work itself and the critical writing around it have developed in tandem. Never before have scholars at the university level taken such an interest in Indigenous literary production, as exemplified in the number of Indigenous literature courses offered across the country—courses that in large part did not exist twenty-five years ago.

The idea of putting together this anthology of selected essays came about when we were discussing the Indigenous literature classes we were teaching at both the introductory and upper levels. Because in our case Indigenous literature was attached to the English Department, we found that the majority of students enrolling in our classes had little or no idea about Indigenous histories or cultures and had preconceived ideas on how to approach literature. In other words, they saw no difference in the way Indigenous literature and any other kind of literature should be approached and studied. [See Jo-Ann Episkenew's "Socially Responsible Criticism: Aboriginal Literature, Ideology, and the Literary Canon" (2002).] By this we mean that since they were studying Indigenous literature while taking other courses—ranging from Shakespeare to Modern British to Canadian Fiction to Literary Theory—they were simply applying what they had learned in these classes to Indigenous literature. Although ostensibly this seems to make a lot of sense, and we suspect it does for instructors unaware of the socio-political dynamics of Indigenous literary studies, those of us working in the field understand the pitfalls of this approach. [See Kimberly Blaeser's "Native Literature: Seeking a Critical Centre" (1993) on the problem of employing western critical theory as a template to the study of Indigenous literatures.]

Unlike Native Studies programs, English Departments do not attract a lot of Indigenous students who may know something of their cultures and histories, who perhaps may even speak their Indigenous languages. [See Renate Eigenbrod's "A Necessary Inclusion: Native Literature in Native Studies" (2010).] Unfortunately, many Indigenous students have adopted the dominant attitude of western society that literature is a luxury, if not frivolous, and not something that has any real impact on their reality. This attitude is compounded by the fact that most Indigenous literature is written and taught in English, which these students (as do some literary theorists, ethnologists and linguists) consider inauthentic to Indigenous lives. This is certainly a topic in itself, which has been challenged by scholars such as Daniel Heath Justice,[1] and raises what Thomas King has called the "cant of authenticity."[2] [See Emma LaRocque's essay on the role of English in Indigenous literatures, "Preface or Here Are Our Voices—Who Will Hear?" (1990); Margery Fee's essay on orality, "Writing Orality: Interpreting Literature in English by Aboriginal Writers in North America, Australia and New Zealand" (1997); and Kristina Fagan Bidwell's essay on subversion and language, "Code-Switching Humour in Aboriginal Literature" (2009).]

For those of us who have spent a good part of our lives writing, reading, and studying Indigenous literature written in the language of the colonizer, such an attitude flies in the face of our own experiences, and as the authors of these essays indicate, *literature is culture*, certainly one of the earliest expressions of it, and without the existence of vibrant Indigenous cultures all the social programs and money in the world will only serve to hasten assimilation. [See Jeannette Armstrong's "Land Speaking" (1998) in which she connects Okanagan language to her English language poetry.] If in doubt, one can turn to the recent newspaper headlines which have highlighted the salary of a west-coast chief who pocketed nearly one million dollars while many of his people live in substandard housing.[3] Greed, of course, is not foreign or new to Indigenous peoples, and there are stories about it. Such behaviour is presented as monstrous in many Indigenous cultures, certainly contradictory to traditional protocol, and further supports the call for strong traditional cultures grounded in language, literature, and artistic practice. Unfortunately, many of the Indigenous students we

---

1 Daniel Heath Justice, "A Relevant Resonance: Considering the Study of Indigenous National Literatures," in *Across Cultures/Across Borders: Canadian Aboriginal and Native American Literatures*, ed. Paul DePasquale, Renate Eigenbrod, and Emma LaRocque (Peterborough, ON: Broadview P, 2010) 61–76.

2 Thomas King, "How I Spent My Summer Vacation: History, Story and the Cant of Authenticity," in *Landmarks: A Process Reader*, ed. Roberta Birks, Tomi Eng, and Julie Walchli (Scarborough, ON: Prentice Hall and Beacon Canada, 1997) 248–54.

3 Bill Curry and Justin Giovannotti, "B.C. First Nation chief was paid almost $1-million last year." *Globe and Mail* (31 July 2014). Last updated 1 August 2014.

have encountered in our courses have been alienated from their cultures because of histories of oppression, and are only now, as young adults, trying to find their way back "home." Interestingly, they have sought out literature courses to help them get there. [See Neal McLeod's "Coming Home through Stories" (2001) in this context.] All this to say that too often students lack the basics when studying Indigenous literature; moreover, they run into problems when introduced to new material that is premised on foundational concepts.

Thinking about these issues, then, we envisioned a text that would provide an overview of important, if not seminal, essays that have helped shape our understanding of Indigenous literatures in Canada. In other words, we wanted to assemble a teaching text—a "handbook"— which would serve to introduce students to the field by covering all the major themes that have arisen to date. At first the job appeared easy enough. Together we could confidently say that we knew the field. However, we soon realized that like the literature itself, which speaks to community, so too do the essays that examine this literature—either directly through close reading, or indirectly through theory generated by the literature. Furthermore, we reasoned that since it would be our colleagues, among others, who would ultimately be using the text, community should have a hand in determining its contents. And so we set about contacting various colleagues working in the field to solicit suggestions about what should go into such a text. The result was encouraging. They turned out to be enthusiastic about the project and sent us pages of suggestions. The next step was to add our own preferences and then cross-list all the essays suggested, considering what overlap there was, and what themes, if any, might have been overlooked. It was at this point that we again contacted Broadview Press, which had been very supportive of the initial proposal, and told them that we needed more pages. And after more negotiation, we started the heady process of selection.

As it stands, the collection includes those essays most highly recommended by our colleagues, and reflects our desire to cover as many fundamental themes as possible in order to assemble as effective and complete a teaching text as possible. It also means that we tried to be conscious of "voice" and provide potential readers with a variety of perspectives. Readers will therefore immediately notice that a different contributor has written each essay. Such an approach necessarily calls for compromise since we could often have chosen two or three essays by the same author. This means that some of the essays we had expected to include are not here, but, on the other hand, we believe that those we have chosen provide a good cross-section of the themes we wanted to cover, as well as a variety of perspectives that will lead scholars in new directions. Out of the twenty-six contributors, only five are non-Indigenous and the rest are Indigenous voices. This, however, should not come as a surprise to readers since the majority of Canadian scholars writing about Indigenous peoples were, until recently, actually writing about the representation of Indigenous peoples by Canadian authors.[1] As with anything there are exceptions, but it is safe to say that the scholars actually discussing Indigenous literature, whether oral or written, were few and far between; non-Indigenous scholars, such as Penny Petrone, Robert Bringhurst, Julie Cruikshank, and Robin McGrath, making initial forays into the field, were the exceptions to the rule.

Prior to 1990 it was virtually unheard of even for Indigenous peoples to interpret and analyze their own literatures. Certainly there were some essays by Indigenous writers; work by scholars and political figures such as Chief Dan George, Harold Cardinal, Howard Adams, Marlene Castellano Brant, and Wilfred Peltier was published from the late 1960s into the next two decades, but the subject of their essays was either biographical or socio-political, dealing with such topics as education, human rights, and self-governance. The essays of this period may be considered as part of the larger civil rights movement that spread into Canada from the USA, and writing about literature, whether oral or written, was evidently not on anyone's radar. This is not to say that there was *nothing*—research into Indigenous community newspapers and magazines of the period has unearthed the odd literary commentary, but to date nothing of substantial length to our knowledge. The one exception is in the field of Indigenous performance where, as early as the 1970s, nascent artistic development was documented in personal terms by the likes of James Buller, founder of the Association for Native Development in the Performing and Visual Arts in Toronto, and Cree dancer and choreographer Rene Highway.[2] Those writers interested in literature per se, however, were far more focused on creating it rather than commenting on process or extrapolating theory. When we compare Canada to the USA, and consider the educational attainment of the Indigenous populations, we can readily come to some understanding of this situation when we note that writers like N. Scott Momaday, and his contemporaries, such as Vine Deloria Jr., Paula Gunn Allen, and James Welch, were by the early 1970s already obtaining university degrees. Conversely, here in Canada, while a very few individuals such as Basil Johnston, Howard Adams, and Emma LaRocque found their way into institutions of higher learning, the vast majority of Indigenous peoples were living in poverty with little hope of furthering their education; still others were attending one of the many residential schools spread across the country, or trying to deal with the catastrophic results. [See Johnston's "One Generation from Extinction" (1990) and Sam McKegney's interview, "Indigenous Writing and the Residential School Legacy: A Public Interview with Basil Johnston" (2007/2009).] One will notice then a gap of almost one hundred years between the writing of

---

1 Margaret Atwood, *Survival: A Thematic Guide to Canadian Literature* (Toronto: Anansi, 1972); Leslie Monkman, *A Native Heritage: Images of the Indian in English-Canadian Literature* (Toronto: U of Toronto P, 1981); Thomas King, Cheryl Calver, and Helen Hoy, eds., *The Native in Literature: Canadian and Comparative Perspectives* (Toronto: ECW P, 1990).

2 *TAWOW: Canadian Indian Cultural Magazine.* Ottawa: Department of Indian and Northern Affairs. Vol 5. No. 1, 1976. These rare statements can be found in small Indigenous magazines and newspapers of the period.

E. Pauline Johnson and Tomson Highway here in Canada. There are numerous reasons for this, but it is safe to say that whatever writing Johnson's critical and creative work may have encouraged from the next generation it would wither in isolation, neglect, and hostility as epitomized by the residential school system.[1]

In this regard, 1990, the year of the resistance at Kanehsatake ("the Oka Crisis") signifies a watershed for Indigenous literature and literary criticism in Canada. Readers will notice that aside from Pauline Johnson's journalistic piece published in 1892, included as much for historical reasons as for its content, N. Scott Momaday's seminal "The Man Made of Words" (1970), an essay on words, language, and the imagination, which continues to be read on both sides of the border, and Tomson Highway's essay "On Native Mythology" (1987), which he wrote for *Theatrum* after garnering attention for his playwriting, the next four essays are all from 1990 and coincide with the socio-political action associated with "the Oka Crisis." Together the authors of these four essays, Basil Johnston, Lenore Keeshig [Tobias], Thomas King, and Emma LaRocque, raise questions and issues that are indicative of the themes that were to be picked up and explored in further detail throughout the coming decades. As readers will see, appropriation, stereotyping, traditional knowledge, language, orality, land, spirituality, colonialism, post-colonialism, gender, hybridity, authenticity, resistance, literary nationalism, and ethical scholarship reverberate as major themes throughout this collection.

Readers will also notice that we have included only a couple of essays by Native American scholars/ writers. At the outset, we will say that given the current turn towards transnationalism and trans-Indigenous methodologies this decision was probably the most vexing for us. Because this collection is aimed primarily at those young scholars studying Indigenous literature written in Canada, our decisions—along with our colleagues'—were determined by our Canadian context. What essays were fundamental to the study of Indigenous literature here in Canada? Therefore, in looking south of the border we decided to include those few essays that we thought had considerable impact in Canada. Readers may well point to other essays, but in our defence we will say that when push came to shove, if there was a work written in Canada that said much the same thing, and was influential in its own right, we chose it. As for those we included, N. Scott Momaday's aforementioned essay "The Man Made of Words" was seminal to nearly everyone we polled, and we received numerous "votes" for its inclusion. It goes without saying that Momaday's perceptive account of the relationship between the imagination and words—although a product of its time—has influenced countless Indigenous writers. [Consider Thomas King's "Godzilla vs. Post-Colonial" (1990), Jeannette Armstrong's "Land Speaking" (1998), for instance, Bernard Assiniwi's "Je suis ce que je dis que je suis" (1993), or Neal McLeod's "Coming Home through Stories"

---

1 A case in point is the writing of Dawendine, Bernice Loft Winslow, which would be finally published when she was ninety-two years old. (*Iroquois Fires: The Six Nations Lyrics and Lore of Dawendine, Bernice Loft Winslow* [Newcastle: Penumbra P, 1995].)

(2001).] Kimberley Blaeser's "Native Literature: Seeking a Critical Centre" (1993) is also included. Not only was it overwhelmingly suggested by our colleagues, it was initially published here in Canada by Theytus Books and disseminated widely among scholars of Indigenous literature. Accordingly, judging by how often it continues to be quoted, its influence cannot be underestimated. Qwo-Li Driskill's "Stolen from Our Bodies: First Nations Two-Spirits/Queers and the Journey to a Sovereign Erotic" (2004) speaks for itself. At the forefront of advocating for a traditional world-view when it comes to issues of "two-spirit," Driskill's work helps fill a void. [See also Kateri Akiwenzie-Damm's "Erotica, Indigenous Style" (2000).] Included in the text are also Thomas King, Daniel Heath Justice, and Gail Valaskakis, all transplanted Native Americans who took or have taken up residence in Canada and who have made outstanding contributions to the field. We might add that the very presence of these Indigenous American/Canadian scholars in the text emphasizes the current transnational nature of many Indigenous lives. It is a theme that King explores creatively in his short story "Borders,"[1] and which we can consider in Margery Fee's trans-Indigenous approach to "Writing Orality."

Among the other contributors in the collection is Bernard Assiniwi, whose essay, "Je suis ce que je dis que je suis," (1993) is translated from the original French. It needs to be said that Indigenous literature written in French is a field in itself, and there are many more Franco-Indigenous peoples making valuable contributions. We thought, however, that this was important work, which links directly back to Momaday's essay and provides context from a Cree/Algonquin perspective within Canada/Quebec. When we consider the rest of the essays in the collection, one of the central issues that stands out in the writing is the authors' commitment to "literary activism" and ethical scholarship, which harkens back to the themes mentioned earlier and ultimately beyond to cultural and political self-determination. This is hardly surprising, given that the essays reflect the concerns of the literature, and we can easily trace a direct line from Emma LaRocque's seminal "Preface or Here Are Our Voices—Who Will Hear?" (1990) to Lee Maracle's "Oratory: Coming to Theory" (1992), to Armand Garnet Ruffo's "Why Native Literature?" (1997), to Kateri Akiwenzie-Damm's "Erotica, Indigenous Style" (2000), to Qwo-Li Driskill's "Stolen from Our Bodies: First Nations Two-Spirits/Queers and the Journey to a Sovereign Erotic" (2004), right up to Daniel Heath Justice's "The Necessity of Nationhood: Affirming the Sovereignty of Indigenous National Literatures" (2005).

In a similar vein, we can observe that Lenore Keeshig's [Tobias] "Stop Stealing Native Stories" (1990) points in the direction of Indigenous literary nationalism in that it does not shy away from the political in her discussion of the appropriation issue (which is perhaps more relevant than ever), representation, and its implications, and

---

1   Thomas King, "Borders," in *The Harbrace Anthology of Short Fiction*, ed. Jon C. Stott et al. (Toronto: Harbrace, 1998).

connects both backward to E. Pauline Johnson's "A Strong Race Opinion: On the Indian Girl in Modern Fiction" (1892) and forward directly to Gail G. Valaskakis's "Parallel Voices: Indians and Others, Narratives of Cultural Struggle" (1993); connections to other essays in the collection are also apparent, such as to Jo-Ann Episkenew's "Socially Responsible Criticism: Aboriginal Literature, Ideology, and the Literary Canon" (2002), to Renée Hulan's "'Everybody likes the Inuit': Inuit Revision and Representations of the North" (2002), and even to Renate Eigenbrod's "A Necessary Inclusion: Native Literature in Native Studies" (2010).

Other essays pick up on these themes as well while moving in other directions, as in the case of Basil Johnson's contribution, which signals a return to cultural specificity. Thinking of current issues, such as the impact of Residential School and the related questions of Indigenous language and culture, Basil Johnston's "One Generation from Extinction" (1990) leads the way in this respect, speaking as it does of the role of Anishinabemowin in relation to Ojibwe cultural knowledge and survival. We can consider it along with Sam McKegney's "Indigenous Writing and the Residential School Legacy: A Public Interview with Basil Johnston" (2007/2009), Keavy Martin's "Truth, Reconciliation and Amnesia: *Porcupines and China Dolls* and the Canadian Conscience" (2009), and Kristina Fagan Bidwell's "Code-Switching Humour in Aboriginal Literature" (2009).

The issues of interpretation, imposition, and theory were also at the forefront in 1990, and here we begin with Thomas King's "Godzilla vs. Post-Colonial," where he speaks of the problem of applying post-colonial theory to Indigenous literatures. Linking King's essay to Indigenous storytelling practice, we can refer back to Tomson Highway, "On Native Mythology" (1987), and from there move to other essays that grapple with both theoretical and practical questions, such as Lee Maracle's "Oratory: Coming to Theory" (1992), Kimberley Blaeser's "Native Literature: Seeking a Critical Centre" (1993), Armand Garnet Ruffo's "Why Native Literature?" (1997), and Neal McLeod's "Coming Home through Stories" (2001).

One must bear in mind that these thematic "categories" are not absolute but instead fluid, organic like water, and naturally flow into each other. To facilitate the text as a teaching tool, we have listed a number of obvious themes that connect to each of the essays. This too is not fixed, and we are confident that students may find other connections between the essays depending upon their interpretation and analysis. Lastly, we want to reiterate that this collection of essays was conceived as a teaching tool. For example, we included Willie Ermine's "Aboriginal Epistemology" (1995) because, as we indicated earlier, we have found that students come to the literature without any prior experience of Indigenous knowledge systems. Likewise, we included Margery Fee's "Writing Orality: Interpreting Literature in English by Aboriginal Writers" (1997) for its focus on orality from a comparative, trans-Indigenous perspective, which makes important connections between diverse communities and exposes students to "other worlds." Conversely, there are many essays by established and upcoming scholars that could have easily been included in this text. One area that this collection only touches upon is the "trickster figure." The inclusion of short essays by Tomson Highway, "On Native Mythology" (1987), and Daniel David Moses, "The Trickster's Laugh: My Meeting with Tomson and Lenore" (2004), provide important context for the rise in popularity of this traditional Manitou—"transmogrified" by writers of every stripe into a literary device[1]—but there has been a stream of steady commentary over the years. It is in this context that scholars have recently revisited this figure/device with a critical eye, considering both its use and abuse. Readers interested in the topic should therefore consider these seminal essays as a jumping off point for further scholarship.

Again, we conceived of this anthology as a teaching text and a communal project, and in doing so we have done our best to take into account the suggestions of our colleagues in consideration of our own exigencies. Finally, in the construction of any anthology there are implications, such as canonization, and we matter-of-factly want to state that other essays could have easily gone into this collection. Margery Fee has written elsewhere of the "powerful ideological messages" implicit in the "anthology as commodity,"[2] and it is with this in mind that we take heed. That said, if there are any glaring omissions we alone are to blame. There are of course physical constraints, and so it is our hope that the twenty-six essays that we have selected open a window to a better understanding of the wealth of Indigenous poetry, song, fiction, non-fiction, film, and drama that awaits readers and audiences here in Canada and globally.

---

1 In the USA, Gerald Vizenor was one of the first writer-theorists to bring attention to the Trickster figure. Vizenor refers to the "tribal trickster" as "a comic holotrope, and a *sign* in a language game," and thus links him to postmodern theory. Gerald Vizenor, "Trickster Discourse: Comic Holotropes and Language Games" in *Narrative Chance: Postmodern Discourse on Native American Indian Literatures* (Albuquerque: U of New Mexico P, 1989) 187–212.

2 Margery Fee, "Aboriginal Writing in Canada and the Anthology as Commodity," in *Native North America*, ed. Renée Hulan (Toronto: ECW P, 1999) 135–55.

E. Pauline Johnson

"A Strong Race Opinion: On the Indian Girl in Modern Fiction"

E. Pauline Johnson (Tekahionwake, 1861–1913) is one of the most recognized names in Indigenous literature. Born on the Six Nations Reserve near Brantford, Ontario, Johnson was known as much for her performance as she was for her writing—which until recent times has cast a long shadow over her literary career. The daughter of a Mohawk father and a British mother, she was the lone Indigenous female literary voice of her time, and she is often seen to have played the intermediary between Indigenous and non-Indigenous cultures, gaining easy access to imperialist circles, where she would then proceed to celebrate Indigenous cultures as living and vital. As the article in question demonstrates, her work—whether non-fiction, fiction or poetry—is strongest when she is advocating for the rights of Indigenous peoples.

One of the earliest critical essays on the portrayal of Indigenous women in literature, "A Strong Race Opinion," argues not only for the recognition of tribal specificity, but also for the rights of Indigenous people to represent themselves and thus dispel the stereotypes created by settler texts. Remarkably, all of the arguments presented in Johnson's 1892 article continue to hold today, which either shows just how little progress Canadians have made, or how forward thinking Johnson was. She addresses the issue of appropriation of voice explicitly in her conclusion, where she suggests, as does Episkenew and countless critics following her, that writers and critics make an attempt to engage with the people they represent. Johnson's life and career themselves serve to dispel the myths perpetuated by non-Indigenous writers. Sadly, it was in the same year that the article was published, 1892, that the Federal Government in Canada entered into a formal agreement with Christian churches that allowed the religious institutions to operate residential schools.

Johnson, E. Pauline. "A Strong Race Opinion: On the Indian Girl in Modern Fiction." *Sunday Globe Newspaper* (22 May 1892).

A Strong Race Opinion: On the Indian Girl
in Modern Fiction

Every race in the world enjoys its own peculiar characteristics, but it scarcely follows that every individual of a nation must possess these prescribed singularities, or otherwise forfeit in the eyes of the world their nationality. Individual personality is one of the most charming things to be met with, either in a flesh and blood existence, or upon the pages of fiction, and it matters little to what race an author's heroine belongs, if he makes her character distinct, unique and natural.

The American book heroine of today is vari-coloured, as to personality and action. The author does not consider it necessary to the development of her character, and the plot of the story to insist upon her having American-coloured eyes, an American carriage, an American voice, American motives, and an American mode of dying; he allows her to evolve an individuality ungoverned by nationalisms—but the outcome of impulse and nature and a general womanishness.

Not so the Indian girl in modern fiction, the author permits her character no such spontaneity, she must not be one of womankind at large, neither must she have an originality, a singularity that is not definitely "Indian." I quote "Indian" as there seems to be an impression among authors that such a thing as tribal distinction does not exist among the North American aborigines.

The term "Indian" signifies about as much as the term "European" but I cannot recall ever having read a story where the heroine was described as "a European." The Indian girl we meet in cold type, however, is rarely distressed by having to belong to any tribe, or to reflect any tribal characteristics. She is merely a wholesome sort of mixture of any band existing between the Mic Macs of Gaspé and the Kwaw-Kewlths of British Columbia, yet strange to say, that notwithstanding the numerous tribes, with their aggregate numbers reaching more than 122,000 souls in Canada alone, our Canadian authors can cull from this huge revenue of character, but one Indian girl, and stranger still that this lonely little heroine never had a prototype in breathing flesh-and-blood existence!

It is a deplorable fact, but there is only one of her. The story-writer who can create a new kind of Indian girl, or better still portray a "real live" Indian girl who will do something in Canadian literature that has never been done, but once. The general author gives the reader the impression that he has concocted the plot, created his characters, arranged his action, and at the last moment has been seized with the idea that the regulation Indian maiden will make a very harmonious background whereon to paint his pen picture, that, he, never having met this interesting individual, stretches forth his hand to his library shelves, grasps the first Canadian novelist he sees, reads up his subject, and duplicates it in his own work.

After a half dozen writers have done this, the reader might as well leave the tale unread as far as the interest touches upon the Indian character, for an unvarying experience tells him that this convenient personage will repeat herself with monotonous accuracy. He knows what she did and how she died in other romances by other romancers, and she will do and die likewise in his (she always does die, and one feels relieved that it is so, for she is too unhealthy and too unnatural to live).

The rendition of herself and her doings gains no variety in the pens of manifold authors, and the last thing that they will ever think of will be to study "The Indian Girl" from life, for the being we read of is the offspring of the writer's imagination and never existed outside the book covers that her name decorates. Yes, there is only one of her, and her name is "Winona." Once or twice she has borne another appellation, but it always has a "Winona" sound about it. Even Charles Mair, in that masterpiece of Canadian-Indian romances, "Tecumseh," could not resist "Winona."[1]

She is never dignified by being permitted to own a surname, although, extraordinary to note, her father is always a chief, and had he ever existed, would doubtless have been as conservative as his contemporaries about the usual significance that his people attach to family name and lineage.

In addition to this most glaring error this surnameless creation is possessed with a suicidal mania. Her unhappy, self-sacrificing life becomes such a burden to both herself and the author that this is the only means by which they can extricate themselves from a lamentable tangle, though, as a matter of fact suicide is an evil positively unknown among Indians. To-day there may be rare instances where a man crazed by liquor might destroy his own life, but in the periods from whence "Winona's" character is sketched self-destruction was unheard of.[2] This seems to be a fallacy which the best American writers have fallen a prey to. Even Helen Hunt Jackson, in her powerful and beautiful romance of "Ramona,"[3] has weakened her work deplorably by having no less than three Indians suicide while maddened by their national wrongs and personal grief.

The hardest fortune that the Indian girl of fiction meets with is the inevitable doom that shadows her love affairs. She is always desperately in love with the young white hero, who in turn is grateful to her for services rendered the garrison in general

---

1 Charles Mair, *Tecumseh: A Drama* (Toronto: Hunter, Rose & Company; London: Chapman & Hall, 1886).

2 Johnson employs a generalization, or what we would now call a "strategic essentialism," to make her point regarding stereotyping. See Gayatri Chakravorty Spivak, "Can the Subaltern Speak?" in *A Critique of Postcolonial Reason: Toward a History of the Vanishing Present* (Cambridge: Harvard UP, 1999).

3 Helen Hunt Jackson, *Ramona* (Boston: Little Brown, 1884).

and himself in particular during red days of war. In short, she is so much wrapped up in him that she is treacherous to her own people, tells falsehoods to her father and the other chiefs of her tribe, and otherwise makes herself detestable and dishonourable. Of course, this white hero never marries her! Will some critic who understands human nature, and particularly the nature of authors, please tell the reading public why marriage with the Indian girl is so despised in books and so general in real life? Will this good far-seeing critic also tell us why the book-made Indian makes all the love advances to the white gentleman, though the real wild Indian girl (by the way, we are never given any stories of educated girls, though there are many such throughout Canada) is the most retiring, reticent, non-committal being in existence!

Captain Richardson, in that inimitable novel, "Wacousta,"[1] scarcely goes as far in this particular as his followers. To be sure he has his Indian Prose heroine madly in love with young de Haldimar, a passion which it goes without saying he does not reciprocate, but which he plays upon to the extent of making her a traitor to Pontiac inasmuch as she betrays the secret of one of the cleverest intrigues of war known in the history of America, namely, the scheme to capture Fort Detroit through the means of an exhibition game of lacrosse. In addition to this de Haldimar makes a cat's paw of the girl, using her as a means of communication between his fiancée and himself, and so the excellent author permits his Indian girl to get herself despised by her own nation and disliked by the reader. Unnecessary to state, that as usual the gallant white marries his fair lady, whom the poor little red girl has assisted him to recover.

Then comes another era in Canadian-Indian fiction, wherein G. Mercer Adam and A. Ethelwyn Wetherald have given us the semi-historic novel "An Algonquin Maiden."[2] The former's masterly touch can be recognized on every page he has written; but the outcome of the combined pens is the same old story. We find "Wanda" violently in love with Edward MacLeod, she makes all the overtures, conducts herself disgracefully, assists him to a reunion with his fair-skinned love, Helene; then betakes herself to a boat, rows out into the lake in a thunderstorm, chants her own death-song, and is drowned. [...]

Then the young hero describes her upon two occasions as a "beautiful little brute." Poor little Wanda! not only is she non-descript and ill-starred, but as usual the authors take away her love, her life, and last and most terrible of all, her reputation; for they permit a crowd of men-friends of the hero to call her a "squaw," and neither hero nor authors deny that she is a "squaw." It is almost too sad when so much prejudice exists against the Indians, that any one should write an Indian heroine with such glaring accusations against her virtue, and no contradictory statements

---

1 John Richardson, *Wacousta: or, the Prophecy: A Tale of the Canadas* (London and Edinburgh, 1832; Montreal, 1838).
2 G. Mercer Adam and A. Ethelwyn Wetherald, *An Algonquin Maiden* (Montreal: John Lovell & Son; Toronto: Williamson, 1887).

either from writer, hero, or circumstance. "Wanda" had without doubt the saddest, unsunniest, unequal life ever given to Canadian readers. [...]

Perhaps, sometimes an Indian romance may be written by someone who will be clever enough to portray national character without ever having come in contact with it. [...] But such things are rare, half of our authors who write up Indian stuff have never been on an Indian reserve in their lives, have never met a "real live" Redman, have never even read Parkman, Schoolcraft or Catlin;[1] what wonder that their conception of a people that they are ignorant of, save by heresay, is dwarfed, erroneous and delusive.

And here follows the thought—do authors who write Indian romances love the nation they endeavour successfully or unsuccessfully to describe? Do they, like Tecumseh, say, "And I, who love your nation, which is just, when deeds deserve it," or is the Indian introduced into literature but to lend a dash of vivid colouring to an otherwise tame and sombre picture of colonial life: it looks suspiciously like the latter reason, or why should the Indian always get beaten in the battles of romances, or the Indian girl get inevitably the cold shoulder in the wars of love?

Surely the Redman has lost enough, has suffered enough without additional losses and sorrows being heaped upon him in romance. There are many combats he has won in history from the extinction of the Jesuit Fathers at Lake Simcoe to Cut Knife Creek.[2] There are many girls who have placed dainty red feet figuratively upon the white man's neck from the days of Pocahontas to those of little "Bright Eyes," who captured all Washington a few seasons ago.[3] Let us not only hear, but read something

---

1 Francis Parkman, Jr. (1823–93) was an American historian, best known as author of *The Oregon Trail: Sketches of Prairie and Rocky-Mountain Life* and his monumental seven-volume *France and England in North America*. Henry Rowe Schoolcraft (1793–1864) was an American geographer, geologist, and ethnologist noted for his major six-volume study of Native Americans in the 1850s. Jane Johnston Schoolcraft, also known as Bamewawagezhikaquay or "Woman of the Sound the Stars Make Rushing Through the Sky" (1800–42), is the first known Native American literary writer. The wife of Henry Rowe Schoolcraft, she taught her husband the Ojibway language and much of her culture. George Catlin (1796–1872) was an American painter, author, and traveller who specialized in portraits of Native Americans. Catlin travelled to the American West five times during the 1830s.

2 The Society of Jesus arrived in New France in 1610, and travelled to the Lake Simcoe region in 1615. They sought to establish their headquarters near the present town of Midland, but the Iroquois, enemies of the French, destroyed the mission and frustrated the hopes of the missionaries. For further reading see, *The Jesuit Relations and Allied Documents: Travels and Explorations of the Jesuit Missionaries in New France, 1610–1791*, and *The Orenda* (Toronto: Hamish Hamilton, 2013) by Metis novelist Joseph Boyden. The Battle of Cut Knife was fought on 2 May 1885, when a small force of Cree and Assiniboine warriors were attacked by a column of mounted police, militia, and Canadian army regulars near Battleford, Saskatchewan. The warriors defeated the Canadian forces.

3 Susette "Bright Eyes" La Flesche Tibbles was born in 1854, and educated at the Omaha Reservation Presbyterian Mission Boarding Day School in northeastern Nebraska, and at the Elizabeth Institute for Young Ladies in New Jersey. Writer, journalist, teacher, interpreter, lecturer, she advocated on behalf of her people and became nationally known, travelling to Washington, DC, to appear before a congressional committee. Her stature was such that while in the east, she was entertained by the poet Henry Wadsworth Longfellow at his home in Cambridge, Massachusetts.

of the North American Indian "besting" some one at least once in a decade, and above all things let the Indian girl of fiction develop from the "doglike," "fawnlike," "deer-footed," "fire-eyed," "crouching," "submissive" book heroine into something of the quiet, sweet womanly woman she is, if wild, or the everyday, natural, laughing girl she is, if cultivated and educated; let her be natural, even if the author is not competent to give her tribal characteristics.

N. Scott Momaday

"The Man Made of Words"

Navarre Scott Momaday was born in 1937 and is an enrolled member of the Kiowa Tribe of Oklahoma. Among the first generation of contemporary Native American authors to attend university, he received his PhD from Stanford University in 1963 and has since had a distinguished teaching and writing career. Momaday is considered the founding author in what critic Kenneth Lincoln has termed the *Native American Renaissance,* and although his publications are numerous and varied, they all foreground a reverence for language and storytelling. His novel *House Made of Dawn,* which seamlessly combines mythic and modern worldviews, was awarded the *Pulitzer Prize for Fiction in 1969* and is now considered a classic in American Literature. Among his numerous honorary degrees, Momaday received the National Medal of Arts in 2007 for a body of work that celebrates and preserves Native American literary arts and culture.

Published in *Indian Voices: The First Convocation of American Indian Scholars* (1970) and reprinted widely, "The Man Made of Words" is Momaday's most famous essay, and there is no better demonstration of his on-going concern for the imaginative use of language as both a tool for survival and a means of "regeneration." Written at a time when the ethos of the "Vanishing Indian" was still very much a part of popular American culture, "The Man Made of Words" demonstrates the endurance of Native American cultural tradition in the face of the assimilative and destructive forces of colonization. Taking a strong ethical and moral position, Momaday's essay speaks directly to the reader/listener of responsibility to land and community; it equally points out that the language we use daily is one of the most potent elements of existence, and we must not take it for granted as it shapes and defines our existence in the world.

Momaday, N. Scott. "The Man Made of Words." (1970) *Nothing but the Truth: An Anthology of Native American Literature.* Ed. John L. Purdy and James Ruppert. New Jersey: Prentice Hall. 2001. 82–93.

The Man Made of Words

I want to try to put several different ideas together this morning. And in the process, I hope to indicate something about the nature of the relationship between language and experience. It seems to me that in a certain sense we are all made of words; that our most essential being consists in language. It is the element in which we think and dream and act, in which we live our daily lives. There is no way in which we can exist apart from the morality of a verbal dimension.

In one of the discussions yesterday the question "What is an American Indian?" was raised.

The answer of course is that an Indian is an idea which a given man has of himself. And it is a moral idea, for it accounts for the way in which he reacts to other men and to the world in general. And that idea, in order to be realized completely, has to be expressed.

I want to say some things then about this moral and verbal dimension in which we live. I want to say something about such things as ecology and storytelling and the imagination. Let me tell you a story:

One night a strange thing happened. I had written the greater part of *The Way to Rainy Mountain*—all of it, in fact, except the epilogue. I had set down the last of the old Kiowa tales, and I had composed both the historical and the autobiographical commentaries for it. I had the sense of being out of breath, of having said what it was in me to say on that subject. The manuscript lay before me in the bright light, small, to be sure, but complete; or nearly so. I had written the second of the two poems in which that book is framed. I had uttered the last word, as it were. And yet a whole, penultimate piece was missing. I began once again to write.

During the first hours after midnight on the morning of November 13, 1833, it seemed that the world was coming to an end. Suddenly the stillness of the night was broken; there were brilliant flashes of light in the sky, light of such intensity that people were awakened by it. With the speed and density of a driving rain, stars were falling in the universe. Some were brighter than Venus; one was said to be as large as the moon. I went on to say that that event, the falling of the stars on North

America, that explosion of meteors which occurred 137 years ago, is among the earliest entries in the Kiowa calendars. So deeply impressed upon the imagination of the Kiowas is that old phenomenon that it is remembered still; it has become a part of the racial memory.

"The living memory," I wrote, "and the verbal tradition which transcends it, were brought together for me once and for all in the person of Ko-sahn." It seemed eminently right for me to deal, after all, with that old woman. Ko-sahn is among the most venerable people I have ever known. She spoke and sang to me one summer afternoon in Oklahoma. It was like a dream. When I was born she was already old; she was a grown woman when my grandparents came into the world. She sat perfectly still, folded over on herself. It did not seem possible that so many years—a century of years—could be so compacted and distilled. Her voice shuddered, but it did not fail. Her songs were sad. An old whimsy, a delight in language and in remembrance, shone in her one good eye. She conjured up the past, imagining perfectly the long continuity of her being. She imagined the lovely young girl, wild and vital, she had been. She imagined the Sun Dance.

There was an old, old woman. She had something on her back. The boys went out to see. The old woman had a bag full of earth on her back. It was a certain kind of sandy earth. That is what they must have in the lodge. The dancers must dance upon the sandy earth. The old woman held a digging tool in her hand. She turned towards the south and pointed with her lips. It was like a kiss, and she began to sing:

> *We have brought the earth.*
> *Now it is time to play.*

As old as I am, I still have the feeling of play. That was the beginning of the Sun Dance.

By this time I was back into the book, caught up completely in the act of writing. I had projected myself—imagined myself—out of the room and out of time. I was there with Ko-sahn in the Oklahoma July. We laughed easily together; I felt that I had known her all of my life—all of hers. I did not want to let her go. But I had come to the end. I set down, almost grudgingly, the last sentences:

It was—all of this and more—a quest, a going forth upon the way of Rainy Mountain. Probably Ko-sahn too is dead now. At times, in the quiet of evening, I think she must have wondered, dreaming, who she was. Was she become in her sleep that old purveyor of the sacred earth, perhaps, that ancient one who, old as she was, still had the feeling of play? And in her mind, at times, did she see the falling stars?

For some time I sat looking down at these words on the page, trying to deal with the emptiness that had come about inside of me. The words did not seem real. I could scarcely believe that they made sense, that they had anything whatsoever to do with meaning. In desperation almost, I went back over the final paragraphs, backwards and forwards, hurriedly. My eyes fell upon the name Ko-sahn. And all at once everything seemed suddenly to refer to that name. The name seemed to humanize the whole complexity of language. All at once, absolutely, I had the sense of the magic of words and of names. Ko-sahn, I said, and I said again KO-SAHN.

Then it was that that ancient, one-eyed woman Ko-sahn stepped out of the language and stood before me on the page. I was amazed. Yet it seemed to me entirely appropriate that this should happen.

"I was just now writing about you," I replied, stammering. "I thought—forgive me—I thought that perhaps you were…that you had…"

"No," she said. And she cackled, I thought. And she went on. "You have imagined me well, and so I am. You have imagined that I dream, and so I do. I have seen the falling stars."

"But all of this, this imagining," I protested, "this has taken place—is taking place in my mind. You are not actually here, not here in this room." It occurred to me that I was being extremely rude, but I could not help myself. She seemed to understand.

"Be careful of your pronouncements, grandson," she answered. "You imagine that I am here in this room, do you not? That is worth something. You see, I have existence, whole being, in your imagination. It is but one kind of being, to be sure, but it is perhaps the best of all kinds. If I am not here in this room, grandson, then surely neither are you."

"I think I see what you mean," I said meekly. I felt justly rebuked. "Tell me, grandmother, how old are you?"

"I do not know," she replied. "There are times when I think that I am the oldest woman on earth. You know, the Kiowas came into the world through a hollow log. In my mind's eye I have seen them emerge, one by one, from the mouth of the log. I have seen them so clearly, how they were dressed, how delighted they were to see the world around them. I must have been there. And I must have taken part in that old migration of the Kiowas from the Yellowstone to the Southern Plains, near the Big Horn River, and I have seen the red cliffs of Palo Duro Canyon. I was with those who were camped in the Wichita Mountains when the stars fell."

"You are indeed very old," I said, "and you have seen many things."

"Yes, I imagine that I have," she replied. The she turned slowly around, nodding once, and receded into the language I had made. And then I imagined I was alone in the room.

Once in his life a man ought to concentrate his mind upon the remembered earth, I believe. He ought to give himself up to a particular landscape in his experience, to look at it from as many angles as he can, to wonder about it, to dwell upon it. He ought to imagine that he touches it with his hands at every season and listens to the sounds that are made upon it. He ought to imagine the creatures that are there and all the faintest motions in the wind. He ought to recollect the glare of noon and all the colors of the dawn and dusk.

The Wichita Mountains rise out of the Southern Plains in a long crooked line that runs from east to west. The mountains are made of red earth, and of rock that is neither red nor blue but some very rare admixture of the two like the feathers of certain birds. They are not so high and mighty as the mountains of the Far West, and they bear a different relationship to the land around them. One does not imagine that they are distinctive in themselves, or indeed that they exist apart from the plain in any sense. If you try to think of them in the abstract, they lose the look of mountains. They are preeminently an expression of the larger landscape, more perfectly organic than one can easily imagine. To behold these mountains from the plain is one thing; to see the plain from the mountains is something else. I have stood on the top of Mt. Scott and seen the earth below, bending out into the whole circle of the sky. The wind runs always close upon the slopes, and there are times when you can hear the rush of it like water in the ravines.

Here is the hub of an old commerce. A hundred years ago the Kiowas and Comanches journeyed outward from the Wichitas in every direction, seeking after mischief and medicine, horses and hostages. Sometimes they went away for years, but they always returned, for the land had got hold of them. It is a consecrated place, and even now there is something of the wilderness about it. There is a game preserve in the hills. Animals graze away in the open meadows or, closer by, keep to the shadows of the groves: antelope and deer, longhorn and buffalo. It was here, the Kiowas say, that the first buffalo came into the world.

The yellow grassy knoll that is called Rainy Mountain lies a short distance to the north and west. There, on the west side, is the ruin of an old school where my grandmother went as a wild young girl in blanket and braids to learn of numbers and of names in English. And there she is buried.

> Most is your name the name of this dark stone.
> Deranged in death, the mind to be inheres
> Forever in the nominal unknown,
> Who listens here and now to hear your name.
> The early sun, red as a hunter's moon,
> Runs in the plain. The mountain burns and shines;
> And silence is the long approach of noon
> Upon the shadow that your name defines—
> And death this cold, black density of stone.

I am interested in the way that a man looks at a given landscape and takes possession of it in his blood and brain. For this happens, I am certain, in the ordinary motion of life. None of us lives apart from the land entirely; such an isolation is unimaginable. We have sooner or later to come to terms with the world around us— and I mean especially the physical world, not only as it is revealed to us immediately through our senses, but also as it is perceived more truly in the long turn of seasons and of years. And we must come to moral terms. There is no alternative, I believe, if we are to realize and maintain our humanity; for our humanity must consist in part in the ethical as well as the practical ideal of preservation. And particularly here and now is that true. We Americans need now more than ever before—and indeed more than we know—to imagine who and what we are with respect to the earth and sky. I am talking about an act of the imagination essentially, and the concept of an American land ethic.

It is no doubt more difficult to imagine in 1970 the landscape of America as it was in, say, 1900. Our whole experience as a nation in this century has been a repudiation of the pastoral ideal which informs so much of the art and literature of the nineteenth century. One effect of the Technological Revolution has been to uproot us from the soil. We have become disoriented, I believe; we have suffered a kind of psychic dislocation of ourselves in time and space. We may be perfectly sure of where we are in relation to the supermarket and the next coffee break, but I doubt that any of us knows where he is in relation to the stars and to the solstices. Our sense of the natural order has become dull and unreliable. Like the wilderness itself, our sphere of instinct has diminished in proportion as we have failed to imagine truly what it is. And yet I believe that it is possible to formulate an ethical idea of the land—a notion of what it is and must be in our daily lives—and I believe moreover that it is absolutely necessary to do so.

It would seem on the surface of things that a land ethic is something that is alien to, or at least dormant in, most Americans. Most of us in general have developed an attitude of indifference toward the land. In terms of my own experience, it is difficult to see how such an attitude could ever have come about.

Ko-sahn could remember where my grandmother was born. "It was just there," she said, pointing to a tree, and the tree was like a hundred others that grew up in the broad depression of the Washita River. I could see nothing to indicate that anyone had ever been there, spoken so much as a word, or touched the tips of his fingers to the tree. But in her memory Ko-sahn could see the child. I think she must have remembered my grandmother's voice, for she seemed for a long moment to listen and to hear. There was a still, heavy heat upon that place; I had the sense that ghosts were gathering there.

And in the racial memory, Ko-sahn had seen the falling stars. For her there was no distinction between the individual and the racial experience, even as there was none between the mythical and the historical. Both were realized for her in the one memory, and that was of the land. This landscape, in which she had lived for a hundred years, was the common denominator of everything that she knew and would ever know—and her knowledge was profound. Her roots ran deep into the earth, and from those depths she drew strength enough to hold still against all the forces of chance and disorder. And she drew strength enough to hold still against all the forces of change and disorder. And she drew therefrom the sustenance of meaning and of mystery as well. The falling stars were not for Ko-sahn an isolated or accidental phenomenon. She had a great personal investment in that awful commotion of light in the night sky.

For it remained to be imagined. She must at last deal with it in words; she must appropriate it to her understanding of the whole universe. And, again, when she spoke of the Sun Dance, it was an essential expression of her relationship to the life of the earth and to the sun and moon.

In Ko-sahn and in her people we have always had the example of a deep, ethical regard for the land. We had better learn from it. Surely that ethic is merely latent in ourselves. It must now be activated, I believe. We Americans must come again to a moral comprehension of the earth and air. We must live according to the principle of a land ethic. The alternative is that we shall not live at all.

Ecology is perhaps the most important subject of our time. I can't think of an issue in which the Indian has more authority or a greater stake. If there is one thing which truly distinguishes him, it is surely his regard of and for the natural world.

But let me get back to the matter of storytelling.

I must have taken part in that old migration of the Kiowas from the Yellowstone to the Southern Plains, for I have seen antelope bounding in the tall grass near the Big Horn River, and I have seen the ghost forests in the Black Hills. Once I saw the red cliffs of Palo Duro Canyon. I was with those who were camped in the Wichita Mountains when the stars fell. "You are very old," I said, "and you have seen many things." "Yes, I imagine that I have," she replied. Then she turned slowly around, nodding once, and receded into the language I had made. And then I imagined that I was alone in the room.

Who is the storyteller? Of whom is the story told? What is there in the darkness to imagine into being? What is there to dream and to relate? What happens when I or anyone exerts the force of language upon the unknown?

These are the questions which interest me most.

If there is any absolute assumption in back of my thoughts tonight, it is this: We are what we imagine. Our very existence consists in our imagination of ourselves. Our best destiny is to imagine, at least, completely, who and what, and *that* we are. The greatest tragedy that can befall us is to go unimagined.

Writing is recorded speech. In order to consider seriously the meaning of language and of literature, we must consider first the meaning of the oral tradition.

By way of suggesting one or two definitions which may be useful to us, let me pose a few basic questions and tentative answers:

(1) What is the oral tradition?

The oral tradition is that process by which the myths, legends, tales, and lore of a people are formulated, communicated, and preserved in language by word of mouth, as opposed to writing. Or, it is a *collection* of such things.

(2) With reference to the matter of oral tradition, what is the relationship between art and reality?

In the context of these remarks, the matter of oral tradition suggests certain particularities of art and reality. Art, for example...involves an oral dimension which is based markedly upon such considerations as memorization, intonation, inflection, precision of statement, brevity, rhythm, pace, and dramatic effect. Moreover, myth, legend, and lore, according to our definitions of these terms, imply a separate and distinct order of reality. We are concerned here not so much with an accurate representation of actuality, but with the realization of the imaginative experience.

(3) How are we to conceive of language? What are words?

For our purposes, words are audible sounds, invented by man to communicate his thoughts and feelings. Each word has a conceptual content, however slight; and each word communicates associations of feeling. Language is the means by which words proceed to the formulation of meaning and emotional effect.

(4) What is the nature of storytelling? What are the purposes and possibilities of that act?

Storytelling is imaginative and creative in nature. It is an act by which man strives to realize his capacity for wonder, meaning and delight. It is also a process in which man invests and preserves himself in the context of ideas. Man tells stories in order to understand his experience, whatever it may be. The possibilities of storytelling are precisely those of understanding the human experience.

(5) What is the relationship between what a man is and what he says—or between what he is, and what he thinks he is?

This relationship is both tenuous and complicated. Generally speaking, man has consummate being in language, and there only. The state of human *being* is an idea, an idea which man has of himself. Only when he is embodied in an idea, and the idea is realized in language, can man take possession of himself. In our particular frame of reference, this is to say that man achieves the fullest realization of his humanity in such an art and product of the imagination as literature—and here I use the term "literature" in its broadest sense. This is admittedly a moral view of the question, but literature is itself a moral view, and it is a view of morality.

Now let us return to the falling stars. And let me apply a new angle of vision to that event—let me proceed this time from a slightly different point of view:

In this winter of 1833 the Kiowas were camped on Elm Fork, a branch of the Red River west of the Wichita Mountains. In the preceding summer they had suffered a massacre at the hands of the Osages, and Tai-me, the sacred Sun Dance Doll and most powerful medicine of the tribe, had been stolen. At no time in the history of their migration from the north, and in the evolution of their plains culture, had the Kiowas been more vulnerable to despair. The loss of Tai-me was a deep psychological wound. In the early cold of November 13 there occurred over North America an explosion of meteors. The Kiowas were awakened by the sterile light of falling stars, and they ran out into the false day and were terrified.

The year the stars fell is, as I have said, among the earliest entries in the Kiowa calendars, and it is permanent in the Kiowa mind. There was symbolic meaning in that November sky. With the coming of natural dawn there began a new and darker age for the Kiowa people; the last culture to evolve on this continent began to decline. Within four years of the falling stars the Kiowas signed their first treaty with the government; within twenty, four major epidemics of smallpox and Asiatic cholera destroyed more than half their number; and within scarcely more than a generation their horses were taken from them and the herds of buffalo were slaughtered and left to waste upon the plains.

Do you see what happens when the imagination is superimposed upon the historical event? It becomes a story. The whole piece becomes more deeply invested with meaning. The terrified Kiowas, when they had regained possession of themselves, did indeed imagine that the falling stars were symbolic of their being and their destiny. They accounted for themselves with reference to that awful memory. They appropriated it, recreated it, fashioned it into an image of themselves—imagined it.

Only by means of that act could they bear what happened to them thereafter. No defeat, no humiliation, no suffering was beyond their power to endure, for none of it was meaningless. They could say to themselves, "yes, it was all meant to be in its turn. The order of the world was broken, it was clear. Even the stars were shaken loose in the night sky." The imagination of meaning was not much, perhaps, but it was all they had, and it was enough to sustain them.

One of my very favorite writers, Isak Dinesen, said this: "All sorrows can be borne if you put them into a story or tell a story about them."[1]

Some three or four years ago, I became interested in the matter of "oral tradition," as that term is used to designate a rich body of pre-literate storytelling in and among the indigenous cultures of North America. Specifically, I began to wonder about the way in which myths, legends, and lore evolve into that mature condition of expression which we call "literature." For indeed literature is, I believe, the end-product of an evolutionary process, and the so-called "oral tradition" is primarily a stage within that process, a stage that is indispensable and perhaps original as well.

I set out to find a traditional material that should be at once oral only, unified and broadly representative of cultural values. And in this undertaking, I had a certain advantage, because I am myself an American Indian, and I have lived many years of my life on the Indian reservations of the southwest. From the time I was first able to comprehend and express myself in language, I heard the stories of the Kiowas, those "coming out" people of the Southern plains from whom I am descended.

Three hundred years ago the Kiowa lived in the mountains of what is now western

---

1 Karen von Blixen-Finecke (1885–1962) was a Danish author; born Karen Christence Dinesen, she used the pen name Isak Dinesen. The quotation refers to something a friend said about her. Interview with Bent Mohn, *New York Times Book Review* (3 November 1957).

Montana, near the headwaters of the Yellowstone River. Near the end of the 17th century they began a long migration to the south and east. They passed along the present border between Montana and Wyoming to the Black Hills and proceeded southward along the eastern slopes of the Rockies to the Wichita Mountains in the Southern Plains (Southwestern Oklahoma).

I mention this old journey of the Kiowas because it is in a sense definitive of the tribal mind; it is essential to the way in which the Kiowas think of themselves as a people. The migration was carried on over a course of many generations and many hundreds of miles. When it began, the Kiowas were a desperate and divided people, given up wholly to a day-by-day struggle for survival. When it ended, they were a race of centaurs, a lordly society of warriors and buffalo hunters. Along the way they had acquired horses, a knowledge and possession of the open land, and a sense of destiny. In alliance with the Comanches, they ruled the southern plains for a hundred years.

That migration—and the new golden age to which it led—is closely reflected in Kiowa legend and lore. Several years ago I retraced the route of that migration, and when I came to the end, I interviewed a number of Kiowa elders and obtained from them a remarkable body of history and learning, fact and fiction—all of it in the oral tradition and all of it valuable in its own right and for its own sake.

I compiled a small number of translations from the Kiowa, arranged insofar as it was possible to indicate the chronological and geographical progression of the migration itself. This collection (and it was nothing more than a collection at first) was published under the title "*The Journey of Tai-me*" in a fine edition limited to 100 hand printed copies.

This original collection has just been re-issued, together with illustrations and a commentary, in a trade edition entitled "*The Way to Rainy Mountain.*" The principle of narration which informs this latter work is in a sense elaborate and experimental, and I should like to say one or two things about it. Then, if I may, I should like to illustrate the way in which the principle works, by reading briefly from the text. And finally, I should like to comment in some detail upon one of the tales in particular.

There are three distinct narrative voices in "*The Way to Rainy Mountain*"—the mythical, the historical, and the immediate. Each of the translations is followed by two kinds of commentary; the first is documentary and the second is privately reminiscent. Together, they serve, hopefully, to validate the oral tradition to an extent that might not otherwise be possible. The commentaries are meant to provide a context in which the elements of oral tradition might transcend the categorical limits of prehistory, anonymity, and archaeology in the narrow sense.

All of this is to say that I believe there is a way (first) in which the elements of oral tradition can be shown, dramatically, to exist within the framework of a literary continuance, a deeper and more vital context of language and meaning than that which is generally taken into account; and (secondly) in which those elements can be located, with some precision on an evolutionary scale.

The device of the journey is peculiarly appropriate to such a principle of narration as this. And "*The Way to Rainy Mountain*" is a whole journey, intricate with notion and meaning; and it is made with the whole memory, that experience of the mind which is legendary as well as historical, personal as well as cultural.

Without further qualification, let me turn to the text itself.

The Kiowa tales which are contained in "*The Way to Rainy Mountain*" constitute a kind of literary chronicle. In a sense they are the milestones of that old migration in which the Kiowas journeyed from the Yellowstone to the Washita. They recorded a transformation of the tribal mind, as it encounters for the first time the landscape of the Great Plains; they evoke the sense of search and discovery. Many of the tales are very old, and they have not until now been set down in writing. Among them there is one that stands out in my mind. When I was a child, my father told me the story of the arrowmaker, and he told it to me many times, for I fell in love with it. I have no memory that is older than that of hearing it. This is the way it goes:

If an arrow is well made, it will have tooth marks upon it. That is how you know. The Kiowas made fine arrows and straightened them in their teeth. Then they drew them to the bow to see that they were straight. Once there was a man and his wife. They were alone at night in their tipi. By the light of a fire the man was making arrows. After a while he caught sight of something. There was a small opening in the tipi where two hides had been sewn together. Someone was there on the outside, looking in. The man went on with his work, but he said to his wife, "Someone is standing outside. Do not be afraid. Let us talk easily, as of ordinary things." He took up an arrow and straightened it in his teeth; then, as it was right for him to do, he drew it to the bow and took aim, first in this direction and then in that. And all the while he was talking, as if to his wife. But this is how he spoke: "I know that you are there on the outside, for I can feel your eyes upon me. If you are a Kiowa, you will understand what I am saying, and you will speak your name." But there was no answer, and the man went on in the same way, pointing the arrow all around. At last his aim fell upon the place where his enemy stood, and he let go of the string. The arrow went straight to the enemy's heart.

Heretofore the story of the arrowmaker has been the private possession of a very few, a tenuous link in that most ancient chain of language which we call the oral tradition; tenuous because the tradition itself is so; for as many times as the story has been told, it was always but one generation removed from extinction. But it was held dear, too, on that same account. That is to say, it has been neither more nor less durable than the human voice, and neither more nor less concerned to express the meaning of the human condition. And this brings us to the heart of the matter at hand: The story of the arrowmaker is also a link between language and literature. It is a remarkable act of the mind, a realization of words and the world that is altogether simple and direct, yet nonetheless rare and profound, and it illustrates more clearly than anything else in my own experience, at least, something of the essential character of the imagination—and in particular of that personification which in this instance emerges from it: the man made of words.

It is a fine story, whole, intricately beautiful, precisely realized. It is worth thinking about, for it yields something of value; indeed, it is full of provocation, rich with suggestion and consequent meaning. There is often an inherent danger that we might impose too much of ourselves upon it. It is informed by an integrity that bears examination easily and well, and in the process it seems to appropriate our own reality and experience.

It is significant that the story of the arrowmaker returns in a special way upon itself. It is about language, after all, and it is therefore part and parcel of its own subject; virtually, there is no difference between the telling and that which is told. The point of the story lies, not so much in what the arrowmaker does, but in what he says—and indeed that he says it. The principal fact is that he speaks, and in so doing he places his very life in the balance. It is this aspect of the story which interests me most, for it is here that the language becomes most conscious of itself; we are close to the origin and object of literature, I believe; our sense of the verbal dimension is very keen, and we are aware of something in the nature of language that is at once perilous and compelling. "If you are a Kiowa, you will understand what I am saying, and you will speak your name." Everything is ventured in this simple declaration, which is also a question and a plea. The conditional element with which it begins is remarkably tentative and pathetic; precisely at this moment is the arrowmaker realized completely, and his reality consists in language, and it is poor and precarious. And all of this occurs to him as surely as it does to us. Implicit in that simple occurrence is all of his definition and his destiny, and all of ours. He ventures to speak because he must; language is the repository of his whole knowledge and experience, and it represents the only chance he has for survival. Instinctively, and with great care, he deals in the most honest and basic way with words. "Let us talk easily, as of ordinary things," he says. And of the ominous unknown he asks only the utterance of a name, only the most nominal sign that he is understood, that his words are returned to him on the sheer edge of meaning. But there is no answer, and the arrowmaker knows at once what he has not known before; that his enemy is, and that he has gained an advantage over him. This he knows certainly, and the certainty itself is his advantage, and it is crucial; he makes the most of it. The venture is complete and irrevocable, and it ends in success. The story is meaningful. It is so primarily because it is composed of language, and it is in the nature of language in turn that it proceeds to the formulation of meaning. Moreover, the story of the arrowmaker, as opposed to other stories in general, centers upon this procession of words toward meaning. It seems in fact to turn upon the very idea that language involves the elements of risk and responsibility; and in this it seeks to confirm itself. In a word, it seems to say, everything is a risk. That may be true, and it may also be that the whole of literature rests upon that truth.

The arrowmaker is preeminently the man made of words. He has consummate being in language; it is the world of his origin and of his posterity, and there is no other. But it is a world of definite reality and of infinite possibility. I have come to believe that there is a sense in which the arrowmaker has more nearly perfect being than have other men, by and large, as he imagines himself, whole and vital, going on into the unknown darkness and beyond. And this last aspect of his being is primordial and profound.

And yet the story has it that he is cautious and alone, and we are given to understand that his peril is great and immediate, and that he confronts it in the only way he can. I have no doubt that this is true, and I believe that there are implications which point directly to the determination of our literary experience and which must not be lost upon us. A final word, then, on an essential irony which marks this story and gives peculiar substance to the man made of words. The storyteller is nameless and unlettered. From one point of view we know very little about him, except that he is somehow translated for us in the person of an arrowmaker. But, from another, that is all we need to know. He tells us of his life in language, and of the awful risk involved. It must occur to us that he is one with the arrowmaker and that he has survived, by word of mouth, beyond other men. We said a moment ago that, for the arrow-maker, language represented the only chance of survival. It is worth considering that he survives in our own time, and that he has survived over a period of untold generations.

Tomson Highway

"On Native Mythology"

Tomson Highway was born on the land surrounding his Cree reserve near Brochet, in northwestern Manitoba, and grew up speaking Cree. He later moved to southern Ontario, where he studied literature and trained to become a concert pianist. All of Highway's work uses Indigenous language to some degree, and combines the mythological with the contemporary world, which serves to dispel the myth of the "humourless and static Indian" by demonstrating that it is possible to be simultaneously traditional and contemporary. In addition to attaining national acclaim, Highway has achieved considerable success on the international stage and divides his time between France and Canada. He currently works as a playwright, novelist, pianist and songwriter.

Building on the ideas put forward by the "Committee to Re-Establish the Trickster," Highway's 1987 article, "On Native Mythology," promotes the use of theatre to make Indigenous mythology relevant to contemporary audiences. The Committee, established in 1986 by Highway, Daniel David Moses, and Lenore Keeshig Tobias, promoted the incorporation of traditional spirituality and knowledge into Indigenous works in order to demonstrate the continuing relevance and vibrancy of Indigenous culture and spirituality. Highway discusses the challenges of using English to portray spirituality, and refers to his play, *The Rez Sisters*, and his use of the trickster figure, to demonstrate the contemporizing of Indigenous mythologies. As with all the essays in this collection to varying degrees, Highway's short essay concludes with a reference to land, tying the relevance of Indigenous mythology to all people who now inhabit the landscape we call Canada.

Highway, Tomson. "On Native Mythology." *Theatrum* 6 (Spring 1987): 29–31.

On Native Mythology

"Native theatre"—for lack of better terminology—has been around for only about ten years, if that. By "Native theatre," I mean theatre that is written, performed and produced by Native people themselves and theatre that speaks out on the culture and the lives of this country's Native people.

The Indian painters made their first big statement in the early 1960s with the explosion onto the Canadian scene of such names as Norval Morrisseau, Daphne Odjig and others. This event—and particularly in the case of Morrisseau—marked the first time Indian people made available for public consumption their mythology, a mythology considered too sacred, by their own people, for this purpose and, in fact, so potent in its meaning that Christian missionaries did all they could to replace this mythology with their own. Twenty years later, it appears the writers are now finally ready to take the step taken earlier by the visual artists.

If Canada, as a cultural entity, is slowly succeeding in nurturing a literary tradition that has a distinctly and uniquely Canadian voice—albeit, one fashioned out of the melding of any number of other traditions—then the Indian people of this country have a literary tradition that goes back thousands of years. As a people, we are very much aware of the fact that there were mythologies that applied—and applied in a very powerful manner—to this specific landscape since long before the landmark year of 1492 AD. But this literary tradition is an oral tradition, not a written one, and these ancient stories were passed down generation to generation—in Cree, in Ojibway, Mohawk—until they reached us, the present generation, the first, as a group, to have a reasonable grasp of the English language.

But why not write novels? Why not short stories? Why the stage? For me, the reason is that this oral tradition translates most easily and most effectively into a three dimensional medium. In a sense, it's like taking the "stage" that lives inside the mind, the imagination, and transposing it—using words, actors, lights, sound—onto the stage in a theatre. For me, it is really a matter of taking a mythology as extraordinary and as powerful as the human imagination itself and re-working it to fit, snugly and comfortably, the medium of the stage.

The only thing is, this mythology has to be re-worked somewhat if it is to be relevant to us Indians living in today's world. The way these stories go to date, they were meant for a people who lived in a forest environment; we—our family—were all born in tents, grew up travelling by dog-sled and canoe, etc. But, today, as an adult, I am urban by choice. So in order for these myths to be relevant to my life, to my own system of spiritual beliefs, I have to apply these myths, this mythology to the realities of city living. So, "Weesageechak" the trickster figure who stands at the very centre of Cree mythology and who is a figure as important to Cree culture as Christ is to Western culture, still hangs round and about the lakes and forests of northern Manitoba, yes, but he also takes strolls down Yonge Street, drinks beer, sometimes passes out at the Silver Dollar and goes shopping at the Eaton Centre. You should have seen him when he first encountered a telephone, an electric typewriter, a toaster, an automobile. I was there.

Greek drama fascinates me because I feel that the basis for much of that drama is the mythology of that culture: the creatures, beings, the gods and events that inhabit the spiritual world of the Greeks play a central role. In much of Western literature, Christian mythology acts as a central under-pinning. And I believe that for "Native literature" to achieve any degree of universal resonance or relevance, any degree of permanence, Indian mythology must lie at its very root.

The difficulty Native writers encounter as writers, however, is that we must use English if our voice is to be heard by a large enough audience: English and not Cree. The Cree language is so completely different and the world view that that language engenders and expresses is so completely different—at odds, some would say—that inevitably, the characters we write into our plays must, of necessity, lose some of their original lustre in the translation. So, of necessity again, we are very conscious of the fact that we are working with a language that we must reshape to our own particular purpose. I suppose it's a little like trying to imagine what Chekhov's THE THREE SISTERS[1] must look and sound and feel like in the original Russian performed by a Russian company of actors and then seeing it performed in "Oxford" English. We get the general drift, maybe more, but I don't think we get the total reality of it, in the end. At any rate, the English language, as any language does, is changing constantly and we have a say in the changing of that language. It will be interesting to see where we get with it in the next few decades.

Indian mythology is filled with the most extraordinary events, beings and creatures. These lend themselves so well to visual interpretation, to exciting stage and visual creation: the cannibal spirit Weetigo (Windigo in Ojibway) who devours human flesh (in one show, we had him dining out at a Yuppie restaurant in Yorkville); the young man Ayash who encounters a village populated by women with teeth in their vaginas and has to deal with them as part of his vision quest, the woman who makes love to a thousand snakes; and so on and so forth. Not only are the visuals powerful, the symbolism underlying these extraordinary stories is as basic and as

---

1   *The Three Sisters* (1900) is a play by Russian author Anton Chekhov; it was first performed in 1901 at the Moscow Art Theatre.

direct as air. And they come from deep, deep within the flesh and blood of a people who have known this particular landscape since time immemorial and who are so close to it they have become an integral part if it, like rock.

A recent Toronto production provides a good example. In THE REZ SISTERS, the story, essentially, is of the lives of these seven extraordinary Ojibway women, their passions, their tragedies, their exhilarations and of their bizarre and fantastical adventure with a game called bingo, a game otherwise as tawdry and mundane as laundry day on an Indian reservation (the "Rez" to us Indian folk). But on a larger scale, the story is of the Trickster, Nanabush—the Ojibway equivalent of the Cree Weesageechak—and his adventure with these women, the fun he has in "monitoring" the spiritual dimension of their lives. As this spirit figure is the one who straddles the consciousness of Man and that of God, the intermediary between the Great Spirit and his people—he informs the cancer victim among this group of women, Marie-Adele Starblanket, that "it is almost time for you to come with me," all the while disguised as a sea-gull who shits on Marie-Adele's lawn, swings from her clothes-line as she does laundry, etc. Marie-Adele, in some dark corner of herself, knows somehow that she is dying and sort of, though not quite, recognizes the spirit inside the beckoning bird.

Later, as the women are in the van, driving down the highway to Toronto to take part in "the biggest bingo in the world," they stop for a flat tire. In the darkness, Nanabush, now in the guise of a nighthawk, makes another appearance. And he and Marie-Adele have this violent confrontation through which Marie-Adele realizes, for certain now, that she is going to die soon. When the women get to the bingo palace, Nanabush appears to Marie-Adele for the last and final time, this time in the guise of the bingo master—"the master of the game," as Marie-Adele now addresses him—who finally takes her hand at the climax of the game and proceeds to escort her into the spirit world. The other six women, who meanwhile have had varying degrees of awareness with this creature throughout, are left weeping and mourning at her grave. The Trickster has played his "trick" and he chortles. The play, in fact, becomes the tale of small and petty doings of men/women on this earth while only half-aware of some grander, larger "design" that rules their lives.

The mythology of a people is the articulation of the dreamworld of that people; without that dreamlife being active in all its forms—from the most extreme beauty to the most horrific and back—the culture of that people is dead. It is a dead culture and it is, in effect, a dead people we speak of. And, ironically enough, with the threat of nuclear annihilation facing us square in the face, we could be a dead culture and a dead people sooner than we think.

So, I suppose that we Indian people writing for the stage ultimately want to be heard so the dreamlife of this particular people, this particular landscape, can achieve some degree of exposure among general audiences. They just may learn, we keep hoping, something new and something terribly relevant and beautiful about that particular landscape that they too have become inhabitants of.

Basil Johnston

"One Generation from Extinction"

One of Canada's most prolific Indigenous writers, Anishinaabe author, scholar, story-teller, and educator Basil Johnston (1929–2015) was born on the Parry Island Indian Reserve in Ontario and was a member of the Chippewas of Nawash First Nation on Neyaashiinigmiing. He was the recipient of numerous awards, including honourary doctorates from the University of Toronto and Laurentian University, and an Aboriginal Achievement Award. Johnston was a respected authority on Ojibway/Anishinaabe language and culture, and worked for many years with the Royal Ontario Museum in Toronto. From the beginning, his work was profoundly political and he continually advocated for the preservation of Indigenous languages and cultures. A living link to the traditional Elder, Johnston sought to preserve his culture and educate in order to demonstrate that there is much more to Indigenous peoples than material culture.

Johnston's 1990 article, "One Generation from Extinction," addresses many of the same concerns as his landmark article "Is That All There Is? Tribal Literature." Both essays argue that material culture is meaningless without an understanding of a culture's stories and language. In "One Generation from Extinction," Johnston outlines the dire situation facing Indigenous languages in Canada: of the 53 languages originally spoken in Canada, only Inuktitut, Cree, and Ojibway were expected to survive into the next generation. Without knowledge of their language and literature, he argues, communities lose their identities, which is what made the colonial government's "English only" policy such an effective tool of cultural genocide. Johnston, in fact, speaks of Indigenous languages in the past tense, as though already lost, which leaves little hope for Indigenous peoples who don't speak their languages. Ultimately, however, he does offer a solution. The government, he says, must finance language institutes to research and publish in and on Indigenous languages before the last living speakers disappear.

Johnston, Basil. "One Generation from Extinction." *Canadian Literature: Native Writers and Canadian Literature* 124–25 (Spring and Summer 1990): 10–15.

One Generation from Extinction

Within the past few years Gregor Keeshig, Henry Johnston, Resime Akiwenzie, Norman McLeod, and Belva Pitwaniquot died. They all spoke their tribal language, Anishinaubae (Ojibwa). When these elders passed away, so did a portion of the tribal language come to an end as a tree disintegrates by degrees and in stages until it is no more; and, though infants were born to replenish the loss of life, not any one of them will learn the language of their grandfathers or grandmothers to keep it alive and to pass it on to their descendants. Thus language dies.

In some communities there are no more Gregor Keeshigs, Henry Johnstons, Resime Akiwenzies, Norman McLeods, Belva Pitwaniquots; those remaining have no more affinity to their ancestral language than they do to Swahili or Sanskrit; in other communities the languages may not survive beyond a generation. Some tribal languages are at the edge of extinction, not expected to survive for more than a few years. There remain but three aboriginal languages out of the original fifty-three found in Canada that may survive several more generations.

There is cause to lament but it is the native peoples who have the most cause to lament the passing of their languages. They lose not only the ability to express the simplest of daily sentiments and needs but they can no longer understand the ideas, concepts, insights, attitudes, rituals, ceremonies, institutions brought into being by their ancestors; and, having lost the power to understand, cannot sustain, enrich, or pass on their heritage. No longer will they think Indian or feel Indian. And though they may wear "Indian" jewellery and take part in pow-wows, they can never capture that kinship with and reverence for the sun and the moon, the sky and the water, or feel the lifebeat of Mother Earth or sense the change in her moods; no longer are the wolf, the bear and the caribou elder brothers but beasts, resources to be killed and sold. They will have lost their identity which no amount of reading can ever restore. Only language and literature can restore the "Indianness."

Now if Canadians of West European or other origin have less cause than "Indians" to lament the passing of tribal languages and cultures it is because they may not realize that there is more to tribal languages than "ugh" or "how" or "kimu sabi." At most and at best Euro-Canadians might have read or heard about Raven and Nana-bush and Thunderbirds and other "tricksters"; some may have even studied "Culture Myths," "Hero Tales," "Transformation Tales," or "Nature Myths and Beast Fables," but these accounts were never regarded as bearing any more sense than "Little Red Riding Hood" or "The Three Little Pigs." Neither language nor literature were ever considered in their natural kinship, which is the only way in which language ought to be considered were its range, depth, force and beauty to be appreciated.

Perhaps our Canadian compatriots of West European origin have more cause to lament the passing of an Indian language than they realize or care to admit. Scholars mourn that there is no one who can speak the Huron language and thus assist scholars in their pursuit of further knowledge about the tribe; scholars mourn that had the Beothuk language[1] survived, so much more would be known about the Beothuk peoples. In mourning the extinction of the language, scholars are implicitly declaring that the knowledge derived from a study of snowshoes, shards, arrowheads, old pipes, shrunken heads and old bones, hunting, fishing, transportation, food preparation, ornamentation and sometimes ritual is limited. And so it is; material culture can yield only so much.

Language is crucial. If scholars are to increase their knowledge and if they are to add depth and width to their studies, they must study a native language and literature. It is not enough to know linguistics or to know a few words or even some phrases or to have access to the Jesuit *Relations*, Chippewa *Exercises*, Ojibwa *Texts*, or a *Dictionary of the Otchipwe Language*.[2] Without a knowledge of the language scholars can never take for granted the accuracy of an interpretation or translation of a passage, let alone a single word; nor can they presume that their articles, tracts, treatises, essays bear the kind of accuracy that scholarship and integrity demand. They would continue to labour under the impression that the word "manitou" means spirit and that it has no other meaning. Superstitious nonsense, according to the white man. They do not know that the word bears other meanings even more fundamental than "spirit," such as, and/or pertaining to the deities; of a substance, character, nature, essence, quiddity beyond comprehension and therefore beyond explanation, a mystery; supernatural; potency, potential. What a difference such knowledge might have made in the studies conducted by Ruth Landes or Thomas B. Leekley,[3] and others on the Anishinaubae tribe. Perhaps, instead of regarding "Indians" as superstitious

---

1 The Beothuk, an Indigenous people of the island of Newfoundland, were Algonkian-speaking hunter-gatherers who were exterminated by disease and warfare from French and English settlers. Shanawdithit, the last known Beothuk, died in St. John's, Newfoundland, in 1829.

2 Reuben Gold Thwaites, ed., *The Jesuit Relations and Allied Documents: Travels and Explorations of the Jesuit Missionaries in New France, 1610–1791* (Cleveland: Burrows Bros., 1896–1901). R.R. Bishop Baraga, *A Dictionary of the Otchipwe Language* (Montreal: Beauchemin & Valois, 1878). Chrysostom Verwyst, *Chippewa Exercises; Being a Practical Introduction into the Study of the Chippewa Language* (Harbor Springs, MI: Holy Childhood School Print, 1901).

3 Ruth Landes, born 1908 in New York City and died 1991 in Hamilton, Ontario, is considered a "pioneer" in American cultural anthropology and produced a large body of written research, including *Ojibwa Sociology* (1937), *Ojibwa Woman* (1938), *Ojibwa Religion and the Midewiwin* (1968), and *The Mystic Lake Sioux* (1968). Thomas B. Leekley is the author of *The World of Manabozho: Tales of the Chippewa Indians* (New York: Vanguard P, 1965).

for positing "spirits" in trees or in other inanimate or insensate objects, they might have credited them with insight for having perceived a vital substance or essence that imparted life, form, growth, healing, and strength in all things, beings, and places. They might have understood that the expression "manitouwan" meant that an object possessed or was infused with an element or a feature that was beyond human ken; they might have understood that "w'manitouwih" meant that he or she was endowed with extraordinary talents, and that it did not mean that he or she was a spirit.

Language is essential. If scholars and writers are to know how "Indians" perceive and regard certain ideas they must study an "Indian" language. When an "Anishinau-bae" says that someone is telling the truth, he says "w'daeb-awae." But the expression is not just a mere confirmation of a speaker's veracity. It is at the same time a philosophical proposition that, in saying, a speaker casts his words and his voice only as far as his vocabulary and his perception will enable him. In so doing the tribe was denying that there was absolute truth; that the best a speaker could achieve and a listener expect was the highest degree of accuracy. Somehow that one expression "w'daeb-awae" set the limits of a single statement as well as setting limits on all speech.

There was a special regard almost akin to reverence for speech and for the truth. Perhaps it was because words bear the tone of the speaker and may therefore be regarded as belonging to that person; perhaps it is because words have but a fleeting momentary existence in sound and are gone except in memory; perhaps it is because words have not ceased to exist but survive in echo and continue on in infinity; perhaps it is because words are medicine that can heal or injure; perhaps it is because words possess an element of the manitou that enabled them to conjure images and ideas out of nothing, and are the means by which the autissokanuk (muses) inspired men and women. It was not for nothing that the older generation did not solicit the autissokanuk to assist in the genesis of stories or in the composition of chants in seasons other than winter.

To instil respect for language the old counselled youth, "Don't talk too much" (Kegon zaum-doongaen), for they saw a kinship between language and truth. The expression is not without its facetious aspect but in its broader application it was intended to convey to youth other notions implicit in the expression "Don't talk too much," for the injunction also meant "Don't talk too often...Don't talk too long...Don't talk about those matters that you know nothing about." Were a person to restrict his discourse, and measure his speech, and govern his talk by what he knew, he would earn the trust and respect of his (her) listeners. Of that man or woman they would say "w'daeb-awae." Better still, people would want to hear the speaker again and by so doing bestow upon the speaker the opportunity to speak, for ultimately it is the people who confer the right of speech by their audience.

Language was a precious heritage; literature was no less precious. So precious did the tribe regard language and speech that it held those who abused language and speech and truth in contempt and ridicule and withheld from them their trust and confidence. To the tribe the man or woman who rambled on and on, or who let his tongue range over every subject or warp the truth was said to talk in circles in a manner no different from that of a mongrel who, not knowing the source of alarm, barks in circles (w'geewi-anirnoh). Ever since words and sounds were reduced to written symbols and have been stripped of their mystery and magic, the regard and reverence for them have diminished in tribal life.

As rich and full of meaning as may be individual words and expression, they embody only a small portion of the entire stock and potential of tribal knowledge, wisdom, and intellectual attainment, the greater part is deposited in myths, legends, stories, and in the lyrics of chants that make up the tribe's literature. Therein will be found the essence and the substance of tribal ideas, concepts, insights, attitudes, values, beliefs, theories, notions, sentiments, and accounts of their institutions and rituals and ceremonies. Without language scholars, writers, and teachers will have no access to the depth and width of tribal knowledge and understanding, but must continue to labour as they have done these many years under the impression that "Indian" stories are nothing more than fairy tales or folklore, fit only for juvenile minds. For scholars and academics Nanabush, Raven, Glooscap, Weesaukeechauk and other mythological figures will ever remain "tricksters," culture heroes, deities whose misadventures were dreamed into being only for the amusement of children. Primitive and pagan and illiterate to boot, "Indians" could not possibly address or articulate abstract ideas or themes; neither their minds nor their languages could possibly express any idea more complex than taboos, superstitions and bodily needs.

But were ethnologists, anthropologists, linguists, teachers of native children and writers of native literature—yes, even archaeologists—to learn a native language, perhaps they might learn that Nanabush and Raven are not simply "tricksters" but the caricatured representations of human nature and character in their many facets; perhaps they might give thought to the meaning and sense to be found in Weessaukeetchauk, The Bitter Soul. There is no other way except through language for scholars to learn or to validate their studies, their theories, their theses about the values, ideals or institutions or any other aspect of tribal life; there is no other way by which knowledge of native life can find increase. Not good enough is it to say in hushed tones after a reverential description of a totem pole or the lacing of a snowshoe, "My, weren't they clever."

Just consider the fate of "Indian" stories written by those who knew nothing of the language and never did hear any of the stories in their entirety or in their original version but derived everything that they knew of their subject from second, third and even fourth diluted sources. Is it any wonder then that the stories in *Indian Legends of Canada* by E.E. Clark or in *Manabozho* by T.B. Leekley[1] are so bland and devoid of sense. Had the authors known the stories in their "Indian" sense and flavour, per-

---

1   Ella Elizabeth Clark, *Indian Legends of Canada* (Toronto: McClelland & Stewart, 1960). Thomas B. Leekley, *ibid*.

haps they might have infused their versions with more wit and substance. Had the authors known that the creation story as the Anishinaubae understood it to mean was intended to represent in the most dramatic way possible the process of individual development from the smallest portion of talent to be retrieved from the depths of one's being and then given growth by breath of life. Thus a man and woman are to develop themselves, create their own worlds, and shape their being and give meaning to life. Had the authors known this meaning of the Creation Story, perhaps they might have written their accounts in terms more in keeping with the sense and thrust of the story. But not knowing the language nor having heard the story in its original text or state, the authors could not, despite their intentions, impart to their accounts the due weight and perspective the story deserved. The stories were demeaned.

With language dead and literature demeaned, "Indian" institutions are beyond understanding and restoration. Let us turn back the calendar two and a half centuries, to that period when the "Indian" languages were spoken in every home, when native literature inspired thought and when native "Indian" institutions governed native "Indian" life. It was then that a native institution caught the imagination of the newcomers to this continent. The men and women who founded a new nation to be known as the United States of America took as their model for their constitution and government the principles of government and administration embodied in The Great Tree of Peace of the Five Nations Confederacy. The institution of The Great Tree of Peace was not then too primitive nor too alien for study or emulation to the founders of the United States. In more recent years even the architects of the United Nations regarded the "Indian" institution of The Great Tree of Peace not as a primitive organization beneath their dignity and intellect, but rather as an institution of merit. There exist still "Indian" institutions that may well serve and benefit this society and this nation, not as dramatically as did The Great Tree of Peace the United States of America, but bestow some good as yet undreamed or unimagined. Just how much good such institutions may confer upon this or some future generation will not be known unless the "Indian" languages survive.

And what is it that has undermined the vitality of some of the "Indian" languages and deprived this generation and this society the promise and the benefit of the wisdom and the knowledge embodied in tribal literature?

In the case of the Beothuk and their language, the means used were simple and direct: it was the blade, the bludgeon, and the bullet that were plied in the destruction of the Beothuk in their sleep, at their table, and in their quiet passage from home to place of work, until the tribe was no more. The speakers were annihilated; no more was the Beothuk language spoken; whatever their wisdom or whatever their institutions, the whole of the Beothuk heritage was destroyed.

In other instances, instead of bullets, bludgeons, and bayonets, other means were used to put an end to the speaking of an "Indian" language. A kick with a police riding boot administered by a 175-pound man upon the person of an eight-year-old boy for uttering the language of a savage left its pain for days and its bruise upon the spirit for life. A boy once kicked was not likely to risk a second or a third. A slap in the face or a punch to the back of the head delivered even by a small man upon the person of a small boy left its sting and a humiliation not soon forgotten. And if a boot or a fist were not administered, then a lash or a yardstick was plied until the "Indian" language was beaten out.[1] To boot and fist and lash was added ridicule. Both speaker and his language were assailed. "What's the use of that language? It isn't polite to speak another language in the presence of other people. Learn English! That's the only way you're going to get ahead. How can you learn two languages at the same time? No wonder kids can't learn anything else. It's a primitive language; hasn't the vocabulary to express abstract ideas, poor. Say 'ugh.' Say something in your language!...How can you get your tongue around those sounds?" On and on the comments were made, disparaging, until in too many the language was shamed into silence and disuse.

And how may the federal government assist in the restoration of the native languages to their former vigour and vitality and enable them to fulfil their promise?

The Government of Canada must finance the establishment of either provincial or regional language institutes to be affiliated with a museum or a university or a provincial native educational organization. The function of the "institute," to be headed by a native person who speaks, reads, and writes a native language, will be to foster research into language and to encourage the publication of lexicons, dictionaries, grammars, courses, guides, outlines, myths, stories, legends, genealogies, histories, religion, rituals, ceremonies, chants, prayers, and general articles; to tape stories, myths, legends, grammars, teaching guides and outlines and to build a collection of written and oral literature and to make same accessible to scholars, teachers and native institutions; and to duplicate and distribute written and oral literature to the native communities and learning institutions. The native languages deserve to be enshrined in this country's heritage as much as do snowshoes, shards, and arrowheads. Nay! More.

But unless the writings, the essays, stories, plays, the papers of scholars, academics, lexicographers, grammarians, etymologists, playwrights, poets, novelists, composers, philosophers are published and distributed, they can never nurture growth in language or literature. Taking into account the market represented by each tribe, no commercial publisher would risk publication of an "Indian" book. Hence, only the federal government has the means to sponsor publication of an "Indian text," either through a commercial publisher or through the Queen's Printer. The publication of an "Indian" book may not be a commercially profitable enterprise, but it would add to the nation's intellectual and literary heritage.

---

1 Johnston is referring to the banning of Indigenous languages in residential schools. See Sam McKegney, "Indigenous Writing and the Residential School Legacy: A Public Interview with Basil Johnston" (2009).

Lenore Keeshig [Tobias]

"Stop Stealing Native Stories"

Lenore Keeshig [Tobias], Anishinaabekwe, was born on Neyaashiinigmiing (the Cape Croker Reserve) on the Saugeen Peninsula in Ontario. An Ojibway journalist, storyteller, poet, children's author and activist, she is a founding member—along with Daniel David Moses and Tomson Highway—of the influential literary group "The Committee to Reestablish the Trickster," Keeshig [Tobias] fought actively to promote Indigenous voice and writing throughout the 1980s, and into the 1990s—at a time when many Indigenous writers found themselves shut out of the publishing industry. Keeshig [Tobias] became one of the most influential spokespeople of the appropriation of voice controversy which started in the Writer's Union of Canada, when she asked non-Natives to "stop stealing Native stories." The debate then moved to the pages of the *Globe and Mail* newspaper.

"Stop Stealing Native Stories" appeared in the *Globe and Mail* in 1990 and is revolutionary for its condemnation of appropriation of voice. The article appeared as part of a larger debate that condemned the critics of those speaking in the voice of others, accusing them of censorship. Keeshig's [Tobias] article critiques the film *Where the Spirit Lives*, which deals with the residential school experience but was made without the participation of Indigenous peoples. The article contends that not only does the film misrepresent Indigenous identity, but it also commodifies it. Keeshig [Tobias] also argues that it is the privileged who have access to production and filmmaking, taking up space that could be occupied by Indigenous peoples. The article targets unethical appropriation, but does give room for those who speak *with* rather than *for* others. The article cites Métis writer and activist Maria Campbell, who says "[i]f you want to write our stories, then be prepared to live with us," to which Keeshig [Tobias] adds, "[a]nd not just for a few months." Overlooked by non-Indigenous critics focusing on the censorship question, the related issues of retention and promotion of Indigenous language and cultural sovereignty are at the heart of Keeshig's [Tobias] concerns.

Keeshig [Tobias], Lenore. "Stop Stealing Native Stories." *Globe and Mail* (26 January 1990): A7.

Stop Stealing Native Stories

AAA-III-EEE Y-AAh!
Clear the way.
In a sacred manner I come.
The stories are mine!
— Ojibway war song

Critics of non-native writers who borrow from the native experience have been dismissed as advocates of censorship and accused of trying to shackle artistic imagination, but their objections are prompted by something much more.

Where the Spirit Lives may be a bad film. *Bone Bird* by Calgary novelist Darlene Barry Quaife may oversimplify native spirituality.[1] W.P. Kinsella's Hobbema stories[2] may be insulting. But the real problem Is that they amount to culture theft, the theft of voice.

Canada's francophones have a strong and unique voice in North America. Why? Because they have fought to ensure that their language remains intact. Language is the conveyor of culture. It carries the ideas by which a nation defines itself as a people. It gives voice to a nation's stories, its *mythos*.

How do Canadians feel about the US mythos defining them and their country? This is quickly becoming a reality, I fear, because Canadians have been too quick to hand over their voice and their stories to Americans.

Stories, you see, are not just entertainment. Stories are power. They reflect the deepest, the most intimate perceptions, relationships and attitudes of a people. Stories show how a people, a culture, thinks. Such wonderful offerings are seldom reproduced by outsiders.

This is the root of the problem with *Where the Spirit Lives*, which deals with the treatment of native students in government-sponsored residential schools during the

---

1 Darlene Barry Quaife, *Bone Bird* (Turnstone P, 1989), winner of the Commonwealth Writers Prize for Best First Book.
2 William Patrick (W.P.) Kinsella is the prolific and controversial author of what he calls his "Indian stories," set on the Hobbema Reserve in central Alberta. These books include *Dance Me Outside* (1977), also a feature film, *The Fencepost Chronicles*, winner of the 1987 Stephen Leacock Medal, *Brother Frank's Gospel Hour* (1994), and *The Secret of the Northern Lights* (1998).

1930s. The film has been shown on the CBC and TVOntario and as part of Canada Day at the recent festival in Palm Springs, Calif.[1]

So what is it all about, anyway? In the end, a little Indian girl and her brother ride off into the vast, uninhabited wilderness (Anne Shirley goes west?). They ride right out of the sentimentalized Canadian consciousness—stoic child warriors noble in defeat, marching home with Bible in hand. (A book of truth, perhaps, but whose?)

Native people were not involved in any creative aspect of the film. Their voice was heard only through cultural consultants hired to provide the nuances and insights lacked by the movie's writer and producers.

Cultural insight, nuance, metaphor and symbols give a book or film the ring of truth, but their essence—the thing that gives stories universal appeal, that allows true empathy and shared emotion—is missing from *Where the Spirit Lives*, as it is from most "native" writing by non-natives.

Canadians all too often use native stories, symbols and history to sell things—cars, tobacco or movies. But why hasn't Basil Johnston's *Indian School Days* become a bestseller? Why hasn't *Half Breed* by Maria Campbell been reprinted?[2] (Why, for that matter, has Ms Campbell, as one of Canada's "celebrated" authors, never received a writer's grant?)

Where the Spirit Lives, after having squeezed out the native version of what happened in the residential schools, turns around and tells natives to make their own movies. How can we? Even if we had access to financial backers, they would say: "Residential schools? It's been done."

With native people struggling for justice with land claims and in education, what makes Canadians think they have equality in the film industry? In publishing? With agencies that make arts grants? In the arts themselves?

Instead, the Canadian cultural industry is stealing—unconsciously, perhaps, but with the same devastating results—native stories as surely as the missionaries stole our religion and the politicians stole our land and the residential schools stole our language. As Leslie Marmon Silko writes in *Ceremony*,[3] stories "are all we have, you see—all we have to fight off illness and death." As a storyteller I was once advised by an elder that there is a season for storytelling—winter. "Blackflies, mosquitoes and other creatures like those stories," she cautioned.

How quaint, I thought. Nonetheless, I respected her advice and, as time went on, I began to understand it. If storytellers sit around all summer telling stories, then surely they'll become the feast of blackflies and mosquitoes. My elder was telling me that these stories are meant for certain ears only—and native ears.

1 *Where the Spirit Lives* is a dramatic film about Aboriginal children in Canadian residential schools. Written by Keith Ross Leckie and directed by Bruce Pittman, it aired on CBC Television in 1989 and was released in the USA in 1990. It was screened at numerous film festivals, including the Palms Springs International Film Festival.
2 Maria Campbell, *Halfbreed* (Toronto: McClelland & Stewart, 1973).
3 Leslie Marmon Silko, *Ceremony* (New York: Viking Penguin, 1977).

35

So potent are stories that, in native culture, one storyteller cannot tell another's story without permission.

But why are Canadians so obsessed with native stories anyway? Why the urge to "write Indian"? Have Canadians run out of stories of their own? Or are their renderings just nostalgia for a simpler, more "at one with nature" stage of human development? There's a cliché for you.

Maybe Canadian stories about native people are some form of exorcism. Are they trying to atone for the horrible reality of native-Canadian relations? Or maybe they just know a good story when they find one and are willing to take it, without permission, just as archaeologists used to rob our graves for museums.

What about the quest for native spirituality? It is mostly escapist, and people such as Ms Quaife would rather look to an ideal native living in never-never land than confront the reality of what being native means in Canadian society.

For example, residential-school survivors tell of children being forced to eat their own vomit when their stomachs could no longer hold down the sour porridge. They tell of broken knuckles from fingers being rapped. Some even tell of having pins stuck through their tongues as punishment for speaking their own language. (Now, that's censorship.)

And what about the teacher who was removed from one residential school for abusing children? He was simply sent to another, more remote school.

It's not that these stories have never been told; Canadians just haven't heard them. Nor does it mean our writers and storytellers are incompetent and inexperienced, as Mr. Kinsella seems to suggest.

It means our voices have been marginalized. Imagine, Canadians telling native stories because their government outlawed native languages, native culture.

However, as Ms Campbell said on CBC Radio's Morningside, "If you want to write our stories, then be prepared to live with us." And not just for a few months.

Hear the voices of the wilderness. Be there with the Lubicon, the Innu. Be there with the Teme-Augama Anishnabi on the Red Squirrel Road. The Saugeen Ojibway. If you want these stories, fight for them. I dare you.

Thomas King

"Godzilla vs. Post-Colonial"

Thomas King was born in California to a Cherokee father and Greek mother, and immigrated to Canada in 1980, where he holds dual citizenship. He worked at the University of Lethbridge in Alberta, and the University of Minnesota, before moving to the University of Guelph, where he is now Professor Emeritus. More than any other writer, King is responsible for popularizing Indigenous literature in Canada; his first novel, *Medicine River*, was published by a major press, Viking, in 1990, and later made into a movie by the CBC. Known for his use of humour and irony as tools of decolonization, King went on to create and co-star in the CBC radio show *Dead Dog Café Comedy Hour*, while writing major works of fiction, such as *Green Grass, Running Water* (1993), which combines realism with Indigenous mythic elements to create what has been called "mythic-realism." King's work continues to be as popular as ever, and in 2014 he won the RBC Taylor Prize for *The Inconvenient Indian: A Curious Account of Native People* and the Governor General's Literary Award for *The Back of the Turtle*.

King's 1990 essay, "Godzilla vs. Post-Colonial," addresses the domination of post-colonial theory in Indigenous studies in general, and literature in particular during the 1980s and 1990s. It continues to be the most oft-cited work by critics of those applying post-colonial theory to Indigenous texts in Canada. In this influential essay, King argues that applying the term "post-colonial" to work written by Indigenous writers "privileges the arrival of the settlers in North America" in that it excludes all literature pre-dating contact. Progressive positioning, he argues, also contains a value judgement since "post" or "later" is associated with progress, and is therefore privileged. The essay proposes other ways of defining Indigenous literatures, such as tribal (community-based), interfusional (written and oral), polemical and associational (traditional and contemporary), many of which are seen by today's critics as more credible approaches to literature than theories of post-colonialism.

King, Thomas. "Godzilla vs. Post-Colonial." *World Literature Written in English* 30.2 (1990): 10–16.

Godzilla vs. Post-Colonial

I grew up in Northern California, and I grew up fast. I don't mean that I was raised in a tough part of town where you had to fight to survive. I was raised in a small town in the foothills, quite pastoral in fact. I mean I grew up all at once. By my first year of high school, I already had my full height, while most of my friends were just beginning to grow.

We had a basketball team at the high school and a basketball coach who considered himself somewhat of an authority on the subject of talent. He could spot it, he said. And he spotted me. He told me I had a talent for the game, and that I should come out for the team. With my size, he said, I would be a natural player. I was flattered.

I wish I could tell you that I excelled at basketball, that I was an all-star, that college coaches came to see me play. But the truth of the matter is, I wasn't even mediocre. Had I not been so very young and so very serious, I might have laughed at my attempts to run and bounce a ball at the same time. Certainly most everyone who saw me play did.

Now before you think that my embarrassment in basketball was the fault of an overzealous coach, you have to remember that we both made more or less the same assumption. The coach assumed that because I was tall, I would be a good player. And once the coach called my height to my attention and encouraged me, I assumed the same thing. We spent the rest of our time together trying to figure out why I was so bad.

Just before the first game of my second season, I tore my knee, mercifully ending my basketball career. My experience taught me little about basketball, but it did teach me a great deal about assumptions.

Assumptions are a dangerous thing. They are especially dangerous when we do not even see that the premise from which we start a discussion is not the hard fact that we thought it was, but one of the fancies we churn out of our imaginations to help us get from the beginning of an idea to the end.

Which brings me, albeit by a circuitous route, to post-colonial literature. I am not a theorist. It's not an apology, but it is a fact. So I can not talk to the internal structure of the theory itself, how it works, or what it tells us about the art of language and the art of literature. Nor can I participate to any great extent in what Linda Hutcheon calls "the de-doxifying project of postmodernism."[1]

But having played basketball, I can talk about the assumptions that the term post-colonial makes. It is, first of all, part of a triumvirate. In order to get to "post," we have to wend our way through no small amount of literary history, acknowledging the existence of its antecedents, pre-colonial and colonial. In the case of Native literature, we can say that pre-colonial literature was that literature, oral in nature, that was in existence prior to European contact, a literature that existed exclusively within specific cultural communities.

Post-colonial literature, then, must be the literature produced by Native people sometime after colonization, a literature that arises in large part out of the experience that is colonization. These particular terms allow us to talk about Native literature as a literature that can be counterpoint to Canadian literature, a new voice, if you will, a different voice in the literary amphitheatre. I rather like the idea of post-colonial literature, because it promises to set me apart from the masses and suggests that what I have to offer is new and exciting. But then again, I rather liked the idea of playing basketball, too.

I said at the beginning that I was not a theorist and was not going to concern myself with how post-colonialism operates as a critical method. But I am concerned with what the term says about Natives and Native literature and the initial assumptions it makes about us and our cultures.

When I made that rather simplistic comparison between pre-colonial and post-colonial, I left out one of the players, rather like talking about pre-pubescence and post-pubescence without mentioning puberty. My apologies. It was a trick to make you think I was going to say something profound, when, in fact, I was going to make the rather simple observation that in the case of pre- and post-pubescence and pre- and post-colonial, the pivot around which we move is puberty and colonialism. But here, I'm lying again. Another trick, I'm afraid, for in puberty's case, the precedent, the root, and the antecedent are, at least, all part of a whole, whereas in the case of colonialism— within a discussion of Native literature—the term has little to do with the literature itself. It is both separate from and antithetical to what came before and what came after.

Pre-colonial literature, as we use the term in North America, has no relationship whatsoever to colonial literature. The two are neither part of a biological or natural cycle nor does the one anticipate the other, while the full complement of terms— pre-colonial, colonial, and post-colonial—reeks of unabashed ethnocentrism and well-meaning dismissal, and they point to a deep-seated assumption that is at the heart of most well-intentioned studies of Native literatures.

While post-colonialism purports to be a method by which we can begin to look at those literatures which are formed out of the struggle of the oppressed against

---

1   Linda Hutcheon, *The Politics of Postmodernism* (London and New York: Routledge, 2001 [1989]).

the oppressor, the colonized and the colonizer, the term itself assumes that the starting point for that discussion is the advent of Europeans in North America. At the same time, the term organizes the literature progressively suggesting that there is both progress and improvement. No less distressing, it also assumes that the struggle between guardian and ward is the catalyst for contemporary Native literature, providing those of us who write with method and topic. And, worst of all, the idea of post-colonial writing effectively cuts us off from our traditions, traditions that were in place before colonialism ever became a question, traditions which have come down to us through our cultures in spite of colonization, and it supposes that contemporary Native writing is largely a construct of oppression. Ironically, while the term itself—post-colonial—strives to escape to find new centres, it remains, in the end, a hostage to nationalism.

As a contemporary Native writer, I am quite unwilling to make these assumptions, and I am quite unwilling to use these terms.

A friend of mine cautioned me about this stridency and pointed out that post-colonial is a perfectly good term to use for that literature which is, in fact, a reaction to the historical impositions of colonialization. She suggested I look at Maria Campbell's *Halfbreed* and Beatrice Culleton's *In Search of April Raintree*[1] as examples of works for which the term is appropriate. She further suggested that post-colonial was not such a simple thing, that much of what I was concerned with—centres, difference, totalizing, hegemony, margins—was being addressed by post-colonial methodology. If this is true, then it is unfortunate that the method has such an albatross—as the term—hanging around its neck. But I must admit that I remain sceptical that such a term could describe a non-centred, non-nationalistic method.

If we are to use terms to describe the various stages or changes in Native literature as it has become written, while at the same time remaining oral, and as it has expanded from a specific language base to a multiple language base, we need to find descriptors which do not invoke the cant of progress and which are not joined at the hip with nationalism. Post-colonial might be an excellent term to use to describe Canadian literature, but it will not do to describe Native literature.

As a Native writer, I lean towards terms such as tribal, interfusional, polemical, and associational to describe the range of Native writing. I prefer these terms for a variety of reasons: they tend to be less centred and do not, within the terms themselves, privilege one culture over another; they avoid the sense of progress in which primitivism gives way to sophistication, suggesting as it does that such movement is both natural and desirable; they identify points on a cultural and literary continuum for Native literature which do not depend on anomalies such as the arrival of Europeans in North America or the advent of non-Native literature in this hemisphere,

---

1 Maria Campbell, *Halfbreed* (Toronto: McClelland & Stewart, 1973). Beatrice Culleton [Mosionier], *In Search of April Raintree* (Winnipeg, MB: Pemmican, 1983).

what Marie Baker likes to call "settler litter."[1] At the same time, these terms are not "bags" into which we can collect and store the whole of Native literature. They are, more properly, vantage points from which we can see a particular literary landscape.

Two of these terms are self-apparent: tribal and polemical. Tribal refers to that literature which exists primarily within a tribe or a community, literature that is shared almost exclusively by members of that community, and literature that is presented and retained in a Native language. It is virtually invisible outside its community, partly because of the barrier of language and partly because it has little interest in making itself available to an outside audience. In some cases, tribes—the Hopi come to mind—take great pains in limiting access to parts of their literature only to members of their immediate community. Polemical refers to that literature either in a Native language or in English, French, etc. that concerns itself with the clash of Native and non-Native cultures or with the championing of Native values over non-Native values. Like Beatrice Culleton's *In Search of April Raintree*, Maria Campbell's *Halfbreed*, D'Arcy McNickle's *The Surrounded* and *Wind from an Enemy Sky*, and Howard Adams's *Prison of Grass*,[2] polemical literature chronicles the imposition of non-Native expectations and insistences (political, social, scientific) on Native communities and the methods of resistance employed by Native people in order to maintain both their communities and cultures.

The terms interfusional and associational are not as readily apparent. I'm using interfusional to describe that part of Native literature which is a blending of oral literature and written literature. While there are contemporary examples that suggest the nature of interfusional literature—some of the translations of Dennis Tedlock and Dell Hymes work along with those of Howard Norman in *The Wishing Bone Cycle*—the only complete example we have of interfusional literature is Harry Robinson's *Write It on Your Heart*.[3]

The stories in Robinson's collection are told in English and written in English, but the patterns, metaphors, structures as well as the themes and characters come

---

1   Marie Annharte Baker (b. 1942) is an Anishinaabekwe poet and author, storyteller, cultural critic, activist, and performance artist. She is the author of numerous collections of poetry, including *Exercises in Lip Pointing* (New Star Books, 2003) and *Indigena Awry* (New Star Books, 2013).

2   (William) D'Arcy McNickle (1904–77) was an enrolled Salish Kootenai raised on the Flathead Indian Reservation in St. Ignatius, Montana. After studying abroad at Oxford University and the University of Grenoble, he returned to the USA and worked as an educator, anthropologist, and advocate for Native American people. He is the author of the novels *The Surrounded* (1936), and *Wind from an Enemy Sky* (1978). Howard Adams (1921–2001) was born in St. Louis, Saskatchewan, to Cree-Metis parents. After receiving his PhD from the University of California, Berkeley, in 1966, and, disillusioned with both government and Indigenous politics, he remained in the USA and became a professor of Native American studies. A Metis nationalist, he is primarily known today for his autobiographically inspired text *Prison of Grass: Canada from a Native Point of View* (1975).

3   Howard Norman, *The Wishing Bone Cycle: Narrative Poems from the Swampy Cree Indians* (New York: Stonehill, 1976). Harry Robinson and Wendy Wickwire, eds., *Write It on Your Heart, The Epic World of an Okanagan Storyteller* (Penticton & Vancouver: Theytus/Talon Books, 1989).

primarily from oral literature. More than this, Robinson, within the confines of written language, is successful in creating an oral voice. He does this in a rather ingenious way. He develops what we might want to call an oral syntax that defeats readers' efforts to read the stories silently to themselves, a syntax that encourages readers to read the stories out loud.

The common complaint that we make of oral literature that has been translated into English is that we lose the voice of the storyteller, the gestures, the music, and the interaction between storyteller and audience. But by forcing the reader to read aloud, Robinson's prose, to a large extent, avoids this loss, re-creating at once the storyteller and the performance.

> *Yeah, I'll tell you "Cat with the Boots On."*
> *Riding boots on.*
> *That's the stories, the first stories.*
> *There was a big ranch, not around here.*
> *That's someplace in European.*
> *Overseas.*
> *That's a long time, shortly after the "imbellable" stories.*
> *But this is part "imbellable" stories.*
> *It's not Indian stories.*
> *This is white people stories,*
>   *because I learned this from the white people.*
> *Not the white man.*
> *The white man tell his son,*
>   *that's Allison—John Fall Allison.*
> *White man.*
> *He is the one that tell the stories to his son.*
> *His son, Bert Allison.*
> *His son was a half Indian and a half white,*
>   *because his mother was an Indian.*
> *And his father was a white man.*
> *So his father told him these stories.*
> *But he told me—Bert Allison.*
> *So he told me,*
>   *"This is not Indian stories.*
>   *White man stories."*
> *You understand that?*

This metamorphosis—written to oral, reader to speaker—is no mean trick, one that Robinson accomplishes with relative ease. More important, his prose has become a source of inspiration and influence for other Native writers such as Jeannette Armstrong and myself.

Associational literature is the body of literature that has been created, for the most part, by contemporary Native writers. While no one set of criteria will do to describe it fully, it possesses a series of attributes that help to give it form.

Associational literature, most often, describes a Native community. While it may also describe a non-Native community, it avoids centring the story on the non-Native community or on a conflict between the two cultures, concentrating instead on the daily activities and intricacies of Native life and organizing the elements of plot along a rather flat narrative line that ignores the ubiquitous climaxes and resolutions that are so valued in non-Native literature. In addition to this flat narrative line, associational literature leans towards the group rather than the single, isolated character, creating a fiction that de-values heroes and villains in favour of the members of a community, a fiction which eschews judgements and conclusions.

For the non-Native reader, this literature provides a limited and particular access to a Native world, allowing the reader to associate with that world without being encouraged to feel a part of it. It does not pander to non-Native expectations concerning the glamour and/or horror of Native life, and it especially avoids those media phantasms—glitzy ceremonies, yuppie shamanism, diet philosophies (literary tourism as one critic called them)—that writers such as Carlos Castenada and Lynn Andrews[1] have conjured up for the current generation of gullible readers.

For the Native reader, associational literature helps to remind us of the continuing values of our cultures, and it reinforces the notion that, in addition to the usable past that the concurrence of oral literature and traditional history provides us with, we also have an active present marked by cultural tenacity and a viable future which may well organize itself around major revivals of language, philosophy, and spiritualism.

Two of the better examples of associational literature are Basil H. Johnston's *Indian School Days* and Ruby Slipperjack's *Honour the Sun*.[2] Each creates an Indian community, Johnston at a Jesuit boarding school, Slipperjack in northern Ontario. The novels themselves describe daily activities and the interaction of the community itself, and, aside from the first-person narrator, no one character is given preference over another.

---

1 Carlos Castaneda (1925–98) was an American author with a PhD in anthropology. Starting with *The Teachings of Don Juan* (1968), Castaneda wrote a series of bestselling books that describe his training in shamanism. Narrated in the first person, they relate his experiences under the tutelage of a Yaqui "Man of Knowledge" named Don Juan Matus. Critics have claimed that they are works of fiction. Lynn Andrews is an American businesswoman and bestselling author of the "Medicine Woman Series," new age spirituality novels based on Native American traditions. Andrews runs seminars based on the ideas contained in the novels. Critics charge her with commercial exploitation of Native American culture and refer to her as a "plastic shaman."

2 Basil Johnston, *Indian School Days* (Toronto: Key Porter Books, 1988). Ruby Slipperjack, *Honour the Sun* (Winnipeg: Pemmican, 1987).

Because *Indian School Days* is about a boarding school, we might well expect to see a sustained attack on this particularly colonial institution, and, while Johnston does on occasion criticize the expectations that the Jesuits have for their Native wards, he defuses most of the conflicts by refusing to make easy judgements and by granting responsibility and choice to both the Jesuits and the Native boys. The boys are not portrayed as hapless victims, and the Jesuits are not cast as uncaring jailers. Particularly telling are the concerted efforts made by the clerics and the students to care for the very young students, "babies" as Johnston calls them, who "seldom laughed or smiled and often cried and whimpered during the day and at night." While the older boys tried to act "as guardians or as big brothers," the burden of care "fell on the young scholastics, who had a much more fatherly air than the senior boys in Grades 7 and 8."

Ruby Slipperjack concerns herself with an isolated Native community in northern Ontario. Written in the form of a diary, the book follows the everyday life of an extended family. The book has no pretense at plot nor is there a desire to glorify traditional Native life. The story is told in simple and unassuming prose that focuses on relationships:

> There are seven of us in the family, four girls and three boys. My oldest brother got married and went away a long time ago. My other brother, Wess, spends most of his time at the cabin on our old trapline. The rest of us girls are all here. We live in a one-room cabin our father built before he died. Mom got someone to make a small addition at the back a couple of years ago. That's where she sleeps with our little brother, Brian. Brian was just a little baby when my father died and he's about six years old now. The rest of us sleep in the main room on two double beds and a bunk bed.
>
> Three other kids live with us. Mom looks after them because their parents left their home. I guess three more doesn't make much difference aside from the fact the food and clothes have to stretch a little further. The father came to see them once. I heard Mom say that she has never gotten a penny for their keep. Their mother has never come. Actually, I am closer to them than to my own sisters, since mine are gone all winter. Maggie and Jane have become my regular sisters and Vera and Annie are my special sisters when they are home in the summer.

Within the novel, the narrator neither posits the superiority of Native culture over non-Native culture nor suggests that the ills that beset the community come from outside it. Her brother's tuberculosis, John Bull's violent rampages, and the mother's eventual alcoholism are mentioned and lamented, but they are presented in a non-judgemental fashion and do not provide an occasion for accusation and blame either of non-Native culture at large or the Native community itself.

Both books provide access to a Native world, but the access is not unlimited. It is, in fact, remarkably limited access. While Johnston hints at some of the reasons why Indian parents allow their children to be placed at St. Peter Claver's, he does not elaborate on the complex cultural dynamics that have helped to maintain these schools. Much of this is hidden, as are the Native communities outside the school from which the students come. While Slipperjack appears more forthright in her description of the family and the community, she refuses to share with us the reasons for the narrator's mother's alcoholism, the cause of John Bull's violent behaviour, and the reasons for the narrator's leaving the community. In the end, what is most apparent in these two books is not the information received but the silences that each writer maintains. Non-Natives may, as readers, come to an association with these communities, but they remain, always, outsiders.

Now it goes without saying that creating terms simply to replace other terms is, in most instances, a solipsistic exercise, and I do not offer these terms as replacements for the term post-colonial so much as to demonstrate the difficulties that the people and the literature for which the term was, in part, created have with the assumptions that the term embodies.

Unlike post-colonial, the terms tribal, interfusional, polemical, and associational do not establish a chronological order nor do they open and close literary frontiers. They avoid a nationalistic centre, and they do not depend on the arrival of Europeans for their *raison d'être*.

At the same time, for all the range they cover, they do not comfortably contain the work of such Native writers as Gerald Vizenor and Craig Kee Strete. Vizenor's postmodern novels *Darkness in St. Louis Bearheart* and *Griever: An American Monkey King in China* and Strete's short story collections of surreal and speculative fiction *The Bleeding Man* and *If All Else Fails*[1] cross the lines that definitions—no matter how loose—create.

And it may be that these terms will not do in the end at all. Yet I cannot let post-colonial stand—particularly as a term—for, at its heart, it is an act of imagination and an act of imperialism that demands that I imagine myself as something I did not choose to be, as something I would not choose to become.

---

1 Gerald Vizenor, *Darkness in Saint Louis Bearheart* (Minnesota: U of Minnesota P, 1978), revised as *Bearheart: The Heirship Chronicles* in 1990; *Griever: An American Monkey King in China* (Minnesota: U of Minnesota P, 1986). Craig K. Strete, *The Bleeding Man and Other Science Fiction Stories* (New York: William Morrow, 1977) and *If All Else Fails* (New York: Doubleday, 1980).

Emma LaRocque

"Preface or Here Are Our Voices—Who Will Hear?"

Emma LaRocque is Plains Cree Métis from northeastern Alberta. She is a scholar, human rights advocate, poet, author, and social and literary critic. Since 1977 she has taught Native Studies at the University of Manitoba, specializing in Indigenous literatures and advocating for its inclusion in Native Studies departments. Author of the ground-breaking 1975 work *Defeathering the Indian*, LaRocque continues to work towards decolonization in her creative and scholarly work, and is recognized as one of the earliest contributors to Indigenous literary scholarship. Her latest book-length publication is *When the Other Is Me: Native Resistance Discourse 1850–1990* (2010).

LaRocque's 1990 essay "Preface or Here Are Our Voices—Who Will Hear?" appeared as the preface to *Writing the Circle*, an anthology of Indigenous women's writing, and serves as an excellent introduction to the characteristics of Indigenous literature, and the politics surrounding its production and reception. In fact, one can say that LaRocque's essay has become a model for the energy and political engagement that is the hallmark of contemporary Indigenous writing. This article introduces all of the principal themes that were—or would go on to become—central to the study of literature, including colonization, appropriation of voice, language, authenticity, and the ghettoization of Indigenous literature. Echoes of these themes can be found in the various essays throughout this collection.

LaRocque, Emma. "Preface or Here Are Our Voices—Who Will Hear?" *Writing the Circle*. Ed. Jeanne Perreault and Silvia Vance. Edmonton: NeWest, 1990. xv–xxx.

Preface or Here Are Our Voices—Who Will Hear?

To be a Native writer of some consciousness is to be in a lonely place. Happily, our isolation is about to come apart at the seams. This collection, which represents some fifty voices and has already engendered much discussion, is one of a growing number of anthologies reflecting nothing short of a revolution in Native literature.

To discuss Native literature is to tangle with a myriad of issues: voicelessness, accessibility, stereotypes, appropriation, ghettoization, linguistic, cultural, sexual, and colonial roots of experience, and, therefore, of self-expression—all issues that bang at the door of conventional notions about Canada and about literature.

It was not too long ago that Native peoples were referred to as voiceless, even wordless, sometimes with the association of these with illiteracy. But were Indian and Métis voiceless? And what did it mean to be classified as illiterate? To be sure, many Natives were illiterate up to the 1970s, even into the 1990s, due to the unconscionable failure of the Canadian education system to impart to Native youth basic reading and writing skills. And illiteracy does render people voiceless in the life of a country that revolves around the printed word. But what other nuances may be found in these terms? Did it mean Native peoples spoke no words? And since illiteracy is often associated with lack of literature, even lack of intelligence, did it imply that Native peoples were bereft of literature or of knowledge?

In contrast to the inane stereotype of the Indian as soundless, we know from the vast storehouse of our oral traditions that Aboriginal peoples were peoples of words. Many words. Amazing words. Cultivated words. They were neither wordless nor illiterate in the context of their linguistic and cultural roots. The issue is not that Native peoples were ever wordless but that, in Canada, their words were literally and politically negated.

It is now well known that Indian and Métis children in residential or public schools were not allowed to speak their Native languages. What is perhaps less well known are all the ways our words have been usurped, belittled, distorted, and blockaded in Canadian culture. Whether we spoke or wrote in Cree or in English, we had very little access to mainline communication systems.

Literature is political in that its linguistic and ideological transmission is defined and determined by those in power. This is why Shakespeare rather than Wisakehcha is classified as "classical" in our school curriculums. And, of course, the written word is advanced as superior to the spoken word. Oral traditions have been dismissed as savage or primitive folklore. Such dismissal has been based on the self-serving colonial cultural myth that Europeans (and descendants thereof) were/are more developed ("civilized") than Aboriginal peoples ("savage"). So arrogant is this myth and so arrogantly held has this myth been that, except for Christian or scholarly purposes, the colonizers have not bothered to learn Aboriginal languages. To this day, inept and ideologically informed translations of legends or myths are infantilizing Aboriginal literatures.

Power politics in literature is also evident in the decisions of publishers and in audience reception. For example, around the time we were being described as "voiceless," hundreds of us were actually articulating our colonized conditions throughout Canada. Much of this articulation came in the form of speech, but it also came in the form of writing, for there were already a number of very fine Native writers by the later 1960s to the mid-1970s. But rarely were these writers approached or included in the existing literatures of those times. Publishers, including editors and journalists, turned to white authors to speak on our behalf. Just two examples: in *Native Peoples in Canadian Literature* (William and Christine Mowat, eds., Toronto: Macmillan of Canada, 1975), the majority of authors are white, including Hugh Dempsey, Rudy Wiebe, Emily Carr, Al Purdy, and George Ryga; in *Many Voices: An Anthology of Contemporary Indian Poetry* (David Day and Marilyn Bowering, eds., Vancouver: J.J. Douglas Ltd., 1977), there are four poets, one of which is Cam Hubert, whose identities are put in such a way that it is difficult to tell whether they are "Indian poets" or not.

The interplay between audience reception and publishing cannot be minimized. As one of those earlier Native writers, I experienced and studied what may be called the Native-voice/white-audience dynamic. The interactions were often poignant. On another level, we were again rendered voiceless no matter how articulate we were. Apparently unable to understand or accept the truth of our experiences and perceptions, many white audiences, journalists, and critics resorted to racist techniques of psychologically labelling and blaming us. We were psychologized as "bitter," which was equated with emotional incapacitation, and once thus dismissed we did not have to be taken seriously.

We were branded as "biased," as if whites were not! Sometimes, we were even unabashedly charged with lying. The innocence and goodness of white Canada was stridently defended: How could all this oppression happen? How could police, priests, and teachers be so awful?

Our anger, legitimate as it was and is, was exaggerated as "militant" and used as an excuse not to hear us. There was little comprehension of an articulate anger reflecting an awakening and a call to liberation, not a psychological problem to be defused in a therapist's room.

Influenced by uncomprehending critics and audiences, publishers controlled the type of material that was published. It is no surprise that whatever Native protest literature was produced from authors like Harold Cardinal, Howard Adams, George Manual, Duke Redbird, Wilfred Pelletier, or Waubageshig was short-lived. In direct contrast to the hailing given "Black protest literature" as a new genre by white American intellectuals, Canadian critics accused us of "blustering and bludgeoning society." Basically, we were directed just to tell our "stories" (and the more tragic the better) not, in a manner reminiscent of archival descriptions reflecting earlier colonial attitudes, to be so "arrogant" or so daring as to analyze or to call on Canadian society for its injustices.

From about the mid-1970s, there was a noticeable turn to soft-sell Native literature. Personal narratives, autobiographies, children's stories, legends, interviews with elders, cultural tidbits, and "I remember" sorts of materials were encouraged. Here, I must hasten to say that it isn't the Native efforts I am criticizing; given all the suppression, misinformation, and stereotypes that exist, we can never speak enough or do enough correction or debunking. It is the white Canadian response to and use of this literature I am addressing.

Even soft-sell literature has been misunderstood and abused. I recall reading an incoherent review of Beatrice Culleton's moving allegory *Spirit of the White Bison* with the general accusation that "minorities" were "strangling in their own roots" (*Winnipeg Free Press*, 10 August 1986)! Maria Campbell's *Halfbreed* and Culleton's *In Search of April Raintree* have been reduced, at times, to grist for social workers rather than being treated as the powerful mirrors to Canadian society that they are.[1]

Actually, much of Native writing, whether blunt or subtle, is protest literature in that it speaks to the processes of our colonization: dispossession, objectification, marginalization, and that constant struggle for cultural survival expressed in the movement for structural and psychological self-determination. Ruby Slipperjack's gentle and wonderfully written novel *Honour the Sun* and even Chief Dan George's Hiawathian prose reflect protest.[2]

Native writers have been creating new genres in Canadian English literature, but this fact has been largely missed by readers and critics. For example, the more overt protest books of the 1970s often combined their sharp analyses of society with wit, humour, poetry, history, anthropology, and/or personal reflections. Authors turned to facts of biography to humanize the much dehumanized "Indian." Instead of being read as new genres, they were attacked as biased and parochial. Few bookstores, libraries, or professors knew what to do with Native writing that crossed or integrated well-defined, genres, styles, or schools. Native writing soon got thrown into one pot variously called "Native Literature" or "Native Studies."

I have viewed such hashing of our writing with considerable ambivalence. On one hand, Native literature has become a new genre, and Native studies has certainly

1 Maria Campbell, *Halfbreed* (Toronto: McClelland & Stewart, 1973). Beatrice Culleton [Mosionier], *In Search of April Raintree* (Winnipeg, MB: Pemmican, 1983).
2 Ruby Slipperjack, *Honour the Sun* (Winnipeg: Pemmican, 1987). Dan George, *My Heart Soars* (Surrey: Hancock House, 1976).

become a well-respected field of study in the university. On the other hand, categorizing literature on the basis of ethnicity, gender, or politics raises the spectre of ghettoization. While one must be supportive of both Native literature and Native studies, one must be concerned about ghettoization because of its effects on Native writers and writing.

The lumping of our writing under the category "Native" means that our discussion of issues and ideas that are universally applicable may not reach the general public. For example, an analysis of the Canadian school system by a Native author is rarely placed under "education" or "sociology" or "social issues." The poetry and poetic prose in much of the writing of the 1970s is rarely, if ever, placed under poetry or literature proper. And what about Native writers who do not write about Native themes? What about Native women writers who do not write specifically or only about women, and so get excluded from "women's writing" shelves?

Perhaps the ugliest effect of ghettoization is that it raises doubts in the deeps of a writer. Is our writing published because we are good writers or because we are Native? Of course, we may never know, judging from the contradictory responses from editors and publishers. I will never forget a new Winnipeg magazine of poetry returning my poems with a rejection slip that read, "Not Indian enough"! And several years ago, a major literary journal chose a poem (out of perhaps twenty) because, I believe, it has one Cree word at the end. Indeed, one of the editors even suggested that my poems were not authentic because they played too much with words. I do wish I could recall her exact words, since they were quite stunning in their implications—especially since I worry that my poems do not have enough "word play."

Occasionally, I collect my poems, along with my courage, and take them to a reputable poet with the request that he or she critique my works strictly on their poetic merits, not on the basis of my ethnicity or gender. I take some consolation from the fact that there are many white people who get published not necessarily because they are good writers but more because they have access to the publishing world. And that Native writers choose to explore Native themes does not mean they are incompetent. After all, most white writers deal with white issues or characters, but no one thinks of this as either parochial or ghettoized.

Still, the ramifications of ghettoization are unsettling. Generally, the Canadian intellectual establishment has disregarded Native writing. Such disregard reveals a profound Canadian contradiction: even as Native voices are silenced, the writings and movements of other oppressed peoples around the world are saluted. Yet, a study of Albert Memmi's portrait of the colonizer and the colonized in Tunisia reveals a striking similarity to the faces of the colonizer and the colonized of Canada (*The Colonizer and the Colonized*, 1957, 1967).[1] Indeed, the very resistance of the Native's use of the colonizer's language is consistent with this portrait.

So is the belittlement and stereotyping of Native cultures. Canadian society has not understood that earlier Native writing styles have reflected a holistic way of

---

1 Albert Memmi, *The Colonizer and the Colonized* (Boston: Beacon P, 1967).

seeing and placing space and time that produced a sense of integration with the variant aspects of life. This has been confused with the misguided notions of Indian culture (still prevalent today), notions that portray Indians as having taken no direct control over their environment, their children, their urges, their resources, their art, their thoughts, or their knowledge. A presentation that blurs Indians with their landscape only serves to de-culturalize them. In fact, Indians were multifaceted and cultivated peoples who acknowledged and practised a host of distinctions, yet maintained a functional connectedness between parts. And despite the disintegrative forces on Native cultures, many of us grew up with a holistic rather than an atomistic or discrete *Weltanschauung*.

There are numerous Native peoples yet who live or carry this world view. And every Native author of my generation or older has tried, in philosophy and in praxis (in the blending of genres), to teach our audiences our way of seeing and naming our worlds. It appears we have not been received. Superficial, even flaky, conceptions and objectifications of Indian culture have muted the deeper, life-sustaining currents of cultural continuity.

It must also be understood that Native writers have a dialectical relationship to the English (or French) language. Not only do we have to learn English, we must then deal with its ideology. To a Native woman, English is like an ideological onion whose stinging layers of racism and sexism must be peeled away before it can be fully enjoyed. A word must be said about words. Native readers and writers do not look at English words the same way as non-Natives may, for we have certain associations with a host of them. It is difficult to accept the following terms as neutral: savage, primitive, pagan, medicine man, shaman, warrior, squaw, redskin, hostile, civilization, developed, progress, the national interest, bitter, angry, happy hunting grounds, brave, buck, redman, chief, tribe, or even Indian. These are just a few of the string of epithets that have been pejoratively used to *specifically* indicate the ranking of Indian peoples as inferior to Europeans, thus to perpetuate their dehumanization. This is why I often use a lot of quotation marks even though standard editorial practice discourages it. Then, there is the challenge of wanting to use soul language, which for me is Cree, but having to explain it with a running bracketed glossary is distracting. This is made even more difficult by the fact that there is no standard way to spell Cree words in English. Kokom, which can be spelled in at least five different ways, is just such an example. We may also disagree with what is aesthetically pleasing. We may prefer Basil Johnston or Louise Erdrich over Stephen Leacock.[1] We may bring our oratorical backgrounds to our writing and not see it as a weakness. What is at work is the power struggle between the oral and the written, between the Native in us and the English. And even though we know the English language well,

---

1 Basil H. Johnston (b. 1929) is a prolific Ojibway author, language teacher, and scholar. Karen Louise Erdrich (b. 1954) is an award-winning Chippewa/Ojibwe writer from North Dakota. Stephen P.H. Butler Leacock (1869–1944) was a Canadian teacher, political scientist, writer, and humourist.

we may sometimes pay little attention to its logic—perhaps we will always feel a bit rebellious about it all. For, it must be said, that perhaps the height of cheekiness in a colonizer is to steal your language, withhold his from you as long as he can, then turn around and demand that you speak or write better than he does. And when you do, he accuses you of "uppityness" or inauthenticity.

The Native intellectual struggle to maintain our cultural integrity at these profound levels is perhaps most severely tested within the confines of scholarship and scholarly writing. Some of us de-colonizing Native scholars are challenging existing conventions in research methodology, notions of objectivity, and writing styles. So far, there has been little comprehension on the part of our colleagues. The academic world may be the hardest nut to crack. Long-standing conventions hold that objectivity must necessarily entail the separation of the "word" from the "self." As a scholar, I am expected to remain aloof from my words; I am expected to not speak in my own voice. But I am a Native woman writer/scholar engaged in this exciting evolution/revolution of Native thought and action. My primary socialization is rooted in the oral literatures of the Plains Cree Métis, which does not separate the word from the self and certainly knows the difference between atowkehwin (stories of legendary bent or sacred origin) and achimowin (factual and objective accounts). Further, there is ample evidence in the study of justification literature for the argument that objectivity can be a self-serving tool of those accustomed to managing history. This is not to mention my feminist understanding of the use of the English language. So, as an integrated person, I choose to use my own voice whether I am writing history or whether I am writing poetry. I may not always speak in my own voice, but when I do I experience no disconnection between my "self" and my footnotes.

With respect to scholarship and Native literature, many professors still turn to Rudy Wiebe, George Ryga, Robert Kroetsch, or Kinsella[1] when discussing Native themes. Yet, there are numerous Native authors available. To list just a few more (at the risk of offending many, and in addition to the ones referred to already): George Kenny (*Indians Don't Cry*, 1977), Sarain Stump (*And There Is My People Sleeping*, 1971), Marty Dunn (*Red on White: The Biography of Duke Redbird*, 1971), Basil Johnston (*Moosemeat and Wild Rice*, 1980), Jeannette Armstrong (*Slash*, 1985), Lee Maracle (*I Am Woman*, 1988), Maria Campbell/Linda Griffiths (*The Book of Jessica*, 1989), Beth Cuthand (*Voices in the Waterfall*, 1989), Jane Willis (*Geneish: An Indian Girlhood*, 1973), Tomson Highway (*The Rez Sisters*, 1987), Arthur Shilling (*The Ojibway Dream: Faces of My People*, 1986), Rita Joe (*Song of Eskasoni: More Poems of Rita Joe*, 1988). This is not to mention a number of older compilations of Native essays and poetry. And now there is such a spate of new Native writers (in a wild variety of anthologies and special features) that I cannot keep up with them. There are new poets, short story writers, novelists, and playwrights. There are also new

---

1 Rudy Wiebe (b. 1934), George Ryga (1932–87), Robert Kroetsch (b. 1927), and W.P. Kinsella (b. 1935) are well-known Canadian authors who have written about Indigenous peoples.

autobiographies, protest literature, children's literature, and more recollections of legends, myths, and earlier times. Even as I write this preface, I have received three different calls for submissions to Native women's anthologies. So, it cannot be said that we have been wordless from lack of skill or effort. Yet, we have been silenced in numerous and ingenious ways. In effect, we have been censored.

For the last two decades, we have been faced with the weary task of having to educate our audiences before we could even begin dialoguing with them! Our energies have been derailed from purely creative pursuits. Many speakers and writers have been cornered into the hapless role of apologists, incessant (and very patient) explainers, and overnight experts on all things Native. And in response to the negation and falsification of our histories and cultures, some have been pushed to cultural romanticism, even perhaps cultural self-righteousness. But, incidentally, nobody on earth has ever romanticized their culture to such mythic proportions (cowboys moving west and killing Indians being equated with moral and human progress) as white North Americans.

A sentence in Marlene Nourbese Philip's delightful article, "The Disappearing Debate: Or How the Discussion of Racism Has Been Taken Over by the Censorship Issue" (*This Magazine*, July–August 1989), gripped me: "No work is in any full practical sense produced unless it is also received." If Native writers have felt like they have been speaking into a vacuum, it is because we have. Neither the white nor the Native audience has received us. If white audiences have largely misunderstood us, Native audiences have been virtually non-existent. Linguistic, cultural, geographic, and social distances fostered by colonial forces have prevented the development of a broadly based Native intellectual community. And those few of us who have been around for a while do not speak with each other as much as we speak to audiences. This has been due, in part, to unavoidable political and economic circumstances.

The lonely echoes of our own words have been amplified by a strange but perhaps predictable colonial phenomenon: white intellectual judgement and shunning of Native intellectuals. The dearth of Native intellectual voices and artists in the media and in Canadian creative pursuits makes one wonder if the media is aware of our existence. Or are they avoiding us? Or is our invisibility an indication of the extent to which we are ghettoized?

The most distressing thing I have observed is the assumed estrangement between Native intellectuals from "the real people." How it is that white rather than Native intellectuals can better speak for the "real Natives" remains a puzzle. But the following is a typical, if bizarre, scenario: when white journalists "discover" an "articulate" or "bright" Native, they proceed to judge her as an intellectual, then bypass her in their liberal search for the grassroots.

In 1985, Métis writers, including myself, were unearthed. One incident remains for my memoirs: a CBC radio journalist from Regina called for cultural sorts of information. After regaling him (about bears, blueberries, fiddles, ghosts, and things) for about an hour, it somehow dawned on him he was speaking to a professor. He abruptly ended his interview with this request: "Could you tell me where I could find a *real* Métis storyteller?"

During the first Constitutional Conference on Self-Government, Barbara Frum[1] interviewed a white sociologist who off-handedly accused "the Native intellectual elite" of "leading their people down the garden path." (He was from Regina too.) Perhaps because there is no Native intellectual elite, Barbara couldn't find one to interview. Seriously, I know there have not been a vast number of us intellectuals and/or writers around and I know perhaps we do not hustle for the spotlight as much as we should, but we are around. And there are more of us every day.

More seriously, we are not alienated from our roots. Society has made sure of that. And unlike many white intellectuals, we were not born in to our stations in life. This is another reason why our selves are not (yet) separated from our words. To be exceptionalized is but another rung on the ghettoization ladder.

It is against this backdrop of keeping us voiceless that a movement against the appropriation of Aboriginal literatures has been born. There is absolutely no question but that radical intellectual surgery is required in the existing literatures on Aboriginal peoples. There are not enough superlatives in English to say how deeply Aboriginal peoples' worlds have been falsified in white North American literary traditions and popular culture. I, for one, have long been calling for the dismantling of racist thought and language in scholarly and popular works. Again, recently, I addressed my fellow scholars in an essay on the ethics of publishing those historical documents that qualify as hate literature against Indian and Métis peoples ("On The Ethics of Publishing Historical Documents," in Brown and Brightman, 1988). Some missionary and fur-trade journals, even some standard Canadian history books, would qualify as hate literature, even under the most stringent court requirements. But who will go to court against this hate literature? Who will face charges for falsifying Aboriginal histories? For that essay, I have received some thoughtful reviews. But several reviewers have dismissed my legitimate and scholastically sound concerns with the accusation that I am into "censorship."

Ironically, these silly charges came at a time (early 1990) when I was contemplating my continued involvement with this anthology, which was catapulted into the appropriation controversy because several Native women have felt that white editorship of Native women's literature constitutes appropriation. There is an obvious need for clarification and debate on the definition, direction, representation, and strategy of this issue. For now, I will simply submit that the editors of this anthology have not appropriated this literature; instead, they have facilitated its possibilities and transmission. They outline their work and approach in their prefatory comments. If I thought appropriation was involved, I would have removed my materials. For the record, however, I would not have tried to stop the publishing process.

---

1 Barbara Frum (1937–92) was a Canadian radio and television journalist acclaimed for her interviews for the Canadian Broadcasting Corporation (CBC).

But I do call on *all* writers of consciousness to address the continuing dehumanization of Indians as grunting and bloodthirsty savages in the cowboy and Indian movies and comic books, both of which are amply available on late night shows, VCRs, or comic book stands. All must challenge the exploitation of Indian motifs in the media and marketplace. How, I have wondered so many times, is it possible in our era of supposed awareness about "minority rights" that there are still teams called Washington Redskins, Cleveland Indians, Atlanta Braves (hasn't anyone seen their jerseys?), or Edmonton Eskimos? Then there are the archival materials protected as historical documents no matter what racist and inflammatory language they carry. And what could we ever do with the fathomless well of novels that qualify as hate literature but are also protected as classics in our libraries and schools? Then, there are those individual authors who presume to speak from the Native point of view, though this to me is a grey area, depending on how it is done. For instance, I value Cam Hubert's short story "Dreamspeaker" while, on the other hand, David Williams's *The Burning Wood*, Betty Wilson's *Andre Tom Macgregor*, and Mort Forer's *The Humpback*,[1] among many others, would have been better left unwritten. Even so, I have my students read these books for critical purposes. All of this and more needs urgent attention. But what kind and degree of attention? And where might we begin? And since racism informs so much of mainstream literature, surely the onus cannot be on Native writers to address it all. Natives cannot be the only ones responsible for confronting racism and hate literature of this magnitude. Colonized peoples often end up cleaning up the debris colonizers have left—can we refuse to do it this time? That we are raising our voices provocatively (see, for example, Lenore Keeshig-Tobias's important article "Stop Stealing Native Stories" in *The Globe and Mail*, 26 January 1990) should not be used as an excuse to further ignore us or to wash one's hands from the responsibility of fighting racism with respect to Native peoples in literature (and everywhere else, for that matter).

Appropriation is one of many issues that should be addressed by white or Native anthologists of Native literature. The irony is that, after reading this manuscript for purposes of writing the preface, I wanted more editorial changes, particularly with several pieces because they may, however unconsciously, perpetuate stereotypes. After all, much of my life has been spent "defeathering" stereotypes. But my concern (and it is legitimate) is one among many other considerations here. Even though I can rhetorically ask, "What good is the democratization of voice if it is one more avenue for the transmission of stereotypes?," I am painfully aware of the long history of suppressing Native voices, especially women's voices, and I am as anxious as anyone

---

1 Cam Hubert was the legally-changed name of Barbara Anne Cameron, a Canadian novelist, poet, screenwriter, and short story writer. Cameron now uses her birth name Anne Cameron but has written under both names. David Williams, *The Burning Wood* (Toronto: Anansi, 1975). Betty Wilson, *André Tom Macgregor* (Toronto: Macmillan, 1976). Mort Forer, *The Humpback* (Toronto: McClelland and Stewart, 1969).

to help facilitate their/our expression. What a bizarre situation to be in: to know so well the nooks and crannies of colonization that this "knowing" threatens to stand in the way of other voices. Happily, this dilemma was resolved for me because, in the main, this anthology carries many good and worthy words.

And I do care about the quality of writing within the Native community. I do believe in such a thing as literary excellence (albeit dialectical as discussed above) in the tradition of the Cree who were known as Nehiyawak, The Exact Speaking People (although in some dialects it could refer to People of Four Directions). It is in keeping with the spirit of our original cultures to produce excellence in the contemporary context. Accordingly, I do call for an "exact" articulation of our humanity and our oppressed conditions in the advancement of our liberation.

Native peoples, however, are still making a transition from oral to written literatures, from aboriginal to foreign languages. This is both a gift and a challenge. It is a gift to know more than one language, more than one culture. It is a challenge to be able to fly with "the gift," given the colonial state of affairs in our country. But this is 1990. To speak, read, and write in English is the birthright of contemporary Native peoples. It may be said that linguistic "appropriation" can go both ways. My first language is Plains Cree. My parents were forced to allow me to go to school where I was forced to learn English. In due time, I have "appropriated" this language without abandoning my Cree. I have sought to master this language so that it would no longer master me.

Colonization works itself out in unpredictable ways. The fact is that English is the new Native language, literally and politically. English is the common language of Aboriginal peoples. It is English that is serving to raise the political consciousness in our community; it is English that is serving to de-colonize and to unite Aboriginal peoples. Personally, I see much poetic justice in this process.

To be sure, we must attend to the task of "recreating the enemy's language," as Native American poet Joy Harjo put it (at a Native Women Speaker Series in 1989 at the University of Manitoba). This does take some skill, but our survival, as always, depends on skill. Native writers, like all writers everywhere, must have access to and must avail themselves of good and conscious editing and editors. To that end, then, we can make a distinction between editing as craft and editing as ideology. We must make room for the advancement of skill.

Native writers face a monumental but purposeful task: that of giving voice to a people's journey that spans centuries, a journey that at once says so much about white Canada. Alanis Obomsawin, Abenaki filmmaker, singer, and poet from Quebec, in explaining the purpose of her films, said:

> The basic purpose is for our people to have a voice. To be heard is the important thing, no matter what it is we're talking about.... And that we have a lot to offer our society. But we also have to look at the bad stuff, and what has

happened to us, and why.... We cannot do this without going through the past, and watching ourselves and analyzing ourselves, because we're carrying a pain that is 400 years old. We don't carry just our everyday pain. We're carrying the pain of our fathers, our mothers, our grandfathers, our grandmothers—it's part of this land. (Maurie Alioff and Susan Schouten Levine, "Interview: The Long Walk of Alanis Obomsawin," *Cinema Canada*, June 1987: 13)

Much of that 400-year-old pain has been expressed in the war of words against us. And to that, we are pressed to explain, to debunk, and to dismantle. To the war of ways against us, we are moved to retrieve, redefine, and reconcile our scattered pieces. To the voices of despair among us and in us, we are challenged to dream new visions to bring hope for the future.

We are the keepers of time. We must know the places of invasion in our histories and in ourselves so that we may illumine the paths of those who cannot see or who do not know. Because our pain is a "part of this land," we are also the Uncomfortable Mirrors to Canadian society. And few can look at the glaring reflections our mirrors provide. "My knee is so badly wounded no one will look at it / The pus of the past oozes from every pore / ... Anger is my crutch / I hold myself upright with it" writes Native American poet Chrystos (*Not Vanishing*, 1988).[1]

Finally, we cannot be cast as voices of the past, or even of the present. As writers, we are seekers of truth. We are called to transcend our own prejudices and politics, even our centuries-old pain, so that we can do what writers must do—tell the truth about the human condition. In this task, we cannot spare our own human make-up, which, however, must be done with an awareness of the social dimensions influencing it.

This anthology gives voice to Native women, and these women, in unexpected ways, tell the truth about this land, about the oppressor, and about the oppressed in us all. Ideologists will find this wonderfully democratic collection puzzling. It is clear that Native women are not in any uniform stage of political consciousness (but whose "consciousness"?), either about the oppression of Natives or of women. Nor are they at a uniform level of ability. Both are to be expected, because the tidal waves of colonization have hit Native communities at different times in different ways over a span of five centuries. This is not to mention that Aboriginal peoples are also *different* from each other, quite apart from European influences. Represented here are women of different languages, religions, cultures, generations, educational levels, and personal circumstances.

There is a range of movement in theme and style that reflects the transitional nature of contemporary Native consciousness and writing: from oral to written, from ambiguity to clarity, from hesitation to self-assertion, from internalization of

---

1 Chrystos, *Not Vanishing* (Vancouver: Press Gang Publishers, 1988).

stereotypes to an articulation of our colonial experience, and from romanticization to quiet criticism of "our people" and "our culture" (a hint of what is to come). Some themes unique to a people dispossessed stand out: a haunting and hounding sense of loss that drives one to reminisce. "I remember," many of us write, "I remember."

The poignancy of "taking on" the historical millstone of keeping our ancestors' memories alive comes through in our unsettling dreams and visions. "It's with terror, sometimes / That I hear them calling me" wrote Sarain Stump (*And There Is My People Sleeping*, 1971).[1] Then there is the plodding through the maze of identity crises that come from the political burdens and contradictions of our times. Questions of religion, traditionalism, modernism, racially mixed ancestries or offspring, mixed marriages, or feminism all pull at our loyalties.

There is the loneliness that comes from so many places: forced separation from one's children or parents, emotional and intellectual isolation, the experiencing of daily indecencies inherent in a racist society, the grieving that follows death.

Nor is there any escape from having to live in the eye of the storm—a storm one cannot tangibly touch or immediately give voice to, but still it is there. Always there. Like Pakak, the "thousand year companion" who "pierces the heart" with his "socket eyes" (see Halfe).[2] And *forever* trying to remove the speck of self-doubt from one's eyes, and the boulder of arrogance from the whites of others' eyes.

So we share our humanity—over and over again. We share our dreams, our fears, our loves, our hates, our mourning for the dying of the Grandmother, our culture, the Mother, our land, the Children, our future.

Themes specific to Native women are, of course, here: birthing, children, nurturing, sense of vulnerability, fear of violence, wife battering, and sexual assault. And there is some allusion to the developing tensions between male-defined traditions at variance with the women's spirituality, suffering, and perceptions. There is eloquence in the humour, wit, and gentle chiding employed on self and others on issues such as loss of innocence, sexism, hypocrisy, personal foibles, sexuality, and even betrayal.

Finally, a word must be said about the theme of the spectrum of betrayal that permeates these writings. There is betrayal that a child feels about being sent to a hospital, a residential school, or fostering. There is the priestly betrayal of a child in the confessional (see Higgins),[3] of a teenager in "the black sedan" (see Barton).[4] There is the beastly betrayal in the policeman's frenzied raping of a six-year-old child, left alone in the woods during the traitorous treaty days, a story that must be set in a Hiawathian garden to accent the profound loss of innocence (see Gladue).[5] There

---

1   Sarain Stump, *There Is My People Sleeping* (Sidney, BC: Gray's Publishing, 1970).
2   Louise Halfe, *Bear Bones and Feathers* (Regina: Coteau Books, 1994).
3   Barbara Higgins, "God's Man on Earth or First Communion," in *Writing the Circle* (1990).
4   Willow Barton, "Where Have the Warrior's Gone," in *Writing the Circle* (1990).
5   Norma Gladue, "Broken Promises," in *Writing the Circle* (1990).

is "the man in the shadows" who must be "masked" yet (see Chisaakay).[1] There is betrayal by men who jump into children's beds in their own home (see Alice Lee).[2]

The metaphorical layers of betrayal are just as damning, and infinitely more difficult to say: Where were the grandmothers, the mothers, the fathers, the brothers, the "warriors"? Why did they not protect? Too, there is the disloyalty of kin and community in looking the other way, even blaming. And what more can one say about the betrayal of "coldstone Canada" for creating the conditions, then abandoning the oppressed to the oppressed, and to snake priests and yellow-striped sons of…Her Majesty?

To these devastations of war-time proportions, and to all the other indignities available in our society, women here write with such subtlety and restraint, it brought a hammer to my guts and stinging water to my eyes. And with some amazement, I notice a remarkable lack of despair. Or rage.

No one can read these words and say they cannot understand—there is no mystification here. No longer can our words be discarded "as irrelevant as Native poetry" (*The Globe and Mail*, 16 November 1985). Nor should Native women's writing form a new body of ghettoized literature. Both white and Native communities are implicated; both are invited to hear.

Aiy Aiy my sisters for writing with such honesty and courage. Aiy Aiy Jeanne and Sylvia for "sweating" this through. Our loneliness has been lifted.

Aiy Aiy I offer you this poem:

Brown Sister

O my beautiful brown sister
your eyes are deep pools of pain
your face is prematurely lined
your Soul of Sorrow
is the Sorrow of Every Woman
Every Native
My beautiful brown sister
I know you
I know you
you heal me
you sweep sweetgrass over
the scars of my Exile
    Emma LaRocque
    Winnipeg July 1990

---

1 Molly Chisaakay, "Shadows," in *Writing the Circle* (1990).
2 Alice Lee, "child's play," in *Writing the Circle* (1990).

Lee Maracle

"Oratory: Coming to Theory"

Lee Maracle was born into a prominent family of the Stó:lo nation in what is now known as British Columbia. One of Indigenous literature's most uncompromising writers and critics, Maracle is a prolific writer, activist, and performer. She has been active in Indigenous rights movements since the 1970s, and is the author of the highly influential multi-genre *I Am Woman: A Native Perspective on Sociology and Feminism* (1988), as well as numerous works of fiction, such as *Sojourner's Truth and Other Stories* (1990), *Ravensong* (1993), *First Wives Club*—published in 2010, the same year she appeared in the feature film *A Windigo Tale*—and *Celia's Song* (2014). Maracle currently teaches creative writing and Aboriginal Studies at the University of Toronto, where she acts as a mentor to young people on personal and cultural healing and reclamation.

Maracle's 1992 essay argues emphatically that story, or literature, is theory for Indigenous peoples, whereas among settler scholars, theory is separate from story. Words are sacred among Indigenous peoples, and make things real; truth therefore lies in action, not argument. "Coming to Theory" introduces the idea of academic colonialism that Blaeser picks up on one year later, in "Seeking a Critical Centre." Maracle states of mainstream western theory that "[b]y presenting theory in a language no one can grasp, the speaker (or writer) retains authority over thought." This results in academic colonialism, which can only be rectified by an approach to literature that presents thought through interaction, or, as Blaeser puts it, an approach that comes from within the text, or the story's *action*. To demonstrate Indigenous-based methodologies, Maracle methodically deconstructs western notions of theory to demonstrate that these notions mean very little when placed outside human interaction.

Maracle, Lee. "Oratory: Coming to Theory." *Give Back. First Nations Perspectives on Cultural Practice.* Vancouver: Gallerie, 1992. 85–92.

Oratory: Coming to Theory

Theory. If it can't be shown, it can't be understood. Theory is a proposition, proven by demonstrable argument. Argument: evidence, proof. Evidence: demonstrable testimony, demonstration. We are already running into trouble. There are a number of words in the English language with no appreciable definition. Argument is defined as evidence; proof or evidence is defined as demonstration or proof; and theory as a proposition proven by demonstrable evidence. None of these words exist outside of their interconnectedness. Each is defined by the other.

Oratory, on the other hand, is unambiguous in its meaning. Oratory: place of prayer, to persuade. This is a word we can work with. We regard words as coming from original being—a sacred spiritual being. The orator is coming from a place of prayer and as such attempts to be persuasive. Words are not objects to be wasted. They represent the accumulated knowledge, cultural values, the vision of an entire people or peoples. We believe the proof of a thing or idea is in the doing. Doing requires some form of social interaction and thus, *story* is the most persuasive and sensible way to present the accumulated thoughts and values of a people.

Among European scholars there is an alienated notion which maintains that theory is separate from story, and thus a different set of words are required to "prove" an idea than to "show" one. Yet if you take the story out of any school textbook the student is left without proof for the positing of any information. In a science textbook they refer to the story as "an example." The component parts of every example are the same: there is a plot line, tension (conflict), a climax and a conclusion. Mathematical "problems" have the same components. The tension in math is one number versus another, whether they are added or subtracted, multiplied or divided, the tension is resolved into some sort of conclusion different from the two numbers representing the original tension. The numbers have names and the plot line (what to do next) is provided by the theorems and formulae which the student accepts by custom. Numbers lack character—human form. But when we propose them as a problem, confronting real people, they take on a character and human content—social interaction. The number of trees cut to make one edition of a newspaper, for example, or the number of hungry children in a large Canadian city.

Academicians waste a great deal of effort deleting character, plot, and story from theoretical arguments. By referring to instances and examples, previous human interaction, and social events, academics convince themselves of their own objectivity and persuade us that the story is no longer a story. However, *our* intellectuals (elders) know that "$E=MC^2$" means nothing outside of human interaction. Likewise, the concept of zero means nothing. It is represented by a circle devoid of all life. This has no meaning for the living or the dead, but it is useful in teaching young children to interact in a positive social fashion. A child learns that if she doesn't obey the laws of the people, she will suffer great nothingness in her interaction with women and men.

Enough of that talk. There is a story in every line of theory, not in our capacity to theorize. It seems a waste of words to dispassionately delete character from plot line, tension, and conclusion. It takes a great deal of work to erase people from theoretical discussion.

A theoretical proposition advanced by John Stuart Mill in his little essay "Utilitarianism"[1] seems the foundation of theory, law, politics, sociology and culture in North America: "All men are motivated by pleasure and pain." John first has to delete his passion from his theory and his life. The great problem with that, of course, is that people think *being* is a passionate thing.

People are extremely disinclined toward celibacy. "The spirit is strong, but the flesh is weak"—so says Jesus. In contrast, we believe that the human spirit and the body agree: to be passionate is to be alive. You cannot erase passion from the spirit of people. At times people can harness their passionate energy and transform it, putting it to work at endeavors other than sexual expression. But to delete passion from our lives leads to a weird kind of sociopathy—a heartlessness.

Next Mr. John Mill had to delete certain types of people, those who regard "pleasure as a physical thing." Now we have a spirit without passion and a mind without a body. Unfortunately, there is not much left to deal with here because the mind is also physical. What is left is a very cold, calculating and dispassionate Mr. J.S. Mill. It takes a lot of work to delete the emotional and passionate self from story, to de-humanize story into "theory." So we don't do it. We humanize theory by fusing humanity's need for common direction—theory—with story.

Finally, not even Mr. Mill is home. What you have left is a calculator with an attitude. No one in the 1990s is going to reduce themselves to a calculator when you can trot over to K-Mart and buy one for less than twenty dollars. We tend to resent uncaring attitudes. So we don't do it. Our orators know that words governing human direction are sacred, prayerful presentations of the human experience, its direction, and the need for transformation in the human condition which arises from time to time.

---

1 John Stuart Mill (1806–73), the British philosopher, political economist, and civil servant, was an influential contributor to social theory, political theory, and political economy. He is widely known today as the author of *Utilitarianism* (1863).

What is the point of presenting the human condition in a language separate from the human experience: passion, emotion, and character? "If you want people to have confidence in your cure, speak in a language no one understands—Latin. No one speaks Latin anymore, so it is the one we will use." (So said Norman Bethune, delivering a lecture to medical students on medical practice.) By presenting theory in a language no one can grasp, the speaker (or writer) retains authority over thought. By demanding that all thoughts (theory) be presented in this manner in order to be considered theory (thought), the presenter retains the power to make decisions on behalf of others.

Recently, there was a conference at Opitsit (Meares Island) to discuss and shape thoughts on the importance of trees to the environment. Native and European environmentalists both attended. The morning consisted of presentations made by "prominent" environmentalists, who droned on about p.b.m.'s, choloform counts, soil erosion, and so forth—none of which was understood by the Native people there. All of our people spoke and understood English, but none had any background in Latin, so the presentations by the environmentalists went over all their heads. At the end, an old man got up and said he would like to give an Indian point of view. Gratefully, the environmentalists bent their ears to listen. The old man spoke for three hours in his language, then sat down.

The Natives cracked up. The environmentalists sat confused.

Unfortunately, the environmentalists missed the point. We all strive to become orators. An orator is simply someone who has come to grips with the human condition, humanity's relationship to creation, and the need for a human direction that will guarantee the peaceful coexistence of human beings with all things under creation. No brilliance exists outside of the ability of human beings to grasp the brilliance and move with it. Thus we *say* what we think. No thought is understood outside of humanity's interaction. So we present thought through story, human beings doing something, real characters working out the process of thought and being.

For Native people, the ridiculousness of European academic notions of theoretical presentation lies in the inherent hierarchy retained by academics, politicians, law makers, and law keepers. Power resides with the theorists so long as they use language no one understands. In order to gain the right to theorize, one must attend their institutions for many years, learn this other language, and unlearn our feeling for the human condition. Bizarre.

If it cannot be shown, it cannot be understood. Theory is useless outside human application. If only a minority understand theory, only a minority can execute theory; thus theorists require a horde of executives who must control the human condition, control our interactions and our relationships. Because human beings have a tendency to resent such control, we need force to maintain the hierarchy of theorists and executives—police, army, the "enforcers of law."

Despite all academic criticism to the contrary, my book *I Am Woman* is a theoretical text.[1] It was arrived at through my meticulous ploughing of the fields of hundreds of books on the European colonial process—capitalist theory, decolonization, law and philosophy—from the perspective of Indigenous law, philosophy, and culture. My understanding of the process of colonization and de-colonization of Native women is rooted in my theoretical perception of social reality, and it is tested in the crucible of human social practice. The stories and the poetry bring the reality home and allow the victims to de-victimize their consciousness. For Native women, and a good many white women, *I Am Woman* is empowering and transformative.

I Am Woman takes the lives of women very seriously. The book walks gently across the ruined cages, the glass of which I shatter on the very first page.... "How can one reduce one's loved ones small ... minus the colors and the music that moves them..."—to fields of blossoming flowers at the end. The book is filled with story, and it is guided by theory presented through story—the language of people. It is a spiralling in on the self who rose above all the myriad obstacles the colonial and patriarchal process presents for women. More. The book spirals out from the self, in a dogged and heartfelt way, to touch the heart of woman.

By talking to my readers as though they were truly there in my heart, both the point of victimization and the point of resistance become clear. The value of resistance is the reclaiming of the sacred and significant self. By using story and poetry I move from the empowerment of my self to the empowerment of every person who reads the book. It is personally dangerous for me to live among disempowered oppressed individuals. "When they come to get me, I want to know: who is going to be there with me? Because I am not going willingly." So said a young white woman speaking on the possibility of organized state violence against the women's movement in this country; I want to know who is going to be there with me, resisting victimization—peacefully or otherwise, but always stubbornly and doggedly struggling to reclaim and hang on to my sacred self.

---

1 Lee Maracle, *I Am Woman: A Native Perspective on Sociology and Feminism* (Vancouver: Press Gang, 1988).

Kimberley Blaeser

"Native Literature: Seeking a Critical Centre"

Kimberley Blaeser is an Ojibway scholar, educator and poet from the White Earth Reservation in Minnesota. An Associate Professor of English at the University of Wisconsin–Milwaukee, she teaches courses in Native American Literature and Creative Writing, and lectures widely across Canada and the United States. An accomplished poet, who was recently appointed "Wisconsin Poet Laureate," Blaeser is nevertheless known primarily for her critical work, which includes an insightful Indigenous-centred analysis of the work of Ojibway/Anishnaabe writer and scholar Gerald Vizenor, and for her contributions to *Word Warriors*, the multicultural writers' group she helped form in 1991.

Blaeser's essay appeared in 1993 in the first collection of literary criticism in Canada devoted entirely to Indigenous perspectives, *Looking at the Words of Our People*, edited by Jeannette Armstrong. This revolutionary article argues that using established critical frameworks to interpret Indigenous texts is an act of colonization, since meaning is imposed on the marginalized texts by mainstream authorities. In order to remedy this, Blaeser argues that interpretation should come from within the text itself rather than outside the text, and that the removal of the literature from its context is a mistake, since it removes its active function. These ideologies lie at the heart of ethical scholarship, and are among the key tenets of Indigenous literary nationalism. Blaeser also argues that all approaches to Indigenous texts need not be oppositional, since, as Thomas King also notes in "Godzilla vs. Post-Colonial," Indigenous literatures existed long before the arrival of the settlers.

Blaeser, Kimberley. "Native Literature: Seeking a Critical Centre." *Looking at the Words of Our People*. Ed. Jeannette Armstrong. Penticton: Theytus. 1993. 51–62.

Native Literature: Seeking a Critical Center

Uncle Luther, a character in Louis Owens's *The Sharpest Sight*, offers some advice Indian intellectuals should take to heart. In Owens's novel, the old man gives his own reading of Herman Melville's *Moby Dick* and identifies the central failing of Melville's protagonist, claiming that the storyteller in the book "forgot his own story" (91). The antidote to this failing involves a balance: "You see, a man's got to know the stories of his people, and then he's got to make his own story too" (91). But the stakes get higher and the tasks more difficult for Native Americans and mixed-bloods; not only must we "know the stories of our people" and "make our own story," but, Luther warns, "We got to be aware of the stories they're making about us, and the way they change the stories we already know" (91). We must know the stories of other people—stories from the American and world canons—especially the stories told about Indian people; and we must be aware of the way our own stories are being changed: "re-expressed" or "re-interpreted" to become a part of their story or their canon because, as Luther warns, stories have political power: "They're always making up stories, and that's how they make the world the way they want it" (91). As I see it, the lesson for Indian intellectuals involves contemporary criticism and literary interpretation, because literary theory and analysis, even "canonization," can become a way of changing or remaking Native American stories.

This essay extends Luther's (or Owens's) warning and challenge to contemporary scholars: it is a call and, as its title suggests, a search for a way to approach Native Literature from an indigenous cultural context, a way to frame and enact a tribal-centered criticism. It seeks a critical voice and method which moves from the culturally-centered text outward toward the frontier of "border" studies, rather than an external critical voice and method which seeks to penetrate, appropriate, colonize or conquer the cultural center, and thereby, change the stories or remake the literary meaning.

Recognizing that the literatures of Native Americans have a unique voice and that voice has not always been adequately or accurately explored in the criticism that has been written about the literature, I have begun in the last few years to be attentive to other ways of talking about the literature of the First Peoples. Particularly, I have been alert for critical methods and voices that seem to arise out of the literature itself (this as opposed to critical approaches applied from an already established critical language or attempts to make the literature fit already established genres and categories of meaning). So far, I have uncovered only fitful attempts to fashion this interpretive method or give voice to this new critical language. This essay explores the most promising of these endeavors, searches for their points of convergence, and offers some comments on the inherent critical dynamics of Native American literature.

Theorizing American Indian Literature

In her discussion "Toward Minority Theories," Nancy Hartsock writes of "those of us who have been marginalized by the transcendental voice of universalizing theory" (204). Anyone familiar with the history of Native literatures in the Americas, knows well the particulars—translation, re-interpretation, appropriation, romanticizing, museumization, consumerization, and marginalization—generalized in Hartsock's statement. Elements of the native oral tradition, for example, have been dismissed as primitive, rediscovered and translated into "literary" forms, used as models for contemporary literary and cultural movements, altered and incorporated into mainstream works of literature, and almost theorized into their predicted "vanishment."

Indeed, both traditional and contemporary Native works have often been framed in and read from a western literary perspective. Hertha Wong in *Sending My Heart Back across the Years* and Arnold Krupat in *For Those Who Come After*, both talk about and call into question the western theorizing of American Indian autobiography and offer alternative understandings of the form as used by native peoples [1]. William Bevis in "*Native American Novels: Homing In*," and Louis Owens in *Other Destinies* perform similar service for the Native American novel [2]. All four critics recognize in both method and intention a difference from canonical works of the Western literary tradition. Owens's study, for example, recognizes in native stories "other destinies" and "other plots" (1992a, 1). Krupat says of Native texts: "What they teach frequently runs counter to the teaching of Western tradition, and...the ways in which they delight is different from the ways in which the Western tradition has given pleasure" (1989, 54). Quite naturally then, any "transcendental voice of universalizing theory" could not accurately interpret or represent the "other" voice and method of American Indian literature. The insistence on reading Native literature by way of Western literary theory clearly violates its integrity and performs a new act of colonization and conquest.

Hartsock says we should neither "ignore" the knowledge/power relations inherent in literary theory and canon formation nor merely "resist" them; we must transform them (204). Owens, in his discussion of the Native American writers' struggle with language and articulation, the conflicts between written and oral, English and native languages, also calls for a kind of transformation of the existing system. Speaking specifically of N. Scott Momaday, but seeing his case as like that of "his fellow Indian writers," Owens writes: "The task before him was not simply to learn the lost language of his tribe but rather to appropriate, to tear free of its restricting authority, another language—English—and to make it accessible to an Indian discourse" (1992a, 13). His comments here on creative works have implications for the language and articulation of literary criticism as well. What Owens in his own critical work and many other Native American and non-native scholars have attempted is to "tear free of its restricting authority" the existing-critical language and "make that language accessible to an Indian discourse." Scholars like Owens, Gerald Vizenor, James Ruppert, Gretchen Ronnow, Arnold Krupat, Elaine Jahner and myself have employed, for example, postmodern theory, the critical language of the likes of Mikhail Bakhtin, Jacques Lacan and Jacques Derrida[1] in the reading of Native American texts [1]. We have made use of the intersections of Native works with post-colonial and semiotic theory, and with any number of other established critical discourses.

While I believe these theories, like Bakhtin's distinction between monologue and dialogue and between linear and pictorial writing styles, have been helpful, they still have the same modus operandi when it comes to Native American literature. The literature is approached with an already established theory, and the implication is that the worth of the literature is essentially validated by its demonstrated adherence to a respected literary mode, dynamic or style. Although the best scholars in native studies have not applied the theories in this colonizing fashion but have employed them, the implied movement is still that of colonization: authority emanating from the mainstream critical center to the marginalized native texts. Issues of Orientalism and enforced literacy apply again when another language and culture, this time a critical language and the Euro-American literary tradition, take prominence and are used to explain, replace or block an indigenous critical language and literary tradition [2].

This distinction between applying already established theory to native writing versus working from within native literature or tradition to discover appropriate tools or to form an appropriate language of critical discourse, implicates my own work to date just as it implicates the work of most other scholars of native literature. I am not suggesting our critical attempts have all been for naught. However, I am hopeful that future efforts will proceed with greater awareness of the precarious situation that Native American literary criticism is heir to.

In fact, the situation is still more complicated than these comments have so far indicated because the literary works themselves are always at least bi-cultural: Though they may come from an oral-based culture, they are written. Though their writer may speak a tribal language, they are usually almost wholly in the language of English. And though they proceed at least partly from an Indian culture, they are

---

1 Mikhail Bakhtin (1895–1975), Jacques Lacan (1901–81) and Jacques Derrida (1930–2007) are considered influential "master theorists," whose theories on culture and society have impacted critical theory, literary theory, linguistics, 20th-century French philosophy, sociology, feminist theory, film theory, and clinical psychoanalysis.

most often presented in the established literary and aesthetic forms of the dominant culture (or in those forms acceptable to the publishing industry). The writers themselves have generally experienced both tribal and mainstream American culture and many are in physical fact mixed-bloods. Beyond this, the works themselves generally proceed from an awareness of the "frontier" or border existence where cultures meet. The criticism, too, even if written by Native Americans, is also (and for many of the same reasons) at least bi-cultural. Perhaps to adequately open up the multicultural texts of Native American literature, it must be.

Having briefly sketched the complexities of this critical intersection, I still do not rescind my call for an "organic" native critical language. If we need a dual vision to adequately appreciate the richness of Indian literature, the native half to that vision has still been conspicuously absent. Krupat has also articulated a call for new literary criticism, most recently in *Ethnocriticism: Ethnography, History and Literature* and his introduction to *New Voices in Native American Literary Criticism*. He claims, for example:

> "In recent years some academic researchers have wanted very much to take seriously, even, indeed, to base their research upon not only Native experience but Native constructions of the category of knowledge. Still, as I have said, the question remains: How to do so? It is an urgent question" (1993 xix).

Contextual Experiments

Perhaps the most frequently employed mode for articulating what Krupat calls "Native constructions of the category of knowledge" has been oppositional. Lines have been drawn, for example, between cyclical and linear, biological and anthropological, communal and individual. In his 1985 introduction to *New and Old Voices of Wah'kon-tah: Contemporary Native American Poetry*, Vine Deloria, Jr. distinguishes Native poetic expression with just such oppositional rhetoric: "Indian poetry may not say the things that poetry says because it does not emerge from the centuries of formal western thought.... It is hardly chronological and its sequences relate to the integrity of the circle, not the directional determination of the line. It encompasses, it does not point" (ix). Although this and many of the oppositional distinctions may have been necessary early on to underscore the difference, the distinct voice of Indian literature, and although they do contribute to an understanding of the native literary character, they actually proceed from and reinforce an understanding of the dominant position of the Euro-American literary aesthetic, constructing their own identity as they do by its relationship to that master template.

Again taking up the ideas of circularity, Gordon Henry more recently coined the terms "sacred concentricity" to describe both the form and the intention of much Native writing [3]. However, he framed his theory without invoking or writing itself against either the secular or the enshrined linear aesthetic. He simply set out to explain the movement and form he observed in novels like *Ceremony, Love Medicine* and *House Made of Dawn* whose story he felt created a sacred center (which might be place, person, event, etc.) from which emanated ripples of power and connection (and might involve healing, return, forgiveness, etc.). The aesthetic form and movement described in Henry's language has, of course, been noted in various ways and in various degrees by other scholars: the seasonal cycles of *Ceremony* have been noted, the cyclical structure of *House Made of Dawn* explored. Owens writes of the "centripetal" orientation of *Ceremony* and of the "web" it creates. Paula Gunn Allen writes of "the sacred hoop" or "medicine wheel" as the informing figure behind much Native writing (56). The emerging critical language expressing this central aesthetic characteristic of Native literature need not or should not have to base its existence or integrity on an oppositional relationship.

Several of the intriguing experiments in Native critical discourse recognizes both the differences between Native and non-Native perspectives and the complexity of the literary voice that arises from the convergence of these different perspectives. They take as their mode of operation dialogue or mediation between these two critical and cultural centers. Gerald Vizenor's "trickster discourse," Keith Basso's "code-switching" and bicultural "linguistic play," Arnold Krupat's "ethnocritiques" or "ethnocriticism," and Louis Owens's "mixed-blood metaphors" all proceed from an awareness of the border quality of native speech, writing and criticism. Although each scholar theorizes and enacts their theory in varying ways, they all seek to enrich the understanding of native literature by drawing their interpretation from the same multicultural experience which informed the creation of the text. They attempt to explore the wavering and delicate balance in the frontier text between tradition and innovation, to untangle the braided cultural contexts, to acknowledge what James Ruppert calls the "mediational discourse" which "strives to bring the oral into the written, the Native American vision into contemporary writing, spirit into modern identity, community into society, and myth into modern imagination" (210). In Vizenor and in Basso's theories, much of this mediation is accomplished playfully, with humor and self-conscious satire. Beneath or within the humor, cultural contexts and conflicts are bounced off of one another. Understanding here is always in motion.

The Predicament of Theory

However, as Jana Sequoya points out, even the theoretical position of mediation carries with it the possibility for a new form of dominance. The full representation of difference involves multiple sites of literary and cultural knowledge. However in the creation of this multicultural dialogue, this new national story, Native stories may again be changed or taken out of context. "In the oral tradition," Owens has claimed, "context and text are one thing" (1992a, 13); but it is the separation of the two that Sequoya foresees in "their expropriation for the literary market by the cultural mediator"

(467). She writes of the different ways of "having" stories and claims that removing sacred oral stories from their actual culture context to place them within a literary context destroys their social role (460, 468). If this is true, to what degree might all critical endeavors be said to destroy the most immediate social or aesthetic value of those works it seeks to interpret? Alexander Nehamas speaks of the "cruelty of the commentator" and claims that the "elevation" of cultural story to the level of "literature" destroys its moral function [4]. Vizenor warns against the "dead voices" of "wordies" who situate the story in the "eye and not the ear" (7). Krupat, too, discusses the quandaries of criticism particularly as it applies to oral tradition and notes that "Indian people...have no need to produce a body of knowledge about it [oral performative literature] that is separate and apart from it" (1992, 187).

Although the task of the contemporary native theorist seems fraught with difficulty, in the last comment by Krupat we find what may be a direction to take and we find the circularity of this discussion for his comment inadvertently brings us back to the idea of criticism as existing within and arising from the literature itself. Traditional native literature has always entailed both performance and commentary with, in Dennis Tedlock's language, the "conveyer" functioning as the "interpreter" as well. We get, says Tedlock, "the criticism at the same time and from the same person" (47–48). In a similar fashion, contemporary texts contain the critical contexts needed for their own interpretation and, because of the intertextuality of Native American literature, the critical commentary and contexts necessary for the interpretation of works by other Native writers.

If we return to Owens's *The Sharpest Sight*, for example, we find the story centers partly on identity and Cole McCurtain's search for an Indian identity. Cole is told by Hoey McCurtain, "You are what you think you are" which throws Owens's text immediately into dialogue with N. Scott Momaday's "Man Made of Words," especially his oft-quoted statement, "We are what we imagine. Our very existence consists in our imagination of ourselves. Our best destiny is to imagine, at least, completely, who and what, and *that* we are. The greatest tragedy that can befall us is to go unimagined" (55). Owens's Cole disputes Huey (and Momaday) scoffing, "As if...you could really choose what you are going to be instead of just being what it was you had to be" (15). These statements fall early in Owens's novel. The remaining story and the various characters' searches for identity will be read in the broader context Owens has implied. And Momaday is but one of many authors whose ideas or literary works are invoked by Owens in *The Sharpest Sight*. His text comes equipped with many of its own tools of literary interpretation.

Indeed, the dialogues enacted in and between Native texts offer scholars not only rich opportunities for interpretation, but much of the language and organizing principles necessary for the construction critical center. Vizenor, for example, offers us the idea of "shadow writing" and "mythic metaphors." Erdrich offers the possibility of kinship as a formal structuring principal, and the visual images of "buried roots" and "a globe of frail seeds." Momaday gives us the metaphor of the ritual "runners after evil," Owens the metaphor of an "underground river," and Janet Campbell Hale and D'Arcy McNickle offer metaphors of confinement. Our sources also provide intertextual metaphors and critical terms as the texts in their richness quote and comment on one another, and as the authors frame their own works in the context of the writings of other Native authors. Maurice Kenny, for example, titles a collection of tribal poetry "Wounds beneath the Flesh," taking the phrase from Geary Hobson's "Barbara's Land Revisited—August 1978," and Paula Gunn Allen takes the title for one section of The Sacred Hoop from Vizenor's critical commentary on "word warriors." Add to this literary self-consciousness and intertextuality, the multiple connections with oral tradition and the theorizing within the literary works themselves. Add, for example, Silko's intermingling of the traditional and contemporary story, Diane Glancy's and Linda Hogan's comments on the political powers of language and literacy, and Vizenor's theories on trickster.

The critical language of Mikhail Bakhtin and Walter J. Ong may profitably be applied to Native American literature, but as Owens's Uncle Luther reminds us, we must first "know the stories of our people" and then "make our own story too." And, he warns, we must "be aware of the way they change the stories we already know" for only with that awareness can we protect the integrity of the Native American story. One way to safeguard that integrity is by asserting a critical voice that comes from within that tribal story itself.

End Notes

1 See, for example, *Narrative Chance: Postmodern Discourse on Native American Indian Literatures* (ed. Gerald Vizenor, Albuquerque: U of New Mexico P, 1989).

2 I discuss literacy and Orientalism in "Learning 'The Language the Presidents Speak': Images and Issues of Literacy in American Indian Literature." *World Literature Today* 66.2 (Spring 1992): 230–35.

3 From conversations with Henry about his notion of "sacred concentricity" and from his verbalization of it at a lecture at the University of Wisconsin–Milwaukee in 1992.

4 Discussed by Nehamas in a lecture "What Should We Expect from Reading? (These Are Only Aesthetic Values)" given at University of Wisconsin–Milwaukee, 1993.

Works Cited

Allen, Paula Gunn. *The Sacred Hoop: Recovering the Feminine in American Indian Traditions*. Boston: Beacon P, 1986.

Basso, Keith H. *Portraits of "The Whiteman": Linguistic Play and Cultural Symbols among the Western Apache*. Cambridge: Cambridge UP, 1979.

Bevis, William. "Native American Novels: Homing In." *Recovering the Word: Essays on Native American Literature*. Ed. Brian Swann and Arnold Krupat. Berkeley: U of California P, 1987: 580–620.

Deloria, Vine, Jr. "Forward." *New and Old Voices of Wah'kon-tah: Contemporary Native American Poetry*. Ed. Robert K. Dodge and Joseph B. McCullough. New York: International Publishers, 1985: ix–x.

Hartsock, Nancy. "Rethinking Modernism: Minority vs. Majority Theories." *Cultural Critique* 7 (1987): 187–206.

Krupat, Arnold. *Ethnocriticism: Ethnography, History, Literature*. Berkeley: U of California P, 1992.

———. *The Voice in the Margin: Native American Literature and the Canon*. Berkeley: U of California P, 1989.

———. "Introduction." *New Voices in Native American Literary Criticism*. Ed. Arnold Krupat. Washington: Smithsonian Institution P, 1993.

———. *For Those Who Came After: A Study of Native American Autobiography*. Berkeley: U of California P, 1985.

Momaday, N. Scott. "The Man Made of Words." *Indian Voices: The First Convocation of American Indian Scholars*. San Francisco: Indian Historian P, 1970: 49–62.

Owens, Louis. *Other Destinies: Understanding the American Indian Novel*. Norman: U of Oklahoma P, 1992a.

———. *The Sharpest Sight*. Norman: U of Oklahoma P, 1992b.

Sequoya, Jana. "How (!) Is an Indian?: A Contest of Stories." *New Voices in Native American Literary Criticism*. Ed. Arnold Krupat. Washington: Smithsonian Institution P, 1993: 453–73.

Tedlock, Dennis. "The Spoken Word and the Work of Interpretation in American Indian Religion." *Traditional American Indian Literatures*. Ed. Karl Kroeber. Lincoln: U of Nebraska P, 1981: 45–64.

Vizenor, Gerald. *Dead Voices: Natural Agonies in the New World*. Norman: U of Oklahoma P, 1992.

Wong, Hertha. "Sending My Heart Back across the Years": *Tradition and Innovation in Native American Autobiography*. New York: Oxford UP, 1992.

Bernard Assiniwi

"Je suis ce que je dis que je suis" / "I am what I say I am"

Bernard Assiniwi (1935–2000) was born in Montreal, Quebec, to a French-Canadian/ Algonquin mother and a Cree/Algonquin father. He worked for both provincial and national government institutions—including the National Museum of Civilization (now the Canadian Museum of History)—in areas as diverse as the arts, communication, public administration, and biology. Assiniwi published over 30 works of fiction and non-fiction, ranging from historical and contemporary novels to works on the oral tradition and woodcraft. He was the first franco-Indigenous author to be widely published in Quebec, and continues to be read today in both English and French.

This essay addresses what has come to be known in the field of Indigenous literary criticism as questions of hybridity and nationhood. In response to N. Scott Momaday's 1970 essay "Man Made of Words," in which he argues that "we are what we imagine," Assiniwi asserts his right to nationhood based on sense of cultural belonging. Written in 1993, just three years after the Oka Crisis, which served to unite Indigenous peoples from across the continent, the essay takes the "pan-Native movement" one step further, and promotes tribal affiliation as the key to Indigenous survival. In response to debates over "blood quantum" in the United States, Assiniwi asserts that action and experience rather than blood should determine nationhood. In spite of the French in his background, he is, as he declares, 100% Algonquin/Cree, and this is what defines him, and the literature that he produces.

Assiniwi, Bernard. "Je suis ce que je dis que je suis." *Le Renouveau de la parole identitaire*. Ed. Mireille Calle-Gruber, Jeanne-Marie Clerc. Montpellier, France and Kingston, ON: Centre d'Études littéraires françaises du XXe siècle, Groupe de recherche sur les expressions françaises, cahier 2, 1993. 101–06.

Je suis ce que je dis que je suis

En 1966, je prononçais une allocution à l'Université de Colombie Britannique (UBC) dans laquelle je plaisantais en disant que je me demandais « pourquoi le gouvernement canadien tenait tant à changer la façon de vivre des Autochtones du Canada afin de rendre ces gens à l'image des gens de la civilisation ouest-Européenne, alors que dans vingt ans, ces nouveaux arrivants devraient apprendre, de ces mêmes Autochtones, comment ne pas devenir fous au fur et à mesure qu'ils seraient remplacés par des machines, puisque l'époque des loisirs approchait ». Vingt-sept ans plus tard, ces Autochtones ne sont toujours pas assimilés au monde des conquérants du Continent Nord-Américain. Les gens d'ici ne sont toujours pas assimilés à l'identité nationale qu'ont créée les nouveaux arrivants. Pourtant, ils ne sont pas retournés au tribalisme comme les peuples du monde entier sont en train de le faire : car ils ne s'en sont jamais éloignés.

Les Autochtones du Canada, lorsqu'ils s'adressent au public ou aux diverses instances du gouvernement, le font par la bouche de leurs associations nationales, lesquelles se donnent des noms copiés sur ceux qu'utilisent les Anglo- ou les Franco-Européens, tels : l'Assemblée des Premières Nations du Canada ; le Conseil National des Autochtones du Canada ; etc. Mais dès qu'ils se retrouvent entre eux, les Autochtones parlent des Ojibwas, des Cris, des Algonquins, des Mohawks, des Pieds-Noirs. Bien plus, lorsque les nations membres de la nation Algonquine de l'Ouest du Québec discutent entre elles, elles ne parlent plus de « nation » avec un grand N, mais de communautés, telles les Abitibiwinnis ; les Kitigan-Zibi-Anishnabegs ; etc. Le nom bien connu d'Algonquin devient ainsi, soudain, le vocable de la plus petite dénomination : celle de la tribu plutôt que celle de la nation ; et, plus exactement, celle de la nation individuelle plutôt que celle qui désignerait l'Autochtone, l'Aborigène, l'Amérindien ou l'Indien d'Amérique.

Comment pourrait-il en être autrement ? Malgré l'ignorance flagrante des découvreurs du pays, qui parlent des « INDIENS » lorsqu'ils désignent les peuples autochtones d'ici, il faut constater qu'il n'y a pas moins de cinquante-trois cultures bien distinctes, utilisant cinquante-trois langues différentes, reliées entre elles en onze familles linguistiques toutes bien distinctes et disséminées sur plus de quatre mille kilomètres de terres, de l'Atlantique au Pacifique. Cette ignorance de la part de la société dominante fait que lorsqu'un événement particulier se produit, tel la crise de Kanesetake (Oka) pendant l'été de 1990, on l'appelle immédiatement « la crise amérindienne », la « crise indienne », « l'été indien », plaçant, sans discernement, tous les Autochtones d'ici dans un même contexte alors que les Mohawks impliqués dans cette crise sont aussi différents des Cris de la Baie-James que le sont les Français des Turcs. Disséminés dans 613 communautés qui administrent 2241 réserves de terres, les Autochtones ne peuvent se sentir solidaires les uns des autres que lorsqu'ils sont pris à partie, sans autre principe de discernement que le fait d'avoir été là avant la venue des Européens sur notre Continent. Et ces terres de réserve, qui n'appartiennent pas en propre aux individus mais aux communautés qui les administrent, se retrouvent tellement éloignées les unes des autres que les Autochtones se sentent partie intégrante de l'environnement avant de sentir une appartenance « nationale » Autochtone ! Né en Colombie Britannique, l'Haïda se sent beaucoup plus « British Colombian » qu'Autochtone au sens large du mot. Et, de nos jours, s'ajoutant aux 2241 réserves, les nombreuses communautés urbaines et hors-réserves, qui font que les 400.000 Autochtones vivant sur les réserves sont devenus minoritaires par rapport aux quelques 800.000 autres qui vivent dans les centres urbains et ruraux, font aussi que ces gens s'identifient comme Siksikas, Pikunis, Sarcee, Saulteaux, avant de se dire « Autochtones » : car ils ont le sentiment de perdre leur identité dès qu'ils se disent « Autochtones ». Sans une identification particulière, l'homme et la femme d'ici ne sont rien. Et les titres tels que Autochtone, Aborigène, Indien, Amérindien, ne signifient rien s'ils ne sont accompagnés du suffixe Montagnais, ou Micmac, ou Malécite, etc.

Les peuples conquérants, comme les sociétés majoritaires, ont tendance à prendre pour acquis les peuples conquis ou soumis à leurs règles, tout en ignorant, volontairement ou non, les différences et les particularités des minorités. Ces peuples de conquérants sont si sûrs d'eux que quiconque vit ou agit différemment est considéré comme inférieur. Les minorités n'existent pas en tant que peuples ; et elles n'ont pas d'identité propre aux yeux des sociétés dominantes.

Au Québec, depuis la conquête par l'Angleterre d'un pays que ses habitants voulaient « français », la résistance culturelle, sociale, économique et politique s'est organisée. Dans les années 1930, un ordre secret est né, l'ordre de Jacques Cartier, aussi appelé « la patente », afin de contrer l'influence anglophone et de stopper l'assimilation des francophones à la société dominante anglophone. Cet ordre a tenté également d'établir l'identité des francophones catholiques face à l'influence nord-Américaine. Le phénomène n'est donc pas exclusivement autochtone !

C'est au début des années soixante que le mouvement identitaire autochtone est né au Canada. Pendant plus de quatre cents ans, le mot d'ordre fut : « Ne fais pas de bruit, ne dis pas que tu est Cri ou Algonquin, et ton entourage croira que tu fais partie de l'environnement, que tu ressembles à la majorité ». Les Autochtones ont commencé à s'identifier vraiment à ce qu'ils étaient. Mon père, homme fier s'il en fut, me dit alors : « Peut-être cela t'apportera-t-il une plus grande satisfaction d'être, et une plus grande fierté que celles que j'ai eues ». « Dans ma jeunesse, et jusqu'à tout récemment, les gens ne pouvaient pas comprendre ce que nous étions ». Je me souviens que mon père m'avait déjà dit, en 1945, alors que je fréquentais l'école et que les élèves m'avaient pris à partie après la narration du « massacre de Lachine » au temps présent, ainsi qu'on le faisait à l'époque : « Ne crie pas sur les toits que tu es un Sauvage. Cela aiguise leurs instincts guerriers ». L'identité de mon père s'était fondue au sein de la nation dominante, et il ne tentait déjà plus de combattre cet état de la volonté d'être intégré à son environnement.

J'avais 12 ans lorsque j'ai décidé que ma parole serait toute ma vie. Que ma parole serait, désormais, mon identité ; et que plus jamais personne ne serait autorisé à la mettre en doute. Je venais de décider que tout ce que je ferais dans ma vie se rapporterait à ce que je suis. A mon identité. A notre identité qu'on tentait d'endormir par le geste tendre et moelleux de l'assimilation au sein de la majorité. Et qu'on ne pourrait dire plus tard que « mes ancêtres étaient Autochtones ». En 1965, alors que j'annonçais à mon père que je reprenais le nom véritable d'Assiniwi, afin qu'on ne m'appelle plus jamais par le truchement de cette horrible traduction de ce qui voulait dire ce que je suis, il me répondit : « J'espère que tu seras assez fort pour résister aux pressions de l'extérieur comme à celles de l'intérieur, c'est-à-dire à ceux des nôtres qui croient que l'assimilation est préférable ». La parole identitaire qui ne serait pas suivie d'une action positive d'affirmation ne vaudrait pas plus cher que celui qui la prononce. Autrement dit, la parole en ce cas ne serait que verbiage.

Si la parole devient identitaire, elle n'est que le début de l'identité. Il faut pouvoir vivre au niveau de sa parole. C'est d'ailleurs à ce niveau-là qu'on sépare la vraie parole de la fausse. Il fut une époque où il n'était pas de mode de s'identifier aux peuples autochtones d'ici. Seuls les vrais, les fiers, furent assez braves pour le faire. Et à force de le dire, ils ont réussi à convaincre la plupart d'entre nous qu'il était préférable de mourir à grands cris plutôt que de vivre en silence. Alors, beaucoup d'autres se sont levés. Certains, désireux de se trouver une nouvelle noblesse, un lien avec la terre d'ici, afin de perdre leur complexe de dominateur ayant mal agi, se sont trouvés du sang autochtone. Ceux-là se hâtent de vous dire : « Moi aussi, j'ai du sang autochtone dans les veines ». Souvent, celui-là qui parle ainsi n'est pas même capable d'identifier la tribu à laquelle il appartient. Celui-là est un homme faux. Il est porteur de la fausse parole identitaire et fait plus de mal que de bien—avec, souvent, la meilleure volonté du monde. J'ai connu des dizaines d'individus qui avaient fait des recherches (payées, bien entendu) pour le compte de certaines personnes, lesquelles voulaient absolument se trouver DU SANG INDIEN. Toutefois, ces nouveaux alliés sont vite dépassés lorsqu'arrive une crise comme celle de Kanasetake (Oka) : ils redeviennent alors bien vite ouest-Européens d'origine. Croyant que le bateau coule, les rats quittent l'embarcation, disait un jour un capitaine de navire. Et nous nous retrouvons de nouveau seuls, avec nos vérités, nos fiertés, nos langues et nos cultures. On nous a tous accusés en nommant ces événements d'Oka « la crise autochtone ». Nous défendons tous les Mohawks qui sont à l'origine légitime de cette crise, même si nos cultures et nos langues sont diamétralement opposées, car il ne servirait à rien de tenter d'expliquer les traits qui nous rendent différents : les gens ne pourraient comprendre puisqu'ils ont 457 ans de retard sur cette compréhension. Il est plus facile, pour nous, de nous lever, dans un geste de solidarité, pour affirmer ce que nous sommes, ou pour répandre la parole identitaire de « l'Aboriginalité » envers et contre toute compréhension qui nous rendrait, de toute manière, confondus les uns avec les autres. Si les rats n'avaient pas quitté le bateau après la « Crise d'Oka », la parole identitaire n'aurait été que mensonge. Dans le contexte présent, elle demeure vraie en ce qu'elle est un premier geste global d'identité.

Je suis moitié Autochtone et moitié Québécois francophone. J'ai donc en moi autant de sang de la société dominante que de sang autochtone minoritaire. Je pourrais facilement, grâce ou à cause de ce que j'ai l'air d'être, prétendre être l'un ou l'autre. Pourtant, dans les deux cas, j'appartiens à une minorité. La première au sein d'une seconde qui l'est par rapport à la marée anglophone de l'Amérique du Nord. Pourtant, si on me dit métissé, je m'identifie au groupe Algo-Cri. Si je me sens, parfois, Québécois—lorsque les Québécois ne font pas montre de racisme et d'ostracisme envers les miens—, je ne me sens pas du tout Français. Je ne suis pas Métis bien que métissé car, contrairement aux communautés de Métis de l'Ouest canadien, qui ont une langue distincte, faite de Cri, de français et d'anglais, les métissés de l'Est du Canada s'identifient soit aux sociétés dominantes, soit aux sociétés minoritaires autochtones. Même métissés, nous nous identifions à ce qu'ont fait de nous nos cultures : des Algonquins, des Cris, des Atikamekw, des Montagnais, des Abénakis, des Hurons-Wendats, etc. Etre Autochtone, c'est avant tout appartenir à une culture, avoir une façon de vivre différente, un système de valeurs différent, une langue différente—et assez de force de caractère pour le crier à tous vents. Le Chef William Commanda, Chef Suprême des Algonquins d'Amérique, me disait un jour, en parlant d'un homme de sa nation : « Il n'a pas une goutte de sang Algonquin dans les veines, mais il vit avec nous, a épousé une des nôtres, parle notre langue et se conforme à nos coutumes et traditions. Ses enfants sont nés ici. De quel droit le gouvernement viendrait-il nous dire qu'il n'est pas Algonquin ? Il faudrait que nous soyons drôlement mesquins pour lui nier le droit d'être un Algonquin ».

Si l'identité était liée au sang plutôt qu'à la parole, quelqu'un pourrait-il me dire QUI est un vrai Québécois, un vrai Canadien, un vrai Français ? Si l'identité était liée à la couleur de la peau, ou à l'apparence que l'on a, QUI serait donc Américain ou Sud-Africain ? Le fait d'habiter un territoire ou un pays suffit-il à faire de vous ce qu'est ce pays ? Ou faut-il encore savoir et pouvoir l'affirmer ? Et si vous l'affirmez, cette parole suffit-elle ? Ou bien avez-vous besoin de papiers pour le prouver, d'une carte pour le confirmer ?

Bien que je sois, de sang, à moitié Français, Je suis Algo-Cri, du groupe linguistique Algonquien et toute ma vie est orientée vers cette identité…je vous en donne ma parole.

I am what I say I am

In a talk I gave at the University of British Columbia in 1966, I joked that I asked myself "why the Canadian government was so intent on changing the way of life of the Indigenous people of Canada in order to turn them into Western Europeans, when in twenty years these newcomers would have to learn, from the same Indigenous peoples, how to stay sane while being progressively replaced by machines, as the leisure era was approaching." Twenty-seven years later, these Indigenous peoples are still not assimilated into the world of the conquerors of the North-American continent. They are still not assimilated into the national identity created by those newcomers. And yet they are not returning to tribalism, as peoples the world over are now doing: that is because they never left it.

The Indigenous peoples of Canada, when addressing the public or various government bodies, do so through their national associations, named after those used by Anglo- or Franco-Europeans: The Assembly of First Nations of Canada, The National Aboriginal Council, etc. But among themselves, Indigenous people speak of the Ojibwe, Cree, Algonquin, Mohawk, and Blackfoot. Moreover, when members of the Algonquin nation of Western Quebec speak among themselves, they no longer speak about a capital N "Nation," but about communities, such as the Abitibiwinni, the Kitigan-Zibi-Anishnabeg, etc. Thus, the well-known name of Algonquin suddenly becomes the term for the smallest body: the tribe rather than the nation; and, more precisely, the individual nation rather than an Indigenous or Aboriginal person, an Amerindian, or American Indian.

How could it be otherwise? Despite the flagrant ignorance of the discoverers of this country, who spoke of "INDIENS" [Indians] to designate Indigenous people, it should be pointed out that there are no less than fifty-three very distinct cultures, with fifty-three different languages, divided into eleven distinct linguistic families, scattered over more than four thousand kilometres of land from the Atlantic to the Pacific. As a result of the dominant society's ignorance, specific events, such as the Kanesetake (Oka) Crisis of summer 1990, are immediately called "the Aboriginal Crisis," "the Indian Crisis," or "the Indian Summer," which indiscriminately places all Indigenous peoples in the same context, when in fact the Mohawks implicated in the crisis are as different from the James Bay Cree as the French are from the Turks. Scattered among 613 communities administering 2,241 reserve lands, Indigenous peoples can only feel solidarity with one another when they are regarded as a single group, with no other defining characteristic than having been on our continent before the arrival of the Europeans. And these reserve lands, which did not rightly belong to individuals but to the communities that administered them, are so far from one another that the Indigenous peoples feel more connected to their region than to a "pan-Indigenous nation"! Born in British Columbia, the Haïda feel much more "British Columbian" than they do generically Aboriginal. And today, added to the 2,241 reserves are the numerous urban and off-reserve communities, so that the 40,000 Indigenous people living on reserves have become a minority when compared to some 800,000 others who live in urban and rural centres and who self-identify as Siksika, Pikuni, Sarcee, and Saulteaux before calling themselves "Aboriginal," as they feel they will lose their identity as soon as they say "Indigenous." Without a specific identity, the Indigenous man or woman is nothing. And designations such as Indigenous, Aboriginal, Indian or Amerindian mean nothing if they are not accompanied by a suffix, such as Innu, Micmac, Maliseet, etc.

The conquering peoples, like all majority societies, tend to assume that the conquered peoples have submitted to their rule, while also ignoring, willingly or not, the minority's differences and particularities. These conquering peoples are so sure of themselves that whoever lives or acts differently is considered inferior. Minorities do not exist as peoples and possess no identity of their own in the eyes of the dominant societies.

In Quebec, ever since England's conquest of a country its inhabitants considered "French," the people engaged in organized cultural, social, economic and political resistance. In the 1930s, a secret order was created, the "Ordre de Jacques Cartier" (also known as "la Patente" [the thing]), to counter anglophone influence and halt the assimilation of francophones into the dominant anglophone society. The order also tried to establish a francophone Catholic identity in the face of North-American influence. The phenomenon is therefore not exclusively Indigenous!

It was in the early 1960s that the Red Power movement was born in Canada. For over four hundred years, people had been told "Don't draw attention to yourself, don't say you're Cree or Algonquin and everyone will think you're part of the landscape, that you fit into the mainstream." Then Indigenous people began to really identify themselves as what they were. My father, as proud a man as any, told me at that time: "Maybe this will bring you greater satisfaction and a greater pride than mine." "When I was young and until just recently, nobody could understand what we were." I remember my father telling me in 1945, while I was in school and students had taken me to task after speaking about the "Lachine massacre": "Don't cry from the rooftops that you're a Savage. It sharpens their warrior instincts." My father's identity had been absorbed by the dominant culture, and he had already lost the will to fight integration into the world around him.

I was 12 when I decided that my word would be my whole life. That my word would be, from that point on, my identity, and that never again would I allow anyone to question it. I decided that everything I did in my life would be connected to who I was. To my identity. To our identity that the dominant culture has attempted to erase through the soft and gentle process of assimilation. So that later we would no longer be able to say "my ancestors were Indigenous." In 1965, when I announced to my father that I was assuming my true name, Assiniwi, so that never again would I be called by the horrible translation of something I was not, he replied: "I hope you'll be strong enough to resist the external pressures as well as the internal ones—those from our own people who believe that assimilation is preferable." Without positive action, affirmations of identity are as worthless as those who pronounce them. Simply put, the word in this case would be nothing but talk.

Even if your word defines you, it is only the beginning of self identity. One must also be able to walk the talk. This is the only way to separate truth from fiction. There was a time when it was not fashionable to self identify to Indigenous peoples here. Only the true and the proud were brave enough to do so. And by doing so again and again, they managed to convince most of us that it was better to die screaming than to live in silence. Then many others came forward. Some came seeking honour—a link to the land, in order to shed the guilt of the colonizer, and claimed Indigenous blood. They are the first to say, "I, too, have Native roots." These very people are usually unable to name any tribal affiliation. They are fraudulent, and in spite of the best intentions they do more harm than good. I've known dozens of individuals who have done research (paid, of course) for people desperately seeking INDIAN BLOOD. However, these new allies are quickly overwhelmed when a crisis like Kanasetake (Oka) develops, at which point they quickly revert to their Western-European origins. A ship's captain once said that rats flee the boat when they think it's sinking. And so we find ourselves alone again, with our truths, our pride, our languages and our cultures. We've all been accused of calling the Oka events "the Aboriginal crisis." We defend all the Mohawks who are legitimately at the heart of the crisis, even if our cultures and our languages are diametrically opposed, for it would be pointless to try to explain the traits that differentiate us: people are 457 years too late to understand. It's easier for us to stand up and, in a gesture of solidarity, affirm what we are or spread the "Indigenous word" in order to educate those who confuse us with one another. The Indigenous word would have simply been a lie if the rats had not jumped ship after the "Oka Crisis." In the present context, the word is the truth, and is a preliminary gesture toward a pan-indigenous identity.

I am half Indigenous and half francophone Quebecois. I therefore have as much blood from the dominant culture as I do from the minority Indigenous culture. Thanks to or because of my appearance, I could easily claim to be one or the other. Yet in both cases I belong to a minority. The first in the midst of the second, which is a minority in relation to the anglophone tide in North America. If I am to be called "métisse" [mixed blood] however, I identify as Algo-Cree. If at times I feel Quebecois—on those occasions when the Quebecois show no racism and don't ostracize my people—I don't feel at all French. Although mixed blood, I am not Métis. Contrary to the Métis of the Canadian West (who have a distinct language consisting of Cree, French, and English), those of the Canadian East identify themselves either with the dominant cultures or with Indigenous minorities. Even as mixed-bloods, we identify with what our cultures have made of us: Algonquin, Cree, Atikamekw, Innu, Abenaki, Huron-Wendat, etc. To be Indigenous is above all to belong to a culture, to have a different way of life, a different belief system, a different language—and enough strength of character to proclaim it for all to hear. Chief William Commanda, Supreme Chief of the Algonquins of America, spoke to me one day of a man from his nation: "He hasn't got a drop of Algonquin blood in his veins, but he lives with us, married one of us, speaks our language, and conforms to our customs and traditions. His children were born here. What right would the government have to come and tell us that he's not Algonquin? We'd have to be awfully petty to deny him the right to be Algonquin."

If identity were linked to blood rather than speech, would anyone be able to tell me WHO is a real Quebecois, a real Canadian, a real Frenchman? If identity were linked to skin colour, or to appearance, WHO would be American or South-African? Is living in a territory or country enough to make you what that country is? Or must you also be able to know it and affirm it? And if you do, is your word enough to confirm it, or do you need papers and a card to prove it?

Although by blood I am half-French, I am Algo-Cree, from the Algonquian language group, and this identity is the focus of my entire existence...I give you my word.

Gail G. Valaskakis

"Parallel Voices: Indians and Others, Narratives of Cultural Struggle"

Gail Guthrie Valaskakis (1939–2007) was a Chippewa (Ojibwe) scholar, educator, and activist from Lac du Flambeau, Wisconsin. As a scholar, she was instrumental in bringing Indigenous issues to Cultural Studies in North America and had a long and distinguished career at Concordia University in Montreal. A considerable portion of her scholarship examines Indigeneity through the lens of post-colonial theory, and her work using the powwow as an analytical strategy has been particularly influential. Valaskakis also served as Director of Research for the "Aboriginal Healing Founda-tion" in Ottawa. She was awarded a National Aboriginal Achievement Award in 2002.

 Valaskakis's 1993 essay, "Parallel Voices" was inspired by media representations of Indigeneity during the 1990 Oka Crisis, and during the USA's 1992 celebration of Columbus's arrival 500 years prior. Using the terminology of post-colonial theorists such as Gayatri Spivak, Stuart Hall, and James Clifton, Valaskakis describes represen-tations of the "other" or "subaltern," and the stereotypes that such representations create and perpetuate. Accordingly, she examines a range of destructive stereotypes that settlers have created to serve themselves: portrayals of Indigenous women as either princess or squaw, as keepers of the land, Indigenous men as warriors, and Indigenous peoples in general as noble or savage, and above all, as vanishing. She finds resistance to these destructive portrayals through cultural expression.

Valaskakis, Gail Guthrie. "Parallel Voices: Indians and Others, Narratives of Cultural Struggle." *Canadian Journal of Communications* 18.3 (Summer 1993): 283–96.

Parallel Voices: Indians and Others, Narratives of Cultural Struggle

Duke Redbird (1975) tells a story about a non-Indian who is looking for the road to the Duck Lake powwow. He sees an old Indian sitting outside his house and he calls out, "Where's the road to the Duck Lake powwow?" The old man never looks up as he answers, "Don't know." The man in the car mumbles "Dumb Indian." And the old man looks up and says, "I might be dumb, but I'm not lost."

This story held special meaning for First Nations in 1992, a year in which Americans celebrated the quincentennial of Columbus and Canadians continued to digest the meaning of what became known as the "Oka crisis," the 78-day stand-off between Indians and Army which occurred in Quebec in the summer of 1990. Indians know that when Columbus sailed to America, he was lost; and for many Native North Americans, this paradigm of Columbus's encounter with the "New World" is an apt description of the society precipitated through his voyage. The conflicting quincentennial visions of Indians and non-Indians are represented in the titles of the PBS television program *Columbus and the Age of Discovery* and the Indian-made video entitled *Surviving Columbus*. The experiences which are expressed in these very different stories of conquest are indicative of the wider conflict which polarizes Indians and Others in the United States and Canada—which celebrated 125 years of nationhood in 1992. As Coco Fusco (April 6, 1992) suggests, "Columbus" has become a buzzword for a wider, equally polarized debate over identity politics which involves everything from "p.c."—defined by some as "politically correct" and by others as "patriotically correct"—to environmental issues. Indians are deeply implicated in this politicized struggle over national culture and its ethnocentric or pluralist extensions. Some Native people, like Laurie Weahkee (1992) of the Navajo and Cochiti Nations, "see 1992 as a resistance and a memorial..."; other Indians agree with Gerald McMaster & Lee-Ann Martin (1992, p. 12) that 1992 marks a time of reflection on the "'meeting of cultures,' addressing such issues as historicity, cultural conquest, Aboriginal title, identity and sovereignty." And from the perspective of cultural identity, representation, and resistance, the debate over Columbus has been coopted into the essentialist discourse that positions the Indian in an historical past constructed in stereotypes which are removed from the cultural and political reality of contemporary Indian life.

Across North America, there is increasing anger and frustration among people of the First Nations, increasing distrust between Natives and non-Natives: warriors and artists, politicians and writers. Their expressions of anger, frustration, and distrust are grounded in the politics of difference and its oppositional strategies of cultural and political struggle. These are parallel voices, distortions of the communication symbolized in the Two-Row Wampum Treaty of the Iroquois Confederacy, which represents the historical pact between Indians and newcomers in two discreet blue beaded lines that run across a sea of white beads, never intersecting, never imposing upon one another in a respectful relationship of separate nations represented in the Indian canoe and the settler's sailing ship. Today, we are all caught in a web of conflicting interests and actions, confrontations constructed in dominant cultural and political process and the Native experience of exclusion, or stereotypical inclusion and appropriation. For people of the First Nations, this involves the subaltern experience rooted in the lived reality and the representation of the "insider," the "outsider," and the "other." As Coco Fusco (1990, p. 77) writes, "For me, the issue of 'the other' is one of power, of a dynamic between those who impute otherness to some and those who are designated as other. So the questions I ask about otherness have to do with how others or the other are spoken of, who is speaking about them, and why have they chosen to speak of the other at the given historical moment." For Indians at this time in history, otherness is related to issues of identity and cultural struggle entrenched in representation and appropriation, in how they are represented, and how these representations are appropriated by others in a political process which confines their past as it constructs their future.

Discourse and Indians

Indians, of course, have always been spoken of, and have spoken about, the other. The discourse of the Indian as noble and savage, the villain and the victim—most recently represented in the media coverage of the Mohawk warriors of Kahnawake and Kahnesatake and the spear fishing Gitchdon and Gitchedonque of my own reservation in Wisconsin—is threaded through the narratives of the dominant culture. As Robert Berkhofer (1979, p. 72) writes, "For most of the past five centuries, the Indian of the imagination and ideology has been as real, perhaps more real, than the Native American of actual existence and contact." And what Keith Basso (1979) calls in another context "Portraits of the 'Whiteman'" are embedded in the tales of Indian experience which circulate within the oral traditions of First Nations.

But today, there is new concern about competing narratives among artists, writers, and academics. In Canada, what has become known as the Women's Press Debate "began with whether White writers should be allowed to publish work in which they adopted the voices of persons of color" (Begamudre, 1989, pp. 11–12). And among artists and curators, the debate over what one Indian artist calls "the politics of primivitism" (Jacobs, 1986) recently re-emerged in controversy over a painting entitled

Femme aux Bananes, a representation of a "traditional" Black woman painted by a White artist which was rejected from a show sponsored by Concordia University's Women's Centre in Montreal. This struggle over who can represent whom, who can tell the stories of others—and how they should be told—tends to focus on issues of censorship and political correctness, masking the lived experience and problems of people of Colour and people of the First Nations; neglecting the relationship between representation, appropriation and access, and social and political formations which position people of Colour and Native North Americans as other and unequal.

It is, of course, not surprising that the current Canadian debate over representation and appropriation involves images of women. Feminist writing has, along with cultural studies and some ethnographic critique, brought these issues to the surface by posing questions which address the subaltern experience. What does it mean to be placed within competing articulations of power, to be positioned as subaltern, in relation to race, class, and gender, in the hegemony of discursive constructions, academic and popular? How is cultural practice formed and transformed in interwoven experience and memory: historical and current, real and imagined, collective and individual, ambivalent and prescribed, remembered and lived? How is identity negotiated, appropriated, enacted, and acted upon in the discourse of competing representations and narratives? What is the nature of cultural struggle, of power and resistance, exclusion and cultural persistence? And what does all this mean for artistic and media practice?

In addressing these questions, feminist work has recovered the lives and experience of women in research and writing which critique the ways in which gender organizes social experience. But we remain caught in the nexus between competing narratives, between what some call the narrative and the counter-narrative, in trying to find ways to express and act upon the cultural and political reality of difference. It is through the prism of parallel voices, of competing narratives, expressed in public text—in literature, art, music, ceremony, and media—that we can access the subaltern experience, expand our concepts of inquiry, and approach our points of connectedness.

Our stories have always been recognized as a window on who we are, what we experience, and how we understand and enact ourselves and others. But stories are more than a window on identity. We actually construct who we are in discourse through a process which involves an individual's identification with the images and cultural narratives that dominate our ways of seeing and representing the world. The work of Stuart Hall (1985, 1986, 1989) clarifies the importance of cultural narratives and representations in composing our identity as social subjects. For Hall, identity is not formed in internal conceptions of the self, but in the adoption of transforming, openended representations and narratives. These representations and narratives are articulated in the processes of experiencing and forming community within the power relations of different groups and interests. Like the terrain of social struggle in which it is articulated, identity is continually contested and reconstructed. It is built and re-built in the discursive negotiation of complex alliances and relations within the heterogeneity of community; in discourse which is based not in unity or belonging, but in transformation and difference. Within this understanding, representations and cultural narratives are central sites of cultural struggle. As discursive constructions with different ideologies and meanings, representations and narratives are formed in lived experience and public text, in the discourse of everyday action and events—individual and collective, dynamic and diachronic, interactional and mediated. This conceptual framework locates artistic and media images within the ideological struggle of power relations and the dynamic process of building individual and collective identity. And for Indians, this identity has drawn forcefully on the power and purpose of Native narrative.

As Art Solomon (1990, p. 14), an Ojibway Elder who lives in Sudbury, reminds us, Indian stories are teachings, prayers, songs. First Nations reflect different environments, different cultures; but they share this understanding of stories rooted in the common experience of oral tradition. And it is the power of narrative as teaching, prayer, song experienced through collective heritage which makes stories so valued and so important in Indian country.

Indian stories tell experiences in their lives or the lives of people they know—real or imagined—set in narratives that uncoil the spiraled meaning of their reality. Art Solomon (ibid., p. 132) says of his narratives, "I have borrowed this story from someone who had borrowed it from someone else who had borrowed it from someone else...." It is the borrowed quality of Indian stories that stitches narrative to collective heritage, to a polyvocal past experienced in the present. Passed on through kinship and gossip, ceremony and social drinking, stories carry the experience of being Indian from generation to generation. And in Indian country, that experience is rooted in the continuity of a relationship with each other, with the land, and with non-Indians. Robin Ridington (1990, p. 190) writes, "The oral traditions of people who are native to this land are a form of discourse that connects them to the land and to the generations that have gone before." Like Gloria Anzaldua's (1987, p. 67) stories, they are "acts encapsulated in time, 'enacted' every time they are spoken aloud or read silently." It is this imaginative power of the word enacted in the practice of daily life that continually renews the experience of being Indian. As N. Scott Momaday (1976, p. 22) writes about the experience of being Kiowa, "Some of my mother's memories have become my own. This is the real burden of the blood." In our narratives, we transform and live the collective cultural identity which is grounded in our endless connection to the land. Indian stories are, of course, no more monolithic than Indians themselves. Our narratives draw upon the prism of experience which we live, including all the dualities which are rooted in the contingent perspectives of individual and collective memory; Indian and non-Indian experience; historical and transforming culture. Maggie Hodgeson (1990), Director of the Nechi Institute in Edmonton, tells a borrowed story which expresses the significance of this prism. The story she tells is a long and wonderful story, which I have shortened here, about a wolf who was blinded in an accident on his journey through life. In his travels, he comes across a mouse and asks him for his eyes. The mouse agrees to give him one eye, and the wolf continues on his way. But with the mouse eye he can only see one tiny bit of the world at a time, one person, one tree, one footprint. Then he meets a buffalo. He asks him for his eyes. The buffalo agrees to give him one eye, and with this eye, the wolf can see the full range of the world in which he lives. And so the wolf continues on his journey, now able to see with both his mouse eye and his buffalo eye, sight which reveals the simultaneity of past and present, individual and collective, Indian and non-Indian.

Narratives of Indian Women

Within this prism which dynamically interweaves the vision of the mouse eye and the buffalo eye, the narratives and counter-narratives which represent and construct the experience of Indian women occupy a special place. The cultural struggle of Indian women which is revealed in these stories is best expressed, I think, in the images of the "Indian princess" and the "squaw." For Indian men, the dominant image of the last century is clearly the "war-bonneted 'warrior'" (Albers and James, 1987, p. 35). Visual images of Indian women have been less prevalent and more varied; but in their analysis of postcards of Indian women, Patricia Albers and William James point out that "if a uniform caricature (of Indian women) has existed, it has been the image of the Indian 'princess'"; and that "the visual image of Indian women as 'maiden' or 'princess' has increased in popularity over time" (ibid., pp. 35, 48).

The representation of the Indian princess has been of interest to me for a long time. As tourist postcards of Indians, they attracted me because they were such forceful contradictions to the daily life we lived on the Lac du Flambeau Indian reservation. I could not understand the connection between these postcard images— sometimes captioned Indian princesses, sometimes squaws—and my great-grandmother, who lived across the road. I listened to her narratives of our struggle for empowerment until I was eighteen, when I went away to college and she died. I knew women who identified as Indian princesses, and women whom we identified as Indian princesses; but what did this representation mean in the lived experience of my great-grandmother, who was enrolled as a Band member when the reservation was established—and who, at ninety, bought a car and did not speak to my father for two months because he did not want her to get a driver's licence? The ambiguous representation of Indian women has been with us since the colonization of North America. Transformed from the Caribbean and Brazilian Queens of the late 1500s to the Mother-Goddess figure in the 1600s and the more independent Princess image of the 1700s, the Indian woman symbolized the New World (Green, 1976, pp. 702–03). But from the image of the princess Pocahontas to her darker twin, the "squaw," both the nobility and the savagery of Indian woman have been defined in relation to White males—rescuing them, sexually satisfying them, abandoning their Indian nation for them. The progression of the narratives of the Indian princess and the squaw which are so deeply entrenched in North America's history is summarized in an excerpt from Monique Mojica's (1991, pp. 20–21) play, entitled Princess Pocahontas and the Blue Spots:

> Princess, Princess Amazon Queen. Show me your royal blood, Is it blue? Is it green? Dried and brown five centuries old, singed and baked and covered with mold?
>
> Princess, priestess Caribe Queen, What are you selling today, Is it corn, tobacco, beans? Snake oil or a beaver hat. Horse liniment, You just can't beat that!
>
> Princess, Princess, calendar girl, Redskin temptress, Indian pearl. Waiting by the water. For a white man to save. She's a savage now remember—Can't behave.

In later years, representations of Indian princesses move from buckskinclad maidens looking wistfully at handsome warriors through advertising for cigars and Swamp-Root cures and food products, to the "red tunic" stage of the early calendar princesses of the early 1920s and the 1930s, posed with mountains, waterfalls, or moonlit lakes. Later calendar princesses are more enticing, with low necklines, net stockings, and outfits that are more sexually alluring. There are Indian maidens, princesses, and "Chieftain's daughters" in textbooks, stories for children, popular songs, movies, and dime novels. And from the early 1900s to the present, there are postcard images of smiling princesses, some wearing warbonnets. In decided contrast to the representations of the Indian squaw, the images of the princess share one thing in common: they all look like replicas of Brooke Shields. As Virginia Driving Hawk Sneve (1987, p. 72) writes, "The models for the original paintings were not American Indian women but attractive Caucasian women who frequently besieged the artists to be allowed to pose as an Indian princess." These models were engaging in what Rayna Green (1988, p. 30) calls "playing Indian," a "performance" which she finds is "one of the oldest and most pervasive forms of American cultural expression, indeed one of the oldest forms of affinity with American culture at the national level."

The representation of the Indian princess has played a powerful role in constructing the identities of both Indians and non-Indians. Vine Deloria (1969, p. 11) writes in *Custer Died for Your Sins*: Whites claiming Indian blood generally tend to reinforce mythical beliefs about Indians. All but one person I met who claimed Indian blood claimed it on his grandmother's side. I once did a projection backwards and discovered that evidently most tribes were entirely female for the first three hundred years of white occupation. No one, it seemed wanted to claim a male Indian as a forebearer.... A male ancestor has too much of the aura of the savage warrior, the unknown primitive, the instinctive animal to make him a respectable member of the family tree. But a young Indian princess? Ah, there was royalty for the taking. Somehow the white was linked with a noble house of gentility and culture if his grandmother was an Indian princess who ran away with an intrepid pioneer.

Feminist writers recognize the contradictory images of Indian women in the ambiguous, male-oriented representations of all women. But the meaning of the image is negotiated in the context of culture and experience. From the experience of being fur traders' "country wives" which Sylvia Van Kirk (1980) documents in her book, *Many Tender Ties*, to the "Bush Lady" of Alanis Obamsawin's poignant song of a reserve woman in the city, Indian women have re-appropriated and lived the narrative now transformed in Indian country into the representation of the "powwow princess." And their struggle with Indian identity—and Indian men—is complex, confusing, and painful. In Canada, the national Native women's organization sued the Assembly of First Nations for equal status at the Constitutional negotiation table, and lost. In the United States, women continue to challenge the male dominance entrenched in Tribal Councils since their establishment through the Indian Re-organization Act of 1934. And everywhere, Native women struggle to make visible their experience of wife-battering, child-abuse, and sexual abuse.

But Indian women know that the narratives of the princess and the squaw have not been experienced by women alone. Through the difference of their gendered experience, Indian men and women are yoked together in the community of sub-alterns, and in cultural heritage. And women play a special role in the continuity of that community. In the words of Art Solomon (1990, pp. 34–35) "The women is [*sic*] the foundations on which nations are built. She is the heart of her nation. If that heart is weak, the people are weak...the woman is the centre of everything"; and he tells us why: "The women 'were of the earth.' They were connected to the Earth Mother and to the grandmother moon whose work was to govern when all things were to be born, plants, animals, humans."

From a feminist perspective, this essentializing representation of women as close to nature is, of course, problematic. As many writers point out, the assumption underlying this conception is that nature is more basic than culture; and because the project of Western culture is to transform nature, culture is conceived as not only different from, but superior to, nature. Women are defined by essential qualities in opposition to men; and since men, not women, are identified with the institutional and symbolic forms of Western cultural change, this distinction supports the suppression of women. From this perspective, the physiology and social role of women which constitutes women "the heart of the nation" in Native cultures contains the ideology which constructs both the romanticized image of nature's pristine beauty, the Indian princess and her earthy, beast-of-burden sister, the squaw.

Indian women, of course, enact the identity of the contradictory and essentializing images related to the nature/culture paradigm of the dominant society. But their identity is also constructed in the discourses of Native traditionalism and treaty rights, including womens' relationship to the land, to nature, and to each other. Native culture is not frozen in the past of representations forged in ethnographic and artistic practice. And Native traditionalism is neither lost in transformation nor revived as a privileged form of resistance. Native culture is living traditionalism: the practice of everyday life experienced collectively and individually as heritage, a multi-vocal past reenacted daily in the ambiguous play of power and identity. Native women live the meaning of their traditional association with Mother Earth and grandmother moon which is the basis for the unbroken circle unifying nature and culture in all Aboriginal cultures. It is their connection to the power of the earth and the Creator—spiritual and natural—which encodes the practice of Mohawk Clan Mothers and Ojibway Gitchedonque. And within the cultural and political struggle of contested identities among Indian women and men, the unity of culture and nature is grounded in the constant reality of the elders and the land. It is the land—real and imagined, lived in heritage and current political process, and expressed in discourse—which constitutes the connection between nature and culture for Indians. And the struggle over appropriation of the discourse related to land and to nature, over land rights and treaty rights, New Age spiritualism and art, in forms that we often label protest or resistance, challenges the identities and the representations of both Indians and non-Indians. The current contestation of ideologies and the diversity of Indian identities can only be understood in the unity of common culture and history, experience, and political purpose: in collective memory and the continual formation of community. It is the negotiation of relations of power articulated in contested ideology and identity which both fractures and binds Indian communities in their struggle with an oppressive past and an uncertain future. And the reality of this lived experience frames both the current debate over Native representation and appropriation and the possibility of connectedness between Natives and non-Natives, particularly women.

Patricia Montour (1992), a Mohawk lawyer, says in a narrative, "I used to shrivel when people called me a feminist. The issues that feminism has tried to focus on are not the issues that occupy First Nations lives." And she adds, "We have to remember to respect Mother Earth. A lot of ways women are treated on this earth is reflective of the ways Mother Earth gets treated." Today, Indian and non-Indian women recognize a connection between domination of the land and domination of people on the basis of race, class, and gender. In asserting that "ecology is a feminist issue" (Warren, 1987, p. 4) which exposes the link between the oppression of women and the oppression of nature, Eco-feminism suggests the possibility of understanding the connection between what we call ecology today, and the lived reality of traditional Indian life. Eco-feminism, of course, is caught in the circularity of its own essentialist argument. But the point of connectedness among women—and men—which is emerging through the cultural and political struggle over clear-cutting forests and diverting rivers and building nuclear waste dumps, is expanding to include Indian land rights and treaty rights. And this may move Eco-feminism to recognize the reality of difference, to act upon the construction of plural narratives, plural representations.

Appropriating Narratives

To non-Natives steeped in the fictive image of the Indian as noble or savage, land rights and treaty rights are often paradoxical. Non-Indians often view treaties as the historical products of benevolent conquest, artifacts of reasonable (if not equitable) surrender. To First Nations, treaties are a process, exercises of ritualized land acquisition and resource exploitation. For Indians, there is no surrender, only mutual sovereignty, nations abstracted from nation-states, recognized through agreements in which the self-determination of the Two-Row Wampum Belt is the common ground. This is not the self-government of Indian councils grafted onto Canadian and American municipalities; but self-determination "bound up with sovereignty in all its ramifications—social, cultural, political, economic; that which in the Mohawk language, translates as 'carrying ourselves'" (*Tribune Juive*, 1989, p. 5). The political difference between this reality and the historically-bound and current representations of Indians as the villain or the victim is clear. As Margaret Atwood (1972, p. 105) points out, neither representation allows newcomers to identify Native peoples as equal, to recognize them as "real inhabitants of a land." And in fact, these narratives of Indians as romanticized or primitive historical artifacts are used to protest Indian land and treaty rights, and to call for the abrogation of Indian treaties themselves.

The protest against spear-fishing Chippewa of my reservation in Wisconsin, which is led by organizations named "Equal Rights for Everyone" and "Stop Treaty Abuse," has drawn heavily upon the counter-narrative written by James Clifton. His books entitled *The Invented Indian* (1990) and *Being and Becoming Indian* (1989), argue the destructive essentialist perspective that the traditionalism of Indians never existed. In this analysis, the Indians never lived as keepers of the land, in the harmony and circularity of nature and culture. The values which orient traditional Indian cultures, and the treaties which acknowledge them, are fictive inventions of the non-Indian psyche and the manipulation of political process. And, the argument goes, even if there were traditional Indians, there are not any now. Traditional Indian cultures are dead, gone the way of the full-blooded Indians who were the only Indians treaties were meant to recognize. Treaties should be abrogated, making all North Americans "equal," a manoeuvre which would benefit Indians by privatizing land and re-inforcing entrepreneurialism. The argument asserts that Indians today are mixed-bloods living on welfare, in houses not teepees or wigwams, who spear fish during spring spawning season using boats and miner's caps and metal spears—all, from this culturally-oppressive perspective, "non-traditional."

This argument may seem far-fetched; but it is lived daily in the homes and high schools and in the border towns and spearing grounds of Indian country. And the fictive representation it constructs is always present in the ambiguity of images of Indians, no matter how well-intentioned the practice of artists, writers, and the media.

In Canada today, Indians are experiencing a new battlefield of appropriated identity rooted in the salient representation which was constructed during the Mohawk occupation at Oka: the media warrior. In television and newsprint and political cartoons, media's warriors were transformed primitives, monolithic representations of Indian activists: the military masculine, criminalized through association with terrorism and epitomized in the ultimate warrior, Ronald Cross. Cross, code-named "Lasagna," became both the darling of the media and, through the dynamic process of re-appropriating identity, what one reporter called, "a media slut" (Pindera, 1990). As non-Indians transpose this new representation of the savage Indian warrior, Indian communities struggle with the factionalism entrenched in the threats and promises of appropriated identity, narrative and counter-narrative.

The ambiguity of appropriated representations is more subtle but no less problematic in Coco Fusco's (1992) tribute to 1992. She and a colleague presented a piece of performance art at museums in the United States, Spain, and Australia which involved spending three full days in a cage in the museum, dressed as "primitives" who cannot understand English. They danced or sang or posed for photographs for a fee; ate mush; and were taken to the bathroom on a leash. The artists were amazed at how many spectators failed to read their satire on the Indian as museum artifact and were convinced that they were "real Indians." Representations, especially appropriated images, are a double-edged sword, as the White artist discovered when she submitted what she intended as a dignified portrait of a traditional Black woman carrying bananas on her head. Primitive Indians in a museum cage may be conceived as an act of resistance; but the discourse of this performance, like the conception of resistance as movement—either "moving forward" or "moving backward"— negates the most important understanding about Indians: First Nations' resistance is cultural persistence; the social memory and lived experience of traditionalism continually negotiated in the discourse and practice of everyday life. People of the First Nations are "traditional." But in the struggle between pluralism and essentialism, between different forms of resistance to undermine hegemonic constructions, the meaning of Indian traditionalism is masked in conceptions of resistance as action, or identity as historical memory striped off, then pasted back on to become "revitalization" (Minh-ha, 1989, p. 59). And these conceptions are perpetuated in the appropriated voices and representations of Indians through a dangerous game: "playing Indian." What Rayna Green (1988, p. 49) calls the "script" that is enacted in "playing Indian" obscures two important points about North America: "the true Indian-ness of America" and the fact that "the play-Indian roles depend on dead Indians." As Green (ibid.) writes:

> In order for anyone to play Indian successfully, real Indians have to be dead. Americans have to believe them dead or kill them off. The Cult of the Vanishing Indian was merely practice for the ritual enactment. Note, for example, how important it has been historically in America to take fish, water, trees, buffalo and deer away from Indians in order to celebrate their oneness with Nature, their status as First Ecologists. If Indians were still in charge of the land, Americans could not lament their own impoverished stewardship of that land through memorializing the Indians they took it from.

Indians live the political struggle represented in the dead Indian. But appropriation involves other issues of identity and power as well. Filmmaker Loretta Todd (1992, p. 72) tells a borrowed story "of how a European painter in the nineteenth century journeyed into the great plains of this continent to 'record' Native people, a common occurrence of the time, born of the ethnographic. While he was painting a Native man on a horse, another Native man observed the artist's work and remarked how his painting was wrong. The Artist, painting the horse from the side, had shown only two legs of the horse and one leg of the rider. The Native man reminded the artist that the horse had four legs and the rider two, which should all be shown."

The difference between the artist's horse and the Indian's horse is, of course, compounded through appropriation. Whether one is appropriating Native spiritualism through the White Buffalo Society or the books of Lynn Andrews,[1] or representations of Indians in history and art, the horse has only two legs. And in expressing the narrative of the two-legged horse, we limit both Native access to voice and the critique of our own pluralistic experience.

This historical moment moves Canadians and Americans toward discursive constructions of the other drawn from an increasing sense of, on one hand, individual rights and, on the other, collective cultural empowerment. I agree with Gerald McMaster that 1992 was a year for reflection on ourselves, on who we are, and how we are all represented in the discourse of history and art and literature, feminism and resistance, land rights, treaty rights, sovereignty, and self-determination. In 1993, the International Year of Indigenous Peoples, we must recognize—and act upon—the intertwined past and present of our two worlds, our parallel voices.

---

1   Lynn Andrews is an American businesswoman and bestselling author of the "Medicine Woman Series," new age spirituality novels based on Native American traditions. Andrews runs seminars based on the ideas contained in the novels. Critics charge her with commercial exploitation of Native American culture and refer to her as a "plastic shaman."

References

Albers, Patricia C., and James, William R. (1987). "Illusion and Illumination: Visual Images of American Indian Women in the West." In Susan Armitage and Elizabeth Jameson (eds.), *The Women's West.* Norman and London: U of Oklahoma P.

Anzaldua, Gloria. (1987). *Borderlands/La Frontera.* San Francisco: Spinsters/Aunt Lute.

Atwood, Margaret. (1972). *Survival: A Thematic Guide to Canadian Literature.* Toronto: Anansi.

Basso, Keith. (1979). *Portraits of the "Whiteman."* Cambridge: Cambridge UP.

Begamudre, Van. (1989, Fall). *On Cultural Justice and Cultural Revenges.* Saskatoon: Black-flash.

Berkhofer, Robert F., Jr. (1979). *The White Man's Indian.* New York and Toronto: Random House.

Clifton, James. (1989). *On Being and Becoming Indian: Biographical Studies of North American Frontiers.* Chicago: Dorsey P.

———. (1990). *The Invented Indian: Cultural Fictions and Government Policies.* New Brunswick, NJ: Transaction P.

Deloria, Vine. (1969). *Custer Died for Your Sins.* New York: Avon.

Fusco, Coco. (1990, April 6). Lecture at McGill University.

———. (1990, Fall). "Managing the Other." *Lusitania* 1(3).

Green, Rayna. (1988). "The Tribe Called Wannabee: Playing Indian in America and Europe." *Folklore* 99.

———. (1976). "The Pocahontas Perplex: The Image of the Indian Woman in American Vernacular Culture." *The Massachusetts Review* 16(4).

Hall, Stuart. (1985). "Signification, Representation, Ideology: Althusser and the Post-Structuralist Debates." *Critical Studies in Mass Communication* 2(2).

———. (1986). *Journal of Communication Inquiry* 10(2).

———. (1989). "Cultural Identity and Cinematic Representation." *Framework* 36.

Hodgeson, Maggie. (1990, June). *Communities in Crisis Conference: Waseskun Native Halfway House.* Montreal: Concordia University.

Jacobs, Alex Karonialktitae. (1986). "The Politics of Primitivism: Concerns and Attitudes in Indian Art." *Akwekon* 2/3.

McMaster, Gerald, and Martin, Lee-Ann. (1992). *Indigena.* Vancouver: Douglas and McIntyre.

Minh-ha, Trinh T. (1989). *Woman Native Other.* Bloomington: U of Indiana P.

Mojica, Monique. (1991). *Princess Pocahontas and the Blue Spots.* Toronto: Women's P.

Momaday, N. Scott. (1976). *The Names.* New York: Harper and Row.

Montour, Patricia. (1992). *Everywoman's Almanac.* Toronto: Women's P.

Pindera, Loreen. (1990, November). Lecture on the Oka Crisis. Concordia University.

Redbird, Duke. (1975). *Pow Wow at Duck Lake.* National Film Board of Canada.

Ridington, Robin. (1990). *Little Bit Know Something: Stories in a Language of Anthro-*

pology. Vancouver: Douglas and McIntyre.

Solomon, Arthur. (1990). *Songs for the People: Teachings on the Natural Way.* Toronto: NC P.

Sneve, Virginia Driving Hawk. (1987, November). "Remembering Minnehaha." *Country Living.*

Todd, Loretta. (1992). "What More Do They Want?" In Gerald McMaster and Lee-Ann Martin (eds.), *Indigena.* Vancouver: Douglas and McIntyre.

Tribune Juive. (1989). Kahnawake.

Van Kirk, Sylvia. (1960). *"Many Tender Ties": Women in Fur-Trade Society, 1670–1870.* Winnipeg: Watson and Dwyer.

Warren, Karen J. (1987, Spring). "Feminism and Ecology." *Environmental Ethics.*

Weahkee, Laurie. (1992). *Everywoman's Almanac.* Toronto: Women's P.

Willie Ermine

"Aboriginal Epistemology"

Willie Ermine is Cree from Sturgeon Lake First Nation in Saskatchewan. All of his scholarship is informed by his heritage and experience working extensively with elders in his community. As a professor in the Department of Indigenous Studies at First Nations University of Canada, he has worked in the areas of Indigenous thought, health, education, social work, and the humanities. His scholarship aims to promote ethical practices in research and something he terms "ethical space"—a space between different worldviews where the cultures can meet and conduct research. Ermine has presented his work nationally and internationally at academic conferences and knowledge symposiums on Indigenous intellectual traditions.

Ermine's 1995 article, "Aboriginal Epistemology," attempts to provide some crucial context for those unfamiliar with some of the characteristics common to Indigenous worldviews. Though his analysis lacks tribal specificity, and could readily be attacked for essentializing Indigenous cultures, he nevertheless highlights "truths" about Indigenous knowledge that Elders from any number of Indigenous nations reiterate time and time again. Ermine's essay thus focuses on harmony with, rather than control over the environment—something termed holism versus fragmentation. The former examines the self in relation to the environment, while the latter seeks to master the environment by defining it. His characterization contributes to a more comprehensive perspective on Indigenous texts—something Episkenew has also promoted as necessary for providing socially responsible criticism. Ermine, like Episkenew, cautions against the academic tendency to define rather than to accept mystery, or the indefinable.

Ermine, Willie. "Aboriginal Epistemology." *First Nations Education in Canada: The Circle Unfolds.* Ed. Marie Battiste and Jean Barman. Vancouver: U of British Columbia P. 1995. 101–12.

Aboriginal Epistemology

When I heard the learn'd astronomer,
When the proofs, the figures, were ranged in columns
before me,
When I was shown the charts and diagrams, to add,
divide, and measure them,
When I sitting heard the astronomer where he
lectured with much applause in the lecture room,
How soon unaccountable I became tired and sick,
Till rising and gliding out I wander'd off by myself,
In the mystical moist night air, and from time to time,
Look'd up in perfect silence at the stars.

           —Walt Whitman

The year 1492 marked the first meeting of two disparate world-views, each on its own uncharted course of exploration and discovery for purposeful knowledge. The encounter featured two diametric trajectories into the realm of knowledge. One was bound for an uncharted destination in outer space, the physical, and the other was on a delicate path into inner space, the metaphysical.

The Aboriginal world has since felt the repercussions of that encounter of world-views. The relentless subjugation of Aboriginal people and the discounting of their ideas have hurt those aboard the Aboriginal voyage of discovery into the inner space. The tribal crews, along with their knowledge and secrets, came precariously close to aborting their inward missions. Meanwhile, the Western world-view and the concomitant exploration of the outer space continued unabated for the next five centuries. Acquired knowledge and information were disseminated as if Western voyages and discoveries were the only valid sources to knowing. The alternative expeditions and discoveries in subjective inner space by Aboriginal people wait to be told.

This chapter aims, first, to discuss ideology in relation to the Aboriginal world-view. The ideology that directs information- and knowledge-gathering determines the purpose and method of knowing. Second, the chapter examines the premise that Aboriginal people were on a valid search for subjective inner knowledge in order to arrive at insights into existence. What Aboriginals found in the exploration of the self became the basis of continued personal development and of Aboriginal epistemology. This chapter's basic assumption is that individuals and society can be transformed by identifying and reaffirming learning processes based on subjective experiences and introspection. For Aboriginal people, first languages and culture are crucial components in the transformative learning process. The three specific orientations of the transformation are: skills that promote personal and social transformation; a vision of social change that leads to harmony with rather than control over the environment; and the attribution of a spiritual dimension to the environment (Miller, Cassie, and Drake 1990, 4).

Ideology is one determinant of the quality of research on epistemology. Early ideas such as Destutt de Tracy's (1801) definition of ideology as the science of ideas used to distinguish science from the metaphysical suggest the Western world's direction and purpose in seeking the nature and origin of knowledge. Subsequent categorization and selective validation of knowledge by Western science has inevitably influenced Western ideology as the driving force behind knowing. Engels's later definition of ideology as the "attitudes and ideas concealing the real nature of social relations to justify and perpetuate social dominance" (1893) also illustrates the Western world's degenerate outlook on knowledge. For Engels, Western attitudes and ideas were such that knowledge was being used for dominance and in effect produced a state of "false consciousness." The implication of this "false consciousness" is that the Western world is guided by invalid criteria in its synthesis of total human knowledge. In short, the Western world has capitulated to a dogmatic fixation on power and control at the expense of authentic insights into the nature and origin of knowledge as truth.

The greater menace to Aboriginal thinking are the assumptions that drive the search for knowledge in the Western world. One assumption is that the universe can be understood and controlled through atomism. The intellectual tendency in Western science is the acquisition and synthesis of total human knowledge within a world-view that seeks to understand the outer space objectively. In the process, Western science, the flagship of the Western world, sought answers to the greatest questions concerning our existence and our place in the universe by keeping everything separate from ourselves. In viewing the world objectively, Western science has habitually fragmented and measured the external space in an attempt to understand it in all its complexity. Fragmentation of the universe has led to what Bohm (1980) calls a "fragmentary self-world view."

The fragmentation of the constituents of existence has invariably led to a vicious circle of atomistic thinking that restricts the capacity for holism. Western science's division of the universe into neatly packaged concepts has permeated Western understanding of the world. We see the wretchedness and world despair that Western science has produced based on this fragmentary self-world view, in Purpel's words a "moral and spiritual crisis" (1989, 28). Fragmentation has become embedded in the Western world-view and is the cornerstone of Western ideology. Aboriginal people should be wary of Western conventions that deny the practice of inwardness and fortitude to achieve transformative holism.

Those people who seek knowledge on the physical plane objectively find their answers through exploration of the outer space, solely on the corporeal level. Those who seek to understand the reality of existence and harmony with the environment by turning inward have a different, incorporeal knowledge paradigm that might be termed Aboriginal epistemology. Aboriginal people have the responsibility and the birthright to take and develop an epistemology congruent with holism and the beneficial transformation of total human knowledge. The way to this affirmation is through our own Aboriginal sources.

As with many other cultures around the world, the holy people and philosophers among Aboriginal people have explored and analyzed the process of self-actualization. The being in relation to the cosmos possessed intriguing and mysterious qualities that provided insights into existence. In their quest to find meaning in the outer space, Aboriginal people turned to the inner space. This inner space is that universe of being within each person that is synonymous with the soul, the spirit, the self, or the being. The priceless core within each of us and the process of touching that essence is what Kierkegaard called "inwardness" ([1846] f96S, 24). Aboriginal people found a wholeness that permeated inwardness and that also extended into the outer space. Their fundamental insight was that all existence was connected and that the whole enmeshed the being in its inclusiveness. In the Aboriginal mind, therefore, an immanence is present that gives meaning to existence and forms the starting point for Aboriginal epistemology. It is a mysterious force that connects the totality of existence—the forms, energies, or concepts that constitute the outer and inner worlds. Bohm has written that this way of looking at the totality can best be called "undivided wholeness in flowing movement" (1980, 11). Couture has described this immanence as "the pervasive, encompassing reality of the life force, manifest in laws—the laws of nature, the laws of energy, or the laws of light" (1991a, 208). To the Cree people it is *muntou*, the mystery. For our Aboriginal scientists, the potential and implications of such insight were gripping. With this "force," knowing becomes possible. The Old Ones focused on this area for guidance and as the foundation of all Aboriginal epistemology.

The idea of our progenitors was to try to gain understanding of many of the greatest mysteries of the universe. They sought to do this by exploring existence subjectively; that is, by placing themselves in the stream of consciousness: Our Aboriginal languages and culture contain the accumulated knowledge of our ancestors, and it is critical that we examine the inherent concepts in our lexicons to develop understandings of the self in relation to existence. The Cree word *mamatowisowin*, for example, describes the capability of tapping into the "life force" as a means of procreation. This Cree concept describes a capacity to be or do anything, to be creative. Couture (1991a, 208) has said that "elders are familiar with Energy on a vast scale, in multiple modes, e.g., energy as healing, creative, life-giving, sustaining." *Mamatowisowin* is a capacity to tap the creative force of the inner space by the use of all the faculties that constitute our being—it is to exercise inwardness. Bohm (1980) has discussed Aristotle's notion of causality. His life force or "energy on the vast scale" is the "formative cause" that creates *mamatowisowin*. This energy manifests itself in all existence because all of life is connected, and all of life is primarily connected with and accessed through the life force. Huston Smith has said, "there is, first, a reality that is everywhere and always the same; and second, that human beings always and everywhere have access to it" (1953, 276). To Smith, this is the "primordial experience." The Cree concept goes further than Smith, however. For the Cree, the phenomenon of *mamatowan* refers not just to the self but to the being in connection with happenings. It also recognizes that other life forms manifest the creative force in the context of the knower. It is an experience in context, a subjective experience that, for the knower, becomes knowledge in itself. The experience is knowledge.

Indication that Aboriginal people were attaining knowledge of a very different nature and purpose from Western peoples is evident in Aboriginal language and culture. Ancestral explorers of the inner space encoded their findings in community praxis as a way of synthesizing knowledge derived from introspection. The Old Ones had experienced totality, a wholeness, in inwardness, and effectively treated a physical manifestation of the life force by creating community. In doing so, they empowered the people to become the "culture" of accumulated knowledge. The community became paramount by virtue of its role as repository and incubator of total tribal knowledge in the form of custom and culture. Each part of the community became an integral part of the whole flowing movement and was modelled on the inward wholeness and harmony.

The various Aboriginal cultural structures that have survived attest to the conviction of our progenitors and to the depth of their explorations and understanding of the cosmology of the inner world. The deliberate probing of the incorporeal by tribal groups reveals similar experiences and themes in the inner space. Each successive generation of Aboriginal people inherited the fascination with inwardness and has continued the quest for enlightenment in existence. The value of the ancient "cultures" and of the education system through time is borne out by the persistence of the promise of introspection in constructing meaning for contemporary Aboriginals.

Inquisitiveness about mystery and continued exploration of the inner space is a legacy we must promote in our own time. The accumulation and synthesis of insights and tribal understandings acquired through inwardness, and the juxtaposition of knowledge on the physical plane as culture and community, is the task for contemporary Aboriginal education. The necessary capacity and willingness to be creative by developing *mamatowisowin* is achievable through Aboriginal systems of education.

We have within our tribal communities and cultures vestiges of extraordinary journeys into the unknown by our people. For example, we have from the mists of unremembered time a character in our traditional oral narratives who speaks to us about how we may travel the path into knowing the unknown. The trickster-transformer continues to guide our experiences into the deep reaches of the psyche and the unfathomable mystery of being. The Old Ones knew of this character who directs us around the inner space and saw in him the potential for much deeper exploration into and knowledge from the very self. For this reason, our people's education systems esteemed the Old Ones highly. It was the Old Ones, from their position in the community, who guided young people into various realms of knowledge by using the trickster. The Old Ones, above all, knew the character of the trickster and his capacity to assist with self-actualization. The fact that this trickster-transformer continues to intrigue us speaks of our unfinished exploration of the inner space.

The rituals and ceremonial observances still practised by our Old Ones in our tribal communities compel us to make more inward journeys. Tribal rituals are the calculated trajectories to the world within and any such journeys can only be propelled by the collective energy of a people ordained to explore that domain. The tribal ceremonies display with vivid multidimensional clarity the entries and pathways into this inner world of exciting mystery that has been touched by only the few who have become explorers of sacred knowing. Rituals and ceremonies are corporeal sacred acts that give rise to holy manifestations in the metaphysical world. Conversely, it is the metaphysical that constructs meaning in the corporeal. Continuation of rituals and ceremonies will enable the children of those early spiritual explorers to advance the synthesized understanding of inner space.

We have, as well, the physical clues of valuable conceptualizations. The outcrops of stone and rock known as medicine wheels survive from a time when our people were actively exploring the inner space. These wheels convey concepts derived from introspection and illustrate the pathways to self-discovery, the first door to mystery. They speak, in the silence of the unknown, about the progressive growth of self through a cyclical journey of repetition, experience, and construction of meaning. The wheels mirror the cosmology of the inner space. *The Sacred Tree* states the following:

> The medicine wheel can be used as a mirror by any sincere person. The medicine wheel not only shows us who we are now, it can also show what we could be if we developed the gifts the Creator has placed in us... Many of these hidden gifts might never be developed if we do not somehow discover and nurture them. The great spiritual teachers have taught that all the gifts a person has are like the fruits hidden within a tree. (Bopp et al. 1988, 35)

These stone circles and the indestructible fragments constituting the whole wheel infuse us with thoughts of a universe depicting the wholeness found in the inner space. The stones reveal our subjection to the metaphysics of the inner space. They give us insight into our common humanity and our connectedness. The ancient ones recorded their findings in the inner space in simple stone, and it is only by analyzing and synthesizing the truths of inner space that we can fully decipher the messages of the wheels.

There are also the people of the animal and plant world who steward certain doors to knowledge of the inner space. The Old Ones and the keepers of the earth among our people tell of the rich information about the inner space contained in these life forms. When Old Ones speak of the "great Peace, the still, electrifying awareness one experiences in the deep woods," (Colorado 1988) or of the mesmerizing effect of the total interaction in nature, one understands that these are subjective accounts of those who know what it is to tune into the inner world. Deloria has said:

> Here, power and place are dominant concepts—power being the living energy that inhibits and/or composes the universe, and place being the relationship of things to each other...put into a simple equation: power and place produce personality. This equation simply means that the universe is alive, but it also contains within it the very important suggestions that the universe is personal and, therefore, must be approached in a personal manner. The personal nature of the universe demands that each and every entity in it seek and sustain personal relationships. (Deloria 1991, 4)

It is for this reason that the Old Ones, the guides of our communities, have instilled in the young a sense of wonder and have sought to encourage young minds to recognize and affirm mystery aesthetically and spiritually. Thomas similarly stresses the value of searching for knowledge at the conjunction of physical and metaphysical realities:

> Teach on the outset, before any of the fundamentals, the still imponderable puzzles of cosmology. Let it be known, as clearly as possible, by the young minds, that there are some things going on in the universe that lie beyond comprehension, and make it plain how little is known...Teach ecology later on. Let it be understood that the earth's life is a system of interlinking, interdependent creatures, and that we do not understand at all how it works...teach that. (Thomas 1983, 213)

The guides knew what they were doing and what they were talking about. Much like Thomas, the Old Ones talked about the inner cosmology. The plants and animals were a vital nexus in comprehending the sophisticated directional maps into the metaphysical. Only by understanding the physical world can we understand the intricacies of the inner space. Conversely, it is only through journeys into the metaphysical that we can fully understand the natural world. Those Old Ones who made countless journeys into the inner space have embedded these principles in Aboriginal education systems so that future generations can continue the research.

The language of the people provides another valuable indication of an inner space. The word for "mystery" usually refers to a higher power and also connotes our own deeper selves as a humble connection with the higher mystery. In conceptualizing this existence of "ponderable" mysteries, our languages reveal a very high level of rationality that can only come from an earlier insight into power. Our languages suggest inwardness, where real power lies. It is this space within the individual that, for the Aboriginal, has become the last great frontier and the most challenging one of all.

Yet, within the Aboriginal community a paradox seemingly exists. In no other place did the individual have more integrity or receive more honour than in the Aboriginal community. The individual's ability as a unique entity in the group to become what she or he is ultimately meant to be, was explicitly recognized. There was explicit recognition of the individual's right in the collective to experience his or her own life. No one could dictate the path that must be followed. There was the recognition that every individual had the capacity to make headway into knowledge through the inner world. Ultimately, the knowledge that comes from the inner space in the individual gives rise to a subjective world-view out onto the external world.

Aboriginal epistemology is grounded in the self, the spirit, the unknown. Understanding of the universe must be grounded in the spirit. Knowledge must be sought through the stream of the inner space in unison with all instruments of knowing and conditions that make individuals receptive to knowing. Ultimately it was in the self that Aboriginal people discovered great resources for coming to grips with life's mysteries. It was in the self that the richest source of information could be found by delving into the metaphysical and the nature and origin of knowledge. Aboriginal epistemology speaks of pondering great mysteries that lie no further than the self.

The spirit is the haven of dreams, those peculiar images that flash symbolic messages to the knower. Dreams are the link to the spiritual world from whence our spirit comes, and they are linked with "undivided wholeness in flowing movement" (Bohm 1980). Our progenitors knew and believed in the power of dreams; it is only through dreams that sacred undertakings are attempted. Dreams are the guiding principles for constructing the corporeal. Dreams, the voice of the inner space, give rise to the holy and prescribe all ceremonies on the physical level. Conversely, the physical ceremony, as an enactment of the holy, nourishes the spirit and the energy of the "vast scale" (Couture 1991a, 208). The Old Ones, and the culture they developed, understood that dreams were invaluable in understanding self and sought to manipulate the external so that dreams might happen. It is through dreams that the gifted in our Aboriginal communities "create" experience for the benefit of the community through the capacity inherent in *mamatowisowin*. We have the shaking tent rituals and other "channelling" capabilities that are great avenues for out-of-body knowledge. Blessings and other assorted gifts that permeate Aboriginal thought all stem from dreams. The fruit of this cyclical process involving dreams is the invaluable experience that we call knowledge. Experience is knowledge.

Visions also derive from the inner space. Aboriginal people greatly valued the quest for visions as one of the primary sources of knowing. Many tribal cultures insist on having and fulfilling visions as part of their grand design and purpose. According to Johnston:

It is said and believed, "that no man begins to be, until he has seen his vision." Before this event, life is without purpose; life is shallow and empty; actions have no purpose, have no meaning… What makes the search difficult is that the vision is not to be sought outside of oneself: nor is it to be found outside of one's being. Rather it must be sought within one's inner substance and found therein. Since it will be found within a person's inner self, the search must be conducted alone. (Johnston 1976, 114)

The Old Ones promoted the significance of visions and constructed the community to accommodate their fulfillment. In turn, visions received by individuals allowed people to understand and provided the necessary meaning for the continuity of the community. This is reciprocity between the physical and the metaphysical, the wholeness.

Prayer is another significant aspect of the inner space. Colorado states:

Prayer as a Medicine—Gii Laii is the quiet, still place (a round hole in the bed of a stream or lake of water and the quiet, still place of balance within ourselves). Prayer is a medicine where all life begins, exists within, without and between us and our relationships. It is an actual place and state of being that marks the endpoint/beginning of our science. (Colorado 1988, 54)

In Aboriginal epistemology, prayer extracts relevant guidance and knowledge from the inner-space consciousness. It is the optimal metaphysical idiom that is recognized in corporeal form as chants, dances, language, and meditation. The Old Ones know the intricate and tedious task of fusing the energy that emits from the place of prayer within. Prayer becomes power and by its very nature becomes another instrument in Aboriginal ways of knowing.

In summary, Aboriginal people have inherited from earlier ages a mission to explore and seek metaphysical knowledge. We know that this quest for knowledge took place along various avenues. Mythology, ritual, and ceremonies, the medicine wheel, nature, and language all reveal vestiges of grand discoveries and communion with the universe within. However, the greatest legacy of our ancestors is in what they discovered within individuals of tribal communities. *Mamatowisowin* is the capacity to connect to the life force that makes anything and everything possible.

The recording of ancestral pioneering expeditions and associated community structures helped individuals hone their self-development by developing *mamatowisowin* through dreams, visions, and prayer. The culture of the Aboriginal recognized and affirmed the spiritual through practical application of inner-space discoveries.

Aboriginal education has a responsibility to uphold a world-view based on recognizing and affirming wholeness and to disseminate the benefits to all humanity. Our ancestors have done their part in blazing the initial trail into the inner space. Our task is to continue the exploration and ensure that successive generations persist. In *The Sacred Ways of Knowledge, Sources of Life*, Beck and Walters state:

> Native American sacred ways insist on learning, or education, as an essential foundation for personal awareness. A knowledgeable human being was one who was sensitive to his/her surroundings. This sensitivity opened him/her to the Grand mysteries and to the possibility of mystical experiences, which was considered the only way to grasp certain intangible laws of the universe. (Beck and Walters 1977, 164)

The "fragmentary self-world view" that permeates the Western world is detrimental to Aboriginal epistemology. The Western education systems that our children are subjected to promote the dogma of fragmentation and indelibly harm the capacity for holism. The mind-set created by fragmentation impedes the progress towards inwardness that our ancestors undertook. Only through subjectivity may we continue to gain authentic insights into truth. We need to experience the life force from which creativity flows, and our Aboriginal resources such as language and culture are our touchstones for achieving this. It is imperative that our children take up the cause of our languages and cultures because therein lies Aboriginal epistemology, which speaks of holism. With holism, an environmental ethic is possible.

The last word should come from Cecil King (1989), an Aboriginal educator who, after presenting a paper at the 88th Annual Meeting of the American Anthropological Association in 1989, concluded with this story:

> I had a dream that all the people of the world were together in one place. The place was cold. Everyone was shivering. I looked for a fire to warm myself. None was to be found. Then someone said that in the middle of the gathering of Indians, what was left of the fire had been found. It was a very, very small flame. All the Indians were alerted that the slightest rush of air or the smallest movement could put the fire out and the fire would be lost to humankind. All the Indians banded together to protect the flame. They were working to build the fragile feeble flame. They added minuscule shavings from toothpicks to feed it.
>
> Suddenly, throughout the other peoples, the whisper was heard. "The Indians have a fire." There was a crush of bodies stampeding to the place where the

flame was held. I pushed to the edge of the Indian circle to stop those coming to the flame so that it would not be smothered. The other people became hostile saying they were cold too and it was our responsibility to share the flame with them. I replied, "It is our responsibility to preserve the flame for humanity and at the moment it is too weak to be shared but if we all are still and respect the flame it will grow and thrive in the caring hands of those who hold it. In time we can all warm at the fire. But now we have to nurture the flame or we will all lose the gift."

Note

This chapter originated as a graduate paper for a course entitled "First Nations Curriculum: Theory and Practice" at the University of Saskatchewan and received the Alumni Association Award.

References

Beck, Peggy, and Anna Walters. 1977. *The Sacred Ways of Knowledge, Sources of Life.* Arizona: Navajo Community College P.

Bohm, David. 1980. *Wholeness and the Implicate Order.* London: Routledge and Kegan Paul.

Bopp, J. et al. 1988. *The Sacred Tree.* Lethbridge: Four Worlds Development Project.

Colorado, Pam. 1988. "Bridging Native and Western Science." *Convergence* 21 (2/3): 49–68.

Couture, Joseph E. 1991a. "The Role of Native Elders: Emergent Issues." In John W. Friesen, ed., *The Cultural Maze.* Calgary: Detselig Enterprises.

———. 1991b. "Explorations in Native Knowing." In John W. Friesen, ed., *The Cultural Maze.* Calgary: Detselig Enterprises.

Deloria, Vine. 1991. "Power and Place: Equal Personality." In Vine Deloria, ed. *Indian Education in America.* Boulder, CO: American Indian Science and Engineering Society.

Johnston, Basil. 1976. *Ojibway Heritage.* Toronto: McClelland and Stewart.

Kierkegaard, Soren. [1846] 1965. "Truth Is Subjectivity." In H.J. Blackham, ed., *Reality, Man and Existence: Essential Works of Existentialism.* Revised. London, ON: Bantam.

King, Cecil. 1989. "Here Come the Anthros." Paper presented at the 88th Annual Meeting of the American Anthropological Association, Washington, DC.

Miller, John P. 1988. *The Holistic Curriculum.* Toronto: OISE P.

Miller, John P., J.R. Bruce Cassie, and Susan M. Drake. 1990. *Holistic Learning.* Toronto: OISE P.

Purpel, David E. 1989. *The Moral and Spiritual Crisis in Education.* New York: Bergin and Garvey.

"Reading the World and Reading the Word: An Interview with Paulo Freire." 1985. *Language Arts* 62 (1).

Solecki, Sam. 1993. "Ideology." In *Encyclopedia of Contemporary Literary Theory.* Toronto: U of Toronto P.

Smith, Huston. 1953. "Philosophy, Theology, and Primordial Claim." *Crosscurrents* 28(3): 276–88.

Thomas, Lewis. 1983. *Late Night Thoughts on Listening to Mahler's Ninth Symphony.* New York: Viking.

Whitman, Walt. 1948. *The Complete Poetry of Walt Whitman.* Garden City, NY: Garden City Books.

Margery Fee

"Writing Orality: Interpreting Literature in English by Aboriginal Writers in North America, Australia and New Zealand"

Margery Fee is a settler scholar who has worked on Indigenous literatures and the politics of language since the inception of Indigenous literary studies in the academy. A professor in the Department of English at the University of British Columbia, Fee has authored numerous papers on Indigenous literatures, taking on such topics as language, land, literacy, health, identity, and the "anthology," and continues to work on ethical scholarship and on decolonizing the academy. From 2007 to 2015 she was the editor of *Canadian Literature*: *A Quarterly of Criticism and Review*, and is currently associate editor of the *Dictionary of Canadian English on Historical Principles* (2nd online ed.).

Taking a pan-Indigenous approach to English-language texts by Indigenous writers in North America, Australia, and New Zealand, Fee examines the invocation of the oral in the written text, calling it a "living communicative practice." Valuable for its comparative approach and decolonizing focus, Fee's 1997 article uses traditional western critical parameters and linguistic theory in order to demonstrate the immediacy and decolonizing impact of the oral in the written. To support her position, she uses examples from Indigenous authors to show how Indigenous texts destabilize the privileging of the written over the oral. Like most of the critics whose work is reproduced in this anthology, Fee argues for the importance of context in the study of Indigenous literatures.

Fee, Margery. "Writing Orality: Interpreting Literature in English by Aboriginal Writers in North America, Australia and New Zealand." *Journal of Intercultural Studies* 18.1 (1997): 23–39.

Writing Orality: Interpreting Literature in English by Aboriginal Writers in North America, Australia and New Zealand

Thomas King's novel *Green Grass, Running Water* (1993) begins with a disembodied voice telling a story:

> "So.

In the beginning, there was nothing. Just the water." This sounds like a familiar story: Genesis. Then comes the next line: "Coyote was there, but Coyote was asleep. That Coyote was asleep and that Coyote was dreaming" (King, 1993: 1). Now the story doesn't sound so familiar. But another group of readers (figured as implied listeners) will think that this still sounds like a familiar story. Coyote stories are a genre of traditional stories from a wide range of Aboriginal cultures in western North America (see Bright, 1993). King has quickly invoked two cultural traditions, Western and Aboriginal, as well as the storytelling situation itself, in the first four lines of a postmodern novel. This invocation of an oral tradition is commonplace in writing in English by Indigenous peoples in Canada, the United States, Australia and New Zealand/Aotearoa. It plays off and with Western ideologies about orality and writing, as well as Western literacy practices. It asserts that this literature is distinctive and authentic, because it is marked as coming out of a long-standing cultural tradition.

In much the same way, English studies valorizes the whole tradition of English literature by forcing its most highly accredited practitioners, usually doctoral students, to learn to read Old English, particularly *Beowulf*, which derives from an oral epic. This grounding of national literatures in oral forms, particularly myths, epic poetry and folk tales, comes out of Romantic literary theory. Friedrich von Schlegel, for example, states that

> Given a nation unendowed with poetic stores that date from some time prior to the period of regular artistic culture, and it may safely be asserted of the same, that it will never attain to any nationality of character, or vitality of genius. (Bohn, 1859: 159)

British-descended settler critics in outposts of Empire, acutely aware of the thinness of their national literatures, struggled to try to produce the requisite antiquity. J.D. Robins[1] concludes in "The Backgrounds of Future Canadian Poetry" (1915) that myths are "more myths of the soil than of the race" which means that since English-Canadians had taken over Canadian soil, they could also take over the myths of the Aboriginal peoples, who were widely believed at this time to be on the verge of what was always characterized as a regrettable extinction: If this be so, it only serves as an excellent precedent for embodying in this background the weird and fascinating legends of the soil that are to be found in Canada among our Indians, whose spirit breathes so strongly and beautifully through the work of Pauline Johnson [Mohawk]. Of these we are the sole heirs, and the necessity of preserving them is urgent (Robins, 1915: 316).

Thomas King and other contemporary Indigenous writers combat this appropriative move and assert their claims, both to the oral tradition and to the land, by adapting oral stories and the story-telling situation to the written text, a move which marks both content and form.

This move is made more difficult because even those few Aboriginal writers who are fluent in their languages write in English, since the readership in Indigenous languages for literature is close to nil. Eric Hobsbawm has examined how societies constantly invent traditions in order to "inculcate certain values and norms of behaviour by repetition" (Hobsbawm, 1983: 1), often tying these invented traditions to past forms to enforce the sense of longevity. He notes that the invention of tradition occurs more frequently when a rapid transformation of society weakens or destroys the social patterns for which "old" traditions had been designed, producing new ones to which they were not applicable, or when such old traditions and their institutional carriers and promulgators no longer prove sufficiently adaptable and flexible, or are otherwise eliminated (King, 1993: 4–5).

Here then, after the cultural crisis of dispossession and forced linguistic assimilation, textual markers of orality substitute for the near-extinct Aboriginal language and the writer takes on the mantle of the oral story-teller. As David Murray notes in his comment on Leslie Marmon Silko's practice of fusing myth with realism in her novel *Ceremony*, this move is "an attempt to create or assert a continuum in which American Indian literature would run from oral narrative and ceremony straight through to novels written in English" (Murray, 1991: 87). But just because the invention of tradition is an adaptive move shared by many (all?) cultures, the educated critic cannot dismiss the invention of this tradition as simply parallel to the grounding of English literature in *Beowulf*. If one of these moves is fraudulent or inauthentic, the other is equally so. Both moves, admittedly, come out of an assertion of nationalism. But all such traditions are deliberately tied to a particular cultural context and in this case, the Aboriginal context is one that embodies difference from and resistance to many facets of Western culture. Thus, Indigenous literature cannot be understood completely from a Western perspective, even though most Indigenous writers have been educated in an assimilative Western system, in what Ron and Suzanne Scollon call "essayist literacy" and what Greg Sarris's Aunt Mabel calls "school way." Knowing that he is puzzled by a story she has told him, she laughs and says "I know you. You'll... you're school way. You'll think about it and then write something" (Scollon and Scollon, 1984: 48). Sarris, like many other anthropologists and some literary critics, is struggling to revitalize the conventions of oral performance in writing, because these conventions have implications for intercultural social relations, pedagogy, and, not least, the survival of Indigenous culture as a set of living communicative practices, rather than as a set of "dead" texts and artifacts.

Many of these texts destabilize the convention[al] Western distinction between oral and written. In Ruby Slipperjack's *Honour the Sun*, Owl, the narrator, tells us that every night her mother reads to her children:

> There's a thick, red Cree Bible which no one understands but it's read anyway. The other is a thin, black prayer book in Ojibway that she's reading now. Then, there's the thin, black one that holds the hymns which Mom sings, more often than we kids care to listen to.... [then] The jokes and stories start. Sometimes we tell old Indian legends with some hilarious mistakes. When we know them well enough, Mom tells us another and we keep repeating it again till we can tell it correctly. (Slipperjack, 1987: 15)

This brief account begins the story of a young girl growing up in a small village on the rail line in Northern Ontario, simultaneously being instructed in the discourses of her Native culture and, through school, those of standard English and Western culture. The discourses of her traditional "oral" culture,[2] of a nineteenth-century Christian culture supported by minimal literacy, and of a twentieth-century modern literacy all intersect in this novel, which is itself presented as an artifact of literacy: selections from the Owl's diary. Further, the diary is presented as a translation into English from Ojibway, a language frequently seen as belonging to an "oral" or pre-literate culture. The situation clearly cannot be explained by classifying the young narrator as either illiterate or literate, her culture as oral or not, the author's language as "simply" English. When dealing with writing that is produced in direct resistance to their settler cultures, non-Indigenous critics must realize that they are no longer post-colonials "writing back" to Empire: they are now the target of a colonized people's resistance. In this situation, critics must use all the knowledge they have gained from their own experiences as colonized to consider their role as colonizers, to interrogate their own political and psychological investments in reading Indigenous literature in ways that produce themselves as Subject, the Indigene as Other, themselves as ordinary citizens of a self-evident nation, the Indigene as deviant or rebel.

They must remember, as Julia Emberley puts it, how "in the hegemonic practices of postcolonial knowledge, representations, images and stereotypes of the Native become the abstract figures of a late-capitalist currency" (Emberley, 1990–1991: 50). Any reading of indigenous literature must be problematized by the understanding that critics and authors, whether Indigenous or not, are affected by ideologies concerning the processes of reading, writing and speaking, ideologies that are spread by the formal education that is the usual contemporary transmitter of literacy. As D.F. McKenzie writes of the Treaty of Waitangi, "signed" in 1840 by forty-six Maori chiefs, interpretation of such intercultural documents requires that the Pakeha, the non-Maori, recognize "their own myth of literacy" (McKenzie, 1985: 46).

This myth is particularly suspect in that it invariably privileges literate culture over oral, the phonetic alphabet over the pictorial,[3] and those who speak and write a distinctive language over those who speak and write in English, whether standard or not. These valorizations permeate the discourses in which literary works by Indigenous writers are written and received. Most Indigenous cultures used oral forms to convey their cultural knowledge, and many still do; if they developed writing, it was pictographic or was taken to be so (see Coe, 1992). The use of Indigenous languages in North American, Australia and New Zealand has been severely reduced in the last two generations by a system of enforced formal education that frequently removed children from their parents and home culture and punished them for communicating in their native languages, and even further by the pressures of a dominant English-language culture on all minority languages. Thus Indigenous writers face the uphill battle of having to identify, as usual, with the stigmatized half of the opposition; not only are their cultures Other, but so are those means of cultural production most closely allied with these cultures in both popular and scholarly thought. Finally, they are required to disseminate their words in print, rather than speech, and in English, rather than in a native language. This would not be a hardship if the social valorizations were different. As it is, however, they often face accusations of inauthenticity, such as Simon During's comment on Mudrooroo Narogin's proposal for *Aboriginality in Writing from the Fringe: A Study of Modern Aboriginal Literature*: "Any primordial Aboriginality would itself be hybridized, textualized as soon as it is expressed in writing" (During quoted in Hodge and Mishra, 1991: 113). Somehow, the literate Indigene cannot be Indigenous.[4] Jacques Derrida's analysis of Claude Lévi-Strauss makes it clear, however, that one can just as easily argue that the Indigene was never illiterate. In Lévi-Strauss's idealizing account of the Nambikwara as innocent and non-violent, the "ethnocentrism which, inspired by the model of phonetic writing, separates speech from writing with an ax, is thus handled and thought of as anti-ethnocentrism," but, as Derrida notes:

> the difference between peoples with and peoples without writing is accepted, but writing as the criterion of historicity or cultural value is not taken into

account; ethnocentrism will apparently be avoided at the very moment when it will have already profoundly operated, silently imposing its standard concepts of speech and writing. (Derrida, 1974: 121)

Derrida dissolves the ideological distinction between the oral and the written: speech is no closer to presence, no more authentic, however much Western culture may nostalgically idealize a certain kind of "authentic" speech. However, Western culture also valorizes writing of a certain kind, and imposes idealizations derived from this standardized writing back *onto* speech. Roy Harris explains that although Western education is filled with this "scriptist bias," nonetheless "writing and speech in Western civilization have for centuries been locked in a relationship which is essentially symbiotic" (Harris, 1986: 46). Thus speech is preferred over writing in some arguments and writing over speech in others:

> At first sight the insistence that writing is only a representation of speech may appear to run quite counter to the prevailing scriptism of European culture. But that appearance is deceptive. The doctrine that writing represents speech becomes a cornerstone of scriptism once the written representation is held to be not a slavish or imperfect copy but, on the contrary, an idealization which captures those essential features often blurred or distorted in the rough and tumble of everyday utterance. Thus it is possible for the written representation to be held up as a model of what the spoken reality ought to be. (Harris, 1986: 46)

Significantly, the study of writing systems has historically been allied with the ideological project of establishing alphabetic script as the most developed in an evolutionary scheme of writing systems (what Harris calls "the evolutionary fallacy") and with the project of using the absence or presence of writing systems and the kinds of systems used as means to determine which cultures can be represented as more civilized than others. This study had predictable results, with those engaged in the study finding their own culture to be the most civilized. A long list of the best-known writers on the issue, such as Walter Ong, Jack Goody, Marshall McLuhan, and Eric Havelock, "claim, roughly, that writing is necessary for the forms of consciousness found in modern western thought" (Feldman, 1991: 47). At this point, allied with a rise in a linguistics focused on speech, "interest in writing systems declined abruptly" (Basso, 1989: 425). After all, if the Western system is the most developed, all other systems become of merely antiquarian interest.

In brief, the distinction between oral and written is profoundly ideological, deployed to favour particular classes, cultures and interests. In fact, as Joel Scherzer and Anthony C. Woodbury, editors of *Native American Discourse*, point out "there is no simple dichotomy between oral and written discourse, between literate and nonliterate societies" (Scherzer and Anthony, 1989: 10). Indeed, as many studies have argued, we need to talk about oralities and literacies (see, for example, Gee, 1990, Whiteman, 1981).

M.A.K. Halliday makes it clear that although there are differences between speech and writing, these are not necessarily the differences that have been constructed. For example, he demonstrates that contrary to the commonplace belief that language is more fragmented than writing, "spoken language tends to be grammatically intricate, but lexically sparse" (Halliday, 1987: 66). Despite such findings based on empirical research, the construct of "oral vs. written" rolls on in both Western and non-Western theoretical and fictional writing. The tendency for literary critics to avoid using linguistic and sociolinguistic studies to aid their readings is itself based on the Western academy's distinction between the written and the spoken, as well as on the distinction between the literary and the non-literary that grounds the disciplinary boundary between literary and linguistic studies. This disciplinary boundary is, of course, a construct, one that in the nineteenth century assimilated literature to nationalism in the service of empire and philology to the related task of standardizing the national language through dialectology, lexicography and grammar.

In Western culture, the oral provides the epic roots of the literary tradition, but the roots, however sacred, ultimately are seen as necessarily flowering into the highly complex literate culture supposedly required for modern technological development. That even we are, for much of our social lives, oral creatures, is usually forgotten, perhaps because Western élite culture is transmitted mainly through written texts and formal instruction in standard "essayist" literacy. In fact, the oral-written distinction makes less sense than distinctions based on cultural situation, some of which call for informal, fragmented speech, others for highly ritualized and planned speech, still others for various kinds of writing, from the informal letter to the legislative document (Gee, 1990: 56). Further, all of these situations are embedded in discourses, whole sets of cultural practices that bear the belief systems of particular cultural groups.

To resurrect or construct the spoken dialect into something resembling a national language with its canon of written literature has been a goal of liberation movements since the rise of European nationalism in the eighteenth century. Many postcolonial critics have supported this move as vital to the liberation of any colonized group (see, for example, Brathwaite, 1984, Mazrui, 1975, Ngugi, 1986). Often, however, the move is accompanied by a repetition of an act of symbolic territorial conquest and an ascription of a natural link between language and place that, whatever its temporary strategic value, can lead to all kinds of political exclusions. This move thus has its dangers, as do most such simple reversals, which explains W.D. Ashcroft's comment: "I must reject the notion that language is itself the peculiar embodiment of culture" (Ashcroft, 1987: 116). For Indigenous writers in Canada, the United States, Australia and New Zealand/Aotearoa, this point is particularly important, because many Indigenous languages are near extinction. Unlike many African writers, for example, such Indigenous writers do not normally come from a large community of Indigenous language speakers who are either literate or potentially literate in that language. Further, schooling in their own languages is still rare, with a few exceptions at the early primary and the post-secondary level. Thus one finds Native critic Lee Maracle writing that "Language is one means of expression of culture, but it is not the main expression.... Black North Americans, Mexican North Americans, Native North Americans, Asian North Americans and White North Americans speak English—many as their *only* language. We are not the same culturally" (Maracle, 1990: 169). In other words, the unavailability of a language or language variant suitable for construction into a distinctive national language may complicate the struggle for Indigenous liberation, but it certainly does not stop it. As Beth Cuthand remarks, "Maybe one of the most valuable gifts the colonizers gave us was the English language, so that we could communicate with each other" (Cuthand, 1985: 53). It is high time to reexamine the idea that true language difference rests only in highly distinctive standardized national languages and that peoples without such languages can have neither a legitimate claim to self-government, nor anything but a defective culture. In Europe, these languages have been standardized over centuries; it is highly ironic that former colonies, whose struggles for decades to liberate themselves from English culture in English, are now turning these arguments on their own internal colonies, arguing that what they themselves have accomplished (national independence) is impossible without a distinctive national language.

Nonetheless, as Ashcroft comments, "the inscription of language variants in the text is one of the most exciting tools available to the cross-cultural writer" (Ashcroft, 1989: 116) and Indigenous people, embedded in a dominant European settler culture, are almost of necessity cross-cultural. Whether a language variety is the bearer of a culture or not, the inscription of language variants can serve to metonymically signal cultural difference. Certainly many Indigenous writers have used the representation of their local variant of English and actual words and phrases from Indigenous languages in their work. Others echo syntax. Still others engage in self-translation, like Ngugi (for an excellent account of these practices in West African writing, see Zabus, 1991). Some incorporate traditional tales or allusions to them in their writings, while others imitate these tales. (Compare the modern Coyote stories of Beth Brant and Thomas King, in Moses and Goldie [1992] with the more traditional ones of Harry Robinson [1989], for example). However, it is impossible to generalize about this practice as a whole if Ashcroft's caveat is taken seriously, as I believe it should be. There is no necessary virtue in incorporating representations of the oral in written texts, *pace* Bakhtin (1981). Michel Pêcheux has stated that "words, expressions, propositions, etc., change their meanings according to the positions held by those who use them" (Pêcheux, 1982: 111), and any examination of how literature represents the oral must take into account not only the context of this use within the work, but the literary, linguistic, material and socio-political contexts of the work itself—that is, the discursive context. However, this is not to say that in studying language use it is enough to focus on the purely local. Rather than simply applying the meta-frameworks of the discipline of English to the local artifact, Western literary theory to Indigenous fiction, as many relevant cultural and institutional discourses as possible must be articulated, so as to avoid as many category traps as possible. Many Indigenous writers, not surprisingly, have incorporated theoretical discussions of these problems into their own writing. For example, Rose, a character in a story by Patricia Grace, "A Way of Talking," makes the same point as Pêcheux: "It's not so much what is said, but when and where and in whose presence" (Grace, 1975: 5).

An examination of the metaphors used of language in particular discourses makes clear some of the differences in language attitudes. Rose's position differs from the commonplace Western view that language is like a commodity or perhaps a commodified body (one that can, for example, be contaminated and degraded by mingling with impure dialects, even sicken and die, just like such a body). This view, in which a word carries its meaning along with it from situation to situation, is constructed by the artifacts required by a standard language: written texts, language conventions consolidated by grammars, dictionaries and usage guides (on the standard language, see Crowley [1989], Joseph [1987]). In this view, a word, like a suitcase, carries its meaning inside it. But language also works like a tool or a weapon, building up or breaking down social barriers. Halliday calls it a "social semiotic": in his terms, "language actively symbolizes the social system" (Halliday, 1987: 3). Pierre Bourdieu (1991) describes it as a medium of exchange, like money; some inherit it, some acquire it and proceed to accumulate it, while others remain impoverished. As with fashion, it marks distinction, including power and cultural differences, and aspects of it, the lexicon, idiom, and speech style in particular, vary like fashion to keep mimicry at bay and social distinctions obvious.

Lennard Davis, in *Resisting Novels: Ideology and Fiction* (1987), shows how novelistic conventions of dialogue, along with standard orthography, create the myth that there is a grammatical, accent-free speech. This myth is easily undermined by listening to a tape of a conversation among members of the elite while following along with a transcription. The ideological effect of this convention of novelistic dialogue, however, makes it nearly impossible to represent distinctive spoken dialects in a way that does not make its speakers look ill-educated and inferior.[5] The representation of dialect in literature is not intended to be accurate, anyway, but rather to mark a particular group of speakers as outside the norm implied in the narrative for both author and audience. Thus, the traditional function of dialect representation in literature has been to mark the lines of social difference. And yet the myth that all members of the elite speak the "same" dialect survives, buttressed not only by popular beliefs, but also by academic practice, ranging from composition class (where "rules" are often imposed that have little to do with the actual practice of professional writers) to the valorization of theory as embodied in recognizably theoretical discourse over theory embodied in other text-types, such as poetry or fiction. In North American linguistics, Noam Chomsky's ideal speaker-hearer belongs to a non-existent homogeneous speech community; however useful a fiction this may be for linguistics it supports the ideology that universalizes Western conventions about language. Bourdieu, however, has shown how this act of universalization of Western conventions of literacy through formal education serves to privilege those whose parents' speech and attitudes have already prepared them to produce the standard norm while "those least able to accept and adopt the language of the school are also those exposed for the shortest time to this language and to educational monitoring, correction and sanction" (Bourdieu, 1991: 62; see also Gee [1990]). This point only begins to explain why Indigenous peoples, not to mention members of other minorities, often do poorly at school and in any other part of the public sphere ruled by standard language conventions, such as courts of law and political arenas. (The Owl, for example, has been trained at home in a system that deprecates "showing off" and designates children as observers, adults as actors. As a result, her chances of becoming fluent in English through schooling are slim: "I wouldn't dare talk English in school. I'd be embarrassed and teased to death if I dared ever to talk English in front of the whole classroom" [Slipperjack, 1987: 77].)

The cultural capital of academics—what we've accumulated—is in decontextual-ized forms of knowledge and distanced representation. Arguably, the more abstracted our knowledge from society, the purer, and therefore more intellectually valuable it becomes, at least in the eyes of the university. When Saussure divided language into *langue* (the idealized "grammatical" form) and *parole* (what goes on in real language encounters) he made it possible for linguistics to aspire to the status of a science by marginalizing the social, and more importantly, the political. Ashcroft argues then, that a postcolonial linguistics must focus "on the message, reinstating the parole as the realisation of the code in social life..." Such a focus, he continues, would be "instrumental in conceiving the discourse of the post-colonial as rooted in conflict and struggle, as 'counter-discourse,' since the perpetual confrontation with a 'standard code' is that which constructs the language" (Ashcroft, 1989: 62).

The tendency in looking at the incorporation of dialect or language variation into English texts is to focus on words and sentences, just as Chomskyan linguistics does, as if a word by word, sentence by sentence translation could do the whole job. This method is a reflection of majority language practices, which reflect the modern Western tendency to isolate and bracket components of a problem for analysis and then to fail to return the components to their holistic context for re-evaluation. This tendency leads to various disasters, ranging from the wholesale misinterpretation of cultures to the destruction of the ecosphere. Nature certainly can be studied bit by bit, and indeed must be, but nature (and language is, at least in part, a natural evolutionary phenomenon) *works* as a whole. In other words, it is high time to reexamine the idea that true language difference rests in highly distinctive standardized national languages and that, therefore peoples without such languages can have neither a legitimate claim to self-government nor anything but a defective culture. Each cultural group acquires its variant of English through widely differing processes and assimilates it to widely differing cultural discourses.

Although I agree that a postcolonial linguistics requires a move back to *parole* and that the struggle with the standard language is an essential feature of contemporary Fourth World discourse, Ashcroft has made too much of this "perpetual confrontation." Indigenous English derives its nature also from the discourse conventions of the Indigenous language, lost or not. John J. Gumperz and J. Cook-Gumperz point out that "even where the original native language is lost the old discourse conventions tend to persist and to be taken over into the group's use of the majority language. In fact these conventions come to reflect the identity of the group itself..." (Gumperz and Cook-Gumperz, 1982: 6). In their study of Athabaskan narrative traditions, Ron and Suzanne Scollon go even further, noting that although two Athabaskan languages, Koyukon and Dogrib, are "morpheme by morpheme and word by word" mutually unintelligible, "a Koyukon woman hearing a tape of a Dogrib storytelling says that she can almost understand everything being said" (Scollon and Scollon, 1984: 173). Thus, they continue, "we have been concerned to understand how a tradition of communication can remain intact despite changes in virtually all the obvious contents" (Scollon and Scollon, 1984: 174). Thus the influence of standard English on Indigenous writers may be far from central and we, as literary critics, cannot rely on our knowledge of our own discourse conventions to see us through an interpretation of their work.

Further influences on Indigenous Englishes are the generally non-standard dialects of English spoken by those from whom the group learned English and contact with pidgins and creoles (see Dillard [1975], Todd [1990]). A corrective view of Ashcroft comes from *Mudrooroo's Master of the Ghost Dreaming*, which focuses on the struggle for leadership between Fada, the Superintendent of the Government Mission for Aborigines and aspiring member of the Royal Anthropological Society and Jangamuttuk, a *maban* and elder. Fada, described by his wife as "all...words" (Mudrooroo, 1991: 9) is "writing the definitive text" (Mudrooroo, 1991: 10) about his charges. He has learned how to derive symbolic power from the employment of the standard language. But what is most significant about Fada is that he has dragged himself out of London's slums by selling his body to a gentleman and his soul to the Church in return for the cultural capital of an apprenticeship in upper class discourse conventions and a formal education. His wife, who has herself risen far above her birth class, thinks contemptuously "Him and his practicing hour after hour to find and keep his aitches" (Mudrooroo, 1991: 8). In other words, both Fada and his wife leave in their wake a lot of Cockney-accented Aboriginal English. And

Jangamuttuk has also learned a "way of talkin'" from Wadawaka, an escaped slave who reached London only to be sent as a convict to Australia, where he teaches West African proverbs and pidgin to Jangamuttuk. The point is that standard English plays a minor role in the formation of Jangamuttuk's English, as it does in the formation of many Indigenous Englishes.

Discourse conventions, as Gumperz (1982) notes, can distinguish different groups who speak the same language, for example those who speak the local standard or prestige dialect from those who speak varieties of Indigenous English. Not only a variant phonology, but also such things as conversational turn-taking, code-switching, amount of talk, verbal deference, directness of questions or answers, control of topic, self-presentation, and attitudes to other language varieties are all governed by such conventions, which are also reflected in methods of socializing and educating children, and, more importantly for this paper, in narrative style and structure.

In ignorance of such conventions, literary texts may be imperialistic by assimilating them to majority conventions of literary discourse. In all innocence, that is to say ignorance, critics may intend to praise literary texts by showing how they fit the most cherished and admired fictional and theoretical conventions of the current discipline; in doing so, however, these texts may well be assimilated to a convention against which they are fighting. Christopher Miller points out that although deconstruction has valorized difference, it has done so in such a way that such difference can be totalized. He counters:

> But suppose we had to care what the difference is, even faced with all the "vertiginous possibilities of referential aberration" associated with literature? Suppose that we could no longer afford the mandarin detachment from messy differences in the plural; that the matter of difference were simply too urgent to be glorified and homogenized as differance-with-an-A.... The challenge now is to practice a kind of knowledge that, while remaining conscious of the lessons of rhetorical theory, recognizes European theory as a *local phenomenon* and attempts dialogue with other localized systems of discourse. (Miller, 1990: 8)

In two books, *Linguistic Convergence: An Ethnography of Speaking at Fort Chipewyan, Alberta* (1979) and *Narrative, Literacy and Face in Interethnic Communication* (1981), Ron Scollon and Suzanne Scollon examine the discourse conventions of Athabaskan speakers as opposed to those characteristic of Westernized speakers. They term the former "bush consciousness" the latter "modernist consciousness." (I find these terms unfortunate, both because of the connotations of "bush" and "modernist," and because "consciousness" seems too all-encompassing a term for what is a set of learned conventions.) Many of the Athabaskan speakers they studied were literate and spoke at least two of English, Cree and Chipewyan. Most spent at least some of their time engaged in subsistence hunting and gathering. Those possessed of "bush consciousness" defer to elders and strangers, speak little and slowly, and allow for longer pauses before taking their conversational turn, all of which means that a "modernist consciousness" interlocutor is likely to assume they are hostile, shy, or stupid. Further, the Scollons explain:

> To the individualistic and integrative bush consciousness, language is also highly integrated to the personal experience of the speaker. There are no normative standards or higher values placed on the speech of others [except, I would add, that of elders]. Thus language is seen as highly individualized and variable. This contrasts, of course, with the normative standards of the modern consciousness. We have our dictionaries, grammars, and good speakers... (Scollon and Scollon, 1981: 206–07)

Not to mention the literary canon. As a result of their discourse conventions, Athabaskan storytellers tend to tell stories characterized by what the Scollons call thematic abstraction. This abstraction serves the major goal of storytelling in Athabaskan culture: "to get the listener to provide and remember the abstract in his or her own words" (Scollon and Scollon, 1984: 178). The result is a minimalist style that does no more than suggest themes, except in cases where the audience does not appear to follow. To explain every detail is to impose on the individual listener, who is supposed to be able to figure out the story for herself. Members of the local audience have generally been instructed from childhood with such stories and by example, rather than by direct explanation and instruction (see also Scollon and Scollon, 1984: 176 on "the importance of the riddle as training for the 'high language'"). This paradigm fits what Lee Maracle writes in *Sojourner's Truth and Other Stories*: "We firmly believe as eight-year-olds that school is stupid, repetitive, and lacking in dignity.... Not much is left to the imagination in European stories either. The answer to the question posed lies within the lines of the story.... *Our* stories mainly pose the dilemma..." (author's emphasis, Maracle, 1990: Preface 12).

Because much of the work an English student is likely to be familiar with on the nature of oral cultures is derived from the study of Classical literatures and Old English, our tendency may be to assume that all oral cultures are what Scollon and Scollon call the "bard-and-formula oral tradition" (Scollon and Scollon, 1984: 179). Unlike a typical performance in this tradition, however, the Athabaskan performing a story "shows no interest in embellishment, no unilateral attempt to control the flow, little use of time-honored formulas or epithets" (Scollon and Scollon, 1984: 178). Audience interaction is crucial. Further, this is a culture where there is no specialization in the bardic role: everyone is trained to tell stories, as in Slipperjack. Different cultures have different oral conventions as well as different written ones.

Culturally distinct learning strategies also affect the ways stories are told. Verbal explanation is not a feature of traditional Native learning where the learner observes, often for a long time in silence and then attempts the task without help. Majority culture teachers constantly intervene and explain; obviously this intervention would reduce the independence needed by future hunters who will repeatedly find themselves thrown back on their own intellectual, emotional, and physical resources for survival.

Slipperjack's *Honour the Sun* (1987) is often illuminated by the Scollons' analyses. Explanation and interpretation is not a feature of this novel: among the few instructions the young narrator receives are "listen to the silence" (Scollon and Scollon, 1984: 184) and "honour the sun." Events are described and left unglossed. In Indigenous writing, what look like failures or gaps to a Western reader may simply mark a reluctance to impose interpretation. Or there may be other cultural reasons for the refusal of the omniscient prying into every detail (and not just of sex) that characterizes much of the most popular Western realist writing. Studies of courtroom miscommunication between white Australian Court personnel and Aboriginal witnesses have revealed many such reluctances: "There are examples of witnesses exhibiting reluctance about giving information about secret sites or dangerous practices, uttering the name of a recently deceased person...answering for another person, or providing information that only senior people have a right to talk about" (Koch, 1991: 102). Speakers of Aboriginal English grant privacy in a very kin-oriented and public life by an "indirect style of verbal interaction" (Eades, 1991: 86). A Westernized reader may be unable to understand or appreciate cultural accounts that represent these conventions.

The more obvious or self-conscious any integration of the spoken into the written becomes in a fiction, the more likely is the cry "postmodern," but the particulars of the text may reveal a political stance that has nothing to do with the valorization of the contemporary postmodern. In Grace's story, for example, Rose, who has rebuked Jane, a Pakeha woman, for failing to distinguish Maoris as individuals, has to face her angry and embarrassed sister, who has just introduced Rose to Jane: "At last I said, 'Rose, you're a stink thing...Gee Rohe, you made me embarrassed.'" Rose's response is "Don't worry Honey she's got a thick hide." The narrator says Rose's words startled her "because it's not our way of talking to each other": "Usually we'd say, 'Never mind Sis,' if we'd wanted something to be forgotten" (Grace, 1975: 4). The narrator, the embarrassed sister, although she comments on how unlike this response is to the local norm, does not remark on its roots in Rose's university experience, where Rose has clearly been reading African American writers. What the sister does realize is that she has consistently let Rose speak for her in similar circumstances, and that it is time for her to speak for herself. The story speaks to two audiences. One, like the sister, has never been to university, but will, like her, receive the political message of the story from Rose. The other audience will appreciate the self-conscious theorizing and the play with language varieties. Indigenous writers' struggle to bridge the wide gap between the older generation (Rose's sister) and their own and the one following them, represent the spoken for many purposes other than those promoted either by nationalism or by postmodernism. In representing speech they are breaking with the standard language promoted by the educational apparatus that denied many of their people functional literacy. To represent the colloquial talk of the ordinary people, to incorporate tales, gossip, jokes, stories, is to demonstrate solidarity with an audience that rarely reads, and perhaps may even attract this audience as readers. A way of talking is not simply a deviation from the standard norm, but represents a whole system of solidarities and identifications.

Another commonplace move made in the consideration of writing from cultures regarded as primarily oral is to equate the oral with an illiterate urban culture, i.e., to the culture of the so-called *lumpenproletariat*, an equation that does violence to both sides. This move obscures the significance of the oral in those cultures where public speaking is as formal and as institutionally regulated as in our own—perhaps more so. Witi Ihimaera's *The Matriarch* (1986) centres on a scene where a woman violates the conventions of the ceremonial debate which is part of the gatherings called *hui* in Maori culture: "In any *hui*, a ritual response must be matched to the relative prestige and social distance of the other group: to score points over the other side by producing a particularly elaborate or appropriate response.... The audience takes careful note of each victory or loss of face" (Edwards, 1990: 95–96). Victory in such encounters depends on years of apprenticeship in the traditions of a culture, and a great deal of *The Matriarch* is devoted to an account of such an apprenticeship. Ihimaera's account dramatizes the issue of the right to speak of members of Maori society not traditionally permitted to do so, for example, women: "The matriarch, a woman and therefore not tapu, was standing where men only stood. Yes, she was high-born, and she had spoken on marae in her own lands, but this marae was outside her tribal boundaries and therefore could give her no genealogical and spiritual protection. In the old days, standing like this, she would have been killed" (Ihimaera, 1986: 111). The non-Maori critic is likely to assume that Ihimaera has been influenced by contemporary feminism in the production of this scene (as I confess I did at first). However, he has in fact based this scene, bowdlerizing it somewhat in the process, on an event that happened around fifty years ago, when a high-born East Coast chieftainess was attending a funeral in a part of the country where women ranked lower than men. She dared to speak before the men in her party, as was the custom on the East Coast; her chant was interrupted by the hosts. Anne Salmond describes the rest:

> The old chieftainess serenely ignored them and continued her speech to the end; then she looked over to the local elders and addressed them with all the pride of her descent: "You Arawa men! You tell me to sit down because I am a woman, yet none of you would be in this world if it wasn't for your mothers. This is where your learning and your grey hairs come from!" And turning her

back on them, she bent over and flipped up her skirts in the supreme gesture of contempt. The Arawa men sat speechless, dumbfounded by the grandeur of the insult, and in that silence, the old woman became a legendary figure. She left the marae unrebuked, and East Coast people have been telling the story ever since. (Salmond, 1989: 212)

Here, the cure for misinterpretation is more local knowledge. Ihimaera also focuses on the use of traditional debating skills as part of the struggle for land rights by dramatizing the Matriarch's attempt to change tradition and by incorporating transcripts of the speeches of Maori parliamentarian, Wi Pere. Here the similarity of a powerful way of speaking in Maori society to English parliamentary debate means that a Maori skill can be transferred to a new forum where it can support the political goals of its adherents, even though these goals are completely opposed to those of the English settler government. The novel focuses on the fight to adapt traditional conventions of discourse to the needs of the Maori in the modern world (Simms, 1991: 46), and this is indeed what much of this invention of a tradition is about.

Leslie Marmon Silko's *Storyteller* (1981) is explicitly aimed at valorizing orality as a characteristic of traditional Laguna culture to permit the struggle for Native survival:

> *The storyteller keeps the stories*
> *all the escape stories*
> *she says "With these stories of ours*
> *we can escape almost anything*
> *with these stories we will survive."* (Silko, 1981: 247)

These writers are constructing their cultures now, in the present, in the same ways in which majority cultures have always constructed themselves through discourse, in order to survive. What unites Indigenous writers across cultures is a common desire to preserve Indigenous cultures against the totalizing monoculture of capitalist development, to valorize their cultures and to thus promote the struggle for Indigenous political control of their institutions, traditional territories and social practices. And this valorization may become at least as empowering as, say, the Euro-American valorization of phonetic script. And it has different implications. To make the struggle between them more equal works to integrate what has been "separated...with an ax."

Notes

1 Robins became Head of English at Victoria College, University of Toronto (one of the largest English departments in Canada) in 1938.

2 In fact, Cree and Oji-Cree speakers in this area have been literate for 150 years in a syllabic script that, although invented by a Christian missionary, James Evans,

around 1840, spread in advance of the missionaries throughout the region. See Bennett and Berry (1989).

3 For example, Robert K. Logan's *The Alphabet Effect: The Impact of the Phonetic Alphabet on the Development of Western Civilization* (1986), synthesizes a wide range of scholarship for a popular audience to convey the thesis that the phonetic alphabet puts Western culture at the pinnacle of an intellectual hierarchy: "Phonetic writing was essential to the intellectual development in the West. No such development occurred in the East" (p. 24). Not only is intellectual development affected, implies Logan, but also cognitive development and even the nature of the brain itself: "Eastern and Western thought patterns are as polarized as their respective writing systems" (p. 47).

4 This is not the place to go into the recent controversy about Mudrooroo's ancestry being Black American rather than Aboriginal, except to quote Cassandra Phybus's comment in a guest editorial for the *Australian Book Review* (1996), where she remarks that his blackness has been "erase[d] ... by the mass media because it is not proper blackness, that is not Aboriginal," while the family members who have talked about his ancestry "are constructed, in this telling, as the authentic ones, truthful because they are white; not you will notice, Afro-American." I thank Sneja Gunew for bringing this piece to my attention.

5 Zora Neale Hurston manages to get around this difficulty in *Their Eyes Were Watching God* (1937) by coupling the faithful representation of Black dialect with a high poetic style that allows her to counter the conventional representation of the speakers of such dialects in mainstream fiction as comic and stupid; see, for example, her last few pages.

References

Ashcroft, W.D. (1989) Constitutive Graphonomy: Post-Colonial Theory of Literary Writing, in: S. Slemon and H. Tiffin (Ed.) *After Europe: Critical Theory and Post-Colonial Writing* (Sydney, Dangeroo), pp. 58–73.

Ashcroft, W.D. (1987) Language Issues Facing Commonwealth Writers, *Journal of Commonwealth Literature*, 22.1 pp. 99–118.

Bakhtin, M. (1981) *The Dialogic Imagination* (Ed.) M. Holquist. Trans. Caryl Emerson and Michael Holquist (Austin, U of Texas P).

Basso, K.H. (1989) The Ethnography of Writing, *Explorations in the Ethnography of Speaking*. 2nd ed. R. Bauman & J. Scherzer (Ed.) (Cambridge, Cambridge UP) pp. 425–32.

Bennett, J. and Berry, J.W. (1991) *Cree Literacy in the Syllabic Script* in Olson and Torrance, pp. 90–104.

Bourdieu, P. (1991) *Language and Symbolic Power.* Ed. and Intro. J.B. Thompson. Trans. G. Raymond & M. Adamson (Cambridge, Polity P and Basil Blackwell).

Brathwaite, E. (1984) *History of the Voice: The Development of Nation Language in Anglophone Caribbean Poetry* (London, New Beacon).

Bright, W. (1993) *A Coyote Reader* (Berkeley, U of California P).

Brotherston, G. (1992) *Book of the Fourth World: Reading the Native Americas through Their Literature* (Cambridge, Cambridge UP).

Coe, M.D. (1992) *Breaking the Maya Code* (London, Thames and Hudson).

Crowley, T. (1989) *Standard English and the Politics of Language* (Urbana, U of Illinois P).

Cuthand, B. (1985) Transmitting Our Identity as Indian Writers, in: A. Dybikowski and Others (Ed.) *In the Feminine: Women and Words/Les femmes et les mots* (Edmonton, Longspoon), pp. 53–54.

Davis, L.J. (1987) *Resisting Novels: Ideology and Fiction* (New York, Methuen).

Denny, J.P. (1991) Rational Thought in Oral Culture and Literate Decontextualization. In Olson and Torrance, pp. 66–89.

Derrida, J. (1974) *Of Grammatology*. Trans. G. Spivak. (Baltimore, MD, Johns Hopkins UP).

Dillard, J.L. (1975) *Perspectives on Black English* (The Hague, Mouton).

Eades, D. (1991) Communicative Strategies in Aboriginal English, in: S. Romaine (Ed.) *Language in Australia* (Cambridge, Cambridge UP) pp. 84–93.

Edwards, V. and Sienkewicz, T.J. (1990) *Oral Cultures Past and Present: Rappin' and Homer* (London, Basil Blackwell).

Emberley, J.V. (1990–91) A Gift for Languages: Native Women and the Textual Economy of the Colonial Archive, *Cultural Critique* 17, pp. 21–50.

Feldman, C.F. (1991) Oral Metalanguage. In Olson and Torrance, pp. 47–65.

Gee, J. (1990) *Social Linguistics and Literacies: Ideology in Discourses. Critical Perspectives on Literacy and Education* (London, Falmer).

Grace, P. (1975) A Way of Talking, *Waiariki and Other Stories* (Auckland, Penguin), pp. 1–6.

Gumperz, J.J. and Cook-Gumperz, J. (1982) Introduction: Language and Social Identity, *Language and Social Identity* (Cambridge, Cambridge UP), pp. 1–21.

Halliday, M.A.K. (1978) *Language as a Social Semiotic: The Social Interpretation of Language and Meaning* (London, Edward Arnold).

Halliday, M.A.K. (1987) Spoken and Written Modes of Meaning, in: R. Horowitz and S.J. Samuels (Eds) *Comprehending Oral and Written Language* (San Diego, Academic), pp. 55–82.

Harris, R. (1986) *The Origin of Writing* (London, Duckworth).

Hobsbawm, E. (1983) Introduction: Inventing Traditions, in: E. Hobsbawm & T. Ranger (Eds) *The Invention of Tradition* (Cambridge, Cambridge UP), pp. 1–14.

Hodge, B. and Mishra, V. (1991) *Dark Side of the Dream: Australian Literature and the Postcolonial Mind*. Australian Cultural Studies (North Sydney, Allen and Unwin).

Hurston, Z.N. (1990) *Their Eyes Were Watching God* (New York, Harper Perennial).

Ihimaera, W. (1986) *The Matriarch* (Auckland, Heinemann).

Joseph, J.E. (1987) *Eloquence and Power: The Rise of Language Standards and Standard Languages* (London, Frances Pinter).

Koch, H. (1991) Language and Communication in Aboriginal Land Claim Hearings, in: S. Romaine (Ed.) *Language in Australia* (Cambridge, Cambridge UP), pp. 84–93, 94–103.

Logan, R.K. (1986) *The Alphabet Effect: The Impact of the Phonetic Alphabet on the Development of Western Civilization* (New York, William Morrow).

Maracle, L. (1990) *Sojourner's Truth and Other Stories* (Vancouver, Press Gang).

Maracle, L. (1990) Ramparts Hanging in the Air, in: (Ed.). Telling It Book Collective, *Telling It: Women and Language across Cultures* (Vancouver: Press Gang), pp. 161–72.

Mazrui, A. (1975) *The Political Sociology of the English Language: An African Perspective* (The Hague, Mouton).

McKenzie, D.F. (1985) *Oral Culture, Literacy and Print in Early New Zealand: The Treaty of Waitangi* (New Zealand, Victoria UP).

Miller, C. (1990) *Theories of Africans: Francophone Literature and Anthropology in Africa* (Chicago, U of Chicago P).

Moses, D.D. and Goldie, T. (Ed.) (1992) *An Anthology of Canadian Native Literature in English* (Toronto, Oxford UP).

Mudrooroo [Colin Johnson]. (1991) *Master of the Ghost Dreaming* (Sydney, Angus and Robertson).

Murray, D. (1991) *Forked Tongues: Speech, Writing and Representation in North American Indian Texts* (Bloomington, Indiana UP).

Olson, D.R. and Torrance, N. (Ed.) (1991) *Literacy and Orality* (Cambridge, Cambridge UP).

Pecheux, M. (1975) *Language, Semantics and Ideology: Stating the Obvious.* Trans. (1982) Harbans Nagpal (London, Macmillan).

Pybus, C. (1996) Editorial. *Australian Book Review*, October, p. 2.

Robins, J.D. (1915) The Backgrounds of Future Canadian Poetry, *Acta Victoriana* 36, pp. 312–16.

Robinson, H. (1989) *Write It on Your Heart: The Epic World of an Okanagan Storyteller.* Comp. and (Ed.) W. Wickwire (Vancouver, Talonbooks/Theytus).

Salmond, A. (1989) Rituals of Encounter among the Maori: Sociolinguistic Study of a Scene, in: R. Bauman & J. Scherzer (Eds) *Explorations in the Ethnography of Speaking,* 2nd ed. (Cambridge, Cambridge UP), pp. 192–212.

Sarris, G. (1993) *Keeping Slug Woman Alive: A Holistic Approach to American Indian Texts* (Berkeley, U of California P).

Scherzer, J. and Woodbury, A.C. (Ed.) (1987) *Native American Discourse: Poetics, Rhetoric and Literate Culture.* Cambridge Studies in Oral and Literate Culture (Cambridge, Cambridge UP), pp. 192–212.

Schlegel, F. von. (1815) *Lectures on the History of Literature, Ancient and Modern.* Trans. H.G. Bohn (1859) (London, H.G. Bohn).

Scollon, R. and Scollon, S.B.K. (1984) Cooking It Up and Boiling It Down: Abstracts in Athabaskan Children's Story Retellings, in: D. Tannen (Ed.) *Coherence in Spoken and Written Discourse. Advances in Discourse Processes* 12 (Norwood, NJ, ABLEX), pp. 173–97.

Scollon, R. and Scollon, S.B.K. (1979) *Linguistic Convergence: An Ethnography of Speaking at Fort Chipewyan, Alberta.* Language, Thought and Culture (New York, Academic P).

Scollon, R. and Scollon, S.B.K. (1981) *Narrative, Literacy and Face in Interethnic Communication. Advances in Discourse Processes* 7 (Norwood, NJ, ABLEX).

Silko, L.M. (1981) *Storyteller* (New York, Little Brown, Arcade).

Simms, N. (1991) *Points of Contact: A Study of the Interplay and Intersection of Traditional and Non-Traditional Literatures, Cultures and Mentalities* (New York, Pace UP).

Slipperjack, R. (1987) *Honour the Sun* (Winnipeg, Pemmican).

Todd, L. (1990) *Pidgins and Creoles*, 2nd ed. (London, Routledge).

Wa Thiong'o, Ngugi (1986) *Decolonising the Mind* (London, Heinemann).

Whiteman, M.P. (Ed.) (1981) *Variation in Writing: Functional and Linguistic-Cultural Differences.* Vol. 1 of *Writing: The Nature, Development, and Teaching of Written Communication,* 2 vols. (Hillsdale, NJ, Laurence Erlbaum).

Zabus, C. (1991) *The African Palimpsest: Indigenization of Language in the West African Europhone Novel. Cross Cultures* 4 (Amsterdam, Rodopi).

Armand Garnet Ruffo

"Why Native Literature?"

Armand Garnet Ruffo (Ojibway) is from Chapleau, in northern Ontario, with family ties to the Sagamok Ojibway First Nation and the Chapleau Fox Lake Cree First Nation. He is recognized as one of Canada's earliest contributors to both Indigenous literature and literary criticism, and one of the earliest scholars to promote Indigenous literary studies at the university level. A poet, activist, filmmaker and scholar, Ruffo teaches Indigenous literatures at Queen's University in Kingston, Ontario. Ruffo's multi-genre approach to writing is perhaps nowhere better illustrated than in his 1997 text, *Grey Owl: The Mystery of Archie Belaney*, which combines poetry, prose, fact, and fiction to explore the controversial British writer and conservationist.

Published shortly after *Grey Owl*, Ruffo's landmark 1997 essay "Why Native Literature?" is one of the most frequently cited articles on the subject of Indigenous writing. According to Ruffo, Indigenous literature was born out of a collective need to reclaim voice and resist colonialism, and he traces its beginnings to letters and petitions written for political ends. He references his own poem "Sahquakegick," as well as the work of other Indigenous writers as examples of both literary resistance and belonging to land. Land, he argues, is one of Indigenous literature's defining features, and he describes the sense of belonging on land as holistic, and an organic part of both traditional and contemporary works. Finally, Ruffo defines two branches of contemporary Native literature: the mythic-sacred and the historical-secular. Most work, he concludes, contains both these branches. These characteristics—the contemporary, the mythic/sacred, and the historical/secular—define the resilience, endurance, and continuity of Indigenous cultures.

Ruffo, Armand. "Why Native Literature?" *American Indian Quarterly* 21.4 (Fall 1997): 663–74.

Why Native Literature?

If we consider the titles of Jeannette Armstrong's essay "The Disempowerment of First North American Native Peoples and Empowerment through Their Writing," Emma LaRocque's "Here Are Our Voices—Who Will Hear?" or even Jordan Wheeler's "Voice," we come to some understanding of the position in which many Native writers see themselves in relation to their work, their people, and Canadian society at large. In fact, it would not be hyperbole to say that the kind of writing to which these writers refer faces with an unblinking eye the realities of what it means to be a people under siege. For Native people, this is the history of the Americas and the legacy of colonialism. We only have to think back to the 1990 Oka Crisis, or the confrontation at Ipperwash and the death of Dudley George (who was shot by an Ontario Provincial Police officer), to consider the appalling social conditions in which most Native people are forced to live. Indeed, the situation at the end of the twentieth century for Native people is critical. For many, it is a matter of life and death. In a 1994 interim report, the Royal Commission on Aboriginal Peoples documented that the suicide rate among young Native people is five to six times higher than it is among their non-Native peers—and rising. In a country that boasts one of the highest standards of living, obviously something has gone terribly wrong.

This intolerable situation, as Wheeler sees it, is only exacerbated by having the Native voice stymied by the dominant society, where "a novel written by a non-aboriginal writer [about Native people] sell[s] millions of copies when it is riddled with stereotypes, racial attitudes, shallow, one-dimensional characters and cultural inaccuracies. Tell a people that they are poor and hopeless enough times and they will begin to believe it" (40). Clearly, the only alternative to this kind of colonizing imposition is for Native people to claim their own voice and thereby give insight into their own values, traditions, concerns, and needs. It is a reality that for the most part is still unheard and unheeded in a country whose first inhabitants are but a mere afterthought, an anachronism to be dealt with, at best "material" for constructing a sense of Canadian national identity in a multicultural state. Any wonder that Elleke Boehmer, in her *Colonial and Postcolonial Literature*, observes that "Indigenous writers rightly remain wary of... [the] implications of the postcolonial. For they see themselves as still colonized, always-invaded, never free of a history of white occupation" (229).

As an expression of voice, or, more correctly, a community of voices, Native writers are attempting to find expression in a society that does not share their values and concerns. The form of these voices, like content itself, varies according to individual author, but as community, theirs is a collective voice that addresses the relationship between colonizer and colonized, the impact of colonialism, and, moreover, functions on a practical level by striving to bring about positive change. Thus, my claim is that Native literature, while grounded in a traditional, spiritually based worldview, is no less a call for liberation, survival, and beyond to affirmation. As the tradition of Native spirituality is inherent in the literature, beginning with European contact, so, too, is the tradition of addressing historical, secular concerns. To proceed with this position, I will foreground a number of prominent theoretical and functional perspectives in the context of the relationship between language and power to point out that Native people were subjected to ideologies that have had very real and dire consequences. In doing so, I will confirm that while Native culture may be appropriated due to the imbalance of power between colonizer and colonized, it is ironically this very imbalance that makes it impossible for the dominant culture to position itself within the Native worldview. Finally, I will consider some prominent characteristics and motifs of Native literature in order to arrive at a methodology for understanding and approaching it.

Back in the mid-seventies, prior to the popularizing of such terminology as *postcolonial* and *postmodern*, Canadian literary critic and theorist Northrop Frye, in an essay entitled "Haunted by Lack of Ghosts: Some Patterns in the Imagery of Canadian Poetry," stumbled upon the difference between Native and non-Native perception. He writes:

> I said in an article on Canadian literature that the Canadian problem of identity seemed to me primarily connected with locale, less a matter of "Who am I?" than of "Where is here?" Another friend, commenting on this, told me of a story about a doctor from the south (that is, from one of the Canadian cities) travelling on the arctic tundra with an [Inuit] guide. A blizzard blew up, and they had to camp for the night. What with the cold, the storm, and the loneliness, the doctor panicked and began shouting "We are lost!" The [Inuit] looked at him thoughtfully and said, "We are not lost. We are here." (27)

It is through this simple anecdote that Frye goes on to observe that "a vast gulf between an indigenous and an immigrant mentality opened at that point" (27). In his text *The Bush Garden*, Frye presents a thematic analysis of Canadian literature, referring to what he calls the "garrison mentality," which he says has had the tendency to manifest itself as a "tone of deep terror in regard to nature" (225). This theme supposedly persists throughout Canadian literature and, in fact, has developed as the literature itself developed, moving from the physical to the psychological, a position that Margaret Atwood further developed into her thematic guide to literature, *Survival*. Thus, Frye moves us along a trajectory in which nature becomes the embodiment of the unanswerable denial of human and moral values, equated with all that is uncivilized.

It goes without saying "that where Native people figure in Frye's Canadian landscape they are inevitably connected to the land, and, as the land is considered terrifying, the embodiment of a denial of Western cultural values, so too do Native people symbolize this perception" (*Bush Garden* 140). (Although Frye does not provide a detailed analysis of this observation, one only has to consider his reference to E.J. Pratt's martyrdom of Brébeuf. In a contemporary context, one might consider the portrayal of the Mohawks on the front page of *Maclean's* during the Oka Crisis.) Accordingly, as it has been illustrated by Daniel Francis in *The Imaginary Indian: The Image of the Indian in Canadian Culture* and Leslie Monkman in *A Native Heritage: Images of the Indian in English-Canadian Literature*, these imaginings run a gamut of variations from the noble savage embodying spirituality to the savage lacking spirituality with a myriad of versions of the degraded and doomed. In the American context, Robert Berkhofer picks up a similar theme. He writes that "Only civilization had history and dynamics in this view, so therefore Indianness must be conceived of as ahistorical and static" (27).

With the rapidly depleting natural environment, however, and the New Age, posthippy search for spiritual enlightenment in a wasteland of mass consumerism, contemporary Western writers have come to realize that their own humanity is indelibly linked to nature. Accordingly, this notion of Native as anachronism, of being static and locked into the past, has of late been viewed in a positive light and has gained new prominence. It is this latest incarnation that has recently become the most problematic, namely, "We as Native," which is essentially a reworking of the noble savage motif tempered by the contemporary agenda of self-fulfilment and preservation. In this context, the writer dons the persona (or shall I say headdress) of the Native, as indicated in Doug Fetherling's poem "Explorers as Seen by the Natives" (463). As with older variations, again, the dominant merely perpetuates stereotypes and continues the legacy of objectifying Native people.

Francis succinctly sums up these transitory imaginings. He concludes that "Our thinking about Indians relates to our thinking about ourselves as North Americans" (222). Likewise, Berkhofer writes that "American authors increasingly looked to the experiences of other peoples to criticize their own society" (107). Without getting into the whole appropriation issue, I will merely say that this is most controversial in that it raises issues of exploitation, power relationships, and domination, all of which are put into sharp relief against questions of freedom of expression, artistic licence, and censorship. (Interestingly, one of the finest works written about Native people, Rudy Wiebe's Governor General's Award-winning novel *The Temptations of Big Bear* [1973], ultimately presents Big Bear not merely as a Christian but even as Christlike. That Wiebe's title is reminiscent of Nikos Kazantzakis's *The Last*

Temptation of Christ [1951] seems hardly a coincidence. For some, such a portrayal may not be necessarily negative; nevertheless, for others, it is certainly a cause for concern. Gail Anderson-Dargatz's bestselling novel *The Cure for Death by Lightning* provides a recent example of a controversial representation of Native culture by the dominant. This, however, is a topic of discussion in itself.)

The important thing to consider among these numerous variations of the "Imaginary or Whiteman's Indian" is that historically each of these imaginings has been projected and readily imposed upon Native people for the purpose of subjugation, whether it be physical, psychological, or spiritual. What makes this all the more insidious is that these projections have taken on a life of their own. According to Albert Memmi, "racism appears...not as an incidental detail, but as a consubstantial part of colonialism" (74). Janice Acoose explains the impact of such imagery in the portrayal of Native women in Canadian literature: "They were generally represented in Canadian literature somewhere between the polemical stereotypical images of Indian princess...and the easy squaw. Such representations create very powerful images that perpetuate stereotypes and perhaps more importantly, foster dangerous cultural attitudes that affect human relationships and inform institutional ideology" (39). To be sure, this imagery and the language associated with it are far from neutral. We only have to consider the term *Indian*, which as an imperial construct serves to wipe out any trace of a unique culture and history among individual First Nations. Consider also the social policy that was implemented in response to the stereotypical and racist perception of Native people as being "uncivilized," particularly as it pertains to the residential school system. I need not dwell on the catastrophic results.

Reconsidering Frye's anecdote as it relates to perception of place and, accordingly, identity, in light of the kinds of stereotyping that has been imposed upon Native people over the centuries, we can begin to see how the imposition of language has not only compounded the problem of meaningful communication between Native and non-Native peoples but has resulted in those catastrophes for Native people in the real world. This legacy leads us to consider the theories of Edward Said, particularly that of the relationship between discourse and power and its impact on what we may term "historical truth." From this perspective, "the power to narrate, or to block other narratives from forming and emerging, is very important to culture and imperialism, and constitutes one of the main connections between them" (Said xiii). Hence, the unabated misrepresentation and appropriation of Native voice. Yet, despite it all, the colonizer, no matter how hard he tries to get out of his skin, must always remain the colonizer because, simply put, he is the one wielding power.

According to George Steiner, "One need not subscribe to romantic 'personalism' in order to know that it is mere artifice to seek to immunize the meanings of a work of literature from the life and milieu of the writer" (8). Considering the cataclysmic postcontact experience of Native people on this continent, we can conclude that Native literature represents a response to an experience that literally turned life and milieu upside down. Moreover, this expression is of an experience of such magnitude that it has moved beyond an individual response and into the realm of the collective psyche of a people. Where new experiences come into play, the individual translates these into the context of this communal experience, which has never been forgotten but passed from one generation to the next (Gunn Allen 8). In other words, Native writers, while writing from their individual perspectives, are in a sense adjuncts of the collective experience, of what we may call "community." This is no doubt a very different frame of reference from that of non-Native writers, who traditionally place great emphasis on individuality and hence personal isolation.

Considering these observations, then, in regard to what I have termed the imposition of language, its codification signifying a relationship to real power, the question "Why Native literature?" becomes at least partially answered. It arises because it must if authentic Native voices are to be heard and addressed within a country that to date has been satiated by projections of what Native people are supposed to be, projections that have been used to keep "The Native under Control" (Said 162). What this leads us to, however, are even more questions, such as, "What is this Native voice?" And, ultimately, "What is Native literature?" In the words of Thomas King, "perhaps our simple definition that Native literature is literature produced by Natives will suffice for the while" (xi). At this point, I will say only that the literature itself tells us what it is; theories of criticism, ways of approaching the literature, will necessarily come from the literature and not be foisted upon it.

What we see in turning to the writing itself is a body of work that differs remarkably from that of non-Native people. Beginning with the oral tradition, nowhere does the land appear; in Frye's words, "immoral and terrorizing" (*Bush Garden* 225); on the contrary, it is considered a living entity, a mother who must be respected and honoured even at the harshest of times. As such, one only has to consider the relationship to the land and environment, relationships to people and other life forces, to material possessions, and, certainly, to the Creator. It is these inherent traditions and values, then, emphasizing what we may call a holistic, connected, or integrated approach to life, that one finds throughout the work. However, for those who may think that Native literature is solely about spiritual matters (which much literature *about* Native people tries to be), I must reiterate that the contemporary Native worldview is postcontact and therefore also inherently secular/political.

At this point, I will shift the discourse to a more personal level and present a poem of mine entitled "Sahquakegick." The reason for choosing the poem is twofold: first, because it provides an effective and immediate way to illustrate my position; and second, because it was recently reprinted in a McGraw-Hill Ryerson Senior Issues school anthology (the significance of this second point will become clear by the conclusion of this essay). To proceed, I will use the poem as a starting point to illustrate my central thesis, that of liberation, survival, and beyond, while examining some of the common motifs that one finds throughout Native literature.

Sahquakegick

Although I never knew him
I am told when my great-great-grandfather
signed away miles of home and bush
   campfires hugged Lake
   Biscotasing like moons
in treaty, with the government of Canada
   official men in official
   black suits
It is a special day he pronounced
looking stern and proud
   in this photograph
   shot in front of the Hudson Bay Company
   store
while faces in the background
looking bewildered looked on

And he knew also the momentous day
meant change
   change, yes, like the seasons
   he knew that
and standing like the trunk of a tree
dressed in leather and balancing
his rifle, I am told he said slowly
in grave concern
looking beyond the heads of all
to me now, squarely,
some will learn and speak. (24)

The central theme is clearly the land, particularly its passing from Native control to Canadian control during the treaty process. As well, there is the idea of passing the torch, so to speak, from one generation to the next, the writer using his knowledge of the English language to address the ramifications of the treaty process and loss of land. The significance of this cannot be overstated. From the earliest prayers and songs, the land and all the forms of life upon it have always been regarded as sacred by the people. That is a constant, a given. An example of this may be found in a traditional Midewiwin (Anishnaabe Medicine Society) death song, which, translated, reads:

You are a spirit,
I am making you a spirit.
In the place where I sit,
I am making you a spirit.

The speaker centres himself on the land, which becomes an integral part of the process of communication with the spirit world. When we speak of the land, it is not any land but a specific piece of Mother Earth that is as much spiritual as physical. For me, in "Sahquakegick," it is the land of northern Ontario, Biscotasing, Anishnaabe country. As for the Midewiwin singer, it is literally the land beneath his feet.

Another theme evident in the poem, one that is considered among the most predominant in Native literature, is that of community and a sense of family. What we notice is a return to the community rather than a going away. In "Sahquakegick," the return is metaphorical as well as spiritual; the poet finds his great-great-grandfather speaking to him through an old photograph. In numerous other Native works, the movement is in fact physical with spiritual overtones. For example, one only has to think of Richard Wagamese's *Keeper 'n Me*, in which a Native protagonist finds strength and well-being by returning to his community after a life in the non-Native world. Community is necessarily linked to identity, the return to community signifying the protagonist's recognition of himself as a Native person who has survived the colonizing and assimilating forces of the dominant society.

Garnet Raven, the young Anishnabe protagonist in Wagamese's novel, returns to White Dog Reserve after twenty years of trying to be everything from Mexican to African. Through it all, he comes to learn that his identity and well-being are inseparable from the traditions of his own Anishnabe community. "What I'm tryin' to say is tradition gives strength to the culture," he later concludes. After remaining on the reserve for two years, he comes to further understand that "the land is a feeling" (155). In other words, he discovers that it is just as much inside his people as it is under their feet. While his return to the community signals a movement towards spiritual enlightenment, particularly the knowledge of who he is and what it means to be Anishnabe, it also finally gives him a role and identity within the community, that of storyteller; the book we are reading is his contribution to community life.

In "Sahquakegick," the theme of identity and voice is implied in the writer's identification with his relations who appear in the background of the photograph "looking bewildered." The task of learning and speaking has been passed on to him, and he, through writing the poem, has taken up the call to speak for those who cannot. This, of course, is a theme that has pervaded much contemporary Native literature. In this regard, we can consider Maria Campbell's *Halfbreed* and Beatrice Culleton's *In Search of April Raintree*. In both, the author employs a first-person, autobiographical perspective. Certainly, these authors go a long way towards breaking the silence and showing "what it was like ... what it still is like," to be a Native person in Canada (Campbell 9). Theirs are moving testimonies that are not unique to a few Native people in this country but relate the racism and oppression that is the norm for so many. In Campbell's case, her narrator's poverty and destitution lead her to a life of prostitution, drugs, and alcohol. Through it all, she manages to move away from her despair and begin a process of healing, eventually returning to her community where she once again finds "happiness and beauty" (2). Campbell refers to ·herself as "a community healer and teacher" (Griffiths and Campbell 69), and it is in the writing of *Halfbreed* that she most forcefully expresses the healing process. April Raintree, the protagonist of Culleton's work, likewise goes through a personal hell of family suicide and sexual abuse. In the end, she, too, comes full circle, "accepts who she is" as a Native woman (Culleton 228), and learns the value of speaking out for herself and her people.

I would like to take this idea of voice a step further and note that the historical branch of Native literature can be traced directly through such poems as "Sahquakegick" to a central concern: the pressure put on Native people to sign away their land for immigrant settlement, when they had little knowledge of the significance of their signature and little or no command of the English language. This branch, then, begins with the genre of petitions and protest letters, which were a direct response to the rapid influx of settlers and the deteriorating living conditions of Native people. From the letters of Joseph Brant, writing to the colonial government in 1798 to demand control of his lands along the Grand River, and Catherine Sonee-goh Sutton, writing in 1860 to the editor of the Owen Sound *Leader* to protest against speculators buying up Native land, this spirit of indignation can be traced to the poetry and fiction of contemporary writers. One only has to consider the work of renowned Mohawk poet Pauline Johnson, whose poem "The Cattle Thief" is essentially a woman's protest against the racist treatment of her husband and family. In her essay "Here Are Our Voices—Who Will Hear?" Emma LaRocque remarks that "much of Native writing, whether blunt or subtle, is protest literature in that it speaks of the processes of our colonization, dispossession, objectification, marginalization, and that constant struggle for cultural survival expressed in the movement for structural and psychological self-determination" (xviii). In fact, it is said that one cannot be a Native writer and not be political; it comes with the territory.

The other branch of Native writing to which I would like briefly to allude is that of the spiritually based mythological. Although "Sahquakegick" does not use mythology per se, it does refer to sacred elements: *gisiss*, the moon; and *ishkote*, fire. The "campfires hugged Lake/Biscotasing like moons"—the metaphor here draws the reader into the relationship between community and time. Prior to the arrival of white settlers, Native literature in its oral form was spiritually centred in that it was, and is, informed by an Indigenous worldview that sees humans not at the top of an evolutionary pyramid but rather as a link in a circle of creation in which every entity is endowed with spirit. Essentially, this body of literature revealed through culturally specific myth(s) the values, customs, attitudes, and religious and philo-sophic beliefs of a particular nation.

As a consequence of contact, however, these myths and sacred songs of the oral tradition, which had flourished as part of daily life prior to the arrival of the Euro-peans, were forced to go underground in order to survive the onslaught of zealous Christian missionaries. Some also found their way into the hands of professional and amateur ethnologists. The point is that many of these myths and songs managed to survive and remain intact, and it is this wealth of material that has provided an alternative to the influence of the so-called historical/secular writing that Native people found themselves by necessity forced into doing. Moreover, it is this branch, originating in the earliest stories of the Manitous, such as Trickster, in all his/her guises from Coyote to Weesaykayjac to Nanabush to Raven, as well as in the prayers and chants of the earliest poems and songs, that is having a profound influence on contemporary Native writers. In light of the work of Tomson Highway, whose plays *The Rez Sisters* and *Dry Lips Oughta Move to Kapuskasing* are constructed around the transformative qualities of the mythological Nanabush, or Thomas King, whose short stories in addition to his novel *Green Grass, Running Water* feature a sly and mischievous Coyote as a central character, this branch appears, ironically, to offer new possibilities for literary creation.

In contemporary Native literature, these two influences (or branches, as I have called them)—the mythic/sacred and the historical/secular—are not exclusive. For while Highway and King both draw on mythological sources, their work is still profoundly historical/political in that it challenges the dominant power structures, be it the church and its impact on Native people (as in Highway's *Dry Lips Oughta Move to Kapuskasing*) or the state and its officially sanctioned history (as in King's "The One about Coyote Going West"). This, of course, is not to say that the force of the political message does not vary depending on the individual author. According to Gerald Vizenor, "comic signs and tragic modes are cultural variations... they are not structural opposition" (introduction 9). Writers such as Highway and King are not bound to what Vizenor refers to as the tragic language of the social sciences. Rather, in using mythic trickster figures, they move towards a "comic narrative" ("Trickster Discourse" 195), which, of course, does not mean that the work shouldn't be taken seriously. On the contrary, the use of humour as an important survival tool is evident in the work of numerous serious writers.

Finally, I draw attention to the words of the late Anishnaabe Elder Art Solomon, who, in his last collection of poems and essays, *Eating Bitterness*, appears to set out the task, or perhaps the challenge, for the contemporary Native writer: "When enough Native people feel good about themselves, about their beliefs, spiritual-ity and culture, then we have hope for the future simply because we may express ourselves according to the way we are" (58). The message here is clear: the need for healing, the need for expression, go hand in hand with each other. To bring hope to young Native people so they too can express themselves and heal is a communal task. With new writers continually emerging in the communities, where once there were a handful of Native people expressing themselves creatively there is now no less than a flowering, what has been termed an "Aboriginal renaissance." In the recent community-based publication *Steal My Rage*, Joel Maki, the editor, says that "we had envisioned producing a thin volume featuring perhaps a dozen authors. This changed with the response to our advertisement: only a week after sending out a call for unpublished Native writers, the submissions began to flow in until we had received almost four hundred works" (1).

Why Native Literature? For an answer we can turn to the work of these young authors. What they write about—in poems such as "Prayer for Oka," "The Survivors," "Healing Begins with Me," and "Guardian Spirit Winds," which begins with the line "steal my rage"—is none other than liberation, survival, and beyond... to affirmation. This is not to say that the work of these writers is not at times dark and despondent, but, nevertheless, it is in the very act of expressing themselves, of ironically putting down words in the language of the colonizer, that these authors reveal their determination to liberate themselves and to choose life over death. To address Native people themselves so that they can empower and heal themselves through their own cultural affirmation, as well as to address those in power and give them the real story: this too is the answer. And if collections such as *Steal My Rage* are any indication of things to come, then it is evident that there is no lack of creativity and self-expression among Native people. The last word, however, goes to Art Solomon, who succinctly grounds us in reality: "We can only make ourselves understood if others are willing to listen" (58).

Works Cited

Acoose, Janice. *Iskwewak—Kah' Ki Yaw Ni Wahkomakanak: Neither Indian Princesses nor Easy Squaws.* Toronto: Women's, 1995.

Berkhofer, Robert F. *The Whiteman's Indian: Images of the American Indian from Columbus to Present.* New York: Vintage, 1979.

Boehmer, Elleke. *Colonial and Postcolonial Literature.* Oxford: Oxford UP, 1995.

Campbell, Marcia. *Halfbreed.* Toronto: McClelland, 1973.

Culleton, Beatrice. *In Search of April Raintree.* Winnipeg: Pemmican, 1983.

Fetherling, Doug. "Explorers as Seen by the Natives." *The New Oxford Book of Canadian Verse in English.* Ed. Margaret Atwood. Toronto: Oxford UP, 1982.

Francis, Daniel. *The Imaginary Indian: The Image of the Indian in Canadian Culture.* Vancouver: Arsenal, 1992.

Frye, Northrop. *The Bush Garden: Essays on the Canadian Imagination.* Toronto: Anansi, 1971.

———. "Haunted by Lack of Ghosts: Some Patterns in the Imagery of Canadian Poetry." *The Canadian Imagination.* Ed. David Staines. Cambridge: Harvard UP, 1977.

Griffiths, Linda, and Maria Campbell. *The Book of Jessica*. Toronto: Coach House, 1989.

Gunn Allen, Paula. Introduction. *Spider Woman's Granddaughters: Traditional Tales and Contemporary Writing by Native American Women*. Ed. Gunn Allen. New York: Ballantine, 1990.

King, Thomas. Introduction. *All My Relations: An Anthology of Contemporary Canadian Native Literature*. Ed. King. Toronto: McClelland, 1990.

LaRocque, Emma. "Preface: Or, Here Are Our Voices—Who Will Hear?" *Writing the Circle*. Ed. Jeanne Perreault and Sylvia Vance. Edmonton: NeWest, 1990.

Maki, Joel T. Introduction. *Steal My Rage: New Native Voices*. Ed. Maki. Toronto: Douglas, 1995.

Memmi, Albert. *The Colonizer and the Colonized*. Boston: Beacon, 1965.

Monkman, Leslie. *A Native Heritage: Images of the Indian in English-Canadian Literature*. Toronto: U of Toronto P, 1981.

Ruffo, Armand Garnet. "Sahquakegick." *Opening in the Sky*. Penticton, BC: Theytus, 1994.

Said, Edward W. *Culture and Imperialism*. New York: Vintage, 1994.

Solomon, Arthur. *Eating Bitterness: A Vision beyond the Prison Walls*. Toronto: NC P, 1994.

Steiner, George. *George Steiner: A Reader*. New York: Oxford UP, 1984.

Vizenor, Gerald. Introduction. Vizenor, ed.

———. "Trickster Discourse: Comic Holotropes and Language Games." Vizenor, ed.

———, ed. *Narrative Chance: Postmodern Discourse on Native American Indian Literatures*. Norman: U of Oklahoma P, 1992.

Wagamese, Richard. *Keeper 'n Me*. Toronto: Doubleday, 1994.

Wheeler, Jordan. "Voice." *Aboriginal Voices: Amerindian, Inuit, and Sami Theatre*. Ed. Per Brask and William Morgan. Baltimore: Johns Hopkins UP, 1992.

Jeannette Armstrong

"Land Speaking"

One of the foremost scholars and educators of Okanagan language, literature and knowledge, Jeannette Armstrong was born and raised on the Penticton Indian Reserve in British Columbia. An accomplished speaker and writer of essays, poetry, and fiction, Armstrong's ground-breaking publications include the novel *Slash* (1987), the poetry collection *Breath Tracks* (1991), and the edited collection of essays *Looking at the Words of Our People*: *First Nations Analysis of Literature* (1993). Armstrong is also the founder and director of the En'owkin Centre, an Indigenous educational institution located in Penticton. She is recognized internationally for her contribution to Indigenous move-ments of resistance and empowerment, and as testament to her achievement currently holds a Canada Research Chair at the University of British Columbia.

At the centre of Armstrong's work is the concept of interdependence and the centrality of land and language to Indigenous existence. "Land Speaking," originally published in 1998, uses poetry as a means of expressing the way in which Indigenous language is born from the land, and thus carries sacred and sustaining powers. Substantiating Lee Maracle's assertion in "Oratory: Coming to Theory," Armstrong writes that from her Okanagan perspective speaking is doing, since Okanagan words describe action. This conforms to her conviction that cultural empowerment is inte-gral to environmental preservation—a principle increasingly embraced by Indigenous cultural and environmental activists today.

Armstrong, Jeannette. "Land Speaking." *Speaking for the Generations: Native Writers on Writing.* Ed. Simon Ortiz. Tucson: U of Arizona P, 1998. 174–95.

Land Speaking

I want to discuss the intensity of my experience as an Okanagan who is indigenous to the land I live on, and how that experience permeates my writing. It is my conviction that Okanagan, my original language, the language of my people, constitutes the most significant influence on my writing in English. I will discuss how my own experience of the land sources and arises in my poetry and prose and how the Okanagan language shapes that connection.

I want to comment on the underlying basis for how this occurs within my personal experience of the land as an Okanagan-speaking writer. I will emphasize the significance that original Native languages and their connection to our lands have in compelling the reinvention of the enemy's language for our perspectives as indigenous writers.

As I understand it from my Okanagan ancestors, language was given to us by the land we live within. The land that is the Okanagan is part of the Great Columbia River Basin on the interior plateau of Washington State and British Columbia. The Okanagan language, called N'silxchn by us, is one of the Salishan languages. My ancestors say that N'silxchn is formed out of an older language, some words of which are still retained in our origin stories. I have heard elders explain that the language changed as we moved and spread over the land through time. My own father told me that it was the land that changed the language because there is special knowledge in each different place. All my elders say that it is land that holds all knowledge of life and death and is a constant teacher. It is said in Okanagan that the land constantly speaks. It is constantly communicating. Not to learn its language is to die. We survived and thrived by listening intently to its teachings—to its language—and then inventing human words to retell its stories to our succeeding generations. It is the land that speaks N'silxchn through the generations of our ancestors to us. It is N'silxchn, the old land/mother spirit of the Okanagan People, which surrounds me in its primal wordless state.

It is this N'silxchn which embraces me and permeates my experience of the Okanagan land and is a constant voice within me that yearns for human speech. I am claimed and owned by this land, this Okanagan. Voices that move within as my experience of existence do not awaken as words. Instead they move within as the colors, patterns, and movements of a beautiful, kind Okanagan landscape. They are the Grandmother voices which speak. The poem "Grandmothers" was written in N'silxchn and interpreted into English. The English term *grandmother* as a human experience is closest in meaning to the term *Tmixw* in Okanagan, meaning something like loving-ancestor-land-spirit.

Grandmothers

In the part of me that was always there
grandmothers
are speaking to me
the grandmothers in whose voices
I nestle
and draw nourishment from
voices speaking to me
in early morning light
glinting off water
speaking to me in fragile green
pushing upward
groping sun and warmth
pulling earth's breath
down and in
to join with porous stone
speaking to me
out of thick forest
in majestic rises to sheer
blue
in the straight slight mist
in twigs and fur
skin and blood
moon and movement
feathers stroking elegant curves against wind
silent unseen bits
in the torrent of blood
washing bone and flesh
earth's pieces
the joining of winds
to rock
igniting white fire
lighting dark places
and rousing the sleeping moment
caught in pollen
a waking of stars

inside
and when blue fire
slants to touch this water
I lift my eyes
and know I am seed
and shooting green
and words
in this hollow
I am
night glittering
the wind and silence
I am vastness stretching to the sun
I am this moment
earth mind
I can be nothing else
the joining of breath to sand
by water and fire
the mother body
and yet
I am small
a mote of dust
hardly here
unbearably without anything
to hold me
but the voices
of grandmothers[1]

The language spoken by the land, which is interpreted by the Okanagan into words, carries parts of its ongoing reality. The land as language surrounds us completely, just like the physical reality of it surrounds us. Within that vast speaking, both externally and internally, we as human beings are an inextricable part—though a minute part—of the land language.

In this sense, all indigenous peoples' languages are generated by a precise geography and arise from it. Over time and many generations of their people, it is their distinctive interaction with a precise geography which forms the way indigenous language is shaped and subsequently how the world is viewed, approached, and expressed verbally by its speakers.

I have felt within my own experience of travel to other lands of Salishan-speaking people an internal resonance of familiar language and familiar land. I can hear the

---

1 *Gatherings*, vol. 3 (Penticton, BC: Theytus Books, 1992).

N'silxchn parts in all Salishan languages. I have been surprised by how unfamiliar sounds in those languages resemble and resonate closely with the physical differences between their land and mine. The language lets me feel the points where our past was one and lets me "recognize" teaching sites of our common ancestry. The poem "Ochre Lines" imitates the way N'silxchn engages a constant layering of land and human experience within its imagery.

Ochre Lines

skins
drums
liquid beat fluttering under the breast
coursing long journeys
through blue
lifelines
joining body to body
primeval maps
drawn under
the
hide
deep
floating dreams past
history
surging forward
upward
through indigo passages
to move on the earth
to filigree into fantastic
gropings over the land
journeys marking
red trails
a slow
moving earth vision[1]

I experience land as a fluent speaker of Okanagan. N'silxchn, the Okanagan land language, is my first language, my Earth Mother language. When I close my eyes and my thoughts travel, N'silxchn recreates the sounds, the smells, the colors, the taste and texture precisely. N'silxchn emulates the land and the sky in its unique flow around me. I feel its vast outer edges touching the sky and the horizon in all that I experience as life. I feel it speaking the oldness of earth, speaking to us. I have given

---

1 *Gatherings*, vol. 4 (Penticton, BC: Theytus Books, 1994).

English voice to this sense of N'silxchn land presence in my grandmother landscape poems. The poem "Winds," from that series, intertwines land presence through my human voice presence.

Winds

Winds	moving			clouds
past		earth		sky
are		one		moves
around	me	silent		colors
drifting	sometimes	present		dark
with	soft		white	
			flakes	touching
life		rich	lacework	unknown
	hands		twined	with care
a place	forever	still	tracing	quietly
a line	stretched	to a	horizon	
fading			with time	and gently
ending		breath[1]		

As it is spoken today, the Okanagan language carries meanings about a time that is no more. Its words speak of a world different in experience from this one. Its words whisper more than the retelling of the world. Through my language I understand I am being spoken to, I'm not the one speaking. The words are coming from many tongues and mouths of Okanagan people and the land around them. I am a listener to the language's stories, and when my words form I am merely retelling the same stories in different patterns. I have known this about my language since learning English as a second language. Learning English as a second language allowed me to "hear" the different stories in English words from those that N'silxchn brings forward from its origins. I now know this is true of any language. I hear words speak old stories. The poem "Words" emerged through an exercise in both languages to capture N'silxchn imagery interpretive of such an illusive and abstract concept as meaning.

Words

Words are memory
a window in the present
a coming to terms with meaning
history made into now
a surge in reclaiming
the enormity of the past

---

1 *Breath Tracks* (Stratford, ON, and Penticton, BC: Williams-Wallace/Theytus Books, 1991).

a piece in the collective experience of time
a sleep in which I try to awaken
the whispered echoes of voices
resting in each word
moving back into dark blue
voices of continuance
countless sound shapings which roll thunderous
over millions of tongues
to reach me
alive with meaning a fertile ground
from which generations spring
out of the landscape of grandmother
the sharing
in what we select
to remember
the physical power in thought
carried inside silently
pushing forward in each breathing
meaning wished onto tongues transforming with each utterance
the stuff of our lives
to travel on wind
on air
to bump wetly
against countless tiny drums
to become sound
spasms coursing upward into imagine
there to turn gray silence
into explosions of color
calling up the real
the physical
the excruciating sweetness of mouth on mouth
the feltness of the things of us
then settling soundless
colorless
into memory
to be hidden there
reaching ever forward into distances unknown
always linking to others
up to the last drum
vibrating into vast silence[1]

---

1 Ibid.

By speaking my Okanagan language, I have come to understand that whenever I speak, I step into vastness and move within it through a vocabulary of time and of memory. I move through the vastness into a new linking of time to the moment I speak. To speak is to create more than words, more than sounds retelling the world; it is to realize the potential for transformation of the world. To the Okanagan, speaking is a sacred act in that words contain spirit, a power waiting to become activated and become physical. Words do so upon being spoken and create cause and effect in human interaction. What we speak determines our interactions. Realization of the power in speaking is in the realization that words can change the future and in the realization that we each have that power. I am the word carrier, and I shape-change the world. The poem "Threads of Old Memory" was an inquiry in English-language imagery of the N'silxchn concept of speaking as a profound and sacred responsibility.

Threads of Old Memory

Speaking to newcomers in their language is dangerous
for when I speak
history is a dreamer
empowering thought
from which I awaken the imaginings of the past
bringing the sweep and surge of meaning
coming from a place
rooted in the memory of loss
experienced in ceremonies
wrenched from the minds of a people
whose language spoke only harmony
through a language
meant to overpower
to overtake
in skillfully crafted words
moving towards surrender
leaving in its swirling wake
only those songs hidden
cherished
protected
the secret singing of which
I glimpse through bewildered eyes
an old lost world
of astounding beauty

When I speak
I attempt to bring together
with my hands
gossamer thin threads of old memory
thoughts from the underpinnings of understanding
words steeped in age
slim
barely visible strands of harmony
stretching across the chaos brought into this world
through words
shaped as sounds in air
meaning made physical
changers of the world
carriers into this place of things
from a place of magic
the underside of knowing
the origination place
a pure place
silent
wordless
from where thoughts I choose
silently transform into words
I speak and
powerfully become actions
becomes memory is someone
I become different memories to different people
different stories in the retelling of my place
I am the dreamer
the choice maker
the word speaker
I speak in a language of words formed of the actions of the past
words that become the sharing
the collective knowing
the links that become a people
the dreaming that becomes a history
the calling forth of voices
the sending forward of memory
I am the weaver of memory thread
twining past to future
I am the artist

the storyteller
the singer
from the known and familiar
pushing out into darkness
dreaming splinters together
the coming to knowing

When I speak
I sing a song called up through ages
of carefully crafted rhythm
of a purpose close to the wordless
in a coming to this world from the cold and hungry spaces in the heart
through the desolate and lost places of the mind
to this stark and windswept mountain top
I search for sacred words
spoken serenely in the gaps between memory
the lost places of history
pieces mislaid
forgotten or stolen
muffled by violence
splintered by evil
when languages collide in mid-air
when past and present explode in chaos
and the imaginings of the past
rip into the dreams of the future

When I speak
I choose the words gently
asking the whys
dangerous words
in the language of the newcomers
words releasing unspeakable grief
for all that is lost
dispelling lies in the retelling
I choose threads of truth
that in its telling cannot be hidden
and brings forward
old words that heal
moving to a place
where a new song begins
a new ceremony

through medicine eyes I glimpse a world
that cannot be stolen or lost
only shared
shaped by new words
joining precisely to form old patterns
a song of stars
glittering against an endless silence[1]

The Okanagan language, as I have come to understand it from my comparative examination with the English language, differs in significant ways from English. Linguists may differ from my opinion, arguing that the mechanics of grammar differ but the functional basis of the two languages does not. I will not argue. I will only say that I speak Okanagan and English fluently, and in so doing I perceive differences that have great influence on my world-view, my philosophy, my creative process, and subsequently my writing.

Okanagan is completely vocally rooted in that it has never been written down. It is a language devised solely for use by the human voice and the human body. The elements inherent in that are straightforward. A good example is the N'silxchn method of differentiating between the word for "this," *axa* (used only with something you can touch), and "that," *ixi* (used only with something near, as in a room) and "that over there," *yaxis* (used for something farther away but still only when you can point at it), the last with a voice stretching of the vowels to indicate far away. In a vocally rooted language, sound, with all its emotive qualities, determines how words are used and forms a backdrop in meaning, as do gesture, stance, and facial expression.

While this seems to impose limitations on what one has available for descriptive imagery in written languages, actually the opposite occurs. The range is broadened by the way the sounds in words can be combined and the way each sound can be used, in much the same way that classical music stretches the imagination by the various mathematically possible ways sound elements can be combined.

Over time, the Okanagan language has acquired a music-based sensitivity in the creation of meaning. The sound elements of tempo, beat, rhythm, volume, and pitch have a greater significance for comprehension than in languages that rely on visually based imagery. The language re-sounds patterns of action and movement as imagery. This is what the Okanagan people mean when they say that everything is a singing. Sounds solicit emotion even in babies; certain sounds cause sadness, and certain rhythms cause excitement. Sounds "speak" in particular ways of inner response. Music relies on such responses to communicate its message. In the same way, Okanagan, as a vocally based language, relies heavily on sounds and sound patterns to communicate meanings.

---

1 Ibid.

N'silxchn recreates sounds of the land in its utterance, but it also draws on the natural human emotional response to sound and rhythm to contain and express a philosophical or spiritual idea. The poem "Frogs Singing" is the result of a long discussion on our language and worldview with my sister Delphine, who spoke only Okanagan until age twelve. She pointed out that the stars and the frogs in the Okanagan summer nights have the same rhythm and that in saying it to recall the sound and the night filled with stars, the rhythm filled her soul and became hers.

Frogs Singing

my sister did not dream this
she found this out when she walked
outside and looked up and star
rhythms sang to her pointing their spines of light
down into her and filled her body with star song
and all around her
frogs joined the star singing
they learned it
long ago[1]

It has become apparent to me that, for the most part, English lacks this kind of musical coherence. For the most part, the "sounds" of the words and the rhythms created in their structure clearly are not constructed to draw a musical response. In fact, the language is deaf to music and only chances on it through the diligent work of writers. Perhaps this has to do with the loss of the body as the sole carrier of words. Perhaps literacy—with its marks on stone, wood, paper, and now in electronic impulses—silences the music that writers are able to retrieve.

Okanagan is a language guided by active components of reality. Syllables form base units that carry meaning in the language. Root syllables are where meanings reside rather than only in whole or complete words. Words are a combination of syllables, each of which carries meaning and contains function. Each word, when examined, can be broken down into root syllables, each of which has an active meaning and when combined activates a larger animated image.

An example is the Okanagan word for dog: *kekwep*. The word has two syllables. The first syllable, *kek*, is an action syllable meaning something like "happening upon a small (thing)," and the second syllable, *wep*, meaning something like "sprouting profusely (as in fur)." In English, the two together would not make specific sense. However, when these two syllables are combined in Okanagan, they immediately join together to become an activator of a larger image. They create an action together—

---

1 "Frogs Singing," in *Durable Breath*, ed. John E. Smelcer and D.L. Birchfield (Anchorage, AK: Salmon Run P, 1994).

fur growing on a little living thing—made familiar only by a connective experience.

When you say the Okanagan word for dog, you don't "see" a dog image, you summon an experience of a little furred life, the exactness of which is known only by its interaction with you or something. Each such little furred life is then significant in its own unique way. Although each dog bears the commonality of having fur and being little and particularly familiar, no *kekwep* can ever be just a dog.

Speaking the Okanagan word for dog as "an experience" is quite different semantically from reading the English word *dog*. The English word solicits an inanimate generic symbol for all dogs, independent of action and isolated from everything else, as though a dog without context and without anything to which it is connected could really exist. It must be a frightful experience to be a dog in English.

In Okanagan, then, language is a constant replay of tiny selected pieces of movement and action that solicit a larger active movement somehow connected to you by the context you arrange for it. Times, places, and things are all made into movement, surrounding you and connected to you like the waves of a liquid stretching outward. The following excerpt from my novel *Slash* gives an example of this sense of time and place merging into one through imagery in my prose.

> She came and knelt in front of me. She took my hands and spoke my Okanagan name softly. I had a strange feeling like I did when I heard the dance songs inside my head. I felt like I was made of mist or something and I melted into the scene around me. She said in our language, "We are now more than one. We have become three. Your son will be born in the springtime when the saskatoon flowers bloom. He will be named to your side of the family."
>
> I couldn't speak. All I could do was reach out and pull her to me and rock her while the feeling washed over us. I knew she felt it. Somewhere in my head, I saw us from another point of view, just a little above us, like through clear glass. I saw us kneeling and moving with the rhythm that flowed around us in shimmering waves, then we grew smaller and smaller until we were just a speck on top of that mountain and our land was vast and spread out around us, like a multicolored star quilt.[1]

In the Okanagan language, perception of the way reality occurs is very different from that solicited by the English language. Reality is very much like a story: it is easily changeable and transformative with each speaker. Reality in that way becomes very potent with animation and life. It is experienced as an always malleable reality within which you are like an attendant at a vast symphony surrounding you, a symphony in which, at times, you are the conductor.

---

1 *Slash* (Penticton, BC: Theytus Books, 1985).

Fluent speakers of both English and indigenous languages sometimes experience a separation of the two realities. I have experienced this separation, and it has fascinated me since my formative years as a learning storyteller and later as an interpreter for my elders at ceremonial and political gatherings. My concern as a writer has been to find or construct bridges between the two realities.

In the use of English words, I attempt to construct a similar sense of movement and rhythm through sound patterns. I listen to sounds that words make in English and try to find the sounds that will move the image making, whether in poetry or prose, closer to the Okanagan reality. I try, as in the example below, to create the fluid movement of sounds together with images in a fashion that to me resembles closely the sounds of the Okanagan.

Tonight, I sit up here at the Flint Rock and look down to the thousands of lights spread out in the distance where the town is creeping incessantly up the hillsides.

Across the Okanagan valley the sun begins to set. Blazes of mars-red tinged with deep purple and crimson brush silvery clouds and touch the mountain tops. The wind moans through the swaying pines as coyotes shrill their songs to each other the gathering dusk. Long, yellow grasses bend and whip their blades across cactus, sand and sage.[1]

In North American colloquial English, I have found some of the rhythms I search for. I find them more abundant in Rez English, so I often use Rez English in the prose I write, as in this example from "This Is a Story":

Actually Kyoti himself was getting pretty sick and gaunt from eating stuff that didn't taste or look like food. Especially real food like fresh salmon. But the headman would just shake his head and say, "Get out of here, Kyoti. Your kind of talk is just bullshit. If you say them things, people will get riled up and they might start to raise hell. They might even try to do something stupid like break the dams."[2]

Okanagan Rez English has a structural quality syntactically and semantically closer to the way the Okanagan language is arranged. I believe that Rez English from any part of the country, if examined, will display the sound and syntax patterns of the indigenous language of that area and subsequently the sounds that the landscape

---

1 Ibid.
2 *All My Relations: An Anthology of Contemporary Canadian Native Fiction*, ed. Thomas King (Toronto: McClelland and Stewart, 1990).

speaks. I believe it will also display, through its altered syntax, semantic differences reflecting the view of reality embedded in the culture.

An example is the Rez English semantic pattern that subverts and alters the rigid sequential time sense compelled by the way the English language grammatically isolates verb tense. Standard English structures a sentence like this: Trevor walked often to the spring to think and to be alone. Rez English would be more comfortable with a structure like this: Trevor's always walking to the spring for thinking and being alone. The Rez style creates a semantic difference that allows for a fluid movement between past, present, and future.

Another example is the way spoken Rez English often seeks to supplant a divisive disposition in human interaction revealed in English grammar through the designation of gender-based pronouns. Mother-tongue speakers of Okanagan experience great difficulty in the use of the gender-based pronouns. They most often seek to leave them out. An example of spoken Rez English that seeks a balance would be structured something like this: Mary was talking with Tommy about the balky car and then the talking was on how to fix it. In English this would be: Mary spoke to Tommy about the balky car, and then she talked with him about how it could be fixed.

In Okanagan storytelling, the ability to move the audience back and forth between the present reality and the story reality relies heavily on the fluidity of time sense that the language offers. In particular, stories that are used for teaching must be inclusive of the past, present, and future, as well as the current or contemporary moment and the story reality, without losing context and coherence while maintaining the drama. There must be no doubt that the story is about the present and the future and the past, and that the story was going on for a long time and is going on continuously, and that the words are only mirror-imaging it having happened and while it is happening.

I concern myself with how to capture and express that fluidity in my writing. I have found a serious lack of fluidity in English grammatical structure. Perhaps here may be found the root of the phenomenon that gives rise to the discussion about linear and nonlinear reality.

My writing in English is a continuous battle against the rigidity in English, and I revel in the discoveries I make in constructing new ways to circumvent such invasive imperialism upon my tongue.

Kateri Akiwenzie-Damm

"Erotica, Indigenous Style"

Kateri Akiwenzie-Damm is an Ojibway poet, editor, and publisher born in Toronto with roots to the Nawash First Nation at Neyaashiinigmiing (the Cape Croker Reserve). Educated at York University and the University of Ottawa, she is known for writing some of the earliest essays on Indigenous literature in Canada. She is the author of a collection of poetry, *my heart is a stray bullet* (1994), and two poetry and music CDs, and has been published internationally. She is best known as editor and publisher of Kegedonce Press, the Indigenous publishing house she established in 1993, which has gone on to publish award-winning authors such as Richard Van Camp, Basil Johnston, and Gregory Scofield.

Kateri Akiwenzie-Damm's playful and seminal essay, "Erotica, Indigenous Style," is indicative of her early interest in erotic expression—or rather the lack of it—in contemporary Indigenous literary arts in Canada, the USA, Australia, and Aotearoa (New Zealand), and the implications of this phenomenon. Her essay uses a comparative approach to link erotic expression to healthy Indigenous sexuality, and culture in general, and conversely the lack of it to colonization and genocide. Heartened by writers such as Metis poet Gregory Scofield and Creek poet Joy Harjo, who have both explored the subject, Akiwenzie-Damm says that to be part of the movement is to consider "the huge and vast array of issues that surround it." Like Qwo-Li Driskill's "Stolen from Our Bodies," Akiwenzie-Damm's essay contends that a healthy sexuality is indicative of political empowerment.

Akiwenzie-Damm, Kateri. "Erotica, Indigenous Style." *Journal of Canadian Studies* 35.3 (September 2000): 97–104.

Erotica, Indigenous Style

"Many artists recognize that stories of the erotic have long been the source of inspiration and renewal in their communities."

—Lee-Ann Martin[1]

Sex in the First Person

About five years ago, I started thinking about sex. Seriously. I mean, I started thinking seriously about sex, about sexuality and about the utter lack of it in Indigenous writing. Or so it seemed to me. I've since realized that, of course, there was some erotic writing by Indigenous writers around—it just took some searching. A lot of searching. Too much searching. A person could reach puberty, live her entire adult life, go through menopause and still not have stumbled across a single erotic poem or story by a First Nations writer. Or, to make it even more depressing, I realized one could live and die as an Indigenous person and not come across a single erotic poem or story by an Indigenous writer from Canada, the United States, Australia, Aotearoa (aka New Zealand).... I know, I looked. And while I didn't quite reach menopause before I found some, in a sense I cheated—I asked Indigenous writers to send erotica to me and I started writing it myself.

What Is Indigenous Erotica?

Indigenous erotica is political. It's also many other things, of course. It's stimulating, inspiring, beautiful, sometimes explicit. It's written by Indigenous writers, painted by Indigenous painters, filmed by Indigenous filmmakers, photographed by Indigenous photographers. But, for better or worse, because of the societies surrounding us, it, like everything else we do, is political. When one asks "what is Indigenous literature?" it's a political question and the answer is political regardless of one's personal politics. Until now, it wouldn't have occurred to most people that Indigenous literature could encompass not only "protest" literature, creative non-fiction, biography, autobiography, poetry, drama, fiction and various forms of storytelling but erotica as well. Somehow erotica was separated, excluded to the point that for the most part, we didn't even think of it. Yet, we know that our teachings and our perspectives as Indigenous peoples are inclusive and holistic. We know that "First

Nations languages contain numerous words, stories and jokes depicting sexuality and the erotic as an important, and frequently humourous, aspect of life, love and spirituality."[2] All the more strange, therefore, that this aspect of our creative cultural and personal expression should be so absent.

Jo-Anne Grace, a Maori friend in Aotearoa who is a weaver and student in an arts program at a Maori university, tells me that many of the old waiata (or chants) were beautifully "erotic" and that the erotic was so much integrated into life and arts and song that these waiata or songs were not considered at all shocking or even different, despite their explicitness. This, as I understand it, is similar to the attitudes and traditions of the Anishnaabek and other First Nations and Inuit in North America. Old-time stories included all aspects of life, and sexuality was certainly not excluded. It was an accepted aspect of life. Another friend, Haunani-Kay Trask, a Native Hawaiian poet and leader in the Hawaiian sovereignty movement, once told me that for Native Hawaiians, the world is eroticized: often food, the land and all elements of the natural world are eroticized in Native Hawaiian song and poetry. Certainly this is evident in Haunani's poetry. In Indigenous societies like the Anishnaabe, the earth and all who dwell within it contain a "manitou," a vibrant energy that is creative and procreative, and thus sexual.

So What Happened?

In my estimation, the answer is simple: colonization and genocide. When the colonizers arrived, who we are as Indigenous peoples was no longer a natural result of us living as we always had in our homelands. On the one hand, we were defined and categorized by the colonizers. Set on small parcels of land called reserves or marae or missions, we were renamed, and then those names were defined and legislated so as to separate Us from Them. On the other hand, we were beset by missionaries bent on offering us "salvation" for our sinful ways, and in their view sex was a sin, unless for procreation. This was the message of many of the missionaries.

Anyway, neither the colonizing governments with their missions of genocide and assimilation nor the missionaries with their sexually repressive dogma of "good" and "evil" cared to accept our attitudes to sexuality and certainly not any open expressions of it, cultural, artistic or creative! Certainly they didn't want us procreating. That wasn't the solution to "The Indian Problem." We were supposed to vanish, to die, not procreate, for God's sake! Miscegenation was not acceptable, it was tolerated because at least it fit in with the Master Plan of wiping us out. After a few generations of mixing our recessive genes with their dominant ones, we'd be as good as White, no problem. Besides, we were simple creatures who needed to be taught proper civilized behaviour. So a good many of our ceremonies were banned, and of course we were taught that those "erotic" songs and stories were unacceptable in a civilized society.

Why? As Joy Harjo has said, "To be 'in the erotic,' so to speak, is to be alive. Yes, eroticism presents political problems, cultural difficulties, religious problems because the dominant culture can't function with a society of alive people."[3] To deny the erotic, to create an absence of erotica, is another weapon in the oppressor's arsenal. When this part of us is dead, our future survival is in jeopardy.

So What Happened?

Well, for one thing, it seems that many of the songs were "translated" into English in a way that changed them into something more acceptable. The stories were repressed and hidden away like some dirty secret. Or they were collected and retold by people like Herbert Schwartz in *Tales from the Smokehouse*, in such a way as to be more acceptable (though still titillatingly risqué and scandalous) for a non-Native audience. As Lee-Ann Martin says, "The legacy of colonialism contributed to the collision between the worldviews of Aboriginal and Euro-Canadian communities. Eventually, many Aboriginal stories became silenced and the images invisible."[4] The stories, it seemed, were acceptable only within academic contexts, for the gaze and study of anthropologists and such. Fascinating.

Unfortunately, it seems we got the message. By the late 1980s and early 1990s, when I was working on an AIDS awareness campaign for First Nations communities in Canada, I realized that in terms of sexuality many of our communities were at least as repressive (and hypocritical) as the colonizing cultures that surround us. Though I didn't know it at the time, this was when my awareness of the sexual repression of Indigenous peoples began. Imagine trying to inform vulnerable First Nations communities of the potential onset of a health disaster like AIDS and being told that in some First Nations communities, it wasn't acceptable to discuss sex publicly. How do you inform people of the risks so they can protect themselves if you can't make any reference to sex? In retrospect, we did a lousy job of it as a result. Today AIDS is rampant in some First Nations communities, just as was predicted. So is it political? Damn right it is.

Erotic without Reservation

Since I woke up to this, I have spent more than four years collecting and editing erotica by Indigenous writers. From the outset, the intention of the project was to advance an alterNative to some of the stereotypes and misconceptions about Indigenous peoples, particularly about relationships and sexuality. Like many others, I was tired of images of Indigenous men as violent, monosyllabic studs, abusers of Indigenous women and ravishers of white women or as noble savage type shamans, warriors and chiefs. I was sickened by stereotypes of Indigenous women as promiscuous, drunken whores or sexless Mother Earth types. All of those stereotypes and images that make us less than the whole, complex, loving, sexual, spiritual beings we are.

I began to realize that there were few positive, affirming portrayals of relationships, especially romantic and sexual relationships, between Indigenous peoples in the arts or mass media, even by our own artists and communicators. Janice Acoose, in one of her essays in *Iskwewak*—"Kah' Ki Yaw Ni Wahkomakanak, Neither Indian Princess nor Easy Squaws," asks, "how stereotypical images like the Indian princess or easy squaw affect our values, beliefs, and attitudes."[5] I also began to wonder how the stereotypes, combined with the lack of realistic images, were affecting our self-image, especially in the minds of our young peoples, many of whom have dealt with violence, abuse, cultural deprivations and the forced imposition of foreign values.

It seems to me that the repression of erotic art is symptomatic of our oppression and signifies a deep psychological and spiritual break between a healthy and holistic tradition and an oppressed, repressed, shamed and imposed sense of reality. If erotic art is "a vital aspect of the human condition—of being human,"[6] then our very humanity is attacked and skewed when our erotic arts are repressed. Writing particularly about Native women, Acoose says that

> Stereotypic images of Indian princesses, squaw drudges, suffering helpless victims, tawny temptresses, or loose squaws falsify our realities and suggest in a subliminal way that those stereotypic images are us. As a consequence, those images foster cultural attitudes that encourage sexual, physical, verbal, or psychological violence against Indian women.[7]

Not only do these images affect us and our communities, they are absorbed by the societies around us and provide a sort of self-fulfilling justification of their genocidal actions on both political and social levels. Racism, violence and disrespect are so much easier when the targets of it have been dehumanized.

Eroticism is uniquely human. To deny it in any culture or individual is to deny humanity. "Erotic art determines the boundaries of sexuality that are permissible within historical and cultural categories of the aesthetic."[8] The silencing of our erotic expression says our sexuality is not "permissible," that its expression is unacceptable, that we must remain unseen and ignored, that we must accept the dehumanizing effects of being oppressed and colonized.

I, like others, absolutely refuse! The erotic must be reclaimed, expressed and celebrated as an aspect of our humanity. When I became conscious of the importance of being alive and whole in the erotic, I decided to put together an anthology of Indigenous erotica. And I began to discuss "erotica" with other Indigenous writers. I wanted to break down some of the barriers within our communities and within ourselves. How can we be healthy in a holistic way, if we are deprived this view of ourselves or if we only see ourselves portrayed as damaged and unhealthy? I don't believe we can. Overcoming this requires that we rid ourselves of the poison of those stereotypes and lies. To heal I believe that our own stories, poems and songs celebrating our erotic natures are part of the antidote. As Linda Hogan says in *Listening to the Land*:

... [W]ords have a great potential for healing, in all respects. And we have a need to learn them, to find a way to speak first the problem, the truth, against destruction, then to find a way to use language to put things back together, to live respectfully, to praise and celebrate earth, to love.[9]

We need to see images of ourselves as healthy, whole people. People who love each other and who love ourselves. People who fall in love and out of love, who have lovers, who make love, who have sex. We need to create a healthy legacy for our peoples.

The response to the anthology has been extremely enthusiastic! I have spoken to quite a few writers, many in person, to tell them about the project and why I am devoting so much time and energy to such a seemingly outrageous and potentially embarrassing pursuit. Remember, although erotica has become somewhat more mainstream in the few years since I undertook this crusade, it was not so initially. More to the point, when I started it was not at all so in the Indigenous community. There was no talk about erotica within the Indigenous community. I was determined to change this, but I was a little nervous initially that I would be laughed at or shunned. I imagined whispered conversations at Native lit gatherings filled with speculations about the real reasons I was asking people to send me erotica *nudge nudge wink wink.*

Thankfully, these small fears were unfounded. There was no laughing. Well, actually, there was a great deal of laughing but none aimed at me. No shunning. And, to the best of my knowledge, no speculating. Like the serious artists we are, we discussed it seriously. Because it is serious. There is something seriously wrong when sexuality and erotic expression are repressed. In an individual person, it might raise a few eyebrows. Amongst a whole people, it raises a red flag. Amongst Indigenous peoples from various parts of the world, it raises serious concerns with huge implications about our futures.

What is interesting (though not surprising) is that the underlying political aspect of Indigenous erotica was a reality that virtually everyone I spoke with seemed to recognize immediately. Although I was prepared to explain the deeper significance of my undertaking, it was unnecessary. As in so many cases when Indigenous peoples speak with each other, there was an unspoken understanding of our situation that did not require explanations. Nevertheless, I did have some wonderful discussions and conversations with other Indigenous artists and writers including Lee-Ann Martin, Jo-Anne Grace, Haunani-Kay Trask, Joy Harjo, Sherman Alexie, Richard Van Camp, Morgan Wood, Geary Hobson, Melissa Lucashenko, Armand Ruffo, Briar Grace-Smith, Beth Cuthand, Joseph Bruchac and many others. Engaging in these discussions has been one of the most inspiring, gratifying, worthwhile and fun aspects of this quest.

Defining the Ineffable

So what is Indigenous erotica? From the outset, in my discussions and in collecting material for an anthology, I resisted defining "erotica" as I prefer to allow the writers and their work to define their terms using their own aesthetics and cultural perspectives. This is also what I have chosen to do in my own work. To rediscover the erotic voice. To give voice to the erotic, the loving, the sexual, the repressed, the oppressed, the "dirty," outrageous, intimacies of womanhood and sexuality that had only been hinted at in my earlier work. With the anthology, I was interested in providing the opportunity, or at least the catalyst, for other writers and artists to consider the erotic and what it means for us, as writers from specific cultures and homelands, with our own artistic, cultural and literary traditions.

To be so much a part of the movement to look at erotica and, consequently, the vast array of issues that surround it, is a gratifying and passionate pursuit. Because I see very clearly that this is a huge political statement. To reclaim and express our sexuality is part of the larger path to de-colonization and freedom.

In selecting work for the anthology, what I have looked for is well-written poetry, songs, stories, scripts, and experimental forms of writing that positively portray Indigenous sexuality and healthy sexual, romantic, loving relationships between Indigenous partners. Of special interest is original, previously unpublished work, particularly humourous pieces, fiction and international submissions. Two-spirited, gay, lesbian, bisexual and transgender submissions have been invited and welcomed. To me, diversity is important. By defining, limits are set and barriers created. By leaving it open so that we can create it together, for ourselves, is to allow our erotica to be free of those imposed boundaries. Erotica without reservation.

The result is a manuscript that is soon to be published by a Maori publisher in Aotearoa/New Zealand: *Without Reservation*.[10] The work in this collection explores erotica from the perspectives of Indigenous writers from different nations and cultures. All of the work included is superbly written, provocative and beautifully crafted. Beyond that, it is a long overdue exploration and celebration of the eros of Indigenous people.

Indigenous erotica, as the work in this collection will show, speaks about the healing nature of love, about love that celebrates us as whole people, about love that is openly sexual, sensual, emotional, and spiritual. Love, and the expression of it, is a medicine to heal the pain of oppression, hatred, lovelessness and colonization. In this collection Indigenous writers freely express themselves and their ideas about love and sexuality without being constrained by imposed moral codes or definitions.

Someday soon I hope to find the North American publisher who will join me in pushing the boundaries so that *Without Reservation* can be enjoyed and celebrated here on Turtle Island, as well. So far, though responses have been very encouraging, no one has been brave enough to take up the offer. I suspect that in part it's because those who are interested in Indigenous literature cannot see beyond their own confined definitions to understand what it means to embrace fully a collection of literary erotica. Although it might be easier to find a publisher if I dropped the word "erotica" from the subtitle, it would diminish the point and cater to the limitations that have so long constrained us. Like the works in the visual art exhibit "Exposed,"[11] these works "reject the colonial history that has hidden Aboriginal erotic images for too long... [and] reaffirm the important place of the erotic in human existence."[12]

In my own work, I believe I am finally breaking through most barriers and can write freely, without obliviously dragging along the hang ups that I acquired as an Anishnaabe woman who was raised under the Indian Act, as a Roman Catholic, without having seen an erotic story or poem by an Indigenous writer until I was in my late 20s. I can be, and have been, undaunted in giving readings where the mention that I might read some love poetry or erotic poetry produces initial shock and surprise. No worries. I enjoy it. I enjoy writing it, reading it, presenting it, talking about it. In a way, it's like sex—once you do it, it becomes a part of who you are. Just one more aspect of life, one more element of what you do.

And so the work continues because I believe passionately that when Indigenous people de-colonize ourselves we'll not only free our minds, we'll free our bodies, our spirits, our whole selves. We'll live without reservation.

Without reservation. Mashkow-aendun!

Notes

1 Lee-Ann Martin, "Reclaiming Desire," *Exposed: Aesthetics of Aboriginal Erotic Art* (Regina: The MacKenzie Art Gallery, 1999) 44.

2 Martin 36.

3 Joy Harjo, "The Spectrum of Other Languages: Interview with Bill Aull, James McGowan, Bruce Morgan, Fay Rouseff-Baker, and Cai Fitzgerald," *The Spiral of Memory: Interviews*, ed. Laura Coltelli (Ann Arbor: U of Michigan P, 1996), 108.

4 Martin 36.

5 Janice Acoose, Iskwewak: Kah' Ki Yaw Ni Wahkomakanak, *Neither Indian Princess nor Easy Squaws* (Toronto: Women's P, 1995), 49.

6 Davis, Kate. "Foreword." *Exposed: Aesthetics of Aboriginal Erotic Art.* Ed. Lee-Ann Martin. Regina: MacKenzie Art Gallery, 1999. 7.

7 Acoose 55.

8 Martin 36–37.

9 Linda Hogan, *Listening to the Land: Conversations about Nature, Culture, and Eros*, ed. Derrick Jensen (San Francisco: Sierra Club Books, 1996), 122.

10 Kateri Akiwenzie-Damm. *Without Reservation: Indigenous Erotica* (Neyaashi-inigmiing, Cape Croker: Kegedonce, 2003).

11 *Exposed: Aesthetics of Aboriginal Art* (Regina: Mackenzie Art Gallery, 2000).

12 Martin 44.

Neal McLeod

"Coming Home through Stories"

Neal McLeod is a Cree-Swedish multilingual poet, artist, and scholar who has taught literature and Indigenous studies at First Nations University in Regina, and at Trent University in Peterborough. Raised on the James Smith Cree First Nation reserve in Saskatchewan, McLeod grew up in a multi-lingual household and has studied at both the University of Saskatchewan and the Umea Konsthogskola—Academy of Fine Arts—in Umea, Sweden. In addition to his academic work, McLeod has two books of poetry to his credit and has exhibited his paintings widely. His knowledge of Cree language, land, and culture informs all of his work. His latest book is the groundbreaking *Indigenous Poetics in Canada* (2014).

McLeod's seminal 2001 essay, "Coming Home through Stories," is one of the first texts in Canada to discuss Indigenous displacement from traditional lands in terms of diaspora. Using examples of Cree stories from his own family, McLeod demonstrates how it is possible to keep culture and home alive through stories, which act as a form of resistance. He also discusses renowned Chippewa (Ojibway) writer and scholar Gerald Vizenor's theory of "trickster hermeneutics," which describes how trickster stories are a form of "passive resistance." Picking up on a topic that was just starting to become prevalent, McLeod concludes by describing the term "hybrid" not in negative terms, but rather positively, describing how "hybridization" modifies the culture of the colonizer to suit Indigenous cultures. The hybridity that he describes strengthens Cree culture rather than weakening it, thus problematizing arguments that suggest that a traditional, stagnant culture is the only "authentic" culture.

McLeod, Neal. "Coming Home through Stories." (*Ad*)*Dressing Our Words: Aboriginal Perspectives on Aboriginal Literatures*. Ed. Armand Garnet Ruffo. Penticton: Theytus Books, 2001. 17–36.

Coming Home through Stories

Dwelling in the Familiar

"To be home" means to dwell within the landscape of the familiar, a landscape of collective memories; it is an oppositional concept to being in exile. "Being home" means to be a nation, to have access to land, to be able to raise your own children, and to have political control. It involves having a collective sense of dignity. In a post-colonial situation, in the subversion of the stories by the colonizer, one is able to reassert one's narratives. A collective memory emerges from a specific location, spatially and temporally, and includes such things as a relationship to land, songs, ceremonies, language and stories. Language grounds *Nehiyâwiwin* (Creeness). To tell a story is to link, in the moments of telling, the past to the present, and the present to the past.

My *Nicapân* (great-grandfather) Peter Vandall used to tell stories of his uncle Big John and the Northwest Resistance of 1885. His stories were about surviving and remembering. Part of surviving is through remembrance: when you remember, you know your place in creation. Keith Basso in *Wisdom Sits in Places* uses the example of the Western Apache to discuss the importance of the relationship between narrative and space. While he notes the importance of earlier writers that discussed the importance of place names, such as Boas and Sapir (Basso 43), he extends earlier writing by showing that the narrative is an ongoing, organic activity. Basso speaks of narrative as a "spatial anchor" (91). In his view, space is more important in understanding the Apache than time. It is through memory, which is located in the landscape, that people are able to situate themselves in the world: "the meaning of landscape and acts of speech are personalized manifestations of a shared perspective on the human condition" (Basso 73).

Thus narrative memory, according to Basso, situates understanding through an interconnection between space, memory and ancestor. Essentially, Apache memory is the building of stories upon one another, and the accumulation of meaning and interpretation. Wisdom in Basso's account emerges from this layering process. Basso writes:

> The commemorative place-names, accompanied by their stories, continue to accumulate, each one marking the site of some sad or tragic event from which valuable lessons can be readily drawn and taken fast to heart. (28)

Over a period of time the stories become internalized by the individual, and there is a dialectical play between tradition and the present, between individual and collective memory. Basso writes:

> For the place-maker's main objective is to speak the past into being, to summon it with words and give it dramatic form, to produce experience by forging ancestral worlds in which others can participate and readily lose themselves. (ibid: 33)

In this context narratives are thus essentially maps which emerge out of a relationship to a specific area, whereas wisdom emerges from voice and memory within that landscape. Basso notes that the process of narration is as though "the ancestors were speaking to you directly, the knowledge the stones contain. Bring this knowledge to bear on your disturbing situation…" (ibid: 91). The culmination of wisdom, then, is "extremely personal" as the past is understood as a function of a person's life experience (ibid: 32), and as it used to make sense of life and to live a good life.

Diaspora

Often when one group becomes dominated by another, the dominated group tends to lose some of its narratives; history shows that the dominator imposes its narratives upon the dominated group. To describe the two groups in this dynamic I will use the term colonizer for the group that has power, and I will use the term colonized for the group which is dominated. These terms are by no means static, as many Indigenous groups which were later dominated by Europeans, were themselves colonizers in their own right. The Cree (*Nêhiyawak*), for instance, displaced other groups such as the Blackfoot and Dene in their territorial expansion of the late seventeenth to the first half of the nineteenth century.

However, while it is important to note that the *Nêhiyawak* were themselves a colonizing power at one time, the imposition of English rule altered our lives. English control over Cree territory, especially after *ê-mâyihkamikahk* ("where it went wrong"/The Northwest Resistance) of 1885, radically altered Cree ability to govern ourselves and to perpetuate our stories. The English through a systematic process attempted to alienate *Nêhiyawak* from our land and in turn alienate us from our collective traditions.

I will argue that the process of alienation occurred in two interrelated ways (and these were concurrent). First, the English gradually alienated *Nêhiyawak* from our land, a process which was accelerated with the Fur Trade winding down and also through the Treaty process (which was accompanied by increased settlement). Second, the English alienated *Nêhiyawak* from our stories and languages, and set up coercive legislation in regards to our religious ceremonies. These ceremonies were outlawed in the *Indian Act* (Section 114) and mandatory attendance to residential schools was imposed.

I define the removal of an Indigenous group, in this case the *Nêhiyawak*, from their land as *spatial diaspora*. Once *Nêhiyawak* were removed from their land and put on reserves, there was a gradual decay of the "spatial anchor" (in which *Nêhiyawak* had grounded themselves. I call the alienation from one's stories *ideological diaspora*: this alienation, the removal from the voices and echoes of the ancestors, is the attempt to destroy collective consciousness. Undoubtedly, spatial diaspora and ideological diaspora are interrelated. Both aspects of diaspora, as I have defined them, emerge from a colonial presence.

In contrast to "being home," diaspora is the process of being alienated from the collective memory of one's people. *Nêhiyawak* have been forced into diaspora in two overlapping senses: spatial and ideological. Canada has often been the land where people from around the world have come to avoid persecution and oppression in their homelands; it is my contention, however, that Indigenous people within Canada have also been placed into a state of exile within this country.

I will use the term *ideological home* to refer to the interpretative location of a people. An ideological home provides people with an Indigenous location to begin discourse, to tell stories and to live life on their own terms. An ideological home is a layering of generations of stories, and the culmination of storyteller after story-teller, in a long chain of transmission. To be home, in an ideological sense, means to dwell in the landscape of the familiar, collective memories, as opposed to being in exile. "Being home" means to be part of a larger group, a collective conscious-ness; it involves having a personal sense of dignity. Furthermore, an ideological home, housed in collective memory, emerges from a specific location, spatially and temporally. An ideological home needs to have a spatial, temporal home as well.

Narrative Maps

I believe that *Nehiyâwiwin* (Creeness) developed organically and will continue to develop if people choose to take the time to learn the stories and the language. How-ever, some people such as Simon During argue against the organic development of the traditions of colonized people. During describes the post-cultural as a state of being where the "'cultural' products are not essentially bound to the life-world that produced them" (36–37). During seems to imply that attempts at recovering stories and a narrative home, essentially the attempt to move beyond the domination of the mainstream culture, are bound to fail because they are intertwined with the discourse of the colonizers.

The process of "coming home" through stories could be thought of as the expe-rience of discerning the liminal space between Cree culture and the mainstream society. There are discursive differences between the colonized and the colonizer as they are embedded within different interpretative vantage points. The "'reality' represented...by the map not only conforms to a particular version of the world but to a version which is specifically designed to empower its makers" (118).

Trickster-Treaty Stories

It is my contention that spatial diaspora occurred first and was followed by an ideological diaspora. Frizzly Bear, an Elder from the Onion Lake Reserve in Saskatchewan, described the spatial sense of diaspora as was prophesied by the old people: "[y]ou won't be able to stop anywhere on your journeys because there will be a steel rope everywhere" (Frizzly Bear 1976). The steel rope would cut the land into different sections with a grid imposed upon the landscape. Bear noted that he thought that the "steel rope...is the wire they use for fencing" (ibid). Through the process of "fencing" the land, *Nêhiyawak* (the Cree) were marginalized. The first type of diaspora (spatial) had thus occurred.

However, despite an encroaching colonial presence, there were leaders who resisted the impending diaspora (in both senses of the word as I have defined it). Some of the strongest leaders of this resistance were *Mistahi Maskwa* (Big Bear), *Minahikosis* (Little Pine) and *Payipwât* (Piapot). There are many stories of resistance to the new colonial order. There is a story of Indigenous resistance to colonial power that was told to *Nimosôm* (my grandfather) by an Elder in Saskatchewan:

> One of the Queen's representatives had come to negotiate with the Indians. His aides treated him very grandly and even had a chair for him to sit on. A cloth was spread on the ground and several bags of money were placed on it. The representative explained through an interpreter how many bags of money the Queen had sent. [A Chief] was told this and said, "Tell the Queen's representative to empty the money and fill the bags with dirt. Tell him to take the bags back to England to the Queen. She has paid for that much land." (McLeod 1975: 6)

The story illustrates the irony in the encounter of two worldviews. In this story, the chief, *Kawâhkatos* (Lean Man), questioned the imposition of the Treaty in the context of his own worldview and his concept of the land. To use Vizenor's terminology, the story bespeaks of a Trickster encounter (1994). The Trickster-Treaty story is about transforming assumptions: *Kawâhkatos* understood his life through the stories and the concrete world around him, whereas the Treaty commissioner understood the world (at least the Treaty) within the perspective of a written legal agreement.

Another humorous resistance story exists of the Treaties. Unfortunately, the storyteller was not recorded when it was transcribed:

> So I'm going to tell a story about this woman who was kind of spry. She knew five dollars wasn't enough [amount of Treaty annuity]. So she got this notion to get herself pregnant as she'd get paid in advance. She put a pillow under her skirt; so she walked up the paymaster. When he saw her he said, "So you're pregnant. Then we'll have to pay you an extra five dollars in advance." When

she received her money she fumbled a dollar bill on to the floor, then she bent down to pick it up. Her string bust, and she had a miscarriage; her pillow fell out. So this was the end of advances on pregnant women. They have to be born before they receive $5.00. This is the little story that I wanted to tell. (*Indian Film History Project*, IH 427)

The story is a manifestation of a hermeneutical encounter between the new colonial order and *Nêhiyawak*: the story, while humorous, is one of resisting the imposition of Treaty and of the reserve system. Despite having to live on reserves, *Nêhiyawak* had the power of passive resistance. Stories, such as the ones above, in the spirit of the Trickster, seek to transform the circumstances that the people were living in.

Vizenor's notion of "trickster hermeneutics" is very similar to Bhabha's notion of "space of translation" (Vizenor 1994: 25). There is a need for "discursive space" to mediate these two worlds and sets of knowledge and experience. Bhabha calls such a place "a place of hybridity" (25) and offers many insights in regards to how colonized people make attempts to survive changes to their life-worlds. The strength of his position is that he does not see the various cultures as victims, but rather celebrates their ability to recreate themselves in the face of new circumstances. The attempt to move beyond the limitations of colonial discourse is indeed the process behind Trickster-Treaty stories.

My uncle, Burton Vandall, once told me yet another Trickster-Treaty story. At Treaty payment time, people would borrow children from other families. They would walk up to the paymaster, who was handing out Treaty annuity payments, over and over again; everyone would take turn using the same children. Eventually, the paymaster caught on, and he started to paint a mark on the faces of the kids once they got their first and "final" payments.

Spatial Diaspora

The effects of spatial diaspora are devastating upon Indigenous people, and this condition of alienation exists both in our hearts (ideological diaspora) and in our physical alienation from the land (physical diaspora). Exile involves moving away from the familiar into a new set of circumstances.

Caribbean writer George Lamming, who lived for many years in England, writes of the process of diaspora:

We are made to feel a sense of exile by our inadequacy and our irrelevance of function in a society whose past we can't alter, and whose future is beyond us. (12)

To be in exile, at least on one level, is to live a disjointed life. In this state, the discourse and the physical reality surrounding this discourse are imposed upon the people thrown into diaspora. Yet, the person in exile has no control over this imposed national discourse and corresponding material reality. To live in exile, to live in diaspora, is to have the difficult task of keeping one's dignity, one's story, in the face of the onslaught of a colonial power.

The process of diaspora for *Nêhiyawak* (the Cree) began in the 1870s when the British Crown extended its influence into western Canada through a Treaty process. In the period after the Treaties, 1878–1885, all of the major *Nêhiyawak* chiefs on the Canadian prairies had taken Treaty. Minahikosis (Little Pine) took Treaty in 1879 and Mistahi Maskwa (Big Bear) in 1882. By this time, *Nêhiyawak* were starving, and the buffalo, their lifeblood, had vanished from the land. The diaspora was an alienation and a removal from the land. *Nêhiyawi* life-world foundations were under siege, and the ability to perpetuate *Nehiyâwiwin* (Creeness) was greatly undermined. The Treaties and the incursions of Europeans upon the Plains transformed the land: a new, colonial order had been imposed.

New Order Upon the Land

My great-grandfather, *Kôkôcîs* (Cree nickname for Peter Vandall) himself lived at the crossroads of great historical and social change, and he had the fortune of being able to sit with people who had experienced the changes of the 1870s and 1880s first hand. *Kôkôcîs* spoke of how during the time of these upheavals, the buffalo used to go to Redberry Lake, which is south of the Sandy Lake Reserve. He said that the buffalo would go out on the lake when the ice was thin. There would be thousands of them in long lines. The buffalo would then drown in the lake. My great-grandfather used the expression *ê-mistapêsocik*. The expression could be translated as "they drowned themselves." It was reasoned that they drowned themselves because the order of the land had been transformed. Instead of being able to roam the land freely, the buffalo, like the Native people, were being increasingly confined to smaller and smaller areas. It was as though the whole order of the landscape was radically changing. A word that I have heard to describe this time of massive change is *pâstahowin*. This word could perhaps be translated as "transgression" or perhaps as "when one does something wrong it comes back to them." The word was used to refer to the way in which the changes brought about by Europeans had caused the various animals and spirit beings to retreat into the earth.

Despite the efforts of *Nêhiyawak* to resist the colonial presence, the events of 1885 strengthened the colonial grip on *Nêhiyâwaskiy* (Cree territory). Because of frustration with the government, coupled with mass starvation, events culminated in the violence in 1885. Different armed conflicts, such as at Frenchman's Butt, Cutknife Hill and Batoche, broke out between Indigenous people and Canadians. In speaking of 1885, Edward Ahenakew, a Cree clergyman and for a time political activist, spoke of the "scars [that] remain in our relationship with the white man" (71). After the troubles, the Canadians exercised their domination of the new region: they were able to impose the new, colonial order and met with markedly decreased resistance. The

Cree word for all of the events of 1885 is *ê-mâyihkamikahk* "where it went wrong"; *ê-mâyihkamikahk* represents the culmination or spatial diaspora.

One of the strategies used to deal with the imposition of a colonial order is the creation of discourse within a liminal space. It is the testing of discourse and narration, the attempt to try to find the possibilities which could emerge in the face of changing circumstances. Bhabha uses the term "poetics of exile" (5) to refer to the liminal space between the colonized culture and the culture of the larger power. The space-in-between is where people make sense of their worlds; it is the location wherein they situate their consciousness, in the space wherein they try to make sense of their world. Indeed, this is the situation the Cree people were facing after 1885: the world had radically changed, and would change even more, and the collective discursive action of the Cree would reflect this.

Hybridity and Survivance

There is a trend in contemporary Indigenous discourse to create a bi-polar differentiation between colonizer and colonized: within this creation of a discursive dichotomy, the past is sometimes romanticized. Such a romanticization of the past distorts the experiences of those who lived through these times of change, and distorts present realities as well.

One reason that there was a shift in religion is due to the fact that there was widespread use of bad medicine during the time of the 1870s and 1880s. People saw how some were using the old plants and rituals to harm other people. Oftentimes people would use these powers to harm someone perhaps due to jealousy or perhaps due to anger. There was a story of Chief *Atâkahkohp* who had an encounter with a strong Swampy Cree medicine. The Swampy Cree medicine man tried to use medicine on *Atâkahkohp*; the chief in turn had to use medicine to defend himself. Edward Ahenakew notes: "...Ah-tah-ka-hoop was high in the secret society of medicine men..." (1995: 97). *Atâkahkohp* then "sang a song and chanted words that the others could not understand" (97). This song then subdued the old man and all of his negative energy fell back on himself. The Cree word to describe this is "*pâstâhowin*."

There are other stories along this line. For instance, Andrew Ahenakew notes: "There are some things about Indian custom that are not nice. Medicine Men and Cultural Doctors were the boss of people. They were taught some of the medicine that was nice, but they had some of these bad medicines" (1976). He then adds: "An old man told me once when I was visiting him, 'We were given our Indian custom ever since we've lived, to pass from generation to generation, but these old men are using these things, like medicine and visions, in the wrong way. They should use the medicine right—it was for a good purpose" (1976). Thus, Andrew Ahenakew thinks that one of the reasons why the customs were fading is that people were misusing tradition.

In the spirit of Trickster hermeneutics, one of my ancestors, Big John, adopted elements of the colonial presence and transformed them to subvert them. He was a successful farmer on the Sandy Lake Reserve in Saskatchewan, and he taught my great-grandfather *Kôkôcîs* (Peter Vandall) how to farm. In addition to being a successful farmer, and despite the difficulties many Indigenous farmers faced during this transitional time, Big John was also a photographer; Metis author Maria Campbell told me that he had a darkroom in his basement. He had a Bible in Cree syllabics which he read regularly; I have handled this book myself many times. While he adopted a hybridized form of Christianity and adopted elements of modern technology such as the camera, he was still a Cree. In the face of colonial pressure, one can struggle to retain an Indigenous identity through a process of "hybridization" (Bhabha 35). The narratives of the colonizer can be subverted through a shifting of interpretative reality and space.

In addition to being influenced by his uncle Big John, *Kôkôcîs* was heavily influenced by his grandfather, *Wîcihkos* [diminutive form of *Wîtihkokân*]. The way in which *Kôkôcîs* negotiated between the world of Christianity and the world of traditional Dene/Cree hunting beliefs is certainly an example of what Vizenor calls Trickster hermeneutics and what Bhabha calls hybridity. My great-grandfather wove the narratives of Cree/Dene hunting beliefs with those of Christianity and tried to find new ways of applying old concepts in light of new situations. While *Wîtihkokân* used dreams and intuition, Big John, his son, learned to use some of these techniques as well, but only in a new context. My father noted: "He really believed in God. Those old people who raised him talked to him about God" (McLeod 2000).

There is an interesting story of how *Wîtihkokân* would go into the Church. The word that he would say was "*sah-sîciwisiwak*. He was sitting in church and this man was preaching. He used to go there and smoke his pipe and listen. Mostly he went because the Minister at the time used to invite him. He tried to solicit him to turn to Christianity. Out of the kindness of his heart he [*Wîcihkos*] used to go to listen and smoke his pipe. He couldn't understand why they would talk about Jesus, that they would save human beings yet they killed him. He used to think they were afraid that they killed him and that they would be punished. He used to think these people were afraid" (McLeod 2000). *Kôkôcîs* was raised by this old hunter who, while curious about Christianity, saw contradictions in it, and saw how it was used to scare people.

Big John, the son of *Wîtihkokân*, was important because he represented the transitional period when people were moving from agriculture to farming. My father noted: "At the time when people were forced to move on to the reserves he adapted quite rapidly" (McLeod 2000). My father shared the following narrative with me regarding Big John: "he used to look at the soil and he could tell by its texture how fluffed up it was, the colour of it was grey-light, it was worked properly. It had to do with circulating the soil once a year. He used to plough his land about six inches deep . . . no deeper than that. He would do this every year so the soil kept circulating. He studied the texture to see how much fibre there was in it. It was almost like he could feel the land." (McLeod 2000)

Big John left the earth during the sickness of 1918, the person who had bravely helped negotiate a new narrative space for Cree consciousness through his actions, farming and photography. Maureen Lux notes that "50,000 Canadians died from influenza" (4) and adds: "During the epidemic the Royal Canadian Mounted Police (RCMP) were sent to reserves to enforce strict quarantines, preventing Native people from leaving reserves" (ibid: 10). The sickness had a large impact upon the people.

Despite the shifts that were occurring in the peoples' lives, they still relied a great deal on older ways of doing things, including traditional medicinal practices. People in my family have told me that people from all over would come to see *Kwêcic* in order to get medicine for a variety of things. I have heard that people from Montana would come to see her in order to get plants to help with various illnesses. She never had children, but did raise *Kôkôcîs* for a period of time after the death of his natural mother. *Kwêcic* died when I was about seven or eight at the age of about 110.

Slowly but surely there was a shift from traditional healing to modern healing techniques; I think that one has to be careful about ascribing causation. I do not think that one can say it was simply the shift to Christianity and farming that brought about the change. With increased hospital availability people began to frequent them more often and gradually the old techniques fell out of use. I think that it would be possible to draw a comparison to the changes that occurred in the field of education, the replacement of old pedagogical techniques with new ones.

Diaspora Story
Kôkôcîs (my great-grandfather/Peter Vandall) told this story at *Nôhkom's* (my grandmother's) funeral. It is also recorded in *The Stories of the House People* (Vandall 1987). *Kôkôcîs* opens the story:

> *aya, ê-kî-âcimostawit ôtê ohci kihci-môhkomâninâhk-nitâ-têminânak êkotê itâ-mowak ôta kâ-mâyahkamikahk-êkwa, êwako awa pêyak nisis aya, kî-pê-takotêw tânitahtw-âskiy aspin ôma otâhk*

> It was told to me by a man from the United States—friends of ours had fled there at the time of *ê-mâyihkamikahk*—and this one was my uncle, he had come back a few years ago. (Vandall 65)

It was through the storytelling that his uncle came home from the exile caused by *ê-mâyihkamikahk*: he had managed, through stories, and the humour of the stories, to preserve his dignity as a *Nêhiyaw* person. Furthermore, it is through these stories that these people attempted to find a way home. *Kôkôcîs* reported that his uncle said, "I do not have much to give you, but I will give this story, my nephew."

The story is about a man who went fishing. This man liked to drink and was sipping whiskey while he was fishing. He needed bait and saw a snake with a frog in its mouth. The man took the frog out of the snake's mouth, but he had pity on the snake: he knew that the snake was as hungry as he was. This man, after having taken the frog, gave the snake some whiskey in exchange. The snake, after a while, came back with another frog to trade for a drink.

This uncle of *Kôkôcîs* had fled during the troubled times: he was forced into exile because he had made a stand for his rights and dignity. The story was given to *Kôkôcîs* and was an important element of his repertoire. The story speaks of being generous and of having pity on those with less power; it talks about the changes which were emerging, and the effort that the people were engaged in trying to negotiate this emerging space.

Old Man *Kiyâm*

The process of diaspora involves both physical and spiritual enclosement. It is the move away from the familiar towards a new alien "space." This new space attempts to transform and mutate pre-existing narratives and social structures. It was not only the old people who were imprisoned and put into diaspora, but also those who went through the residential school system. Bhabha writes: "The social articulation of difference, from the minority perspective, is a complex, on-going negotiation that seeks to authorize cultural hybridities that emerge in moments of historical transformation" (2). The story from my great-grandfather is one example of this, and so is the story of *Mistânaskowêw*. Stories are told to try to negotiate through the field of experience.

Ideological Diaspora: Residential Schools

Ideological diaspora was the internalization of being taken off the land. A central manifestation of this occurred through the residential school system, which was established as a way of "educating" Indigenous people. There were several such schools set up through western Canada, and they were operated by various Churches. Children were taken away from their homes and their communities. Instead of being taught by the old people in the traditional context, children were being taught in an alien environment which stripped them of their dignity; it was a process of cultural genocide and spiritual exile. Once put away in both an ideological and spatial sense, many children never came "home": instead they spent their lives ensnared in alcoholism and other destructive behaviours.

In the 1930s, *Nimosôm* (my grandfather) went to residential school on the Gordon Reserve which is north of Regina, Saskatchewan. At first, he was happy to go; a friend of his, Edward Burns, even remembered him clapping his hands in anticipation

(Regnier 4). He was anxious to see the world beyond the borders of the Reserve: however, his experience of the school was far from what he expected.

He came back and told his father, Abel McLeod, what was going on in the school: the beatings, the naked children and the hunger. The authorities came for my *mosôm* a second time. *Nicapân* (my great-grandfather/Abel McLeod) did not want his son to go back, but he was told by the Mounties that they would arrest his son if he resisted. The Mounties knew that *Nicapân* was a man of influence in the community, and an arrest would be difficult as the people supported him. He told the Mounties that they would also have to arrest him. He could not let them take his son again. They subsequently used force to take my *mosôm*, a boy of twelve, who spent the next three nights in jail cells throughout the province as he was taken back to the school.

This experience of residential schools exemplifies the process of ideological diaspora. Alienation from the land, political pressure and the use of force were all parts of a larger effort to destroy *Nehiyâwiwin*. The schools solidified the polarization of the entities "*Nehiyâwiwin*" (Creeness) and "Canadian." All things Cree were taken to be dangerous and not worthy to exist, whereas all things Canadian were exemplified and taken as prototypes: *Nehiyâwiwin* acted as a foil which helped to create a "Canadian" identity. The schools did much to create a sense of spiritual and ideological diaspora.

It is interesting to note how the narrative I gave of *Nimosôm* functions as a map to an old prophecy told by Frizzly Bear in 1976 (though the prophecy itself is from the late nineteenth century):

If you don't agree with him [the whiteman], he'll get up and point at you with a revolver, but he can't fire. He'll put his gun down and everything will be over. You will agree with him and what he's going to teach you is nothing that is any good for us. (Frizzly Bear 1976)

These schools were the vehicles of cultural genocide with concerted attempts to destroy language and stories. This was forced exile, the separation from the security of culture and the wisdom of the "Old Ones." The survivors of this school are modern day *okicitawak* (Worthy Men—"warriors"). Instead of fighting in the world, they fight against the memories of these schools that linger in the landscapes of their souls.

Residential schools nearly silenced *Nêhiyawak* stories forever. In "One Generation from Extinction," Basil Johnston stresses the importance of language and stories, in the context of their fragility:

Therein will be found the essence and the substance of tribal ideas, concepts, insights, attributes, values, beliefs, theories, notions, sentiments, and accounts of their institutions and rituals and ceremonies. (102)

Johnston comments on the effects of ideological diaspora, the alienation from collective memory: "With language dead and literature demeaned, 'Indian' institutions are beyond understanding and restoration" (103).

Tootoosis and Political Revival

John Tootoosis saw the brainwashing effects of the schools and the way that the Church was using its power to destroy traditional teachers in regard to the way we understood ourselves in the world. He often talked about how hard it was to organize people: "Indians weren't organized before. They were so damn dominated by the government" (Tootoosis 1977). People were seemingly unable to make decisions, as they had very little control over their lives. As Native people began to organize in the twenties and thirties, they began to break the yoke of domination; indeed, one of the central demands of Native political leaders and organizations was to end the domination of schooling by the Churches. Speaking of the League of Indians organized in the early 1920s, Tootoosis said: "The League opposed residential schools, the church wanted to dominate the people and keep the schools" (1977).

While there were severe pressures on our culture and on the people at that time, they found ways to preserve their identity and their place in the world. Stories and languages led some of the people back to their identities; it is only through our own stories that we can find true dignity and integrity in the world.

The late Wilfred Tootoosis, the oldest son of John, reflected on his experiences at residential school, and how he was singled out because of his father's activities:

I had quite an experience in school. I'd get picked on. The nuns and priests spoke against my dad's movement, everywhere, in church, in the classroom. And when somebody did something wrong they ganged up and blamed me for it...They could have had my dad shot if they had a chance to. (1999: 314)

The children of activists and spiritual leaders were often hit the hardest, and they were attacked and singled out in the schools. My father told me that the priests used to call John Tootoosis's children "communists." There are many stories of John Tootoosis and his struggle to fight for the rights of the Cree people.

Coming Home through Stories

The effects of going to school have to be understood us a radical separation with the past, as a disjunction in the daily experience of the people. People were no longer allowed to acquire language and socialization in the normal way; the economic life of the people had also changed and would in turn affect their discursive action. Bhabha calls an "unhomely moment [that] which relates the traumatic ambivalences of a personal, psychic history to the wider disjunctions of political existence" (11). He then goes on to say that "the personal is the political" (ibid); indeed, the Crees of the twentieth century became increasingly aware of the limitations that were put upon them, and the systematic attempts that were made to wipe out their culture. The effect of being in exile and the trauma associated with it are manifested in the stories told and ensuing political action.

But our battle to survive as a people certainly goes beyond the issue of residential schools. Smith Atimoyoo, one of the founders of the Saskatchewan Indian Cultural Centre, spoke of the "new arrows" that people are presently facing (23): today we have a different kind of arrow to fight for our collective existence. Here I borrow the term "wordarrows" from Gerald Vizenor (1978): words are like arrows that can be shot at the narratives of the colonial power. Wordarrows have transformative power and can help Indigenous people "come home"; wordarrows can help to establish a new discursive space. Every time a story is told, every time one word of an Indigenous language is spoken, we are resisting the destruction of our collective memory.

Stories act as the vehicles of cultural transmission by linking one generation to the next. There are many levels to the stories, and many functions to them: they link the past to the present, and allow the possibility of cultural transmission and of "coming home" in an ideological sense. Our task today is to retrieve tribal narratives and paradigms, and to reaffirm our tribal identities in the face of the overwhelming pressure of diaspora.

Despite the fact that the original colonizing power, Britain, has been reduced in influence, there is still an attempt to maintain cultural hegemony:

> through canonical assumptions about literary activity and through attitudes to post-colonial literatures which identify them as isolated natural off-shoots of English literature and which therefore relegate them to marginal and subordinate positions. (Ashcroft et al. 7)

Within this context, Cree narratives are still marginalized and kept on the periphery of Canadian consciousness. This marginalization is not only a result of canonical assumptions but also the foundation for the privileging of European narrative paradigms over Indigenous paradigms. I want to suggest that the metaphorical discursive pattern of Nêhiyawak needs to be taken into account in order to come to a complete phenomenological understanding of the history of Canada.

Finally, I would like to share a diaspora story which has been passed on to my family for one hundred years. It was told to my great-great-grand mother Kêkêhkiskwêw (Hawk Woman), then to Nimosôm (my grandfather), and then to my father Jerry McLeod. I have also heard elements of the story from Clifford Sanderson and Bill Stonestand. All of these people are from the James Smith Reserve.

There was a group of people from the Cîkâstêpêsin (Shadow in the Water) Reserve. There was a large flood on Sugar Island which is close to Birch Hills, Saskatchewan. Many people died during this flood. There was one woman who climbed up a tree with her baby; she tied a cloth around the tree and moved up the tree to escape the water. The cloth was used to hold her up there. Eventually, the flood went away, and the people left the area. Also, about eleven people from the Band had been involved in the troubles at Batoche in 1885. There were too many bad feelings associated with the land there, at Sugar Island, so they left. Some of them went to camp with the people of the James Smith Reserve. However, a group also went to the Sturgeon Lake Reserve.

The camps were close together. Back then people had pity on each other; they shared more with each other. They had pity on their fellow *Nêhiyawak*. That is why the people of *Cîkâstêpêsin* (Shadow on the Water) stayed there. There was a man who had prophecies of the *Cîkâstêpêsin* people. His name was Pîkahin Okosisa ("the son of Pîkahin"). He died about 1897, which is about 12 years after *ê-mâyihkamikahk*. My dad said that they wrapped his body up with cloths. They had a wake for him. Then, one person noticed that Pîkahin Okosisa's feet were starting to warm up, and told the others. And the man came back to life.

Pîkahin Okosisa spoke of many things. He spoke of great fires in the northern skies; also, this is what my dad told me, that there would be a great war. Pîkahin Okosisa said that families would split up more in the future. He spoke of the kind of houses that we would live in. He even foretold that people would fly in the sky. Pîkahin Okosisa saw all of these things. He also said, "My people will have good hunting near *Mêskanaw*" (a town in Saskatchewan). He lived for forty more days and then he died for good. His reserve was "surrendered" in the 1890s, but before the Christmas of 1997, a letter was received stating the government would recognize the *Cîkâstêpêsin* (Shadow on the Water) claim. This is the story of Pîkahin Okosisa as I have heard it and as it has been passed on to me.

I think of *Nehiyâwiwin* (Creeness) as a large collective body. When I was born in 1970, there were so many people who knew so many beautiful things about *Nehiyâwiwin*. As *Nêhiyawak*, when we listen and tell our stories, when we listen and hear our language, we have dignity, because we are living our lives as we should. We are living our lives on our own terms; our stories give us voice, hope and a place in the world. To tell stories is to remember. As Indigenous people, we owe it to those still unborn to remember, so that they will have a "home" in the face of diaspora.

Thus, in a sense, the process of "coming home" is an exercise in cartography; it is trying to locate the place of understanding and culture. To "come home" is to dwell in liminal space, and the process of "coming home" is not so much returning to some idealized location of interpretation: rather, it is a hermeneutical act, perhaps an act of faith. It is the attempt to link two disparate narrative locations, and to find a place, a place of speaking and narrating, wherein the experiences of the present can be understood as a function of the past. At the same time, a culture is a living organism, with many layers and levels, and there will always be a manifold of interpretations of this culture. I would argue, in a similar way to David Newhouse

(1999), the emerging forms of Aboriginal consciousness, including Cree forms, will be hybridized forms.

The metaphor of an anchor is helpful here in talking about narrative tradition. If a ship is tied to the anchor it will not rest in one spot forever. The ship will shift around, alternating locations. However, it will stay in the same general area, the same general location over a period of time. However, if the ship is cut off from that anchor, then it will drift beyond the known. For some time, the experiences will still be familiar; however, once the anchor is cut, and the ship moves beyond the familiar, narrative memory is lost forever.

To "come home" through stories is to anchor ourselves in the world. Many people, including my *mosôm*, John R. McLeod, and the great Cree leader John Tootoosis, survived the residential school experience and attempted to make sense of that experience and the world around them. While being thrown from their ideological home, through tremendous efforts, they were able to find their anchor again and to "come home" through stories and narrative memory. And because of them, we have that anchor today, and it is our time, it is our responsibility to keep that anchor, if Cree narrative memory is to survive through the coming generations.

Works Cited

Ahenakew, Andrew. (1976) *Kâtâayuk: Saskatchewan Indian Elders*. Saskatoon: Saskatchewan Indian Cultural College.

Ahenakew, Edward. (1995) *Voices of the Plains Cree*. Ed. Ruth Buck. Foreword by Stan Cuthand. Regina: Canadian Plains Research Centre.

Armstrong, Jeannette C. (1998) "The Disempowerment of First North American Native Peoples and Empowerment through Their Writing." *An Anthology of Canadian Native Literature in English*. 2nd ed. Ed. Daniel David Moses and Terry Goldie. Toronto: Oxford UP. 239–42.

Ashcroft, Bill, Gareth Griffiths and Helen Tiffin. (1993) *The Empire Writes Back: Theory and Practice in Post-Colonial Literatures*. New York: Routledge.

Atimoyoo, Smith. (1979) Proceedings of the Plains Cree Conference. Held in Fort Qu'Appelle. October 24–26, 1975. Regina: Canadian Plains Research Centre.

Basso, Keith. (1996) *Wisdom Sits in Places: Landscape and Language among the Western Apache*. Albuquerque: U of New Mexico P.

Bhabha, Homi. (1997) *The Location of Culture*. Routledge: New York.

Cruikshank, Julie. (1990) *Life Lived Like a Story*. Vancouver: U of British Columbia P.

Darnell, Regina and Michael K. Foster (eds). (1988) *Native North American: Interaction Patterns*. Hull, QC: National Museums of Canada.

Demallie, Raymond J. (1982) "The Lakota Ghost Dance: An Ethnohistorical Account." *Pacific Historical Review*. 51(2): 385–405.

Dempsey, Hugh. (1984) *Big Bear and the End of Freedom*. Lincoln: U of Nebraska P.

During, Simon. (1989) "Waiting for the Post: Some Relations between Modernity, Colonization and Writing." *Ariel: A Review of International English Literature.* 20(4): 31–61.

Dyck, Noel. (1992) "Negotiating the Indian 'Problem.'" David Miller et al. *The First Ones: Readings in Indian/Native Studies.* Piapot Reserve: Saskatchewan Indian Federated College P. 132–40.

Fenton, William N. (1998) *The Great Law and the Longhouse: A Political History of the Iroquois Confederacy.* Norman: U of Oklahoma P.

Frizzly Bear (1976) *kâtâayuk.* (Ed.) Donna Phillips, Robert Troff and Harvey White-calf. Saskatoon: Saskatchewan Indian Cultural College.

Galbraith, John S. (1982) "Appeals to the Supernatural: African and New Zealand Comparisons with the Ghost Dance." *Pacific Historical Review.* 51(2): 115–33.

Goodwill, Jean and Norma Sluman. (1984) *John Tootoosis.* Winnipeg: Pemmican Publications.

IH-427. (Sept. 1973) "Saulteaux Elders Workshop #1." Speakers are unidentified. Saskatchewan Indian Cultural College. Part of Indian Film History, housed at the Saskatchewan Indian Federated College Library.

Johnston, Basil. (1998) "One Generation from Extinction." *An Anthology of Canadian Native Literature in English.* 2nd ed. Ed. Daniel David Moses and Terry Goldie. Toronto: Oxford UP. 99–104.

Lamming, George. (1995) "The Occasion for Speaking." *The Post-Colonial Studies Reader.* Ed. Bill Ashcroft, Gareth Griffiths and Helen Tiffin. New York: Routledge. 12–17.

Lux, Maureen. (1997) "'The Bitter Flats': The 1918 Influenza Epidemic in Saskatchewan." *Saskatchewan History.* 49(1): 3–17.

Mandelbaum, David. (1994) *The Plains Cree: An Ethnographical, Historical, and Comparative Study.* Regina: Canadian Plains Research Centre.

McLeod, Jerry. (25 June 2000) Dialogue with Neal McLeod. Location: James Smith Reserve (Cree), Saskatchewan.

McLeod, John R. (11 Dec. 1975) Minutes from "Treaty Six General Meeting. Onion Lake Band Hall." Interpreter and Transcription: Anna Crowe. Onion Lake, Saskatchewan. From the private papers of John R. McLeod.

Milloy, John. (1990) *The Plains Cree.* Winnipeg: U of Manitoba P.

Pflüg, Melissa A. (1997) *Ritual and Myth in Odawa Revitalization: Reclaiming A Sovereign Place.* Foreword by Lee Irwin. Norman: Oklahoma UP.

Regnier, Robert. (1997) "John McLeod: First Nations Educator." Unpublished Paper.

Tonkin, Elizabeth. (1992) *Narrating Our Pasts: The Social Construction of Oral History.* Cambridge: Cambridge UP.

Tootoosis, John. (9 Sept. 1977) Interviewer: Murray Dobbin. Interview Location: Poundmaker Reserve. *Towards a New Past* (collection). A1178/1179. Saskatchewan Archives Board.

Tootoosis, Wilfred. (1999) *In the Words of Elders: Aboriginal Cultures in Transitions*. Ed. Peter Kulchyski, Don McCaskill, and David Newhouse. Toronto: U of Toronto P.

Vandall, Peter. (1997) *Wâskahikaniwiyiniw-âcimowina/Stories of the House People*. Ed. and trans. Freda Ahenakew. Winnipeg: U of Manitoba P.

Vansina, Jan. (1985) *Oral Tradition as History*. Madison: U of Wisconsin P.

Vizenor, Gerald. (1994) *Manifest Manners: Postindian Warriors Of Survivance*. Hanover, New England: Wesleyan UP.

———. (1978) *Wordarrows: Indians and Whites in the New Fur Trade*. Minneapolis: U of Minnesota P.

Jo-Ann Episkenew

"Socially Responsible Criticism: Aboriginal Literature, Ideology, and the Literary Canon"

Jo-Ann Episkenew is a Métis scholar and activist born in Manitoba and living in Saskatchewan. She is Professor of English at First Nations University of Canada, and is currently working as the Director of Indigenous Peoples' Health Research Centre at the University of Regina. Her role in what might seem to be two divergent fields indicates her ongoing efforts to integrate life experience and academic studies, for, as all of her work indicates, Indigenous literature reflects living, breathing experience. Drawing on her Métis background, she works in the areas of literature, trauma, healing, health, drama, and ethical scholarship. She is the author of the award-winning *Taking Back Our Spirits: Indigenous Literature, Public Policy, and Healing* (2009).

Of increasing concern in the academic industry is the danger that criticism supersede literature and become in itself the primary text. This is the subject of Episkenew's 2002 essay "Socially Responsible Criticism." In an age when competition for academic jobs and funding is fierce, there is the continual danger that non-Indigenous scholars "forget" their privilege and act out of self-interest. Episkenew argues that these scholars must be cognizant of the authority dominant society accords them and work at understanding the context surrounding the works they're examining in order to avoid destructive misinterpretations. To illustrate her point Episkenew provides concrete examples of misreadings by non-indigenous scholars intent upon ascribing texts by authors such as Leslie Marmon Silko, Maria Campbell, and Beatrice Culleton-Mosionier with western worldviews and characteristics. Episkenew argues that since Indigenous literature is not objective, criticism shouldn't claim or pretend to be, and states, "(t)o really understand the context of the literature, the scholars must leave the ivory tower and talk to Aboriginal people."

Episkenew, Jo-Ann. "Socially Responsible Criticism: Aboriginal Literature, Ideology, and the Literary Canon." *Creating Community*. Ed. Renate Eigenbrod and Jo-Ann Episkenew. Penticton, BC: Theytus Books, 2002. 51–68.

Socially Responsible Criticism: Aboriginal Literature, Ideology, and the Literary Canon

During my most cynical moments I believe that the literary canon—that collection of "great" works of literature—is merely a creation of academics looking for teachable works of literature, and publishers looking for the profits that are likely to ensue if their texts are taught in university English classes. Works of literature, then, become incorporated into the canon when a significant number of academics teach them. At some point in our development, most burgeoning academics deduce—or are told—that we must have a specialization, our "turf" if you will, an area in which we are the experts. Tenure and promotion depend on it. As a result, we look for some area of study that piques our interest and, with luck, has enough room to enable us to carve out an intellectual space for ourselves. If Shakespeare is our passion, our challenge is a large one; after all, it is hard to make a space for one's self in such an occupied area. Clearly it is easier to find a space in an area that is new and unoccupied, one like the area of Canadian Aboriginal Literature. That choice, however, brings with it its own challenges.

Unlike its relatives south of the border, writing by Canadian Aboriginal authors still occupies the literary margins of the canon. While the works of Native American authors, such as Silko, Momaday, and Erdrich, appear in every new anthology of modern American literature, the works of Canadian Aboriginal writers, especially early writers, such as Clutesi, Campbell, and Culleton, are absent. In the US, the canonized Native American writers are well-educated in a western sense and are often academics themselves. Although their works include many allusions to Native American epistemology, they are complex in a way with which academics are comfortable. Canadian Aboriginal Literature is not comfortable for many academics for a number of reasons, not the least of which include its apparent lack of academic sophistication and complexities in the conventional sense. We can find a reason for this when we examine the social and political context from which it came into being.

Although governments on both sides of the 49th parallel used education as a weapon of colonization, they wielded this weapon in different manners. Both colonial governments chose to use residential schools as a strategy to assimilate the Indians; however, in the US, many Native Americans[1] were encouraged to obtain further education—usually in the trades—after finishing boarding school. Some

Native Americans found their way into universities. The government hoped that educated Native Americans would gain employment in the cities and assimilate, thus abandoning the resource-rich reservations or selling their land to mainstream Americans. In Canada, attitudes were much different, and First Nations people were sent back to their reserves when their tenure at residential school was complete. Smaller and rarely rich in natural resources, reserve land was not coveted to the same extent. It was valued more as a place to confine First Nations people. First Nations people were typically discouraged from attempting to gain access to higher education, and Métis people were often denied access to any education at all.[2] In the unlikely event that they did gain access to a university, status Indians could lose their legal status as Indians if they received a university degree.[3] Métis and Non-status Indians' access to education was inconsistent. They were allowed to attend residential schools if there were vacancies, but forced to leave when the schools became full of status Indians.[4] If living near town, they found themselves at the mercy of the white property owners who could deny their children access to school, which they often did, especially if the Métis families did not own property.[5] Canadian Aboriginal literature reflects this history. Most early writers, therefore, were not well-educated and could not be expected to be familiar with the language of academia. Later writers, although more educated, are cognizant that many of their people are not, and so they write in a way that their works are accessible to a variety of educational levels and not solely for an academic audience.

Many academics believe that Canadian Aboriginal Literature is inferior in that it is flawed in its lack of complexity and, therefore, is not "teachable." After all, how does one handle a simple narrative when one has been trained to analyze and deconstruct complexities? Nevertheless, some academics are choosing to teach Canadian Aboriginal Literature as witnessed by the growing number of "Native Lit" sessions at mainstream academic conferences. It is only a matter of time before works of Aboriginal literature begin to appear regularly in anthologies of Canadian literature. Canadian Aboriginal Literature is knocking on the door of the Canadian literary canon, and scholars are already publishing articles about this new area. The challenge that they face is finding something to say about these seemingly uncomplicated works of literature when they have been trained to look for and analyze complexities.

Even before works of Canadian Aboriginal literature begin to make regular appearances in anthologies of Canadian Literature, articles about them have begun to form a canon of interpretations. Although scholars write ostensibly to analyze works of literature to make them better understood, we also write to refute or augment the ideas presented in the critical writings that precede ours. And so, critical works beget more critical works, and often the literary works that are their subjects often become mere examples illustrating the critical thoughts of the academics who create them. I see this happening with Canadian Aboriginal literature, and as an Aboriginal academic it concerns me.

When analyzing literary works, most scholars are very conscious that ideology is embedded in the text; what they often forget is the ideology that they bring to their reading. I use the term "ideology" to refer to those ideas and beliefs that we take so for granted that we do not hold them up for critical examination and consider them to be "just the way it is." Interpretations are grounded in this kind of ideology. It is important to note that almost all of the scholars who create these interpretations are not Aboriginal people. Most are members of the colonizer culture and, therefore, cannot possibly share the same ideology as Aboriginal people, whether they be the authors who create the literature, the people about whom they write, or the few Aboriginal students in their classes. Let me give you an example from my own experience.[6]

As an undergraduate student majoring in English, I registered in a class in literary analysis based on New Criticism. The assigned text was an anthology entitled *Literature: An Introduction to Reading and Writing*, 2nd edition, (1989), which included Leslie Marmon Silko's story "Lullaby" (1981). "Lullaby" was the topic of the first writing assignment the professor gave the class. Although I cannot remember the topic of the assignment, I can remember my grade. I received a D+/C-, which I remember vividly because it hurt my pride. At the end of the essay the professor left a note explaining that my low mark resulted from my not addressing the suicide at the end of the story. I was stunned. I had seen no suicide and asked my professor to explain. My professor, a Montreal anglophone, pointed out that when the central character Ayah, an older Dene (Navajo) woman wraps herself and her drunken husband, Chato, in a blanket, curls up beside a rock, and prepares to go to sleep she is committing suicide. The text, he said, clearly reveals that the old woman, unable to bear the weight of her tragic life, chooses death for herself and her husband. I suspected that he had heard stories of old Native people who, weary of life, walk out into the wilderness to die. If one is analyzing only the text of "Lullaby," this is a plausible interpretation. What is missing, however, is the context of both text and readers.

It is important to consider the context of "Lullaby," in that both Silko and her characters are Indigenous to the American South-West. The land that seemed so frightening and dangerous to my professor is their home. Ayah and Chato live in a hogan, a structure made out of rocks, earth, and wood, which is as much a part of the land as the cluster of rocks beside which they spent the night. It is not suicidal for them to take shelter beside these rocks and cover with their blankets; indeed, they carry blankets along with them for just such an occasion. They are old people, and despite their tragic lives, they have survived. To an Aboriginal reader, "Lullaby" is not a story of suicide; it is one of survival, albeit filled with references to the suffering that result from a lifetime of colonization and oppression.

As reader, my context differs radically from that of my professor. Although I too spent my early years in a large urban center, I moved to northern Saskatchewan as a teenager. What is a cold winter night in Arizona, would likely be a nice day in late autumn in Saskatchewan. I have lived with trappers who regularly go out on foot to check their trap lines regardless of the weather. Sometimes they sleep out in the bush—albeit by a fire—wrapped in blankets in temperatures falling below -20°C. This is how Aboriginal people who live on the land exist; this is how we have always lived. My husband grew up on a reserve near Fort Qu'Appelle in southern Saskatchewan. He tells a story of how he walked from Fort Qu'Appelle to Muscowepetung Reserve, a distance of about 40 km., one cold winter night. When he found that he was too tired to go on, he made a shelter in a farmer's field by piling bales of hay around himself. He slept there for the night and finished walking to the reserve in the morning. My brother-in-laws found it necessary to do the same thing from time to time. This land is our home, and Aboriginal people have learned to do what they must to survive. I didn't tell this to my professor, however. Somehow, at the time, I felt embarrassed to reveal that I—and my people—still live this way at the end of the 20th Century. Somehow my husband's story smacked of poverty and social problems and all the things that I was sure that my professors associated with Aboriginal people. Even worse, what if I told him and he didn't believe me? What if he accused me of telling or believing tall tales? His was the voice of authority. How could I convince him that my voice contained authority, too? So I silenced my voice, kept my knowledge to myself, and tried to always be cognizant that my professors knew nothing of Aboriginal realities. I followed the rules, tried to anticipate their objections, and wrote "objective" literary analyses that did not reflect my personal context.

Over the last few years, I have become increasingly aware that many interpretations of the works of Canadian Aboriginal Literature lack a fundamental understanding of the ideological context in which the works were written. Worse yet, because the authors of these interpretations are educated people with academic positions at prestigious universities, the general public deems their voices to be ones of authority. However, these interpretations are grounded in the ideology of the colonizer culture, not the ideology of the colonized people who are the authors and subjects of the texts being interpreted. It is important to remember that colonization is not only militaristic, economic, and political; it is also psychological, social, and spiritual.[7] No matter how well-intended, interpretations that lack a fundamental understanding of Aboriginal people as victims of colonization can inadvertently become weapons of colonization themselves because their authors' voices become the voices of authority, authority which could easily overpower the voices of Aboriginal people. That is not to say that only Aboriginal people should be interpreting and critiquing Aboriginal literature. What I am saying is that non-Aboriginal scholars need to be cognizant of the authority that society accords their voices. It is inevitable, then, that their interpretations of Aboriginal literature will have an effect not only on the perceptions that non-Aboriginal people have of Aboriginal society but that Aboriginal people have of themselves. It is important that scholars examine the ideological age they bring to their readings and counter it by looking outside the texts into the contexts in which they were written to some kind of understanding of the ideology of the people whose works they interpret. It is not acceptable to remain secure in the ivory towers writing objective critical articles because these articles, imbued with the voice of authority, have an effect on the social situation of the Aboriginal people who are their subjects. As I said earlier, choosing Canadian Aboriginal Literature as a field of study has its own challenges, especially when Aboriginal people are able to write back.

To illustrate this point, I will examine an interpretation that is both canonized and flawed in that it is based on deeply ingrained ideology of the colonizer culture and is one that many Métis people in this country find particularly problematic. Inevitably, at some point during discussions of identity and representation in Maria Campbell's *Halfbreed* (1973) and Beatrice Culleton Mosionier's *In Search of April Raintree* (1983, 1992, 1999), the icon of the confused and alienated Halfbreed appears. Even though there is abundant evidence to prove that Métis people are not inherently confused, isolated, and alone, this icon remains intact. The Métis Nation of Saskatchewan represents 85,000 Métis in this province, and Métis scholars estimate that there are similar numbers in Manitoba and Alberta. Clearly it is not lonely in the middle.[8] Granted, negotiating identity in a purportedly postcolonial society is a challenge that all Indigenous people face. However, many academics persist in the belief that it is confusion about their identity—and not the racist oppression that is the legacy of colonialism—that cause mixed-blood characters their difficulties. Persons of European ancestry have been indoctrinated into a belief system that views contact, particularly sexual contact, with "the Other"—the non-Christians and non-Europeans—as a constant threat not only to Christian virtue and cleanliness but to the very heart of "social order and continuity" (Farrell Racette, 4). I contend that it is this ideology that many scholars bring to the texts, not the texts themselves, on which they base their interpretations.

Despite the complex legal issues[9] that profoundly influence the social and political context in which *Halfbreed* arises, Maria's Métis family does not experience the confusion and alienation that scholars take for granted. Campbell begins her narration of *Halfbreed* by telling her readers who her people are and where they come from. Campbell identifies her paternal great-grandmother, Cheechum, as "a native woman," a Hudson's Bay Company code word for Métis (Farrell Racette), and as "a Halfbreed woman, a niece of Gabriel Dumont" (Campbell 9). She explains that Cheechum's mother's people were non-status Indians, who "were never part of a reserve, as they weren't present when the treaty-makers came" (10). Cheechum experiences no confusion regarding her identity as a Métis woman. She is not concerned with reconciling her mixed European and First Nations heritage because she neither desires nor requires reconciliation. Cheechum knows that she is Métis and is intensely patriotic despising the European immigrants who displace her people from their land and imposing their religious beliefs on them:

> Cheechum hated to see the settlers come, and as they settled on what she believed was our land, she ignored them and refused to acknowledge them even when passing on the road. She would not become a Christian, saying firmly that she had married a Christian and if there was such a thing as hell then she had lived there; nothing after death could be worse! Offers of relief from welfare were scorned and so was the old age pension. While she lived alone she hunted and trapped, planted a garden, and was completely self-sufficient. (Campbell 11)

Cheechum bequeaths her language, lifestyle, and most importantly, her pride in their Métis identity to her son, her grandchildren, and her great-grandchildren.

Nevertheless, Cheechum is responsible for the injection of Scots blood into the family gene pool through her marriage to Great Grandpa Campbell. However, his Scots' parentage does not draw her son closer to his European heritage. On the contrary, the opposite seems to have occurred. Her son chooses to marry a Métis woman, and "[a]fter their marriage, they lived miles out in the bush and never bothered much with anyone" (Campbell 11). Despite the violence that Grandpa Campbell endures at the hands of his father, "he was a kind, gentle man who spent a great deal of time with his [nine] children" (Campbell 12). As more and more white settlers move onto the land, his children's lives become more difficult.

Many Aboriginal women are ambivalent towards feminism, and many reject it altogether, which bewilders feminist scholars who read Campbell's descriptions of drunken Métis men beating frightened wives. They see violence against women as evidence of a deeply ingrained patriarchal culture although violence against women was not traditional in many Aboriginal cultures. However, the Aboriginal women who shun feminism consider their men to be victims of colonization and oppression as are the Métis men of Campbell's father's generation who find themselves existing in an impossible situation that causes them endless shame. With the twisted logic of the oppressed, they believe themselves to blame for circumstances clearly out of their control. Had their parents and grandparents been present when the treaties were signed—like Big John, Qua Chich, Grandpa Dubuque were—things might have been better. Had they taken treaty rather than scrip,[10] their families might have had land, food, and education. But they have no education, so the only employment for which they would qualify is farm labour, which would put them at the mercy of the white settlers who, unlike the Indians, do not consider the Métis their kin. Their traditional roles of providers and protectors are vulnerable. The Métis men are skilled hunters, but because they do not have Indian status, the law does not allow them to hunt as needed for survival. If they hunt outside of hunting season, they run the risk of prosecution leading to incarceration. With such limited choices Danny Campbell and his brothers choose to ignore the law and do what they have to do to survive: "they trapped, hunted, and sold game and homemade whiskey to the white farmers in the nearby settlements" (Campbell 12). If they obey the law, they doom their families to a life of relief workers, fear, and starvation; if they break the law, they doom their families to a life of police, fear, and shame. Failure meets them at every turn and the chorus of "The White Judges" resounds in their minds: *"You are not good enough, not good enough, obviously not good enough"* (Dumont 11, 13). Readers should not be surprised when the Métis men, more and more often, seek solace in drink.

Non-Native readers usually focus on the tension that Campbell describes as existing between the Métis and the Indians. They interpret this tension as proof that mixed-blood people are alienated from both parent cultures rather than looking at the complex legal issues that divide them. Unable to acquire homesteads, the Métis are squatters on their traditional lands, condemned to live on the unoccupied Crown lands that border the road lines. Their landless state[11] sets them apart from the Indians:

> We all went to the Indians' Sundances and special gatherings, but somehow we never fitted in. We were always the poor relatives, the *awp-pee-tow-koosons.*[12] They laughed and scorned us. They had land and security, we had nothing.... However, their old people "Mushooms" (grandfathers) and "Kokums" (grandmothers) were good. They were prejudiced, but because we were kin they came to visit and our people treated them with respect. (Campbell 25)

The Elders' acknowledgement of their kinship with the Métis is significant because relationships between relatives are sacred in Cree culture.[13] Grannie Campbell's status-Indian sister, Qua Chich, never forgets her Métis relatives and brings her horses every year to help them ready their gardens for planting. Grannie Dubuque's brother, chief of his reserve, dotes on Maria and treats her as if she were his own daughter. Still at this point in history, at least one generation of status Indians would have attended residential schools where the racist attitudes that made them ashamed of their identity would have been internalized. No doubt, these students would have felt some sense of relief upon returning home and learning that the white settlers considered their relatives, the Métis, as being worse than the students had been taught to feel. As the Métis come into more and more contact with the white settlers, they too learn shame. It is their proximity to the white settlers, their legal status, and their poverty—not their mixed blood—that erodes the Métis' sense of pride and security in their identity.

Maria's feelings of shame and self-loathing begin with her first visits to town where she contrasts the Métis' demeanour with that of the white settlers. Maria's childhood abounds with "happiness and beauty" (Campbell 2), which begins to erode as she becomes overwhelmed by the relative prosperity of the townspeople lives and the scorn that they mete out to the Métis. Maria says, "I thought they must be the richest and most beautiful [people] on earth. They could buy pretty cloth for dresses, ate apples and oranges, and they had toothbrushes and brushed their teeth every day.... They didn't understand us. They just shook their heads and thanked God they were different" (Campbell 27). To a child, the shameful demeanour of the adults—their inability to hold their heads high or to look a white person in the eye—seems to acknowledge their guilt, and causes Maria to ask "Mama why [they] had to walk as though [they] had done something bad." Her mother can only reply, "'Never mind. You'll understand when you're older'" (Campbell 37). As she grows older, Maria comes to understand that, to the white settlers, their mixed blood is their crime and the foundation of the Métis' guilt, a crime of which she is also guilty. She comes to believe in a logical fallacy that states that they are poor, untrustworthy, and violent because they are mixed-blood people.

Maria's feelings of shame and self-loathing are exacerbated by her experiences in the education system. She first attends school at the Beauval Indian Residential School, a dubious gift from her Grannie Dubuque, herself a status Indian educated in a convent. It is significant to note that, although Maria remembers little of the one year she spends there, she says that Spring River School, the horrors of which she goes on to recount, is "Heaven compared to the Residential School" (Campbell 49). At the Spring River School, "lunch hours were really rough" (Campbell 50) for the Métis children, who contrast their meager lunches with those of the white children and are reminded of their poverty, sure evidence that their parents had failed, that their people had lost. School and time spent in close proximity to white children teach Maria to hate her mother, father, and all the "no-good Halfbreeds" and teach her that "there was no greater sin in this country than to be poor" (Campbell 50, 61).

Maria is confused but not because of her mixed blood. She is confused because the dominant society has taught her to hate herself and her people. She would like to marry Smoky, but cannot:

When I thought of him and marriage I saw only shacks, kids, no food, and both of us fighting. I saw myself with my head down and Smoky looking like an old man, laughing only when he was drunk. I loved my people so much and missed them if I couldn't see them often. I felt alive when I went to their parties, and I overflowed with happiness when we would all sit down and share a meal, yet I hated all of it as much as I loved it. (Campbell 117)

It is important to note that the Métis community sustains Maria, and only when she leaves it does she experience true alienation. Yet she has been taught to loathe that very community that is her strength. Sadly, the irony here is that her prediction of a future with Smoky is probably accurate given the racism and oppression under which they would live. It is racism that drives Maria to marry a white man, secure in the belief that only white men—not Métis—have the power to deal with the relief workers and the ability to support a family. And, like all racist beliefs, this one proves false.

Beatrice Culleton Mosionier's *In Search of April Raintree* begins with the Raintree family living in Winnipeg in the same sorry state as Maria does in Vancouver but for different reasons. The Raintree family comes from Norway House, a Cree small community on the shores of Lake Manitoba. Unlike Maria's community of Spring River, Norway House in the early 1950s was completely isolated and could only be accessed by boat and airplane.[14] Its people spoke their language and lived off the land by hunting, trapping, and fishing. When Henry Raintree contracts tuberculosis, the family is forced to move south to Winnipeg, an alien environment.

Because Culleton Mosionier chooses April, then of preschool age, to narrate the story, readers have no access to Henry and Alice Raintree's inner lives. Nevertheless, readers can infer that, with the father suffering from a life-threatening disease, this would be a traumatic time for the family. We can also infer from April's recollections that the move would have had a distressing, and ultimately shameful, effect on her father:

> I used to hear him talk about TB and how it had caused him to lose everything that he had worked for.... Although we moved from one rundown house to another, I remember only one, on Jarvis Avenue. And of course, we were always on welfare. I knew that from the way my Dad used to talk. Sometimes he would put himself down and sometimes he counted the days till he could walk down to the place where they gave out cheques and food stamps. (Culleton Mosionier 9)

From these few words it becomes clear that in Norway House the family had a better life than the one they have in Winnipeg and that the loss of this life, "of everything that [Henry Raintree] worked for," damages Henry's self-esteem. We also can infer that when he "put[s] himself down" Henry is blaming himself for the family's loss and their impoverished circumstances. Alienated and confused, not because of their mixed blood but because of their poverty and their displacement from their community and way of life, Henry and Alice Raintree self-medicate with alcohol to relieve their pain for short periods of time.

The Raintree family's physical and temporal settings reveal much about the cause of the Raintree family's alienation. At the start of the novel, the family is physically set in a "rundown house" on Jarvis Avenue. Jarvis Avenue has become a metaphor specific to the City of Winnipeg. Situated in the poorest area of the City, Jarvis Avenue has become infamous to the people of Winnipeg, who have come to associate its name with poverty, despair, and shame. The temporal setting at the novel's start is 1955, a bleak time for Aboriginal people. Because the "Pass Laws" still limited their movements, few status Indians lived in the City of Winnipeg. Canada had no Bill of Rights, and Human Rights legislation had not yet been imagined. In Winnipeg, racist attitudes made it almost impossible for Aboriginal people to gain employment, so those Métis people who could, denied their identity and masqueraded as French and Scots to enable themselves to support their families, always hoping not to be found out. Even if Henry's health permitted him to work, the likelihood of him gaining any employment is slight and good employment nonexistent. April tells us that he is visibly Aboriginal, being "a little of this, a little of that, and a whole lot of Indian" (Culleton Mosionier 9). In her poem "White Belly," Joanne Arnott describes the soul-destroying experience that Aboriginal men of Henry Raintree's generation face in the city when seeking employment. She writes that when a visibly Aboriginal man went looking for work

> [the white people] saw his black hair and brown eyes and redbrown skin. They saw his fear and his pride and his poor man's clothes, and again and again they made the same decision. I can trust you with my truck. I can trust you with a load of bread, a load of milk, a load of laundry. (Arnott 57)

Henry is not even this fortunate and finds no employment. As his tuberculosis goes into remission, his alcoholism deteriorates, and he becomes a permanent welfare recipient.

Although both April Raintree and Maria Campbell are mixed-blood people, it is important for scholars to understand that April's context differs radically from Maria's. Where Maria grows up surrounded by extended family and community, April's only community is a rag tag collection of Aboriginal people whom she calls "aunties and uncles" (Culleton Mosionier 12), and who live on the margins of Winnipeg society. Unlike Maria, April has no Cheechum to teach her pride in her identity, no Native language, and no sun dances. Even with this secure foundation, Maria eventually begins to feel ashamed of her identity when confronted with the relative affluence of the whites and their never-ending racism and oppressive treatment of Aboriginal people. Throughout her life, April learns to associate white skin with goodness, cleanliness, and prosperity, and brown skin with violence, dirt, and poverty. From the margins of the park near her home, April looks at the white-skinned children, "especially the girls with blond hair and blue eyes" and envies them; she imagines "that they were rich and lived in big beautiful houses" (Culleton Mosionier 16). April, as a naive, and therefore unreliable, narrator, cannot know how unlikely it would be that Winnipeg's wealthy children would be playing in a park near Jarvis Avenue. Because April can only describe, rather than analyze, the complexities of her personal context, the analysis of context is left to the scholars who teach and write about this text.

Scholars are not unfamiliar with the requirement to provide students with an understanding of the social, political, and cultural context out of which the texts that they teach arise. Indeed, any class on Shakespeare would not be complete without a comprehensive examination of the political and religious situation in Elizabethan England, no doubt comprised of information that the instructor has gathered from books in the library. These scholars need not worry that there just might be an Elizabethan enrolled in his or her class and that Elizabethan student just might dispute the information given in the lecture. However, this might very well occur in a class on contemporary Aboriginal literature. And, to further complicate things, the instructor cannot always count on the information on the context of Aboriginal literature that she or he has found in the library. At best it is likely to be incomplete and at worst inaccurate. Nevertheless, if one examines the *text* of works of Aboriginal literature without examining the *context* from which it is written, Aboriginal people become abstractions, metaphors that signify whatever the critic is able to prove they signify. However, to write in this way shows a lack of social responsibility because it has an effect on the living people who are the subjects of Aboriginal literature. To really understand the context of the literature, then, scholars must leave the ivory tower and talk to Aboriginal people. This must be done with care and respect.

The narrator of Lee Maracle's short story "Polka Partners, Uptown Indians, and White Folks" describes what *many* Aboriginal people have experienced when interacting with *some* White people (even though she is guilty of essentializing "white people" herself):

> ...white people cannot deal with the beauty in some of us and the crass ugliness in others. They can't know why we are silent about serious truth and so noisy about nonsense. Difference among us, and our silence, frightens them. They run around the world collecting us like artifacts. If they manage to find some Native who has escaped all the crap and behaves like their ancestors, they expect the rest of us to be the same. (Maracle 296)

Maracle's statement reveals that there are risks attached to leaving the ivory tower to investigate the context of the literature. There was a time in the not too distant past when Aboriginal people were the objects of academic discourse rather than the subjects of their own. With Aboriginal people telling and writing their stories, this time has come to an end. By seriously considering Aboriginal literature as an object of academic study, many academics have taken a first step in social responsibility. Now it is time for them to recognize their own limitations and address them by examining context.

Notes

1 In the USA "Native Americans" is a commonly used term to describe the Indigenous Peoples of that country. Under *The Constitution of Canada* (1982), the term "Aboriginal" refers to Indians, as defined by *The Indian Act*, Métis, and Inuit.

"First Nations" is a term now in common usage referring to members of Canada's First Nations, in other words Indians defined by the *Indian Act*.

2 Farrell Racette points out that in Saskatchewan Métis children had no legal right to education until 1944 when the provincial government assumed responsibility for Métis education after a decades-long stalemate with the federal government over jurisdiction (26).

3 Prof. William Asikinack of the Saskatchewan Indian Federated College was stripped of his Indian status and membership in the Walpole Island First Nation in the 1960s after receiving his BEd.

4 Although born on the Cowessess Indian Reserve, my former mother-in-law, Mathilda Lavallie Bunnie, was by law a Non-status Indian, her father having applied for and been granted enfranchisement. In the early 1920s, she attended Marievel Indian Residential School until grade two, when all Métis and Non-status students were required to discontinue, which put an end to her aspirations of receiving an education.

5 Isadore Pelletier, an Elder at the Saskatchewan Indian Federated College, had a similar experience. Also a Non-status Indian, Pelletier lived in Lestock, Saskatchewan, where he attended the town school until grade three. At that time the townspeople decided to expel all Métis and Non-status Indian children from the school on the basis that they were squatters and, therefore, did not pay taxes. Although Pelletier's family owned land, he was expelled along with the others.

6 I remember and appreciate Terry Goldie's cautions that the inclusion of personal reflections in academic writing has the potential to become "self-indulgent" (Edmonton 2000).

7 Winona Stevenson in *To Colonize a People: The File Hills Indian Farm Colony* (Blue Thunderbird Productions, 2000).

8 I credit Sherry Farrell Racette with this observation.

9 Farrell Racette examines these complex legal issues that affect identity:

[T]he pressure to define "Métis" legally and politically is directly relational to the legally and politically defined "Indian." The often arbitrary freezing of an Indian identity and its subsequent administration through the Indian Act is rarely questioned. First Nations bands were given official legal identities; glosses which obscured the same diversity which makes the Métis so difficult to define. The evolution of the legally defined "Indian" through changes and additions to the Indian Act, a piece of federal legislation, has had [an] impact on the Métis. (2)

10 Since Bill C-31 amended *The Indian Act* in 1986, Campbell and her siblings have been eligible to apply for Indian Status. Many of the other Métis families named in this book—Vandals, Arcands, Isbisters, and others—have since become members of the Ahtahkakoop, Muskeg Lake, Big River, and Mistawasis First Nations. Scrip was designed to extinguish Métis Aboriginal title, much as treaties did for First Nations. Scrip commissioners traveled to Métis communities and held

sittings where Métis gathered to fill out applications for their land entitlement. Claimants had to fill out an application, sign an affidavit, and in most cases received their scrip coupon on-site—title to land—if they qualified. The scrip policy, while appearing benevolent, was in reality, through its convoluted procedures of application and corrupt administration, designed to strip the Métis of their land.

11 My husband remembers the Métis from Lebret, Saskatchewan, visiting his family on the Standing Buffalo Dakota First Nation. His father always spoke with great sympathy when he referred to the Métis as "people with no home."

12 Campbell translates this word as meaning "half people" (25). Solomon Ratt, Head of the Department of Indian Languages, Literatures, and Linguistics at the Saskatchewan Indian Federated College, does not agree. Using Standard Roman Orthography, the word is spelled "āpihtawikosisān": "apihtaw" meaning "half" and "kosisan" being derived from "nikosis" meaning "my brother." The Cree word for Métis, then, would literally translate into "halfbrother."

13 In the Cree kinship system, extended family relationships are more important than blood relationships. All of Maria's mother's sisters, had she had any, would also be considered Maria's mothers; all of Grannie Dubuque's sisters would be Maria's grandmothers, and all of her brothers would be Maria's grandfathers. Relatives are wealth.

14 My mother worked for the CBC in Winnipeg at that time and remembers people who came from Norway House to Winnipeg for medical treatment. They often came to the CBC's offices to send messages home on the radio program *The Northern News*.

Renée Hulan

"'Everybody likes the Inuit': Inuit Revision and Representations of the North"

Renée Hulan is a settler scholar living in Nova Scotia, where she teaches Canadian Literature at St. Mary's University. Her work takes an interdisciplinary approach to Canadian literary and cultural history and, among areas of interest such as ethnography, the north, and women's writing, she has published widely in the field of Indigenous literatures. She is one of this country's earliest non-Indigenous advocates for an ethical criticism, and, in 1999, she edited the seminal collection of essays *Native North America: Critical and Cultural Perspectives*.

"'Everybody likes the Inuit'" is excerpted from Hulan's 2002 text, *Northern Experience and the Myths of Canadian Culture*. Picking up where early literary critic of Inuit literature Robin McGrath left off, Hulan's text seeks to "unsettle" colonial ideas of north. Her chapter describes portrayals of Inuit by non-Inuit writers, and the stereotypes these portrayals reinforce. Hulan then goes on to deconstruct these stereotypes by describing the rich tradition of literature that redefines Inuit experience, underlining the political impact of writing, as well as its aesthetic values. Inuit autobiography, she explains, is about representing community and nationhood, since traditionally one does not talk about one's personal accomplishments. In this regard, Hulan contributes to the work of the literary nationalists.

Hulan, Renée. Excerpts from "'Everybody likes the Inuit': Inuit Revision and Representations of the North." *Northern Experience and the Myths of Canadian Culture*. Montreal/Kingston: McGill-Queen's UP, 2003. 60–97. [omitting "Representations of the Inuit" and "The Inuit in Children's Literature" (62–74); "The Reception of Inuit Writing" and "Problems with Authenticity" (78–82)]

"Everybody likes the Inuit": Inuit Revision and Representations of the North

Non-Inuit writing on the north is often preoccupied with two supposed elements of Inuit experience: Inuit access to the Stone Age past as a "contact-traditional" hunting society, and Inuit access to an exotic spirituality. The first element is part of a general trend in the representation of aboriginal people: "real Inuit," like the "real Indians" Louis Owens refers to in *Other Destinies*, are always considered to be part of the past (4). Writers attracted by the idea of the hunt, such as Barry Lopez, are particularly susceptible to this tendency and disseminate masculinist images of the hunting society and how it functions, with men dominating the cultural landscape because they hunt big game. As John S. Matthiasson observes, most literature about the Inuit works this fantasy into "an image of the chauvinistic male hunters dominating their women and trading them back and forth as if they were property" (73); such literature fails to notice the role played by women in the men's hunt or the fact that women hunt sometimes as often as men do. What interests these writers is not how the society works or what hunting represents within the culture; rather, it is the rugged individualism that can be displayed in such deeds, as in the staged hunting scenes in Robert Flaherty's *Nanook of the North* (1922). The importance of the second supposed attribute of Inuit culture, traditional spirituality, can be observed in highly personal travel writing about the north, narratives in which the individual fulfils a quest for self-knowledge or greater wisdom through contact with aboriginal people.

Travel writing, like ethnography, tends to portray Inuit men as hunters, interpreters, and guides, and to leave women out of the picture, creating an image of a culture dominated by masculine pursuits. Yet in their dealings with whites, Inuit men are made subordinate to those who hire them; that is, they occupy the role Inuit women have been assumed to play in Inuit culture. Frequently depicted as poor, defenceless creatures, they undergo a symbolic emasculation that allows them to play a subordinate, passive role, as the feminized counterpart of the masculinized explorers and travellers. The north described in such accounts has been usurped by white men as a playground for their own masculinist fantasies; it is what Margaret Atwood calls "[t]he Robert W. Service North of popular image [which] is assumed to be a man's world; even though the North itself, or herself, is a cold and savage female, the drama enacted in it—or her—is a man's drama, and those who play it out are men" (*Strange Things* 90). By speaking "man to man," to reiterate Trinh's phrase, realist ethnographers cast their subjects in the same way.

Inuit self-representation tells a different story. Both traditional stories and contemporary writing represent Inuit men and women in ways that challenge non-Inuit representation. By merging their traditional conventions with European literary forms such as autobiography, Inuit writing plays a historical role in preserving details of past traditions, a pedagogical role in addressing and educating outsiders, and a political role in making statements on behalf of Inuit.

Images created by ethnographic studies have defined aboriginal peoples, and especially notions of what is traditional in their cultures. Even the term "traditional" synthesizes many perspectives, including those of the ethnographer's culture. Reading these books is an encounter with the images that have allowed sustained paternalism, even neo-colonialism, in Canada's governing of the north.[1] In the wake of the new ethnography and the debate over who speaks for whom, most ethnographers would now insist on the difference between these two practices; nevertheless, the distinction between speaking about others and speaking for others is, as Linda Alcoff shows, often blurred (9).

The debate concerning who speaks for whom in literature can be polarized, with one side advocating the absolute creative freedom of writers and the other insisting that writers should depict only their own experiences. Some writers of the north refuse to become embroiled in this controversy at all, by refusing to write about the Inuit or to report their words. This well-meaning attempt to avoid appropriating the voice of others can have the same effect, however, if the voice of northern inhabitants cannot be heard. These issues bear on the reception of writing by Inuit to be discussed later in this chapter because non-Inuit writers effectively "speak for" Inuit both by reaching an audience that Inuit writers may not have access to and by influencing how that audience will receive Inuit writing.

This criticism is not an argument against the practice of speaking for others; instead, it is a warning of the impact that speaking for others can have in the absence of dialogue, that is, when some have no voice—as has been the case, historically at least, with aboriginal writers. I argue that when Inuit writers speak on behalf of other Inuit it is often in the interest of giving voice to collective concerns. Without a modified version of speaking for others, Robin McGrath would not be able to say that Agnes Nanogak represents the storytellers of the Western Arctic in her collection ("Introduction" xii), nor would Heather Henderson be able to say that Minnie Aodla Freeman "speaks for" her people (62). Without the practice of speaking for others, aboriginal people would not find voices that could reach the people who need to learn most, and non-aboriginal people would continue to imagine aboriginal people according to prevailing stereotypes; thus, "speaking for others" cannot be rejected outright. Inuit self-representation, autobiography in particular, seems to reflect Linda Alcoff's observation that sometimes it is politically expedient to have a spokesperson speak on one's behalf (13).

Inuit Representation

A study of Inuit representation through their literature makes an appropriate and necessary complement to the preceding chapter [on ethnography and the representation of the North], given that their literature has been used for ethnographical purposes. Indeed, as members of a society living in neo-colonial conditions, the Inuit occupy a privileged position in relation to representational issues; that is, as Donna Haraway would say, they are on to the god-trick, the "denial of the critical and interpretative core of all knowledge" (*Simians* 191). Aboriginal people have what post-colonial scholars call "a capacity, far greater than that of white settler societies, to subvert received assumptions about literature" (Ashcroft et al. 144). However, aboriginal writing is valuable beyond how it illuminates non-aboriginal literature and the "received assumptions" the post-colonial theorists mention; the task of literary criticism of aboriginal writing should be understanding its own features, not embedding it in a national or post-colonial canon. Criticism of aboriginal literature should also examine how, just as land is appropriated by the Canadian state, so is the experience and imagination of aboriginal writing appropriated by non-aboriginals. In this context, the uniqueness of the Inuit case lies in the way Inuit culture has been depicted by national discourses of identity.

As early as the 1960s, some anthropologists questioned the accuracy of depicting the Inuit as culturally homogeneous and distinct. While they argued that a contact-traditional lifestyle was emerging in response to rapid social change, the representation of Inuit art and literature, especially by museums, continued to focus on the past life of Inuit culture, commonly figured through a focus on the hunt and the theme of survival (see Matthiasson *Living on the Land*). Today, although Inuit self-representation has evolved, museum exhibits have not, tending still to reflect southern Canadian interest in artifacts from the traditional material culture; in other words, the story of the Inuit as told by another culture for another culture.

With institutional approval to back their position as authorities, anthropologists, explorers, and even curators have come to play a significant role in defining what is authentic about the traditional culture (Harry 148). In this process, they continue to be led by a consuming interest in survival.[7] Traditions—identified, preserved, and, in some sense, created by outsiders—are valued because they are believed to have survived from the pre-contact past. The preference for past tradition, evident in the popularity of Native storytelling, "places Native people in the museum with all the other extinct species" according to Daniel David Moses (Moses and Goldie xiii). In the same way, anthropologists approach Inuit literature as emerging from the Stone Age.

While non-Inuit writers have historically depicted Inuit in ways that enhance and serve their own narrative intentions, Inuit representation deals with local political and material concerns, indicating the tendency Arnold Krupat notes of Native American fiction towards "homing in rather than moving out" through the quest (*Ethnocriticism* 114; see also Bevis). Speaking for others within the culture comes to be an act of political as well as aesthetic representation. This feature of Inuit writing has affinities with post-colonial literature as theorized in *The Empire Writes Back*; for example, in the way African writers stress the social relevance of their work and its importance in the community rather than the individual's career (Ashcroft et al. 126).

Inuit writing does not affirm the attributes conferred by outsiders. Unlike writing about the north by southern Canadians, which situates the north and its inhabitants neatly within the Canadian nation, Inuit writing refuses to invoke a national position; nor does it celebrate its own "Canadianness" or "nordicity." In fact, Inuit leaders usually address Canada on the nation-to-nation basis indicated in John Amagoalik's promise after the 1984 First Ministers' conference to "continue to have discussions with the government of Canada on Nunavut" (qtd in Petrone 264). While Inuit leaders do not reject Canada, they have also maintained the clear sense of separate, ethnic nationalism that led to the creation of Nunavut in 1999.

While contemporary representation of the Inuit romanticizes Inuit culture and homogenizes differences in timeless images, Inuit writing tends to present a complex integration of the insider's information and the outsider's expectations. As members of a minority, the Inuit bear the burden of explanation: southern writers write as if they can imagine the Inuit to be whatever they want, but Inuit writers write knowing they have a responsibility to themselves as a misrepresented or unrepresented constituency. The pressure to explain oneself to those with more power, whose position means not having to know or even to listen, a privilege that exercising tolerance implies (Spelman 182), typically falls on the members of the marginal group. In this abstract sense, the struggle for self-representation accompanying the struggle for self-government in Inuit and other First Nations communities resembles the discovery of subjectivity by other marginalized groups, including women in various societies. Yet Inuit literature in English is distinct in that its political form reflects the traditional belief that words can bring events into being, and it serves a practical political purpose by addressing the national culture in one of its official languages.

Anthropologists seem to agree on the status of Inuit culture as "a way of life that is rapidly vanishing" (Briggs 262) or, more dramatically, "for which the death knell has already been tolled" (Matthiasson 12). When Inuit suggest that their culture is dying, however, their meaning is quite different, because it is inspired by a desire for continuity and renewal, not a wish to commemorate what is past. Many older Inuit people fear that their culture will die with them, and their initiative to maintain continuity has produced collections such as Mark Kalluak's *How Kabloonat Became and Other Inuit Legends* (1974). An example of what Robin McGrath calls "authentic literature," this collection attributes each story to its teller and cites Kalluak as editor and translator. Included in the collection are a variety of tales about traditional figures such as Kiviok, Mahaha, and Kaugyagyuk, as well as traditional stories of orphans and animal spouses.

The stories preserved at the insistence of the older generation do not corroborate observations made in ethnographies; in fact, traditional stories dispute many assumptions held by outsiders, especially those concerning gender roles, passivity, and innocence. The notion of Inuit culture as a pure and dying one allows for the naturalization of gender categories in the writing of outsiders. By concentrating on their perceptions of what constituted traditional Inuit life in the past, outsiders can project naturalized gender differences onto Inuit culture, and, in the worst cases, describe gender in terms which are comforting to those confused about changes in contemporary gender expectations.

The diversity of modern and traditional accounts by Inuit challenges any account of fixed, stable gender roles. For example, while Inuit Alice French mentions female infanticide in her autobiography and echoes Jenness by explaining that a girl was "of little value until she married and brought home a hunter and trapper" (4), traditional stories do not indicate a stable gender hierarchy. Similarly, Jenness's acquiescent Jenny and subservient Icehouse are nowhere to be found in the traditional stories collected by Kappi, Kalluak, and others. Neither are the pliant, silent, Inuit women who populate the adventure stories discussed in chapter 3: Houston's Panee, Horwood's Nasha, or Kelley's Anu. Traditional stories feature strong women, women who act without men, and women who, far from needing to be saved, save others. "The Huntress" tells of a wife who learns from an old woman that her husband is tired of her and plans to kill her. The wife not only escapes him, but travels to another shore where she saves a town from a terrible ogre (Nanogak, *Tales* n.p.). In both "Mother Bear and Two Sons" and "Raven Who Took a Sea Gull Wife," a deserting husband who leaves his wife for another woman is killed when the original wife decides to take revenge (Kappi n.p.). "Flying Sledge" tells of a girl who refuses to take a husband because she is a successful hunter herself and who, when she agrees to marry an orphan boy, is carried away with him on a magic sled as a reward for her act (Kappi n.p.).

Traditional stories restrict no activity to one sex or the other. Instead, the stories suggest, as ethnographer Jean Briggs argues, that "[t]here is nothing holy to [the Inuit] about the sexual division of labour; neither is there, according to the Inuit, anything inherent in the nature of either sex that makes it incapable of doing some of the jobs that the other sex ordinarily does" (270; see also Fienup-Riordan). Despite the interesting opposition these stories make to anthropological accounts, problems arise when moving from the representation of Inuit life in traditional stories to the way Inuit people actually live; these are the problems posed by reading for anthropological meaning and value. Because realist ethnography is based on fieldwork, hence observable data and phenomena, such works of the imagination are often left out. Indeed, Jenness makes it quite clear that stories do not interest him (*People*

142). A literary critical approach can help account for the contribution oral and written literature makes to culture. While Inuit literature attempts to represent real experience, it is not the transparent window realist ethnographers seek, the window on the real life of the Inuit as they are "when only God is looking."

Inuit Autobiography

Inuit literature's accommodation of modernity, which undermines the stability of the "authentic," reflects intersecting linguistic, historical, political, and social pressures. Inuit literature written in English merges oral and written, Inuit and European, and past and present traditions. It has been characterized as attempting to preserve tradition and to accommodate outside influences. For example, some of the earliest Inuit writings in English, autobiographies written by the Inuit of Labrador, show the ambivalence towards identity indicative of the cultural métissage that Dale Blake explores in "Women of Labrador: Realigning North from the Site(s) of Métissage." Some writers used the autobiographical form to espouse English culture while disowning aboriginal identity.

In *Northern Voices* (1988), Penny Petrone traces Inuit autobiography back to testimonials recorded by Moravian missionaries as early as 1776 (58), and continuing in Inuktitut after a written form was developed (103). Writing one's life story began as a religious imperative, encouraged by Christian missionaries, and, as such, early examples tend to show the author's appreciation for and assimilation into the new, colonizing culture. For the missionaries who solicited works by Inuit people, the autobiography testified to their success in converting aboriginal people (57). To them, English ancestry, Christianity, and English literacy, not aboriginal heritage, authorized individuals as writers. In *Woman of Labrador* (1982), Elizabeth Goudie tells how her son was named Robert Bruce to celebrate her husband's Scottish background (53), yet speaks of "Eskimos" with a distance that denies her own Inuit heritage. Almost one hundred years earlier, Goudie's great-aunt, Lydia Campbell, distanced herself from her mother's Inuit identity in her *Sketches of Labrador Life* (1893) by apologizing for her father's choice of bride: "Then of course they had to take wives of the natives of this country. There were very few white men here, much less women" (8). When Campbell describes the decline of the Inuit, which she blames on alcohol and tobacco, she never includes herself among the afflicted population— although she is half Inuit.[9] Dale Blake notes that Campbell's sense of racial identity is "oblique" (168), for although her autobiography is "generally suggestive of Inuit oral myths and legends, with their humour, violence, excitement, superstition, and often unhappy endings" (169), it also relies heavily on Christian themes. In a passage that must have pleased her Anglican clergyman, Campbell engages her religious values by writing that when the Inuit were more plentiful, the "poor souls had no religion whatsoever, besides the rum bottle and biscuits and butter" (11). Campbell concentrates on her father's tales of his home in England (7–8) and continues to describe the poor "Eskimo" as if she has no connection to them (10–11, 29). These two autobiographies show signs of colonial acculturation through identification with the authority figure endorsing the work, and disavowal of the aboriginal mother. At the same time, one hears the voices silenced by ethnographers like Jenness, the voices of Inuit women speaking about their own experiences. As Blake suggests, the two books provide a complex representation of and engagement with aboriginal heritage. The three generations of women who tell their stories in *Saqiyuq: Stories from the Lives of Three Inuit Women* (1999) also provide a history of changes in Inuit communities in the twentieth century, especially with respect to women's roles.

Autobiography became increasingly political in the twentieth century, yet the tradition of white sponsorship continued, albeit with quite different motivation, in publications such as Anthony Apakark Thrasher's autobiography, *Thrasher... Skid Row Eskimo* (1976). According to the book's foreword, Thrasher was first encouraged by his lawyer to write his story, and he wrote it while waiting to stand trial for manslaughter; later, two journalists made it their job to "collate what was essentially a loose-leaf diary into narrative form, authenticate that narrative as thoroughly as possible and expand it" (x). Sceptical about the accuracy of his statements, they verified every detail before publication. In their search for the "facts," they ignored the account's narrative form and literary characteristics; indeed they claim responsibility for changing Thrasher's story into narrative.

Like his contemporary, Minnie Aodla Freeman, who also produced an autobiography, Thrasher first left the north to attend a training course; like Freeman, he suffered the culture shock of coming south. But unlike Freeman, who took a job in Ottawa, Thrasher was deposited in a skid row motel in Edmonton and never got much further. He remembers beatings he received, liquor he drank, and women he slept with, as well as incidents also experienced by Freeman, for example, learning how to cross the street at the traffic light (72–73). While his story concentrates on the sordid aspects of street life, its political subtext can be observed in his nostalgic memories of life in the north and in comments concerning changes to Inuit way of life. Describing his difficulty coping with life in the south, Thrasher writes: "My people in the North were struggling with the same problems. Southern ways were spreading into the Arctic, and my people knew nothing of these new habits and customs, and couldn't grasp many simple things that the white man had accepted for decades" (75–76). Thrasher makes his experience of alienation a political statement on behalf of other Inuit. He idealizes his past life and promotes a view of the Inuit as "a docile people, trusting and loving" (161). By presenting himself as a victim, he undermines his responsibility for his actions, including the death for which he ends up being convicted, so his account seems problematic at best.

There are many narrative inconsistencies in his book; for example, he claims he "read in a medical book that alcohol slows your body's blood pressure down, and gives you resistance to heat," right after he writes: "I couldn't read labels at all, and

I ended up chewing laxatives like candy" (75). If these are exaggerations, they suggest that Thrasher's autobiography might be better understood in the tradition of the song duel, just as *I, Nuligak* (1966) can be better understood as a meeting place for the autobiographical form and the structure of the Kaujjarjuk legend (McGrath, *Canadian Inuit* 103). Thrasher's boastful exaggeration and his unreliability can be read as participating in the general one-upmanship of the song duel form, described later in this chapter, that allows for both the settling of an account and the proof of one's masculinity. However, *Thrasher... Skid Row Eskimo* has been read as a window on the miserable life of urban aboriginal people rather than a book with possible literary merit.

Alice French's *My Name Is Masak*, published the same year as *Thrasher*, features the same integration of romanticized views of traditional life and sordid scenes of the effects of acculturation. French concentrates on her childhood, especially life in residential school, but her autobiography also preserves details of material culture, such as a passage in which she describes the use made of a whale carcass (70). In both the French and Thrasher autobiographies, the author tells the life story of the community while telling her or his personal story, and this gives the autobiography a broader political significance.

Although autobiographies provide valuable ethnographic information to contradict the often skewed perspective of ethnographic representation, they are not simply artifacts of a culture. As products of close collaboration with white editors, the autobiographies by Campbell, Goudie, and Thrasher are what Krupat identifies as "Indian autobiographies" rather than the "autobiographies by Indians" which are self-written and edited (*Ethnocriticism* 219). How much influence can be attributed to editing is uncertain. The editor of Lydia Campbell's sketches admits in the preface to "omitting only a sentence or two of no particular interest," yet although more subtle narrative blanching could have occurred, signs of Inuit culture persist in these texts. For example, Lydia Campbell concentrates on the errors of her youth, because Inuit women are taught that it is "unseemly to discuss their accomplishments, although it is quite acceptable to recall the errors of childhood and adolescence" (McGrath and Petrone 316). French's *My Name Is Masak* and Minnie Aodla Freeman's *Life among the Qalunaat* (1978), though more recent, also deal primarily with childhood experiences. As the cases of *Thrasher... Skid Row Eskimo* and *I, Nuligak* show, autobiographies written by Inuit form a continuum with Inuit oral tradition, and, as *Life among the Qalunaat* and *My Name is Masak* show, their authors act as political spokespeople for the community.

Freeman's *Life among the Qalunaat*, perhaps the best-known Inuit autobiography, exemplifies the important political function of Inuit literature written in English. According to Heather Henderson, Freeman "speaks for" her people (62): by "[m]oving beyond the personal to the public and political, she becomes a spokeswoman protesting injustice" (65). Because the "egotism" needed to write autobiography is antithetical to Inuit ways, Henderson argues, Freeman subverts autobiography by using her life story to voice the collective experience of her people. But Henderson need not submit that the Inuit way, that is, one not driven by ego needs, is the authentic experience underwriting Freeman's authorization as a spokeswoman. One has only to look at the content of the book to understand it as literature with a political value. In fact, Freeman makes her book's thesis plain when she laments the passing of the Inuit culture she knew, writing "I miss my dear people who are becoming stranger, even to me, covering their familiar ways with another culture" (217).

In passages like this one, the self represented is not without individuality, but it is identified with the rest of the community. This is the "part-to-whole" relationship that Krupat has called the "synecdochic self," one marked by a sense of the self "in relation to collective social units or groupings," rather than the more prevalent North American notion that each person possesses an interiorized self separate from other distinct individuals (*Ethnocriticism* 212). It is clear that people who do not revere individualism would not represent themselves as rugged individuals, and this may be the most important factor contributing to the differences between Inuit and non-Inuit representations of the north and the people in it.

Throughout her autobiography, Freeman demonstrates her connection to her community by documenting experiences bearing on political issues, such as the racial prejudice expressed by a teacher who refers to students as "you natives" (195), or the stereotype contained in the white vision of Inuit as "smiling happy people" (194). In an ironic account of how images of the Inuit are made, she describes how she was used to represent the north, while working at the Department of Northern Affairs as a translator: "I found myself one day in a building with a lot of big cameras. Then I was made to put on a parka in the middle of July, when the temperature outside was eighty degrees. It would not have been so bad inside the building, but up I went, right to the roof, where the sun beamed down. A man made a movie of me while I drank ginger ale. I understood that I was advertising the ginger ale" (41). While the irony in the situation gives the passage its humour, Freeman underlines her feeling of exploitation by following it with the understated yet painful observation: "Seeing my picture on the back of Pure Spring Ginger Ale trucks made me feel uneasy" (41).

In another moment when an event in her life takes on a political meaning, she tells how she was asked to pose for a photographer by sitting at a desk with something in her hand, and then later discovered her picture in the newspaper: "The story read: 'Eskimos buying bonds, keeping up with progress,' some remark like that. I felt sick. I had no idea what bonds were. My parents had never even heard about them, let alone buy them. Today my father still has no idea what bonds are, though he has been working with Northern Affairs for the last thirteen years. I felt sick because I was being used to show the qallunaat in the South how well the Inuit are treated in the North" (65). In such passages, Freeman speaks of her own experiences while placing them in the collective context.

Autobiographies, especially those by women, record experience that other accounts downplay or ignore, and for that, they are important as ongoing revisions of ethnographic documents. Lydia Campbell's autobiography contradicts fictional love stories involving white men and Inuit women by describing the cruelty of one Englishman towards his Native wife (27), and by telling a cautionary tale about how a woman who died "under her husband's care" haunted him after he took up with a young girl (14). Meanwhile, her admiration for her sister, Hannah, acknowledges the abilities that go unnoticed in images of passive, silent Inuit women: "I wish there were more Hannahs in the world for braveness. She brought up her first family of little children when their father died, taught all to read and write in the long winter nights, and hunt with them in the day, got about a dozen foxes and as many martens" (6). When Alice French describes how her grandmother Susie runs the household, she adds that many women acted as heads of the household in her community (60). According to French, women also decided who should marry whom (76).

The responsibilities outlined by French stand in sharp contrast to the lack of freedom described by her contemporary, Elizabeth Goudie. Goudie describes the difficulty she had adjusting to her life as a trapper's wife: "I was young and liked gay life. I liked dancing and visiting friends. Jim thought I ought to stay at home with him. Life was very dull for me at first but I got used to it. It was the custom for the man to run the home, the women took second place. A woman could have her say around the house but about the main things in life, the man always had his say. His word went for most everything" (50). Goudie complains of boredom in several instances, as part of her construction of her life as one hardship after another.[10] The discrepancy between Goudie's version of women's place and Alice French's version may be attributed to regional cultural differences or the greater degree to which the Labrador Inuit mixed with Europeans, but it is clear that they stem from different values, with Goudie's experiences most closely resembling those reported by ethnographers.

Although Minnie Aodla Freeman's autobiography does not describe the enforcement of the division of labour according to gender roles, it does articulate certain expectations affecting Freeman during her youth. In one instance, she describes the kind of woman Inuit men dream about as "gentle, kind and understanding" (187); in another, her father's advice suggests that women are expected to take the responsibility for making their marriages work (201). In matters of gender, she wants guidance, and she equates her confusion about gender expectations with the loss of her Inuit identity. At residential school, as she approaches puberty, she experiences a kind of culture shock when she realizes that, in her absence from the community and her family, she has not been trained in the appropriate womanly tasks (140). She feels that her development has been stunted. Yet, she is just as confused and alienated when her period arrives while she is at home in her community, and she complains that no one will tell her what is going on (145).

Introducing Armand Tagoona's *Shadows* (1975), George Swinton recognizes how the fusion of political and personal narratives as well as the ongoing revision of traditional forms meet as the "self becomes part of history—autobiography is extracted from the myths and legends and becomes projected into, and renewed in, myths" (n.p.). *Shadows* consists of twenty-three plates, with commentary by the artist, autobiographical segments, and a number of stories. As Tagoona tells his life, he represents the history of his region and his people with understated clarity: "I am often asked how the Inuit felt about being brought into settlements. It is not an easy thing to talk about; the Inuk himself is not sure how he feels. I myself have lived in settlements almost all my life but I tasted a little 'out there' in the Inuit camps in winter. I love it 'out there'" (n.p.).

Increased interest in the north and activity in the field of communications created an explosion of writing about and by the Inuit in the 1960s and 1970s. Many collections of traditional stories appeared, including those by Kalluak, Kappi, and Nanogak, and many Inuit writers published in northern periodicals such as *Inukshuk, Nunatasiaq News, Inuttitut, Inuit Today, Inummarit, Inuit Monthly,* and *Keewatin Echo.* While this activity continued into the 1980s, a number of anthologies also appeared, including *Paper Stays Put* (1980) and *Northern Voices* (1988), as well as the first study of Inuit writing, McGrath's *Canadian Inuit Literature: The Development of a Tradition* (1984).[11] Illustrated autobiography, such as Normee Ekoomiak's *Arctic Memories* (1988), continues to be an important genre in Inuit literature.

Ruth Tulurialik's *Qikaaluktut: Images of Inuit Life* (1986) precedes Alootook Ipellie's *Arctic Dreams and Nightmares* (1993), but both are examples of the importance of the illustrated text in Inuit representation. Tulurialik's text performs the ethnographic function of cataloguing and interpreting culture. It provides definitions (for example, the passage "Tukipqutaq" indicates the word's denotation of a rock marking a good fishing spot) and stories of cultural practices (significantly, those on traditional birthing do not mention infanticide). Other sections—"The Bay," "Minister," and "Bad Policeman"—describe modern features of northern life, as Tulurialik demonstrates the coexistence of ancient and modern ways.

In *Arctic Dreams and Nightmares* (1993), the stories inspired by the ink drawings collected in the book are intensely personal, but they draw on stories and images from oral literature instead of adopting the western autobiographical form. In fact, Ipellie introduces his book as a "smorgasbord of stories and events, modern or traditional, true or imagined" (xix). Like the Inuit culture represented in ethnography and other forms of writing about the Inuit, Ipellie's Inuit culture revolves around survival. However, unlike other representations, Ipellie's celebrates the "resilient culture" (xiv) for standing up to the "constant threat of cultural genocide" (xv). In the contemporary world, survival means cultural survival: "It is the will and the perpetual pride of our elders that has helped us to retain the old myths, stories and legends so that our present generation can absorb them and pass them on to future generations" (xiv). Part of the goal of Ipellie's work is to continue their work, and by featuring traditional figures like Sedna or stories like "The Woman Who Married a Goose," the Inuit world he creates represents the traditional alongside the modern use of technology and several references to contemporary events.

In "When God Sings the Blues," the narrator's "spirit journey" occurs after he performs a secret chant allowing his spirit helper to travel to the Magical Kingdom where God dwells. The god depicted is an ironic portrait of the Christian God brought to the Inuit with contact. Known by his Inuit name, Sattaanassee, which means Satan, this god possesses a "large array of fax machines" and a "high-powered telescope" with which to look in on humanity (48). Sattaanassee's power comes from technology, yet another ironic comment on the influence of contact on Inuit belief. More concerned with the money going into his coffers than anything else, the economic recession sends Sattaanassee into a depression, causing the narrator to invite him to a blues jam to cheer him up. The satire on the Christian religion is complete when the Arctic audience is entertained by Sattaanassee singing the blues. By borrowing a form (blues) from southern black culture, Ipellie demonstrates the elasticity of cultural meaning, the way cultures intersect and influence each other. His work employs satire, which is a convention of Inuit oral literature, to comment on the aspects of modernity that continue to affect Inuit life.

Inuit Poetry

> *I call forth the song...*
> *I draw a deep breath...*
> *My breast breathes heavily*
> *As I call forth the song.*
> —Akjartoq (qtd in Colombo 44)

"There is no such thing as Eskimo poetry," wrote Edmund Carpenter in 1971, "there are only poetic acts by individual Eskimos" (13). Carpenter's remarks are some of the first in the criticism of Inuit literature as literature. Much of what we know as Inuit "poems" are actually traditional oral songs, chants, and prayers transcribed, collected, and translated by ethnographers, and, therefore, Inuit poetry is subject to the problems of authenticity discussed earlier.[12] While ethnographers who collected traditional songs and stories were moved to do so by their fear that the Inuit traditions were dying, Richard Lewis collected poems for his anthology *I Breathe a New Song* (1971)—whose title alludes to the fact that the Inuktitut word for "to make poetry" means "to breathe"—in order "to help preserve a culture that began to disappear in 1955" (6).

Although Inuktitut does not have an equivalent for the verb "to create," Carpenter describes the Inuit idea of poetic creation thus: "Poet, like carver, releases form from the bonds of formlessness: he brings it forth into consciousness. He must reveal form in order to protest against a universe that is formless, and the form he reveals should be beautiful" (14). Inuit poets are not concerned with representing the landscape, Carpenter asserts; rather, they interact with the environment, which "requires a creative human act before the world explored becomes a world revealed" (15). There is no distance between the poetry Carpenter describes and the prayers and chants of the oral tradition. The poetic brings things into being. In Inuit culture, writes Joseph Epes Brown, "[t]o name or speak of a person, a being, or some phenomenon in Nature, is to make really present that which is named, or indeed is actually to call forth the spiritual essence of that which is named" (142–43). In this Iglulik poem, sung by Aua, the hunter sings for strength "Words Which Make Heavy Things Light":

> *I will walk with leg muscles*
> *which are strong*
> *as the sinews of the shins of the little caribou calf.*
> *I will walk with leg muscles*
> *which are strong*
> *as the sinews of the shins of the little hare.*
> *I will take care not to go toward the dark.*
> *I will go toward the day.*
> (Petrone, *Northern Voices* 7)

Characterized as they are by the repetition of words, phrases, and images, traditional Inuit poems collected and translated for English readers give a sense of the diversity of Inuit culture even if, by taking written form, they cease to be part of the oral tradition. Collections of examples from the oral tradition are synecdochic statements on the culture because they can only evoke the tradition they belong to.

The traditional hunting songs and weather chants that are primarily narrative indicate the male-dominated hunting culture non-Inuit imagine the Inuit to be. In Orpingalik's "My Breath," also collected in Petrone's *Northern Voices*, the speaker mourns his former strength, remembering his hunting prowess and lamenting the state his woman is in:

> *Sad, I would that my woman*
> *Were gone to a better protector*
> *Now that I lack strength*
> *To rise from my couch.*
> *Unaya-unaya.* (24)

The representation of gender difference also inheres in certain distinctly Inuit forms such as the song duel. Song duels, which are also called nith songs, drum songs, or satirical songs, are a form which seems to be unique to Inuit culture. In these, the poet or singer responds to a challenge or challenges another by deriding himself, someone else, a group, or a type of behaviour (McGrath, *Canadian Inuit* 48). Song duels use irony and satire to various ends depending on the purpose they serve, which may include settling disputes, gently criticizing another, accusing another, or binding the friendship between song brothers; they are also intended to amuse listeners. Song brothers engage in duels also to prove their masculinity, and their derisive remarks usually focus on the hunting and sexual prowess of the adversary.

Once they are preserved on paper, these Inuit traditions are claimed within the national literature. In his preface to *Poems of the Inuit* (1981), John Robert Colombo admits that his interest in the Inuit is closely related to his "concern for things Canadian" and his belief that "the oral art of the Inuit adds a distinctive element to the national mosaic" (7). The Inuit represent that absolute difference and identity which justifies the definition of Canada as a multicultural mosaic; moreover, the cultural diversity represented by Inuit poets is as distinctly Canadian as the work of canonical poets: "Aua, Netsit, Uvavunuk, and Orpingalik are new—and strange-sounding—names to place alongside those of Saint-Denys-Garneau, Raymond Knister, W.W.E. Ross and Sir Charles G.D. Roberts, their better-known contemporaries. Yet the mix could occur only in Canada and the two groups of singers have much more in common than is immediately apparent" (7).

Despite Colombo's enthusiasm, however, relatively few contemporary Inuit writers choose poetry as a genre in which to express themselves, preferring the rhetorical advantages of the essay, speech, and even short fiction. Those who do write poetry have reached an audience beyond their community in literary anthologies such as Penny Petrone's *Northern Voices: Inuit Writing in English* (1988). As Petrone remarks, contemporary Inuit writers devote much of their talent to journalism, and "with a new political consciousness, unknown to their ancestors, they are writing a literature of opinion and information, largely derivative and imitative of western models, reflecting the new realities of political and social change" (201).

What little contemporary Inuit poetry there is uses forms and treats themes common to the oral tradition, as the poems collected by Petrone indicate. Robin McGrath argues in her essay "Oral Influences in Contemporary Inuit Literature" that the form and content of Inuit poetry may change, but it is still firmly rooted in the oral tradition. For example, Liz Semigok's "My Cooking Pot" (1988), which was written first in Inuktitut, then translated into English, offers thanks: "Grateful am I when it boils something" (285), and William Kalleo's "The Known Mysteries of Seals" (1982) has the repetition of the hunting chant: "Hunting seals I Hunting different seals" (253). McGrath makes a convincing case for satire as the emerging Inuit form in English, and poems such as Alexis Pamiuq Utatnaq's "Blood Thirsty Enemies" (1974) exemplify the satiric impulse of much Inuit writing:

Our Enemy
Our enemy
They're so many
Our blood they spill
They make us ill
Help us, oh God
From their piercing rods
Our sworn foes
Those mosquitoes.
(Petrone, *Northern Voices* 166)

In this poem, the surprise ending gives pause, reminding readers that, in the Arctic, mosquitoes pose an ever-present threat, as Ivaluartjuk sang in "Cold and Mosquitoes" (1929); however, these mosquitoes also signify invaders from the south too, the image of bloodsucking pests being a particularly evocative one in times of increased resource exploitation.

Ivaluartjuk is just one poet who is also a storyteller and whose work therefore connects directly to the oral tradition. Mary Carpenter Lyons uses poetry and storytelling to voice contemporary political concerns. In "Nunavut?–Denendeh? = Northwesterritories" (1988), the speaker calls on the land to give its people strength to face the "distant men" who watch them die and "Who sit and build / invisible, governing walls." The poem concludes with the lament: "O great land, you are leached by white lies / Lip-serviced, not loved" (Petrone, *Northern Voices* 273). Like the poets of the oral tradition, Carpenter uses the "simplicity of tone, language, and subject matter, all of which combine to suggest the depth of importance of brief moments of emotion" (McGrath, *Canadian Inuit* 45).

As with traditional stories, the reception of Inuit poetry in the south has been deeply influenced by the value of its anthropological content. As part of the essential, sacred culture, poems are treated as artifacts to be collected and preserved. Robin McGrath describes how attempts to popularize Inuit poetry have resulted in "all Inuit poems [being] regarded as sacred, unspoiled flowers that were simply to be admired in a passive way, never subject to the intense light of criticism" ("Inuit Literature" 702). McGrath argues that "Inuit poems in English are not just anthropological enigmas, but are works that are accessible to anyone who brings curiosity and a little imagination to their reading of poetry" ("Reassessing" 19). Unlike the novel, autobiography, and essay, Inuit poetry has not developed primarily through contact with non-Inuit, and it retains strong ties to the oral tradition, but Inuit poems written in English also address a non-Inuit audience. As Petrone remarks, "the sacredness of the word has marked all Canadian Inuit literature. And young Inuit writers today continue to believe, as their forefathers before them, that in language will they find the true meaning of their ancient northern homeland" (202).

The reception of Inuit poetry also demonstrates the popular appeal of anthropological material that the proliferation of ethnography seems also to confirm. Inuit literature in general, and Inuit poetry in particular, has been received this way because the representation of traditional culture confirms preconceptions of the Inuit as a remnant of the Stone Age. These preconceptions include the centrality of hunting in the culture, the cultural significance of survival, and the domination of women within the division of labour, the very same notions that are challenged by contemporary Inuit writers, poets, and storytellers.

In the national discourse that places northern experience at the centre of national identity, Inuit culture can be considered a sort of apex of Canadian nordicity; after all, the Inuit inhabit regions that fulfil Louis-Edmond Hamelin's ten criteria of nordicity. In a 1972 survey, Canadians described Inuit in terms of the noble savage, as a people possessing a pure ideology under threat of southern civilization (Hamelin, "Images" 8), and Hugh Brody observes similar attitudes in *The People's Land*. Inuit culture can be claimed within national discourse, whether that discourse is based on the concept of nordicity outlined by Hamelin or the multicultural values described in government documents.

Images of Inuit life in painting, carvings, and photographs represent "Canada" in public places and publications. Inuit culture plays a dual role in national myth as both the ultimate of identification and the ultimate of difference. That is, as the most northern culture, it represents the idea of north in the Canadian identity, and as a culture under anthropological study, it represents the difference that multiculturalism claims to accommodate. Early criticism of Inuit writing reflects a preoccupation with anthropological content and relevance, and this preoccupation establishes expectations in the non-Inuit audience concerning gender and national identity, which are countered by Inuit writers in their revisions.

While non-Inuit tend to depict the Inuit as ideal Canadians, inhabiting the territory of Canadian national difference, Inuit writers are concerned with the collective experiences and problems of Inuit, not Canadians. As Minnie Freeman's discomfort with the use of her image in advertisements indicates, non-Inuit representations of Inuit do not reflect these concerns. Most importantly, writing by Inuit does not refer to the Canadian identity of the north, recalling Thomas Berger's often quoted observation that its inhabitants view the north as their homeland, not as the national heritage of the multicultural state.

In recent years, multiculturalism has replaced biculturalism as the official discourse of the Canadian government. To understand the ideological ambivalence of multiculturalism it is unnecessary to look further than government publications concerning the renewal of the constitution, which advance tolerance as the multicultural ideal at the heart of Canadian identity. When a 1992 publication asserts that Canadians are "recognized around the world for the values we cherish—tolerance of differences and respect for different cultures and minorities; generosity; compassion for the less fortunate; freedom and opportunity for the individual" ("Our Future Together" 1), it seems clear that the "we" refers to Canadians who share the same things, including the ability to tolerate differences and to respect other cultures. Paradoxically, the "we" does not encompass the object of tolerance, so the passage actually excludes those who are "different" while claiming to accept them. Moreover, the text remains silent about what these cultures are actually different from and thereby implies that the majority members do not have ethnic, gendered, or otherwise defined identities. Such categories (gender, ethnicity, race) serve as repositories of difference that the norm somehow transcends. Whatever the norm tolerates defines it. Both Leslie Monkman (5–6) and Margery Fee ("Romantic Nationalism" 29) identify a similar binary opposition in the constitution of Canadian identity by recognizing how aboriginal difference comes to define the (white) Canadian norm.

The most salient point in the critiques offered by Monkman and Fee concerns the function of aboriginal culture as a point of reference for defining Canadian culture. According to Fee, national models of Canadian literature, and writers who espouse them, have been known to romanticize "the Native" as a means of consolidating ownership of the territory claimed as Canada. Such a romantic image and endorsement of what the Native point of view has to offer readers introduces William Mowat and Christine Mowat's *Native Peoples in Canadian Literature* (1975): "Possibly this book asks the impossible: it asks the reader to step outside his own ethnic consciousness and to walk a mile in Indian moccasins.... If the reader is able to shun any sense of paternalism or superiority that he may hold, if he is able to open himself to upside-down concepts of time, and to fresh relationships with people, society, and the land, he may find his perceptions of Indians and Eskimos jolted but enlarged" (1). In other words, the Native point of view will provide what the national culture, here represented by "non-Indians," lacks. Aboriginal culture plays the same role for Canada that white women have played for white men by representing the "other" by which the "self" can be defined. Mowat and Mowat are right about one thing, however: it *is* impossible to step outside one's own ethnic position in the way they desire, and it is even less desirable to pretend one can. As Linda Alcoff argues, there is an important distinction between the mistaken notion that one can transcend the epistemological and discursive contexts one inhabits as a critic and the potential of "positionality" characterized by continuous shifting between and within those contexts.

Romanticization results from fixing "the Native" in a national image, because to fix something as complex as culture it is necessary to settle on a limited range of attributes. In a well-known passage quoted in Petrone's *Northern Voices*, Inuit writer and politician Nellie Cournoyea sums up the role of the Inuit in Canada: "They glamorize and romanticize the Inuit...and give us status the others don't have. Canadians like to talk about us eating frozen meat and living in the cold. It gives

Canada something that other countries don't have. Everybody likes the Inuit" (286).

The result is a romantic image that characterizes the representation of Inuit culture in Canada as well as the reception of Inuit writing. In the case of Inuit culture, the Native as reference point defining Canadian culture collapses into the north as reference point defining Canadian national consciousness. The Inuit have been imagined as ideal Canadians, as those who can pass on the "autochthonous claim" (Fee, "Romantic Nationalism" 18) to both the land and the north. However, the self-determination of Nunavut will continue to trouble this easy equation of north and the Canadian nation.

Notes

1 That colonialism characterizes the relationship between the Canadian state and the north is a commonplace of northern studies reiterated in, among others, *Canada's Colonies: A History of the Yukon and Northwest Territories* by Kenneth Coates, *The Modern North: People, Politics and the Rejection of Colonialism* by Coates and Judith Powell, and *The Canadian North: Source of Wealth or Vanishing Heritage?* edited by B.W. Hodgins, J. Benidickson, and R.P. Bowles.

[...]

7 Here we see a convergence of anthropological interest in physical survival with a similar preoccupation in literary criticism, as witnessed in Atwood's thematic study in particular. Sherrill E. Grace also notes that Canadians, in inventing themselves, "insist upon surviving" ("Comparing" 247).

[...]

9 In the course of correspondence with Dale Blake, I have come to consider the distance that Campbell creates between herself and other Natives to be part of her assertion of an independent, "authentic" self, and not necessarily a sign of self-loathing. In her essay "Women of Labrador: Realigning North from the Site(s) of Métissage," Blake shows how Campbell and Baikie celebrate mixed blood heritage specifically, and this celebration accounts for the differentiation from other groups.

10 Comparisons can be made between Goudie's experiences as a trapper's wife and those recorded in Olive A. Fredrickson's *The Silence of the North* (1972): Fredrickson, a white woman living in northern British Columbia, focuses on hardships too, but does so in order to glorify the pioneer lifestyle.

11 At the same time, ethnography was proliferating. Writers such as Richard K. Nelson, whose *Shadow of the Hunter* appeared in 1980 along with Michael Mitchell's *Singing Songs to the Spirit: The History and Culture of the Inuit*, and

Fred Bruemmer, whose *Arctic Memories: Living with the Inuit* appeared in 1993, based their texts on brief time spent with the hospitable Inuit, while children's writer Carolyn Meyer collaborated with Bernadine Larsen on a fictional account entitled *Eskimos: Growing Up in a Changing Culture* (1977).

12 Robin McGrath outlines these problems with specific reference to the transcription and translation of the oral in "Editing Inuit Literature: Leaving the Teeth in the Gently Smiling Jaws."

Qwo-Li Driskill

"Stolen from Our Bodies: First Nations Two-Spirits/Queers and the Journey to a Sovereign Erotic"

Qwo-Li Driskill is a Cherokee mixed race, Two-Spirit/Queer poet, writer, scholar, educator, activist, and performer from rural Colorado. Writing from personal experience, Driskill engages themes of inheritance, loss, healing, sexuality, and violence. Driskill's work is at the forefront of advocating for a return to a traditional Indigenous acceptance and accommodation of difference within the community. In addition to lecturing, reading, and performing widely, Driskell is an assistant professor in the Department of English at Texas A&M University. In 2005, her first book of poetry, *Walking with Ghosts*, was nominated for the Griffin Poetry Prize.

In reference to Ernie Crey's landmark study of residential schools, *Stolen from Our Embrace*, "Stolen from Our Bodies," published in 2004, examines the effects of colonization on the body. Driskill's essay, like Andrea Smith's *Conquest*, underlines how sexual assault is an act of colonization which seeks to destroy Indigenous cultures by dominating Indigenous bodies. Borrowing from literary nationalists, Driskill uses the term "sovereign" erotic and describes erotic "wholeness," or the necessity of a return to a physical body distinct from settler society. Driskill includes poetry and song to promote healing, and refers to the body as a critical "homeland" for diasporic peoples.

Driskill, Qwo-Li. "Stolen from Our Bodies: First Nations Two-Spirits/Queers and the Journey to a Sovereign Erotic." *Studies in American Indian Literatures* 16.2 (Summer 2004): 50–64.

Stolen from Our Bodies: First Nations Two-Spirits/ Queers and the Journey to a Sovereign Erotic

This is a Warrior Song
From one poor Skin to another
And I don't know what I'm lookin' for
But I know I've found you

These words will shuffle across concrete
Will float across the Rockies
To the Smokey Mountains
We were stolen from
We were stolen from

We were stolen from our bodies
We were stolen from our homes
And we are fighters in this long war
To bring us all back home

And this is a Warrior Song
From one poor Skin to another
And I don't know what I'm lookin' for
But I know I've found you

U-ne-la-nv-hi U-we-tsi
I-ga-gu-yv-he-yi
Hna-quo-tso-sv Wi-yu-lo-se
But I know I've found you

And this is a Warrior Song
From one poor Skin to another
And I don't know what I'm lookin' for
But I know I've found you[1]

This song came to me one night a few years ago as I began to understand that healing our sexualities as First Nations people is braided with the legacy of historical trauma and the ongoing process of decolonization. Two-Spirits are integral to this struggle: my own resistance to colonization as a Cherokee Two-Spirit is intimately connected to my continuing efforts to heal from sexual assault and the manifestations of an oppressive overculture on my erotic life. Like other Two-Spirit people, I am making a journey to a Sovereign Erotic that mends our lives and communities.[2]

I mention my experiences with trauma in this essay because sexual assault, sexism, homophobia, and transphobia are entangled with the history of colonization. Sexual assault is an explicit act of colonization that has enormous impacts on both personal and national identities and because of its connections to a settler mentality, can be understood as a colonial form of violence and oppression. My own journey back to my body, and the journeys of other First Nations people back to their bodies, necessarily engage historical trauma. In her book *Shaking the Rattle: Healing the Trauma of Colonization* Barbara-Helen Hill (Six Nations, Grand River Territory) writes:

> All of the abuse and addiction that we are seeing in communities are symptoms of the underlying cause, the oppression and the stress of living in isolation on reservations or in Native communities within the larger non-Native communities.... Healing the spirit of the individual will eventually spread to healing the spirit of family and this in turn will spread out into the communities.... (36)

When I speak of a Sovereign Erotic, I'm speaking of an erotic wholeness healed and/or healing from the historical trauma that First Nations people continue to survive, rooted within the histories, traditions, and resistance struggles of our nations. I am in agreement with Audre Lorde when she writes, "Our erotic knowledge empowers us, becomes a lens through which we scrutinize all aspects of our existence, forcing us to evaluate those aspects honestly in terms of their relative meaning in our lives" (57). I do not see the erotic as a realm of personal consequence only. Our relationships with the erotic impact our larger communities, just as our communities impact our senses of the erotic. A Sovereign Erotic relates our bodies to our nations, traditions, and histories.

The term "Two-Spirit" is a word that resists colonial definitions of who we are. It is an expression of our sexual and gender identities as sovereign from those of white GLBT movements. The coinage of the word was never meant to create a monolithic understanding of the array of Native traditions regarding what dominant European and Euroamerican traditions call "alternative" genders and sexualities. The term came into use in 1990 at a gathering of Native Queer/Two-Spirit people in Winnipeg as a means to resist the use of the word "berdache,"[3] and also as a way to talk about our sexualities and genders from within tribal contexts in English (Jacobs et al. 2). I find myself using both the words "Queer" and "Trans" to try to translate my gendered and sexual realities for those not familiar with Native traditions, but at heart, if there is a term that could possibly describe me in English, I simply consider myself a Two-Spirit person. The process of translating Two-Spiritness with terms in white communities becomes very complex. I'm not necessarily "Queer" in Cherokee contexts, because differences are not seen in the same light as they are in Euroamerican contexts. I'm not necessarily "Transgender" in Cherokee contexts, because I'm simply the gender I am. I'm not necessarily "Gay," because that word rests on the concept of men-loving-men, and ignores the complexity of my gender identity. It is only within the rigid gender regimes of white America that I become Trans or Queer. While homophobia, transphobia, and sexism are problems in Native communities, in many of our tribal realities these forms of oppression are the result of colonization and genocide that cannot accept women as leaders, or people with extra-ordinary genders and sexualities.[4] As Native people, our erotic lives and identities have been colonized along with our homelands.

My family is diasporic, descendants of so many removals of so many kinds it becomes difficult to count them all. Survivors of so many genocides that one simply bleeds into the next. As a Red-Black person, the Trail of Tears and other forced relocations are not the first removals of my peoples.[5] I find myself obsessed with the notion of "home" on many levels. I have not only been removed from my homelands, I have also been removed from my erotic self and continue a journey back to my first homeland: the body. "We were stolen from our bodies / We were stolen from our homes."

Sexual assault was not something that was tolerated in most of our cultures before invasion. In Lakota custom, for example, the "Rare Knife" was given to Lakota women to use only to cut off the heads of men who abused her or her children.[6] Consequently, abuse was rare in Lakota lifeways before white supremacist patriarchy enforced violence against women and children. Wilma Mankiller reminds us,

> Europeans brought with them the view that men were the absolute head of households, and women were to be submissive to them. It was then that the role of women in Cherokee society began to decline. One of the new values Europeans brought to the Cherokees was a lack of balance and harmony between men and women. It was what we today call sexism. This was not a Cherokee concept. Sexism was borrowed from Europeans. (20)

Sexual violence is rampant in all communities in the United States. Recent events within the Catholic Church show how often sexual abuse of children is silently condoned. Sexual abuse must be seen with an understanding of the history of colonization, which uses sexuality as a tool to gain power over others and to control women's bodies. In this country the *white wing* attempts to make abortion illegal at the same time women of color and poor women continue to survive forced sterilization. It is no accident that white masculinity is constructed the way it is in the United States, as European invasion of the Americas required a masculinity that murders, rapes, and enslaves Native and African peoples. It is a masculinity that requires men to be soldiers and conquerors in every aspect of their lives. A masculinity rooted in genocide breeds a culture of sexual abuse. It is vital to remember that most of our traditions did not allow such behavior. Healing from assault is intimately joined with decolonization and the reclamation of indigenous understandings of the world.

We were stolen from our bodies
We were stolen from our homes
And we are fighters in this long war
To bring us all back home

A colonized sexuality is one in which we have internalized the sexual values of dominant culture. The invaders continue to enforce the idea that sexuality and non-dichotomous genders are a sin, recreating sexuality as illicit, shocking, shameful, and removed from any positive spiritual context. Queer sexualities and genders are degraded, ignored, condemned, and destroyed. As people often raised under dominant culture's values through our homes, televisions, or teachers, Two-Spirit erotic lives continue to be colonized. Native people survive a legacy of spiritual and sexual abuse at the hands of soldiers, missionaries, clergy, and teachers who have damaged our senses of Self and wounded our sacred connection to our bodies. The boarding school systems in the United States and Canada are one example of the ways our sexualities, genders, and spirits have been colonized by the invaders. Boarding schools continue to have severe repercussions on our communities, including colonized concepts of gender and sexuality. To decolonize our sexualities and move towards a Sovereign Erotic, we must unmask the specters of conquistadors, priests, and politicians that have invaded our spirits and psyches, insist they vacate, and begin tending the open wounds colonization leaves in our flesh.

I have seen no study that tells how many Two-Spirit people commit suicide or turn to drugs and alcohol to cope with the shame colonization brings to our sexualities and genders.[7] How many Two-Spirit people are forced to leave their families and thus their primary connection to their traditions because of homophobia and transphobia? How many of us grapple with deep shame because of our sexualities and/or genders? Our sexualities harbor bruises left by a white supremacist culture. We find ourselves despising our bodies and sexualities, unable to speak of our own erotic lives and desires even with our lovers. We see dominant culture's concepts of the erotic and know they have nothing to do with our Two-Spirit bodies, often causing us to dissociate from our erotic selves or assimilate dominant culture's concepts into our lives. Marilou Awiakta (Cherokee/Appalachian) writes, "Thinking of sex as an it and women as sex objects is one of the grooves most deeply carved into the Western mind. This groove in the national mind of America will not accept the concept of sex as part of the sacred and generative power of the universe—and of woman as a bearer of the life force" (252). It is not only First Nations people who have internalized the dominant culture's concepts of sexuality and gender. The legacy of colonization seeps into every aspect of life in this country, even if only Native folks and other people of color recognize it.

Beth Brant (Bay of Quinte Mohawk) writes about the importance of Two-Spirit engagement in a process of healing from historical trauma:

> Much of the self-hatred we carry around inside us is centuries old. This self-hatred is so coiled within itself, we often cannot distinguish the racism from the homophobia from the sexism. We carry the stories of our grandmothers, our ancestors. And some of these stories are ugly and terrorizing. And some are beautiful testaments to endurance and dignity. We must learn to emulate this kind of testimony. Speaking ourselves out loud—for our people, for ourselves. To deny our sexuality is to deny our part in creation. (63)

To understand our place in creation, I look at the stories within my tradition that celebrate difference. To my knowledge as a non-fluent Cherokee speaker, there is currently no term in Cherokee to describe Two-Spirit people. We simply *are*. However, within our stories are roadmaps for contemporary Cherokee Two-Spirits. Many of our stories address difference, the embodiment of dichotomies, and journeys between worlds. Craig Womack (Oklahoma Creek-Cherokee) reminds us, "Rather than disrupting society, anomalies actually reify the existing social order.... That which is anomalous is also an important source of power. The Southeastern belief system is not an oppositional world of good and evil" (*Red on Red* 244). Our stories as First Nations people keep us alive in a world that routinely destroys and discards us. Though our stories were present as survival cartographies before the invasion of Turtle Island by Columbus and the crowned power of Spain, our stories are perhaps even more vital to our survival now, during the European occupation of our homelands.[8]

It is in our stories, including our written literatures, that I search for meaning and reflection of my Two-Spirit body in order to survive a world in which people like me are routinely killed. How do I make sense of the murder of F.C. Martinez, Jr., a Diné/Cheyenne Nádleeh youth killed in June 2001 in Cortez, Colorado? How do I make sense of the February 2002 murder of Amy/Raymond Soos, a Two-Spirit of the Pima Nation whose naked body was found in Phoenix, Arizona? How do I make sense of the strangled and beaten body of Alejandro Lucero, Hopi Nation, whose body was found on March 4, 2002, also in Phoenix? How do I make sense of the slaughter of "Brandon Teena," always spoken of as white, who was actually of mixed "Sioux" and white ancestry, his life erased by transphobic murderers and his Nativeness erased by white Queer and Trans folks?[9] How do we as Two-Spirits remain whole and confident in our bodies and in our traditions when loss attempts to smother us? I return to our stories.

Many Cherokee stories deal with characters considered outsiders, who live in liminal spaces, help bring about necessary change, and aid in the process of creation. In one story, a water spider brings fire to the other animals after many larger and stronger animals attempt to retrieve it and fail. She creates a bowl and straps it to her back with spider silk in order to carry fire across the water. In another version of the story, a dragonfly assists her by pushing the bowl from behind (Mooney 431). This story is significant to Cherokee Two-Spirits because so much of it deals with the embodiment of opposites. Spider is specifically a water-spider, and in Mooney's recording of the story, a species of spider that is black with red stripes, opposite sacred colors in Cherokee cosmology (Mooney 241). Dragonfly also dwells between worlds of water, air, and earth. In Cherokee cosmology, fire is associated with the female principle and water is associated with the male principle. Dragonfly and spider become beings that help join these realities.

A Sovereign Erotic is a return to and/or continuance of the complex realities of gender and sexuality that are ever-present in both the human and more-than-human world, but erased and hidden by colonial cultures. Oppression is used by the "settlers" to "tame" our "wild" and "savage" understandings of our Selves, to injure our traditional understandings of the world, to pit us against each other along divisions of gender, sexuality, skin tone, geography, "blood-quantum," (dis)ability, and class so that the powers that be have less work to do in maintaining control over our homelands, our bodies, and our spirits.[10]

In discussing the colonization of Queer African and First Nations bodies and sexualities, elias farajajé-jones writes:

> My...African ancestors stood on auctioning blocks in this country where their bodies were offered for sale. They were subjected to the white "gaze" quite literally; their genitalia were touched and inspected in a very public way. The bodies of my First Nations (Tsalagi/Cherokee) ancestors were forcibly removed, infected, massacred, locked up. They were so effectively removed and locked up that they do not even enter into the erotic fictions of the dominating culture. (Kay et al. 328)

Knowing this, Two-Spirit writers, artists, and scholars should turn to and create our own Sovereign Erotic literatures.

In Our Oldest Language

Tsuj'/ Boy, you are ga-lv-lo'/sky
continually above me
I am eloh'/earth your hands reach
inside to aching molten rock
Your fingers gilded wings
that rise and thrust against
dark muscle rhythms
rock me until I am coiled
around you blooming

Your lightning tongue
summons me to skim
the sweltering expanse of your back
tempts me to nv-yo-i/the rocky place
between your thighs where
you are hard as a cedar flute
a-s-da-ya/taut
as a drum

Water swells at your bank
threatens to break loose
But I am slow
so slow and steady as a panther
Nibble and suck
strawberries
Flick my tongue across their dark tips
u-wa-n-sv ale tsu-wo-du/ripe and beautiful
Lure their flavor to the surface of your skin

My mouth hungry for your pulse
even and soft on my lips
My hands blanketed by your hair
Your chest silvered and wet
against mine

V:v/Yes
Our moans a low fierce rumble
a coming storm[11]

Two-Spirit people are creating literatures that reflect Sovereign Erotics, and in doing so participate in the process of radical, holistic decolonization. The erotic within First Nations literatures is rarely examined, and Two-Spirit erotics are often ignored. Womack observes, "I would speculate that a queer Indian presence...*fundamentally* challenges the American mythos about Indians in a manner the public will not accept. Deeply embedded in the romanticism about Indians are ideas regarding gender.... The queer Indian fits none of these popular imaginings" (*Red on Red* 280).

In Her I Am by Chrystos (Menominee) has received praise from other Two-Spirit, Lesbian, and Queer identified women, but has been largely ignored by critics. Not only is this due to the fact that unapologetic Lesbian erotica threatens heteropatriarchal culture, but also because the Sovereign Erotic set forth in her book deals with histories of abuse and colonization that deeply complicate the text. *In Her I Am* demonstrates radical Two-Spirit woman-centered erotics as tools for healing from colonization. The poem "Against" grapples with genocide, abuse, and homophobia and their effects on sexual relationships:

> *We're survivors of childhood violence with black eyes*
> *in common from mothers who hated our difference*
> *[. . . . .]*
> *Your people as well as mine slaughtered in millions*
> *Queer we're still open season*
> *My fingermarks on your ass are loving you*
> *[. . . . .]*
> *Desire red & raw as wounds we disguise*
> *we're open season.* (Chrystos 4–25)

It is poems such as this, which examine the complexities of sexuality within an abusive culture, that are needed in order for Two-Spirit people to engage with healing and (re)creating Sovereign Erotic spaces in our lives and work. Chrystos writes,

> Because sex has been split off from us as women in a colonizer culture, we ourselves police our pleasure.... We need to engage in a radical discussion & redefinition of our sexuality, a discussion which has been co-opted to issues of biology (abortion & conception), rather than sexual freedom, remembering that freedom needs the bones of responsibility to flourish. (83)

Chrystos undertakes this redefinition through the creation of erotic poems for other Native Two-Spirit women that encompass First Nations traditions and histories. In "Woman" the gathering of wild rice is eroticized:

will you come with me moving
through rivers to soft lakebeds
[. . . . .]
Will you go with me
down the long waters smoothly shaking
life into our journey. (Chrystos 1–6)

Likewise, "Tenderly Your" situates the erotic within historical memory:

We're in the grass of prairies our grandmothers rode
Sweet smell of distant cookpots edges the blue
Your kisses are a hundred years old & newly born. (Chrystos 3–5)

The poem continues by discussing the erotic as a tool for healing from trauma:

Flaming ride us past our rapes our pain
past years when we stumbled lost
[. . . . .]
This
is why we were made by creation. (9–14)

Sovereign Erotics are also reflected in Craig Womack's *Drowning in Fire*. Through the narrative of Josh Henneha, lines between historical memory and contemporary lives spiral into one another. The erotic relationship that develops between Josh and Jimmy weaves itself into a history of Creek resistance to allotment and Oklahoma statehood. Snake motifs throughout the text represent both the supernatural tie-snake, an embodiment of opposites, and the Snake faction in Creek resistance history. During a sexual encounter between Josh and Jimmy, snakes appear:

There were snakes everywhere, shimmering rainbows of color and motion, circles and circles.... A copperhead was dancing around one of Jimmy's Air Jordans lying on the floor. A giant rattlesnake sat coiled around the copperhead and the tennis shoes, shaking his tail like an accompaniment to the swaying dance inside the circles they had made, the snakes within snakes.... The whip snake came down from the lamp, crawled over our way, placed his head on the edge of the sparse white sheet, and flicked his tongue at us. (Womack, *Drowning in Fire* 200)

Womack also connects the erotic to the sacred through the relationship between Josh and Jimmy. After the couple makes love in a creek, Josh dreams:

I dreamed that I came back a year later with him and the pond was no longer there, only a large, shimmering mud flat.... In the dried-up creekbed, at the exact spot where Jimmy had come in the creek, had grown a red cedar. My Aunt Lucy stepped out from behind it, and she laughed at the way she'd startled us. "See, boys," she said, nodding at the cedar, "now you know where those trees come from. (*Drowning in Fire* 279)

The Sovereign Erotics created by Two-Spirits are part of the healing of the wounded bodies of ourselves, our lands, and our planet. Collections of First Nations erotic writing that include the work of Two-Spirit writers such as *Without Reservation: Indigenous Erotica* edited by Kateri Akiwenzie-Damm (Anishanaabe) and *Red Ink Magazine*'s Love & Erotic Issue (Volume 11:1) are quickly emerging in North America. We were stolen from our bodies, but now we are taking ourselves back. First Nations Two-Spirits are blooming like dandelions in the landscape of a racist, homophobic, and transphobic culture's ordered garden. Through over 500 years of colonization's efforts to kill our startling beauty, our roots have proven too deep and complicated to pull out of the soil of our origin, the soil where we are nurtured by the sacrifices that were made by our ancestors' commitment to love us.

And we are fighters in this long war
to bring us all back home

Notes
This paper was originally presented as a keynote speech to Portland State University Queers and Allies on April 26, 2002.

1 The Cherokee used in the poem is a translation of "Amazing Grace."

2 My use of the term "sovereign" is in no way an attempt to challenge or replace the legal definitions of sovereignty. As Native nations, sovereignty specifically refers to the legal relationships our nations have with other governments and nations, including the United States. By using the terms "sovereign" and "sovereignty" in relationship to tribally specific and traditional understandings of our bodies, sexualities, genders, erotic senses of self, terms employed in the formation of identities, or other non-legal contexts, I'm using the words as metaphors for relationships between Native people and nations and the non-Native nations, people, values, and understandings that occupy and exist within our traditional lands.

3 Historically, non-Indigenous (i.e., non-Native American) anthropologists used the term berdache to identify the presence of male-bodied transgendered individuals. Derived from a Persian term meaning captive, prisoner, or slave, the term, now considered outdated and offensive, has been replaced by "two-spirited."

4 While I am choosing to focus on erotics as a site of decolonization and sovereignty, it should be made clear that I do not think of the term "Two-Spirit" as a pan-Native term synonymous with "Gay," or "Lesbian." The various traditions being called "Two-Spirit" are often much more about gender identity and gender expression than about sexual orientation. I also realize the problematic nature of using one term for our various and vastly differing tribal traditions, understandings, and identities. I am choosing to use the term "Two-Spirit" throughout this essay because it does not make me splinter off sexuality from race, gender from culture. It was created specifically to hold, not diminish or erase, complexities. It is a sovereign term in the invaders' tongue.

5 It should also be remembered that Cherokees and other First Nations people were sold into slavery. For a thorough discussion of the enslavement of First Nations peoples, see Cherokee/Assateague-Gingaskin scholar Ron Welburn's essay "The Other Middle Passage: The Bermuda-Barbados Trade in Native American Slaves" in *Roanoke and Wampum: Topics in Native American Heritage and Literatures* (2001).

6 Dagmar Thorpe's (Sauk and Fox/Potawatomi/Kickapoo) interview with Charlotte Black Elk (Lakota) (157).

7 As of the writing of this essay, there is a study being conducted, however, through the University of Washington's School of Social Work called the Two-Spirit Honor Project.

8 An invasion, it should be remembered, rooted in the murder and expulsion of Sefardí Jews and Muslim North Africans during the Inquisition.

9 While he used the names Billy and Brandon, "Brandon Teena" is a name created by activists by switching the first and last names given to Brandon at birth. I learned of Brandon's mixed blood ancestry through an unlikely text, *All She Wanted* by Aphrodite Jones. The book is widely criticized in Trans communities for its transphobia and sensationalistic "true-crime" style. In a particularly racist passage that at once romanticizes Brandon's Native features and celebrates his light skin and eyes, Jones writes, "Their grandfather on their father's side was a full-blooded Sioux Indian, so Teena…was an exotic-looking infant. To JoAnn (Brandon's mother), she almost looked black, even though it was only her hair that was dark. Teena was beautiful, blessed with the bluest Irish eyes" (Jones 29). Besides "Sioux," Brandon's tribal affiliation is not mentioned. *All She Wanted* is the only book about Brandon's life and murder, and in some ways remains more factual than the highly popular film *Boys Don't Cry*.

10 (Dis)ability, as an alternative to "disability," was coined in 1999 by radical activist and writer Colin Kennedy Donovan and appears in the 'zine *Fuck Pity: Issue Number One: Not Yr Goddamn Poster Child*. I have chosen to use this term because it draws attention to "disability" as a social and political construct rather than an inherent "condition" blamed on our bodies and minds.

11 By the author, originally published in *Red Ink Magazine*.

Works Cited

Akiwenzie-Damm, Kateri, ed. *Without Reservation: Indigenous Erotica*. Cape Croker Reserve ON: Kegedonce P, 2003.

Awiakta, Marilou. *Selu: Seeking the Corn-Mother's Wisdom*. Golden, CO: Fulcrum, 1993.

Brant, Beth. *Writing as Witness: Essay and Talk*. Toronto: Women's P, 1994.

Chrystos. *In Her I Am*. Vancouver, BC: Press Gang, 1993.

Donovan, Colin Kennedy. *Fuck Pity: Issue Number One: Not Yr Goddamn Poster Child*. Seattle: Independently Published, 2000.

Driskill, Qwo-Li. "In Our Oldest Language." *Red Ink Magazine. Love & Erotics*. Volume 11.1. Tucson: U of Arizona, Fall 2003.

Hill, Barbara-Helen. *Shaking the Rattle: Healing the Trauma of Colonization*. Penticton, BC: Theytus Books, 1995.

Jacobs, Sue-Ellen, Wesley Thomas, and Sabine Lang, eds. *Two-Spirit People: Native American Gender Identity, Sexuality and Spirituality*. Urbana: U of Illinois P, 1997.

Jones, Aphrodite. *All She Wanted*. New York: Pocket Books, 1996.

Kay, Kerwin, Jill Nagle, and Baruch Gould, eds. *Male Lust: Pleasure, Power, and Transformation*. Binghamton NY: Harrington Park, 2000.

Lorde, Audre. *Sister Outsider*. Freedom CA: Crossing P, 1984.

Mankiller, Wilma. *Mankiller: A Chief and Her People*. New York: St. Martin's, 1993.

Mooney, James. *History, Myths, and Sacred Formulas of the Cherokees*. Asheville, NC: Bright Mountain Books, 1992.

Thorpe, Dagmar. *People of the Seventh Fire: Returning Lifeways of Native America*. Ithaca, NY: Akwe:kon P, 1996.

Welburn, Ron. *Roanoke and Wampum: Topics in Native American Heritage and Literatures*. New York: Peter Lang, 2001.

Womack, Craig S. *Drowning in Fire*. Tucson: U of Arizona P, 2001.

———. *Red on Red: Native American Literary Separatism*. Minneapolis: U of Minnesota P, 1999.

Daniel David Moses

"The Trickster's Laugh: My Meeting with Tomson and Lenore"

Daniel David Moses is Delaware and grew up on Six Nations lands on the Grand River near Brantford, Ontario. He is a prolific poet and playwright who has written such acclaimed plays as *Almighty Voice and His Wife* (1991) and *The Indian Medicine Shows* (1996), and a respected professor in the Drama Department at Queen's University in Kingston. Conforming to the ideology of "The Committee to Re-Establish the Trickster," which he created in 1986 with Tomson Highway and Lenore Keeshig [Tobias], Moses's work incorporates western and traditional poetic and dramatic strategies to subvert and resist colonialism.

Moses's 2004 essay describes the 1986 initiative he undertook with Tomson Highway and Leonore Keeshig [Tobias] which led to the creation of "The Committee to Re-Establish the Trickster." The Committee promoted the incorporation of traditional spirituality and knowledge into Indigenous artistic works in order to both preserve culture and demonstrate to audiences that Indigenous culture and spirituality was living and vibrant, and not vanishing. Because the Trickster is emblematic of a different worldview, and common to most Indigenous cultures, the three writers chose it as the cultural symbol that would define their movement. The Committee was immensely successful, in part because of the media attention it received with the spin off from the Oka Crisis in 1990, when Indigenous rights and cultures were in the spotlight. Trickster figures have subsequently become an easily accessible but arguably oversimplified cultural symbol. Recent critical works, such as Deanna Reder and Linda Morra's influential collection *Troubling Trickster* (2010),[1] deconstruct the apparent oversimplification.

Moses, Daniel David. "The Trickster's Laugh: My Meeting with Tomson and Lenore." *AIQ* 28.1–2 (2004): 107–11.

---

1 Deanna Reder and Linda M. Morra, eds., *Troubling Tricksters: Revisioning Critical Conversations* (Waterloo, ON: Wilfrid Laurier UP, 2010).

The Trickster's Laugh: My Meeting with Tomson and Lenore

It is late winter or early spring, 1986, when I get my good idea.

I have worked part-time then on my poetry "habit" for a half-dozen years, in and around the city of Toronto, Ontario, Canada. I have been—here is the sort of soft irony a person with degrees in fine arts can expect—a security officer at the Art Gallery of Ontario. I have also been an assistant immigration officer at Pearson International Airport, where, when I pointed out that harder irony—me, an Indian, doing that job five hundred years too late!—it was a joke not everyone appreciated.

In the meantime, I have met and worked with a circle of other First Nations writers—though I think the term "First Nation" had not yet come into parlance—a circle drawn around the writer/storyteller Lenore Keeshig-Tobias. And I have begun working with a board full of First Nation and other artists and community members who have answered a cry for help from Tomson Highway, the new artistic director of Native Earth Performing Arts, the Native actors' theatre. With him, at this time a fledgling playwright, we are saving the company from dissolution, transforming it into a theatre focused on writers.

So I have seen what we are all doing, that it is good and worthy of attention. Having seen another group of writers in the city getting attention just because they are a group, I decide we too should organize, and I invite my colleagues, Lenore and Tomson, to a meeting. From the outside we may all look alike—there are family resemblances—but from the inside there are differences in cultural values, assumptions, and behaviors that persist now as they did in "time immemorial"—some of our elders really dig the rhetoric—differences that persist despite the best bad efforts of the Canadian government and churches to establish their own cultural values, assumptions, and behaviors among those they would know as "Indians." So the question then is what can a meeting of a Cree musician and playwright (Tomson), an Ojibwa storyteller (Lenore), and a Delaware poet with Iroquoian roots (me) agree to agree on?

I am sure we talk about ourselves, about our different journeys to the city, about the stories we are intent on telling, and about our ways of telling them. These considerations doubtlessly include stories of our families and far-flung communities, stories that are still years later rarely told or heard in the city or any region of Canada other than those areas reserved for those of us who are officially "Indians." Yes, we grew up on reserves, more or less at the mercy of the Department of Indian Affairs and Catholic and Anglican mission churches: Tomson probably more at the mercy, since he dealt with residential school, Lenore less so since her talents took her to a private school on a scholarship, me least of all since I did not have to leave my family until I went to university. But even I am haunted by my grandmother's warning: "What do you want to talk about all that Indian stuff for? It will only get you in trouble."

Whatever sense of our identities as First Nations people we have dared develop, we have done so on purpose, part of a first generation of Indians—that is a legal status in Canada—who have had the option of thinking of themselves as something like citizens. We were finally allowed the vote in 1960 without having to first give up our Indian identity. It is not a franchise we adopt with enthusiasm; the larger society's cultural values, assumptions, and behaviors seem so at odds with our own.

In our meeting, we—Tomson, Lenore, and I—must surely also be considering beauty (if I am remembering correctly Tomson's proclivities), the lessons of our traditions (if I know Lenore's focus), and, if I am consistent in my yearnings, the meaning of it all. We are finding, in our considerations, that we are at odds often but laughing almost always. We find, yes, we find we share a sense of humor that—we remark—we have not usually been able to share with our non-Native peers.

Tomson is already at work on *The Rez Sisters*, a play that will make him famous in Canada, and the thread that weaves his story of a community of First Nations women together is a male character, a playful yet ominous spirit who embodied the hopes and fears of those women characters, a presence who is soon to be perceived as the first salvo in the campaign we are coming up with. (Lenore will use an Every-man/white man/lover sort of presence in her own work.)

What we are coming up with as our area of agreement is a rather rich irony. (The name comes in a laugh after the meeting as I cross the subway platform at Yonge and Bloor on my way home.) We come up with a political-sounding literary/cultural organization we call the Committee to Re-Establish the Trickster.

It seems to us that this bureaucratic convenience, this whitewashing "they all look alike" official government "Indian" label we are saddled with is a stereotype. How seriously can you be taken as a human being or an artist if people think you are heroic or stoic or romantic or a problem? We want people besides ourselves to be dissatisfied with those stereotypes. We do not think they are doing any good. They certainly are not doing us Native writers any good. You get tired of being told your work is not credible because it does not conform to stereotypes. We are interested in getting a bit beyond the stereotypes. We want to try to tell something like the truth, in case somebody out there might be able to hear it. Truth is stranger than stereotypes, than ignorance, stranger even than fiction—which does seem to be a problem with, or for, fiction.

It is not like you can change the truth, take the strangeness out of it, at least in a democracy—and Canada is still tending generally, despite the momentum of capitalism, toward democracy. But why manage truth that way anyway? Variety would seem to be more than the proverbial spice. Especially in a market-driven democracy, it would seem the main course. So why not shift fiction more strangely toward the truth?

We are much younger then, but that is all we want: to open up a space for a little bit of the strange but true about us. (It helps—terrible irony—that the Oka crisis, that standoff between the Canadian military and a Mohawk community over a burial ground, occurs shortly after our own efforts commence, making them for a time a necessary part of what the liberal media frowns over.)

What we choose to lever open that space with is a tool some anthropologist or ethnologist came up with—digging around through our stories, taking them apart, sorting those parts and slapping labels on them, one of those labels being the category "archetype," with a subheading "Trickster." It is in us to hope that if this Trickster character was strange enough to a scientist to be marked and remarked upon, then it might also be true enough to get us all beyond the scientific attention span.

It also does not hurt that the Trickster as we know or rediscover him, as Coyote or Weesageejak or Nanabush, as Raven or Glooscap, is as shifty and shiftless, as horny and greedy, as lucky, as funny, as human as any of us. So we take that archetype up, started waving it around, the banner of our Committee to Re-Establish the Trickster. And for the next couple years, we do lectures and workshops to explain, even put out a couple issues of a little magazine dedicated to the idea that the Trickster is emblematic of our different worldview and the different literature connected to it.

And just what might some of those differences be that this shifty Trickster entity seems emblematic of? Why take the funny seriously? For me, it is something Lenore had said—probably in a writing circle discussion—about storytelling's usefulness from times immemorial always being threefold. The first purpose, to entertain, is clear even within the context of the larger Canadian culture. The laughter of agreement that the Trickster provokes in entertaining us helps us to recognize the familiar, the funny/ha-ha. The second purpose of storytelling, to educate, is not quite as clear in the context I know, is a bit fuzzier, just because my mainstream peers—have they too been at the mercy of churches and schools?—fear being seen as preaching or teaching because it too often means bad writing. The laughter that the Trickster provokes in teaching us helps us recognize the funny/strange. The third purpose of storytelling, to heal, is not clear to me at all at first. Writers are not doctors, witch doctors even, are they?

But it feels so simple and right, maybe too obvious to need articulation, this entire tripartite artistic, meaningful imperative, and it occurs to me that nowhere in my education—and I have managed to attend two universities in pursuit of my writerly art and craft—nowhere has there ever been consideration of the why of being an artist, only of the how, and there has never been interest in who I am, a person from a specific community and culture, only in my talent. The customary first questions First Nations persons ask each other upon meeting are still, Where are you from? Who are your parents? That customary other inquiry I met in school about what I did—they meant genre of writing, poetry or prose—is further along in the conversation, if asked at all.

When you come where I come from, not being asked that question about origins feels at first like not being acknowledged as human, like the questioner is rude or being cruel or does not know any better, or even as if he is imposing another set of cultural values, assumptions, and behaviors upon me. It takes some getting used to. A lot of First Nations people cannot put up with it, do not adjust to the culture of, say, a university, and just make their way, unacknowledged, imposed upon, aching, back to their home reserves. My colleagues and I had managed to put up with it in pursuit of our arts and crafts.

How? What was our strength? If I can take as evidence this story of the three of us, Tomson, Lenore, and I, meeting together that one time, laughing in both recognition and strangeness across our immemorial differences, I have to say that that is how the healing laughter of stories works. The Trickster as we knew or rediscovered him, as Coyote or Weesageejak or Nanabush, as Raven or Glooscap, as ourselves, was so shifty and shiftless, so horny and greedy, so lucky, so funny, it almost did not hurt us to be human.

Daniel Heath Justice

"The Necessity of Nationhood: Affirming the Sovereignty of Indigenous National Literatures"

Daniel Heath Justice was raised in the mining town of Victor, Colorado, and is an enrolled citizen of the Cherokee Nation. He is Chair of the First Nations Studies Program and associate professor of First Nations Studies and English at the University of British Columbia, and lives in the traditional, ancestral, and unceded territories of the Musqueam people. A prolific writer and committed scholar of Indigenous literatures and political self-determination, Justice recently co-edited *The Oxford Handbook of Indigenous American Literature* (2015). In addition to critical work that focuses on Indigenous intellectual production, literary nationalism, and queer literature, he also writes Indigenous and queer fantasy fiction, and has published novels and short stories.

Justice's uncompromising 2005 article, "The Necessity of Nationhood," critiques Canadian perceptions of Indigenous Peoples as cultural rather than national entities. Citing Michaëlle Jean, the Governor General at the time, Justice argues that her promotion of a "unified Canada" erases and displaces indigenous nationhood. The article is particularly revolutionary in that it underlines the distinction between immigrants and First Peoples, the latter who lost land, resources, and political identity to non-Indigenous peoples, whether early settlers or newer immigrants who inherited the legacy. Justice writes: "Indigenousness is *not* ethnic difference; it is both cultural and political distinctiveness, defined by land-based genealogical connections and obligations to human and nonhuman bonds of kinship." He goes on to argue that sovereignty must be part of literary studies since most analyses have been done through an assimilative lens—which doesn't recognize the identity of individual communities. Like so many of the critics included in this collection, Justice argues that culture cannot be separated from politics, since excluding politics divorces literature from reality, and gives access to Indigenous thought and identity without accountability.

Justice, Daniel Heath. "The Necessity of Nationhood: Affirming the Sovereignty of Indigenous National Literatures." *Moveable Margins*. Ed. Chelva Kanaganayakam. Toronto: TSAR, 2005. 143–59.

The Necessity of Nationhood: Affirming the Sovereignty of Indigenous National Literatures

The only obvious difference between the French and the Indians [in Canada] is that the French represent a formidable voting block, which can decide who comes to power and who does not.... So is the right of identity simply a privilege of power?
—Thomas King[1]

The relationship of Aboriginal literatures to the broader Canadian literary canon is not unlike that of Aboriginal peoples in relationship to the Canadian nation-state—in a word, it is vexed. As Kristina Fagan (Métis) points out, "Canadian critics of Aboriginal literature have tended to look through the lenses of culture and colonialism," therefore side-stepping the issue of nationhood, which stands as one of the most significant historical and contemporary concerns for Indigenous peoples worldwide.[2]

This essay is engaged with two primary questions, one prescriptive, the other descriptive: what should be the role of nationhood in the study of Indigenous literatures in Canada today, and what is the significance of political nationhood in broader Canadian contexts? Each question is deeply implicated in the consideration of the other, and it is necessary to address both in the context of thinking of a vibrant and ethical literary criticism in this land. But before commenting at length on the first question, it seems particularly useful to begin with a reflection on the latter.

The "Good of All"?
As I write this essay, the twenty-sixth Governor General of Canada, Adrienne Clarkson, has ended her term, one marked by her well-documented commitment to recognizing the continued presence of First Nations and other Aboriginal peoples. Her successor, Michaëlle Jean, has been officially installed into the position. As I have learned since coming to Toronto three years ago, the Governor General, as Head of State, stands as both representative of the Crown to the Canadian people, and the representative of Canada to the world. As such, Jean's inaugural address—much lauded in Anglophone Canada, much derided in Quebec—gives some idea of how the mercurial public sentiment toward other "solitudes" in Canada colours the relationship of Aboriginal nations to the Crown.

In her inaugural address, Jean made the following bold announcement:

The time of the "two solitudes" that for too long described the character of this country is past. The narrow notion of "every person for himself" does not belong in today's world, which demands that we learn to see beyond our wounds, beyond our differences for the good of all. Quite the contrary: we must eliminate the spectre of all the solitudes and promote solidarity among all the citizens who make up the Canada of today.[3]

While ostensibly commenting on the competing sovereignties of Quebec and Anglophone Canada, Jean's installation speech casts a much wider net, one with implications that quite firmly and predictably displace Aboriginal nationhood. Her support for a single model of Canadian cultural and political supremacy expressly demands an erasure of Indigenous political or social autonomy. By placing immigrants and settlers as both the moral and physical inheritors of a political *terra nullis*, in which the only significance of Aboriginal peoples is their generous facilitation of colonization, Jean presents a multicultural feel-good Canadian Dream that is firmly ahistorical, unabashedly assimilationist, and genealogically dependent upon hundreds of years of brutally repressive public policy toward First Nations and other Aboriginal peoples.

While Jean provides token mentions of "the wisdom of the First Nations," whose great contribution to the Canadian nation-state has been to "pass on to...new settlers the essence of this generous land," her speech presents the place of Indigenousness in Canada as expressly *cultural*, not political. According to Jean, there are many quaint and colourful cultures in Canada, but they are all part of One Canada. National unity makes the dreams of a poor Haitian immigrant a reality, and through hard work and love of Queen and country, she found that she could even rise to the rank of Right Honourable Governor General. Any idea that the unified nation-state of Canada which fulfilled her dreams and ambitions might have been built ingloriously on the bodies of Indigenous peoples is displaced in favour of the more heart-warming and predictable narrative of the Nice Natives sitting down with the Sweet Settlers to weave the grand Canadian tapestry. All we seem to lack from this account is the turkey dinner.

I do not doubt Jean's sincerity, nor her love of the Dominion of Canada. Nor do I dismiss the very real struggles that she and millions of other Canadians have faced in making a place for themselves in this land; as an immigrant myself, I feel some measure of affinity for her quest to find a new home that is free of the constraints of the old one. Yet, as a *Cherokee* immigrant to Canada, I am also very well aware of the fact that my presence in this land is inevitably connected to histories and policies of displacement against the Indigenous nations who were here first, and who are here still. No matter how sympathetic we might be to the very real difficulties and traumas of immigrant experiences, we cannot ignore the fact that the opportunities for non-Natives in Canada come as a consequence of the land loss, resource expropriation, social upheaval, and political repression of Aboriginal peoples. The "good of all" is not, unfortunately, quite as simple as it sounds, nor is it quite true in this case.

Affirming Nationhood

This introductory analysis, though questioning the problematic patriotism of the Governor General's speech, should not be assumed to be either a sweeping dismissal or an unreflective celebration of nationalism. Cultural critics such as Benedict Anderson, Paul Gilroy, Homi K. Bhabha, and others have made clear the constructed nature of collectivized identities, but their most influential analyses are generally concerned with the dominating creeds of nation-states and racialized identities. The political specificities that define the kinship-based ethos of Indigenous nationhood are deserving of a separate consideration, one that engages with both the political concept and reality of Indigenous nations, particularly as those qualities are represented in the literatures of Aboriginal writers in Canada. By doing so, I want to argue not only the necessity of such nationhood in any consideration of Aboriginal peoples, but also, perhaps, the inevitability of such an idea when respectfully approaching Native issues, for the discourses of Indigenousness in North America have always been rooted in political assertions of collective identity through their ties to land, kinship, and history. To deny the centrality of politics from Indigenous identities and cultural and artistic expressions is to dismiss the centuries of armed and ideological struggle of Aboriginal peoples to retain their communal, self-determining sovereignty. Similarly, to be a member of an Indigenous nation in a colonized country is a political act in itself, as the existence of such a collective is an embodied denial of the power of the State to claim either historical or moral inheritance of the land or its memories.

Jean's insistence on the good of all Canadians over the "spectre of all the solitudes"—"all" being a significant modifier, as it unequivocally extends beyond the issue of Quebec separatism—links her words and their implications to a rhetorical tradition that claims Indigenous lands and resources for the appropriative priorities of the nation-state.[4] There is nothing neutral in this language. However well-intended it may have been, such language is ultimately hostile to the survival of Aboriginal peoples as anything other than dispersed and fragmented ethnic individuals, whose identities descend from the assimilative commercial multiculturalism of Canada rather than being rooted in the kinship rights and responsibilities that have defined Aboriginal values, knowledge, and politics for thousands of years.

Indigenousness is *not* ethnic difference; it is both cultural and political distinctiveness, defined by land-based genealogical connections and obligations to human and nonhuman bonds of kinship. "Aboriginal cultures," according to David Bedford and Danielle Irving, "are not simply one more strand of a multicultural tapestry.

Their traditions, which probably most Aboriginal persons want to preserve, are not easily compatible with the bourgeois, liberal democracy to which the remainder of Canada is committed. Being treated as equal Canadians amounts to culture genocide."[5] Cultural and, I would argue, political, as the political has been consistently targeted in Canadian policies toward Aboriginal peoples.

Indeed, re-embedding the political in the analysis of culture is necessary in understanding Aboriginal issues, as Kanawake Mohawk political theorist Taiaiake Alfred demonstrates: "Indigenous governance systems embody distinctive political values, radically different from those of the mainstream. Western notions of dominion (human and natural) are noticeably absent; in their place we find harmony, autonomy, and respect."[6] Cooperative relationship is central to most Indigenous epistemologies, both contemporary and historical; coercion and racial compartmentalization as foundations for social and political control have little common currency in the vast majority of Aboriginal traditions. When humanity is one of many equal peoples in the world—sharing the right of consciousness and significance with the rest of creation—humility shapes both the individual and communal response to the world, and the values of balanced relationship are more important than any individual achievement, especially those that might threaten that balance.[7]

Kinship and community sit at the centre of Indigenous political and cultural expression worldwide. In contrast, individualist Eurowestern politics of majority-rule democracy, along with free trade capitalism, emphasize competition and coercion as fundamental social values, and the dangers posed by these systems to Indigenous peoples are not insignificant, as Maori scholar Graham Hingangaroa Smith notes:

[We must move] beyond the focus on the type of individualism that comes out of the new economic ideologies. The new focus on individual rights and freedoms and on individual choice is at once in conflict with one of the fundamental values associated with Indigenous peoples: the recognition of our collective solidarity. Such collectivity is embedded in our notions of family, tribe, cultural traits, values, and practices.[8]

Yet collectivity is only one part of what has been called "the peoplehood matrix," in which collective Indigenous sovereignty is embedded. According to Tom Holm (Cherokee-Creek), J. Diane Pearson, and Ben Chavis (Lumbee), there are four common and interconnected elements in Indigenous politico-social structures: language, place/territory, sacred history, and ceremonial cycle, all of which are expressed through community in lived experience and socio-political expression. Such a conceptual model, the authors argue, "is a holistic matrix and reflects a much more accurate picture of the ways in which Native Americans act, react, pass along knowledge, and connect with the ordinary as well as the supernatural worlds."[9] This conceptual model of relationship and engagement is far more responsive to the adaptive dynamics of Indigenous epistemologies than are the antiquated progressivist models of "savagism" and "civilization" that still permeate law and popular culture, and which locate Aboriginal sovereignties solely as historical, culture-based structures rather than as expressions of both historical *and* contemporary political concerns.[10]

It is worth noting that the vast bulk of nation-state Indian policy regarding Aboriginal peoples in Canada and the US has specifically targeted Indigenous peoples as peoples, not as individuals. The existence of other sovereignties within the territorial boundaries claimed by these nation-states has been an obsessive topic of concern for both, on both economic and political grounds. As Holm, Pearson, and Chavis note, "colonization is the attempt to dispossess indigenous groups by denying, undermining, or attacking their existence as peoples.... colonizing powers, to further their own goals, attempt to strip from indigenous groups each of the four aspects of peoplehood through the means of territorial dispossession, assimilation, religious conversion, or outright extermination."[11] Even a casual glimpse at the policies of Canada and the US demonstrate the perceived threat of Indigenous nationhood to the nation-state, with assimilation of the tribal body into the state population—and the associated extinguishment of communal cultural, spiritual, land, and resource rights—as the dominant concern of the colonizing enterprise.[12]

If the dynamics of kinship relationships are the political extension of sovereign Indigenous nationhood, as defined by communities by themselves in the context of a physical and spiritual relationship to one another and to a particular land, then it seems reasonable to posit the recognition of nation-to-nation relationship as a useful and ethical foundation for analyzing a wide range of Aboriginal and Canadian issues, from politics, and history to sociology, medicine, and literature. To dismiss nationhood from analysis, especially when it is such a concern of Indigenous peoples themselves, once more silences Native voices and perspectives and reinforces the dominative power of Canadian colonialism.

The acknowledgment of nationhood does not, however, require an oppositional relationship to other sovereignties, as numerous alliances, including that between the Six Nations of the Haudenosaunee Confederation, make clear.[13] Indeed, an inherently antagonistic sovereignty is counter to relational worldviews that emphasize cooperation; kinship requires an adaptability that can accommodate the integration of others into the kinship system, either through adoption or alliance, two much-honoured social and political traditions in Indigenous North America. Alliance can itself be a site of Indigenous political action, according to Malea Powell (Eastern Miami-Shawnee):

> We need a new language, one that doesn't convince us of our unutterable and ongoing differences, one that doesn't force us to see one another as competitors. We need a language that allows us to imagine respectful and reciprocal

relationships that acknowledge the degree to which we need one another (have needed one another) in order to survive and flourish. We need, I would argue, an alliance based on the shared assumption that "surviving genocide and advocating sovereignty and survival" has been a focus for many of the people now on this continent for several centuries and, as such, should also be at the center of our scholarly and pedagogical practices enacted in these United States.... I propose this reimagined alliance not out of idealism, but out of my historical understanding of the ways in which such practices were central to the earliest treaty-relationships between folks who would later be called "American Indians" and the European explorers, traders, and settlers who came to this continent.[14]

Aboriginal peoples need not be seen as inevitable opponents or enemies of those communities that make up the Canadian nation-states. However, for any alliance relationship to truly be successful, it must be built on a foundation of mutual respect and equality, where the sovereignty of each participant is substantively acknowledged and taken into consideration, no matter how large a disparity there may be in size or power between the associated sovereignties. Anything less than full reciprocity of respect—on shared terms and standing, not imposed assumptions—is inadequate to the task of an informed ethical understanding within or among peoples.

Literary Nationalism

Extending this idea of an alliance and respect based on equal sovereignty into the other structural theme of this essay, assimilative multiculturalism simply *cannot* be the assumed common ground for discussion if we are to engage in a responsible and meaningful study of Aboriginal literatures. Although Aboriginal writing has received increasing scholarly and mainstream attention since the 1973 publication of Maria Campbell's autobiography, *Halfbreed*, much of that engagement has been through this assimilative lens, through which Indigenous peoples are read primarily as colourful contributors to the great Canadian socio-cultural mosaic. While this reading is generally intended by scholars and teachers to affirm the human dignity of Aboriginal peoples, it ironically erases one of the most fundamental aspects of Indigenous survival: the status of nationhood.

As Kristina Fagan argues in her incisive literary analysis of Taiaiake Alfred's political treatise *Peace, Power, Righteousness: An Indigenous Manifesto*, the cultural study of Indigenous literatures, though common in academia, is divorced from being relevant to Indigenous lives, and is weakened by its avoidance of political concerns. Yet it is precisely this distance from Native realities that drives its popularity. She writes:

The "cultural" approach (sometimes called "culturalism") has been the most popular way of thinking about Aboriginal literature and identifying particular aspects of Aboriginal cultures (such as tricksters or medicine wheels) in a text. Compared to "nation," however, "culture" can be a politically soft and shifty term. Our ideas about culture walk close to "folklore," associated with identifiable external symbols—distinctive clothing, food, housing, language, and so on. Canada has a long history of fascination with such symbols; they represent a non-challenging form of difference where Aboriginal peoples become yet another culture in the mosaic.[15]

Although culture is an important area of study, when it is separated from the political sphere, readers are distanced from both the uncomfortable personal implications of colonialism as well as decolonizing strategies of intervening in the colonizing processes. "Culture" alone is voyeuristic; it gives access without accountability, and it fetishizes the surface at the expense of deeper significance.

Such avoidance is understandable to a degree, as discussions of colonialism—just like discussions of race, gender, class, sexuality, and other political realities—can evoke feelings of guilt, blame, fear, anger, frustration, and hopelessness. Yet those discussions also open a space for silenced voices to be heard again; they can break open assumptions and expectations, reembody exorcised histories, and open our minds and hearts to other ways of seeing, knowing, and believing. They also provide us with the possibility of developing anticolonial strategies that empower both Native and non-Native peoples toward lasting social justice. Cultural readings, by themselves, distract us, and they fix our attention on shallow surfaces. Culture alone cannot change the world. The power—and danger—of nationhood is that it *can*. Fagan acknowledges this, stating that "Aboriginal nationalism involves specific political demands with which the critic must try to come to terms. If we choose to work with the concept of Aboriginal nationalism, we must consider to what extent we support Aboriginal nationalist claims. And if we do support those claims, what does that mean in terms of literary value?"[16] We are implicated in the ethical consequences of our readings no matter what we do, but only one option gives us the possibility of challenging the terms and effects of that implication.

The critical expression of nationhood in Native literatures—literary nationalism—is a powerful extension of Indigenous intellectual sovereignty, where, according to Robert Warrior (Osage), the purpose is "not a struggle to be free from the influence of anything outside ourselves, but a process of asserting the power we possess as communities and individuals to make decisions that affect our lives."[17] Literary nationalism looks first to Indigenous contexts for interpretive analysis, to social histories, intellectual values, ceremonial traditions, and lived experiences of being both tribal—as in one's specific nation—and being Indian/Native/Aboriginal/Indigenous, a broader category. The plurality of each of these categories is not accidental. There is no monolithic "Native way" of expressing national or individual ideas, no single "Aboriginal worldview" that encompasses the variety of Aboriginal perspectives. Just as there are many First Nations and Aboriginal communities, so too are there many sovereign understandings of all that it is to be Indigenous in Canada.

Placing Indigenous nationhood at the centre of analysis shifts the interpretive lens. Doing so does not assume that non-Natives have no place in the conversation; it does, however, privilege Indigenous sovereignty of expression. Terms such as "mediation," "cross-cultural," "hybridity," and "cosmopolitan" abound in critical studies of Aboriginal literature, and while some good work has been written with a focus on bridging Native and non-Native worlds, the underlying implication is almost always that non-Native understanding is central to the exercise of Indigenous literary criticism. Once again, non-Natives are given a privileged (and, ironically, often central) place in the discussion, and when that point of privilege explicitly displaces Aboriginal nationhood and priorities, it renews and replicates the mechanisms of colonialism that many of the writers claim to reject.[18]

With nationhood and respect as defining principles of analysis, all participants enter with an awareness of their subject positions, and non-Natives cannot assume to be the subject of concern. Rather than Indigenous writers, scholars, and readers being located as optional guests at the Canadian literary table, this shift places the meal firmly in Indigenous hands, where non-Natives understand themselves as guests, and where Native priorities determine the nature of the food and conversations. Such a shift is an idea very much in keeping with Muskogee Creek-Cherokee scholar Craig Womack's call for literary separatism, in which "tribal literatures are not some branch waiting to be grafted onto the main trunk. Tribal literatures are the *tree*, the oldest literatures in the Americas, the most American of American literatures. We *are* the canon."[19]

Engaging Native literary contexts on their own social and political terms is the aim of literary nationalism. How, then, might such an analysis function, and how would it be different from current culturalist readings, especially in Canada, where the critical voices advocating this position are relatively few? The literature itself is a good place to start. Too often we read authors and texts in isolation from any shared context aside from the general "Native Canadian" or "Native American" category. This can certainly give us an idea of the larger commonalities between colonized peoples in North America, but it is a necessarily meager result. What if we either replace or add to that reading one that firmly locates multiple writers of a shared national tradition in conversation with one another?

My own theoretical approach to the question is by examining nation-specific literatures and readings; following the revolutionary Creek-centred work of Craig Womack, my first scholarly book is a study of Cherokee literature through Cherokee political and social history. Given that critics, politicians, and the general public so frequently collapse specific nations into a generalized pan-Native category that erases the distinctiveness of its constituent parts, an approach that privileges specific nations and traditions seems to me an important intervention in the field, and one that gives voice to peoples and worldviews that are often erased or homogenized. Such a model need not be reduced to ethnographic reportage; if done thoughtfully, it will be anything but, as its attention to the socio-political is rooted first in the voices and texts themselves, then radiates outward to encompass the full and varied contexts of internal meaning and significance. A nationhood focus, far from being myopic or parochial in scope, actually necessitates engagement with broader influences, as one cannot know the intimate without understanding the ways in which that intimacy has been shaped by exterior social and environmental forces. A literary nationalist is thus very well placed to study cosmopolitan concerns, and often on a much deeper level than those who take a more generalist approach to Native literatures.

For example, although the term "Aboriginal" in Canada encompasses First Nations, Inuit, and Métis writers, the perspectives, needs, and concerns of each broadly defined group are lost in the general category "Aboriginal," as are the specific impacts and influences of broader social and political pressures. A generalized course on Aboriginal literature has a necessarily limited amount of time and resources to give to these specificities, so any study posited on this model will inevitably provide a very limited understanding of both the cultural and political contexts of the literature, as well as their aesthetic dimensions and functions. Yet if we take a nationalist approach and examine one or a few nations in greater depth—and with it, a smaller body of texts on a more intimate level—we become connected to the lives, hopes, dreams, and imaginations of the people in profound ways.

The Métis literary tradition is a good example. When we read the work of Métis authors as part of a diverse but connected political, historical, and literary genealogy, as well as culture, we not only get a deeper understanding of the conditions under which this literature has been produced, advocated, challenged, and disseminated, we are also more thoughtfully immersed in the relationships between the texts, their times, and their authors *according to Métis priorities*. Although Maria Campbell, Gregory Scofield, Beatrice Culleton Mosionier, Marilyn Dumont, and other Métis writers each have individual voices and perspectives, their diverse works are part of broader expressions of specifically Métis subjectivities. As being Métis means to be in a distinctive political status, both in relation to other Aboriginal peoples and the Canadian nation-state, any literature that expresses Métis subjectivity is inevitably embedded in political questions and concerns. The peoplehood matrix of Métis nationalism provides context and depth that other reading strategies are inadequately situated to engage.

This is not, however, to say that nation-specific analyses are the only thoughtful way of approaching the concept of nationhood in Indigenous literature. A thematic or alliance-based model is also in keeping with Indigenous political priorities, while avoiding the pitfalls of pan-Native or hybridist criticism that displace Native specificities. Cherokee scholar Jace Weaver's 1997 critical study, *That the People Might*

Live: Native American Literatures and Native American Community, examines peo-ple-hood and nationalism across a wide range of texts, authors, and communities, which he links through the neologism of "communitism" ("community" plus "activ-ism"). Looking for these shared links does not necessitate a politically-or culturally-divorced approach; if anything, those links demonstrate the moral imperative of integrating nationhood into the analysis. Weaver says it best when he writes: "Only when we relate literatures to, and situate them in, Native history and the changes in Native cultures can we begin to understand them.... Criticism not focused on and rooted in Native communities only serves the myths of conquest and dominance that seek to subdue and conquer, render tame, our stories."[20]

Imagination

It is the aforementioned moral imperative of highlighting Indigenous nation-hood that seems, to my mind, the most compelling justification for taking such an approach. In the end, literature is an extension of the dreams, hopes, fears, and visions of its creators, and imagination is an essential aspect of any community's survival. In every chapter of *The Truth about Stories: A Native Narrative,* Thomas King writes, "The truth about stories is that that's all we are."[21] In making this statement, King is not diminishing the power of stories; in fact, he is emphasizing their power to transform and shape the very reality in which we exist. Stories are our world; they give dimension and texture to our existence, give us a sense of both the possible and impossible.

Those of us concerned with the continued survival and dignity of Aboriginal peoples have an obligation to expand the imaginative reach of those things that are possible. To teach Aboriginal literature as only quaint cultural artifact is to limit the imagination, to say that nationhood is impossible, that the only way to endure after centuries of genocide and dispossession is by fragmenting and blending in to the very system that created the devastation in the first place. It is to deny Aboriginal peoples the opportunity to heal from the woundings of history, to seek mutually respectful alliances with or strategic separations from non-Natives as they best see fit. It is also to deny non-Aboriginal peoples the chance to intervene in the consequences of their own participation in the colonialist enterprise, to seek a just and equitable future that is mindful of the past.

Imagining new realities is inevitable; it is part of being human. However, the terms of that imagining are always in flux, and here again we come to the moral imperative of doing this work. If, as David Newhouse (Onondaga) asserts, "the creation of the Indian was an act of political imagination," where "Europeans took a thousand different communities and created something that did not exist before: a new people," then it serves to reason that "the created who were made without imagination now have imaginations and are using these imaginations to create a new world and challenge the creators."[22] We can choose to replicate the impotent

Indians of public policy and popular stereotype, or we can affirm the new world to which Newhouse refers, one which represents Aboriginal peoples on their own terms, according to their own diverse and varied histories, priorities, rights, and responsibilities.

Indigenous nationhood, in all its messy uncertainties, inconsistencies, and complications, is an integral part of that challenge, as it places our struggle at the heart of our survival. It is not simply blind jingoism in redface and feathers; if anything, it demands of its practitioners strength, patience, and humility, for it places us firmly in a reciprocal relationship of obligations to living peoples and the kinship networks of which we are all a part. And it posits an understanding where process is more important than product, as kinship is a living system, a set of actions and responses that change and impact others, not a static state of being. Nationhood—the political expression of kinship—is a constant act of creation, one that affirms the lives, dreams, and commitments of Indigenous peoples.

The affirmation of "One Canada"—or even one French Canada and one English Canada—cannot be said to be for the "good of all" when it relegates Aboriginal peoples to the position of bystanders in a land that they have inhabited since time immemorial. To engage honestly, sincerely, and deeply with Aboriginal concerns is to take into account the significance of nationhood to those concerns. Indigenous nations are not now, nor have they ever been, satellites of the nation-state. Yes, they stand as solitudes—not by choice, but by necessity. Colonization has given Aboriginal peoples and their literatures two ultimately untenable options: assimilation, or tokenism. Neither choice acknowledges Native humanity and agency, for both relegate Indigenousness to a secondary consideration in relation to the ambitions and interests of the Dominion of Canada.

Yet there *are* other alternatives, options that come from Aboriginal peoples themselves and grow strong in Native soil, options that open the imaginative possibilities beyond the Hobson's choice of assimilation and objectification. As a political, intellectual, and cultural expression of Indigenous realities and sovereignties, literary nationalism offers a much-needed intellectual and ethical corrective to the colonialist study of Indigenous literatures.

Notes

1 Thomas King, *The Truth about Stories: A Native Narrative* (Toronto: House of Anansi P, 2003), 149.

2 Kristina Fagan, "Tewatatha:wi: Aboriginal Nationalism in Taiaiake Alfred's *Peace, Power, Righteousness: An Indigenous Manifesto*," in *American Indian Quarterly* 28.1 (Winter 2004), 12.

3 Michaëlle Jean, installation speech, 27 September 2005, Governor General of Canada website, <www.gg.ca/media/doc.asp?lang=e&DociD=4574>, 18 October 2005.

4 This statement should not be read as supportive of the Quebec sovereignty movement. Just as the "states-rights" movement in the United States has been consistently anti-Native, often advocating the termination of tribal land and resource rights and the abrogation of treaties between American Indian tribes and the US government, so too has Quebec continually demonstrated its quite selective approach to sovereignty. The Quebec separatist movement is firmly embedded in the hyper-assimilative patriotism model of exclusion, and is thus as compromised as that of the nation-state of Canada. Although Quebec sovereigntists are quite articulate about their own desire for sovereignty, their dismissal of similar Indigenous assertions—which has a much longer genealogy that significantly predates that of Quebec—amounts to an ultimately indefensible hypocrisy.

5 David Bedford and Danielle Irving, *The Tragedy of Progress: Marxism, Modernity, and the Aboriginal Question* (Halifax: Fernwood, 2001), 11–12.

6 Taiaiake Alfred, *Peace, Power, Righteousness: An Indigenous Manifesto* (Toronto: Oxford UP, 1999), 5.

7 In *Honour Earth Mother/Mino-Audjaudauh Mizzu-Kummik-Quae* (Wiarton, ON: Kegedonce P, 2003), Anishinaabe writer Basil Johnston explores this relationship, noting that "What our ancestors found out about the world was sacred; everything was sacred by virtue of its creation by Kitchi-Manitou, and everything was sacred because every form of life had an element of mystery" (148). Much of the book explores the nature of this mystery, in which all peoples—human, plant, animal, mineral, elemental—have consciousness and personalities, and all express themselves in various ways.

8 Graham Hingangaroa Smith, "Protecting and Respecting Indigenous Knowledge," in *Reclaiming Indigenous Voice and Vision*, edited by Marie Battiste (Vancouver: U of British Columbia P, 2000), 214–15.

9 Tom Holm, J. Diane Pearson, and Ben Chavis, "The Peoplehood Matrix: A Model for the Extension of Sovereignty in American Indian Studies," *Wicazo Sa Review* 18.1 (Spring 2003), 15.

10 See again *The Tragedy of Progress*, where coauthors Bedford and Irving analyze the progressivist biases of modernity that have stood as one of the central conceptual underpinnings of social science, and with it public policy toward Aboriginal peoples. Progressivism, as part of the Enlightenment project of infinite human perfectability, implies social evolution from primitive (or savage) states to more advanced and "civilized" ones. In this model, Indigenous nations (as "tribes") have traditionally been seen at the bottom of the evolutionary scale, with free-market Eurowestern nation-states at the top.

11 Holm, Pearson, and Chavis, "The Peoplehood Matrix," 17.

12 In Canada, examples include: the Indian Act regime and the selective use of Indian status to disenfranchise significant numbers of Native women; Métis exclusion from treaty rights and land protections; the residential school system

and the role of religious proselytism, education, and abuse to coercively separate Native children from home, family, language, and culture; the "sixties scoop," in which provincial governments targeted Aboriginal children for removal from their communities and subsequent adoption into Eurowestern families; the proposed White Paper of 1969, which aimed to fully terminate Indian status and land rights and which has, in subsequent years, been a model for incremental implementation, as with the recent controversy regarding the failed First Nations Governance Act. In the US, examples include: the Grant Civilization Policy that paralleled the Canadian residential school system in many regards; allotment of tribal land holdings; termination of federal recognition in the middle of the twentieth century; and relocation of Indian families to urban areas with the express purpose of breaking up reservations.

13 In Iroquois tradition, the Haudenosaunee Confederation—or the Iroquois League—was founded by the Peacemaker along a philosophical and political structure known as the Great Law of Peace, in which warring communities were brought together in a common cause. Although they were bound together in alliance, the distinctiveness of each nation of the Confederation—Onondaga, Mohawk, Seneca, Oneida, Cayuga, and, later, Tuscarora—was recognized as being vital to the totality's success. The Great Law was an expansionist philosophy that encompassed other nations but, unlike Eurowestern expansionism, recognized the sovereignty of those nations that were integrated into the League. See "They Are the Soul of the Councils," chapter three of *Iroquoian Women: The Gantowisas*, by Barbara Alice Mann (Seneca), for an insightful analysis of the Confederation's political and cultural expansionism.

14 Malea Powell, "Down by the River, or How Susan La Flesche Picotte Can Teach Us about Alliance as a 'Practice of Survivance,'" *College English* 67.1 (September 2004), 41–42.

15 Fagan, "Tewatatha:wi," 13–14.

16 Fagan, "Tewatatha:wi," 17.

17 Robert Allen Warrior, *Tribal Secrets: Recovering American Indian Intellectual Traditions* (Minneapolis: U of Minnesota P, 1995), p. 124. Warrior, along with Jace Weaver (Cherokee) and Craig Womack (Muskogee Creek-Cherokee) use the term "literary nationalism" as both the conceptual centre and tide of their forthcoming book, *American Indian Literary Nationalism*, and it is from this and their other varied works that I draw my own understanding of the term.

18 For a very troubling example of such displacement and appropriation, see Elvira Pulitano's *Toward a Native American Critical Theory* (Lincoln: U of Nebraska P, 2003). Womack has written an extended response to her book in the manuscript of *American Indian Literary Nationalism* (see above); I have also discussed the book at length in "Rhetorical Removals: A Review Essay," forthcoming from *Studies in American Indian Literatures*. Pulitano's book is an extended attack on

literary nationalism, drawn from the underlying perspective that colonization in the Americas has compromised Indigenous "purity" to such a degree that no one can really speak with legitimacy as an Indigenous person—except, of course, for non-Native scholars whose "cosmopolitan" perspective places them in an informed and authoritative position to do so. Needless to say, such a claim flies in the face of Indigenous survival.

19 Craig S. Womack, *Red on Red: Native American Literary Separatism* (Minneapolis: U of Minnesota P, 1999), 6–7.

20 Jace Weaver, *That the People Might Live: Native American Literatures and Native American Community* (New York: Oxford UP, 1997), 165.

21 King, *The Truth about Stories*, 122.

22 David Newhouse, "Imagining New Worlds: The Aboriginal Imagination," in *Aboriginal Cultural Landscapes*, ed. Oakes, Riewe, Belanger, et al. (Aboriginal Issues P, 2004), 84.

Sam McKegney

"Indigenous Writing and the Residential School Legacy: A Public Interview with Basil Johnston"

Sam McKegney is a settler scholar living on the traditional lands of the Mohawk and Ojibway peoples, where he teaches Indigenous and Canadian literatures at Queen's University, and works on masculinity theory, Indigenous governance, multiculturalism, hockey culture, and literary activism. In the interest of ethical scholarship, he conducts interviews with Indigenous writers, scholars, and activists and privileges context and action when theorizing his findings. His latest book is *Masculindians: Conversations about Indigenous Manhood* (2014).

McKegney's interview with the renowned Ojibway writer, scholar, and linguist took place in 2007, shortly before the Prime Minister's apology to Indigenous peoples for the government's residential school policy. This period, McKegney explains, was marked by optimism and the feeling that change was in store for Indigenous peoples, and the interview both reflects and problematizes this sense of hope. Johnston discusses residential schools in general, and his own experience in particular, in order to demonstrate the effectiveness of literature—and the inadequacy of historical record—to deal with settler-Indigenous relations and the legacy of the schools. This conforms to the ideas Johnston presents in both his essays "Is That All There Is? Tribal Literatures," and "One Generation from Extinction," the latter reproduced in this collection. It also reinforces Eigenbrod's article stressing the importance of literature in Indigenous studies. Literature and the act of writing, Johnston explains, can reimagine the world and give agency to the powerless. Interestingly however, Johnston disappoints desires for redemptive reconciliation when he concludes by saying, "people don't learn. They make the same stupid mistakes."

McKegney, Sam. "Indigenous Writing and the Residential School Legacy: A Public Interview with Basil Johnston." *SCL/ÉLC* 34.2 (2009): 264–74.

Indigenous Writing and the Residential School Legacy: A Public Interview with Basil Johnston

Throughout his prolific literary career, Anishinaubae[1] elder, orator, and teacher Basil H. Johnston has advocated passionately for Indigenous cultural revitalization in Canada. Several of his fifteen English-language books, including *Ojibway Heritage* (1976), *Ojibway Ceremonies* (1982), *The Manitous* (1996), and *Honour Earth Mother* (2003), participate in the endurance of Anishinaubae worldview by examining the social, political, and spiritual traditions of the Anishinaubaeg. He has also published five books in the Ojibway language and developed an audio program for language retention among Anishinaubae youth. Johnston has been committed, over the past forty years, to ensuring the survival of elements of Anishinaubae culture that the Canadian government and Christian churches sought to eradicate through the disastrous policy of residential schooling, of which Johnston was himself a victim. It has been surprising to some, therefore, that Johnston's writings on the residential school system have avoided explicit condemnation of federal policy.[2] Published in 1988, Johnston's seminal memoir *Indian School Days* employs what Deena Rymhs calls a "mild, nostalgic tone" (5) rather than an overtly critical one to, in Johnston's own words, recall "not the dark and dismal, but the incidents that brought a little cheer and relief to a bleak existence" at Spanish Indian Residential School where Johnston was a student from 1939 to 1947 (*Indian* 11).[3] Avoiding the hyperbole often associated with the system (by both its defenders and its critics), Johnston has acknowledged that "you can't credit [residential] schools with everything, nor can you blame [the] schools for everything" (qtd. in Lutz 239).

I met with Johnston at Toronto's Gladstone Hotel for a public interview to discuss Indigenous writing and the legacy of residential schooling as part of Pages Bookstore's "This Is Not a Reading Series."[4] It took place on 4 December 2007, during a period of profound change in the public discourse on the residential school legacy. After decades of denial and evasion, the federal government had belatedly signed the Indian Residential Schools Settlement Agreement in May 2006; the Common Experience Payments were finally finding their way into the hands of Indigenous survivors by late autumn the following year; and the Official Apology of the Canadian Government to the First Nations, Métis, and Inuit was set to occur on 11 June 2008, during the same month in which the Truth and Reconciliation Commission would begin. The interview thus took place at a time of intense (albeit cautious) optimism regarding the possibility for reimagined relations between Indigenous nations and the Canadian state and for forms of Indigenous empowerment and communal well-being that such relations might augur.

SM   In *Indian School Days*, you stress that the experience of residential school was more difficult for the "wee ones" who were ripped from their families and social systems at the ages of five or six and therefore didn't have the foundation of self-worth and culture that older entrants, like you, might have developed. Tell us about your experience of entering the residential school at Spanish and the feelings of dislocation involved.

BJ   The little ones suffered the most, thrown into the schools, as they were, when they were still really babies. They were outcasts—cast out of their communities, families and homes. And what was worse, they were made to feel unloved and unwanted. They were told, of course, that Jesus loved them, but they were never given the love for which a child's spirit yearns: never hugged, never caressed when they wept, never told "I love you." So when those little ones were released into the world a decade later, they were lost; they were adrift in an alien world that didn't accept them, a world in which they no longer belonged.

I guess, therefore, that I was "lucky"—if you can call it that—to enter the school at ten years of age with some sense of my culture and a sense that my mother loved me. But there was so much pain in that place. I'm talking about students who were violated, students who were raped by their own kind, by older Native students, fifteen to sixteen, and by the priests immediately after mass, by brothers in the various workplaces. And you often wondered what penalties [the perpetrators] had to undergo. Did they go to Father Superior and say, "This is what I had in mind, and this is what I did thereafter"? Not likely.

I didn't know it [then, but] when I was raped by two boys—and, not long after, I was fellated by a priest immediately after mass—I really was thrown into another world. Abuse is too mild a word. It's a violation of the worst kind. It violates not only the body—the flesh—but also the spirit. And you live with this fear of death and fear of being dispatched to Hell.

And I thought, and many of us thought, that we were the only victims.

When I met Lucy—who was my wife and who remained my wife for forty-two years—when I met her and during the...well, thirty-five ensuing years, I never mentioned what happened to me. And when the students at Spanish sued the federal government and the Jesuits, I ended up on the negotiating team. That's when I learned that I was not the only one, that there were hundreds of other youngsters who had suffered the same indignities.

And when you become a victim of this, what happens is that you lose whatever sense of integrity that you've got. You are a worthless thing. And it's confirmed in the gospel readings that Jesus had to die for "our" sins.

Anyway, it's hard to get over that. It takes years, years, years.

And then I met Lucy who—after a year and a half, well, not quite a year and a half, maybe six months after we started going out—said, "I love you," to me. My sense of integrity and sense of worth escalated.

SM   What do you make of the contrition of church and state representatives regarding their roles in administering this system that enabled your violation and that of so many others? Do you feel that the churches—many of which have officially apologized to Indigenous peoples—and the Canadian government—which will purportedly apologize in the coming months—are sincere in their stated regret?

BJ   When I became part of the negotiating team for the suit against the federal government and the Jesuits, I learned a lot of things. At one of the meetings, they had the Father Superior for the Upper Canada Society of Jesus and his assistant, and one of the members of the team from the girls' school spoke. And there were many, many tears in the audience. And I watched the two Jesuits. There was not a sign of sympathy. Not one.

Two years ago this past spring, I was invited up to a spiritual centre up on Anderson Lake, just south of Espanola. And I was called by the Jesuits and the Anglican Church and the United Church ministries. And I told them, "You know, you talk about sympathy, compassion. You don't have any compassion! It's just a word. And it's supposed to have conveyed a sense of feeling, a sense of pity for your fellow human being. But it isn't there. It's an abstract notion."

And that's still my opinion about these institutions.

SM   It's interesting that you identified individual human reactions—or rather, non-reactions—from the Jesuits at that meeting but then finished your comments with "these institutions." This suggests that human behaviour can be circumscribed by systems like that of the Jesuits, which you note in *Indian School Days* prevented the brothers from showing the students any form of love.

Do you feel that appropriate systems have been put in place to deal with the legacy of residential schools? A system of compensation, for instance, has been set in place with the Common Experience Payments, and such vehicles as the Aboriginal Healing Foundation have been financed and given specific mandates. You mentioned healing circles when you and I were speaking a moment ago; do you care to comment on the relevance of the whole "healing industry"?

BJ   You know, I've found that there's an awful lot of charlatans out there, not only Native, but also psychologists. They have an answer for everything. [*laughter*] All we need is a healing circle. "Come on in and we'll heal you. We'll take you to a sweat lodge. Brother, come in and be healed!"

And even though I'm very cynical about these things—a healing circle is not an instantaneous, miraculous healing; it takes a lot of time—one of the conditions [in our legal suit] that never passed was that we have healing from recognized, registered psychologists. And Wilbur Nadjiwon objected. He said, "I'm not havin' no twenty-two-year-old kid with a psychology degree come and try to heal me, looking inside my soul and my spirit!" And I feel the same way. If I want one, I want one who speaks my language.

No. Being healed—the healing has to come from inside, from ourselves. And some don't know it, unfortunately.

I don't think I was able to articulate it, but I used to fight, fight, fight. And each time I fought, there was always some bigger guy, somebody heavier, somebody who knew how to fight a little better, and "Pow!" I'd go down. I'd cry. Somebody would say, "Get up!" And I've taken that as a model for life. When you're felled, you don't wallow in self-pity. You get up.

I don't know if the general asking of forgiveness will do much good. I was asked, "Would you forgive?" I don't know. No one has ever asked me, "Will you forgive me?" for what the church has done, for what the government allowed their church to do. The government is just as much at fault.

I feel like fighting. [*laughter*]

SM I'm glad I'm on this side of the table!

If the goals of the Canadian government and the Canadian population are really "truth" and "reconciliation," how can these be attained in the shadow of trauma? After the racist violence of a system of education designed to tear Indian identity from Indigenous students, how can the righteous rage of the Indigenous population not spill out in forms of hatred toward non-Indigenous Canada?

BJ How? I'm not sure there is one answer. How? Am I a bigot? I don't know. I don't think so. I try not to be.

I used to teach high school in North York. I had one rule: be fair in all your dealings. We had some examples of lies, bigotry. I remember there was a grade 10-11 ST&T [Science, Technology and Trades] class, and one of the boys complained that the boy sitting in front of him always wore the same outfit every single day. And that the boy who wore this outfit smelled.

Well, I didn't know quite what to do. But you know, the boys themselves settled it. They told the complainant that he was a bigot and they apologized to the boy who was being complained on. That was one way. It was the crowd of maybe twenty-five boys of goodwill asserting their displeasure. And altogether, I think too many people stay silent when we've got incidents or articulations of ill will.

SM   Part of the government's strategy for dealing with the residential school legacy has been to historicize the system by requisitioning historical accounts. Certain church groups have financed such publications as well. In *Indian School Days*, you deliberately took an alternative tact by avoiding sources like government policy statements, federal and church archives, newspapers, etc., and focusing on the behaviour of the children—not the typical focus of history.

Do you feel that the history of residential schooling in Canada has been adequately accounted for? What are your thoughts on Canadian history as a discipline?

BJ   I was explaining the causes of the raz[ing] of Fort Ste. Marie in 1648 by the Iroquois to a group of . . . I think they were Mormons. That was in 1968 at the Canadian National Exhibition. And so they went away shaking their heads, you know, wagging their heads in agreement with this stuff that I had found in history books. After they had gone, Howard Skye (Onondaga from Six Nations) plucked me by the sleeve and said, "Would you like to hear *our* story?"

I didn't know that there was another story. The only stories that I knew were those that had been "properly documented." And so he took me aside, and he told me this story:

"When the missionaries settled down in Fort Ste. Marie and Midland, they established a school, and they were teaching the Huron kids and some of the Anishinaubae kids how to read, write, count, and learn all kinds of 'civilized' things that weren't available to the Haudenosaunee youngsters. So the Haudenosaunee or Six Nations asked the missionaries if they could send their boys and girls up to Fort Ste. Marie because this was a good thing.

"In the spring, when they went back up to recover their young boys and girls, some of the girls were pregnant and some of the boys had been violated. So the Six Nations issued a warning. The second year, the same results took place.

"Instead of issuing a third warning, they sent eighteen hundred warriors in March of 1648 and torched Fort Ste. Marie."

So that was the story that he told me. And then that also changed the way I look on history today. There are stories that are not recorded. And there are all kinds of stories of events that have been suppressed; it goes a long, long way back.

And the war today, it's a war for oil. It has nothing to do with the Taliban, nothing to do with al-Qaeda. Oil. And I'm more inclined to believe that than what the president of the United States says.

SM   What about Indigenous understandings of the past? Have Indigenous communities done a better job grappling with the meaning of this history than, say, mainstream historians or the federal government? What do you feel is needed in this regard?

BJ   My next book will be about that. I am giving back to my heritage what it has given me: that is, an understanding of my heritage and my understanding of me. One of the projects is to set down our history from *our* point of view. I'm lucky. I know the stories. I know the words, many of the words. I know how we look on history.

And I'm going to make a real good case for the existence of institutions that the United States took up and adopted in its constitution and part of which Canada has adopted. I know European history and that they didn't have those institutions until they came over here and found them. We had them. We've got words for them. And I know where they fit in.

SM   Is an element of learning that history, and making it relevant to contemporary Indigenous people, encouraging youth and others to learn their Indigenous languages? And how can that be facilitated?

BJ   I've got all kinds of CDs on language...

SM   ...and they can be picked up at your nearest... [*laughter*]

BJ   Write to me!

SM   In terms of action, we've spoken about external strategies for dealing with legacies of acculturation and violence—strategies like psychotherapy, monetary compensation, and church-run healing circles—but what about strategies emerging within Indigenous communities themselves? What needs to be done throughout Indigenous Canada, and on your reserve specifically, to counteract the corrosive influence of a century of residential schooling?

BJ   In teaching, in schools, we have to get back to the old values. For example, I was talking to Joan Roy in May about the loss of the sense of duty. The whole emphasis is on rights. "My rights are being violated." "My rights are being infringed upon." There's not a word about duties.

To us, a right is *debnimzewin*. But each right is also a duty. And we've forgotten to teach those in our Native schools. I've also noticed that they don't teach much in terms of duties to your neighbours in the secular schools and in the public school system of Ontario. And so we have to go back to some of these values: responsibility, duty, right.

And from my readings, I gather that the principal teachers [in Anishinaubae culture] were the grandmothers. They were the holders and keepers of the wisdom.

Not so much the men but it was the women. And they were assigned this duty by the community because the males were out and it was the grandmothers who kept the villages together. And they had the primary responsibility of training the youth.

And I guess there is [a] need to go back to that system, to have grandmothers taking part in schools, teaching language, teaching the literature of the people. Our literature is rich with stories. I know five or six hundred. It's a matter of putting those in sequence.

SM   Do you consider there to be a role for literature in Indigenous empowerment? I'm thinking of a story from your book *The Manitous* (1995) in which the Anishinaubae Trickster/Hero figure Nana'b'oozoo causes the regeneration of the world by breathing life into a tiny ball of mud. You write, "Nana'b'oozoo...had done what everyone is supposed to do, to quest for that tiny knot of soil, the gift of talent, and to make from it one's being and world" (12). Do you feel that literature and storytelling can be used to create one's "being" and one's "world" or at least to augment one's perceptions of those things? Has storytelling assisted you, for instance, in forms of self-realization?

BJ   Well, it confirmed my worth, my sense of worth, but also the worth of my background. And so that, along with Lucy's love and the love of the Native people who offered me guidance, helped me, I think, restore my sense of integrity and sense of purpose.

SM   The impact of literature—or at least literature that finds an audience—moves beyond the author her- or himself. I've often thought of *Indian School Days* as a story designed to celebrate and consolidate the community developed among Indigenous students at Spanish, students torn from their families and home communities. In that way, the story is a social act. At the same time, *Indian School Days* reorients historical focus on residential schooling away from administrators and overseers toward the Indigenous students themselves, thereby recognizing far ahead of most historical accounts the agency retained by Indigenous people throughout situations of acculturation. Do you feel that books like *Indian School Days* facilitate Indigenous empowerment?

BJ   No. I wrote *Indian School Days* with what I knew back in 1979. There were, I think, sixteen of us in Toronto who had attended residential school in Spanish. And we used to talk about the things that amused us when we were there. And I suppose they were little events, silly incidents—that we created—that assisted us in pulling through.

And that was the source of *Indian School Days*. It had nothing to do with trying to change or "empower" anyone. It was just to amuse the readers of, at first, *The Ontario Indian*. I had a definite purpose in writing that book: that is, to make people smile, chuckle, chortle, guffaw... There's altogether too little of that human element in any of the books written by the most prominent authors in Canada. A lot of them aren't humorous.

Now, I will write a very different book this time.

SM A follow-up to *Indian School Days* on the residential school experience? That's exciting! What will that book look like? What will be its shape? Or, are you not in a position to divulge that at this point?

BJ I'd better not.

Ever attuned to audience expectation, the seventy-eight-year-old author concluded the formal interview by leaving his listeners hungry for more details about this work in progress, which was but one of three major projects to which he alluded during the discussion.

During the open question period that followed, one audience member noted the age difference between interviewer and interviewee and asked if it had taken a new generation to start dealing with sins of the past like residential school.

BJ I don't think people ever learn. I really don't think they learn from the mistakes of the past. They don't even learn from their own mistakes. They keep repeating them and repeating them and repeating them. I'm not sure that there's any lesson in residential schools that would, you know, enlighten the nation. Maybe it'll get people more sensitive to our situations.

I think that much of the situations at home on Indian reserves really cannot be attributed too much to the residential school system but to the Indian agency system. They were our managers. They looked after every single aspect of our lives. They're the guys who held us back.

And now we have professional young people—lawyers, businesspeople—they're the people who are going to make a difference. But I really don't believe that people learn from mistakes that were made in the past.

Johnston's response apparently chafed against the desire of some in the audience for validation that Canadian society is progressing in terms of human rights and intercultural empathy. A second audience member pressed Johnston to acknowledge progress by asserting that activists and critical thinkers have accomplished a great deal by analyzing the past and seeking out more just and equitable courses of action.

BJ I don't know if I can articulate it clearer than what I've already given voice to. That's my belief, you know, my observation. People don't learn. They make the same stupid mistakes.

SM Well, does this link back to your unwillingness to simply give up teaching? There are still things to be learned, so you put the ideas out there. You write the books. You want people to read them. You want Anishinaubae children to learn their language, to learn their culture. And just because we don't, I guess, learn the lessons as fully as we should, doesn't mean the teaching should stop.[5]

BJ No. I never would advocate that.

SM So maybe there's some learning that still needs to be done.

BJ There's always hope. [*laughter*]

Notes

1 The Anishinaubaeg are a populous and diverse Indigenous nation whose traditional lands encompass much of what is now Ontario while stretching into Manitoba, Quebec, and the United States. Tribal communities within the Anishinaubae nation include the Ojibway (also known as Ojibwe, Ojibwa, and Chippewa). For this publication, I employ the spelling of Anishinaubae Johnston uses in *The Manitous*, although the spelling "Anishnabe" is more common.

2 This characteristic of Johnston's writing can be traced, in part, to the earliness of his entry into the public debate and also to the peculiarity of his authorial approach. *Indian School Days* was published prior to the disclosures of abuse by Indigenous survivors that catapulted the residential school issue into the public eye at the beginning of the 1990s. As I have written elsewhere, "*Indian School Days*...offers counterbalance to accounts focusing on disclosure of abuses and the malevolent actions of overseers by concentrating narrative attention on the dynamic, precocious, and resistant actions of young students" (*Magic Weapons* 16). Johnston thus diverts attention away from the corrosive influence of culturally genocidal pedagogy toward the retention of agency by Indigenous children who develop senses of community even in profoundly oppressive and disempowering circumstances.

3 Johnston's authorial strategy in the book has actually caused one reviewer, non-Native historian Menno Boldt, to consider the book a "loss" because its author "does not view his experience in the framework of government policy" or provide explicit "analysis of tyranny or oppression" (312).

4 The original interview, which was missing small sections due to recording malfunctions, has been edited and reordered for coherence. Both participants have had the opportunity to review and clarify their comments, but the substance of the interview remains the same.

5 My leading question here betrays my own unwillingness to heed some of the difficult lessons Johnston had shared during the evening, insofar as it seeks to

recuperate the author's prior response into the very narrative of progress he had so eloquently repudiated and thereby placate the generally sympathetic audience.

Works Cited

Boldt, Menno. Rev. of *Indian School Days* by Basil Johnston. *Canadian Literature* 124/125 (1990): 311–12.

Johnston, Basil. *Indian School Days.* Norman: U of Oklahoma P, 1988.

———. *The Manitous.* Toronto: Key Porter, 1995.

Lutz, Hartmut. *Contemporary Challenges: Conversations with Canadian Native Authors.* Saskatoon: Fifth House, 1991.

McKegney, Sam. *Magic Weapons: Aboriginal Writers Remaking Community after Residential School.* Winnipeg: U of Manitoba P, 2007.

Rymhs, Deena. "A Residential School Memoir." *Canadian Literature* 178 (2003): 58–70.

Keavy Martin

"Truth, Reconciliation and Amnesia: *Porcupines and China Dolls* and the Canadian Conscience"

Keavy Martin is a settler scholar living in Treaty 6 territory, where she teaches Indigenous literatures in the Department of English and Film Studies at the University of Alberta. Known for her work on Inuit literature—in particular her award-winning book *Stories in a New Skin: Approaches to Inuit Literature* (2012)—Martin also works on the reconciliation process; Indigenous languages; Indigenous literary nationalism and literary history; and Indigenous rights, treaties, and land claims.

Martin's 2009 essay uses Robert Alexie's 2002 novel about residential schools, *Porcupines and China Dolls*, to deconstruct Prime Minister Stephen Harper's 11 June 2008 apology to Indigenous peoples for the country's residential school policy. Working on the novel's premise that there is "no reliable cure for memory," Martin's analysis deconstructs the apology and addresses scepticism about its sincerity and potential contribution to the healing process. Alexie's characters conclude that healing is not as simple as "talkin' and cryin'," and Martin extends this premise to the apology and the Truth and Reconciliation Commission. Reconciliation, Martin argues, implies resolution and ending, and yet as the novel demonstrates, suffering continues, which reflects the idea that reconciliation is more about relieving the guilt of the dominant culture than it is about the wellbeing of Indigenous communities. Martin accomplishes what so many of the critics in this collection support: an examination of Indigenous literature that considers context, sovereignty, action, and the text itself.

Martin, Keavy. "Truth, Reconciliation and Amnesia: *Porcupines and China Dolls* and the Canadian Conscience." *ESC* 35.1 (March 2009): 47–65.

Truth, Reconciliation and Amnesia: *Porcupines and China Dolls* and the Canadian Conscience

The events of the workshop again made the news that afternoon.... In one week, Chief David, James and Jake would be known all over the NWT. In two weeks, they would be forgotten.—Robert Arthur Alexie, *Porcupines and China Dolls*

In Robert Arthur Alexie's 2002 novel *Porcupines and China Dolls*, three former residential school students shock the fictional hamlet of Aberdeen, NWT, when they disclose the sexual abuse they suffered as young boys under the care of the institution. The people have gathered this day for a healing workshop to address the suffering that alcohol has been causing in their community; the rising action of the novel is devoted to describing this dysfunction, as the narrative follows the main character, James Nathan, through his daily routine of drinking, casual sex, and suicide attempts. But when James and his friends Jake and David—now in their forties—finally put a name to the nightmares that haunt them, they begin the process of taking control of their lives and ending the cycles of abuse. As David says to the assembled people: "I'm tired of runnin'. This is where it ends. Right here 'n right now. This is where we make the change for ourselves 'n for our children. I will run no more!" (198).

The characters' attempts to "face their demons" then becomes literalized, and what follows is an almost-apocalyptic battle scene, as beady-eyed, reeking demons begin to crawl out of the walls and ceiling. The men become Warriors; they grow to impossible heights, and their voices are so mighty that "the roof of the community hall blew off and scattered to the four winds" (204). Armed suddenly with lances and swords, they take their bloody revenge on the "demons, dreams and nightmares" that have been tormenting them (196). The community joins in the epic struggle, and in an orgy of pop-culture references, the victims of residential schools are re-empowered:

> James Nathan was like a knight in shining armour. He was like Kevin Costner in *Dances with Wolves*. He was like Crazy Horse charging into battle. He was like Geronimo at his best.
> Young girls dreamed of marrying him. Young boys dreamed of becoming him. Elders dreamed they were him and cried for the good old days. (205)

Alexie's readers will recognize this scene as the cathartic climax of the healing narrative—even if it is hyperbolic beyond even what Sophocles could imagine. By finally telling their stories in a public setting, the victims seem to have purged themselves of the hurt that has already claimed many lives in Aberdeen. As one of the elder women has told them, "It's gettin' rid of it through talkin' 'n cryin' that's gonna help you. If you don't get rid of it, it'll kill you like it's done to so many of our People" (105). After the battle is over, a cool, cleansing wind sweeps through the hall, and the people soon begin to mark the re-emergence of some of their traditions: they travel out onto the land to carry the body of an abused former student to the Old People—cremating him in the old way—and after decades of obeying the Church's regulations, they witness the return of the drum. Through storytelling, ceremony, and song, the people stitch their community back together again.

It comes as a surprise, then, when James wakes up the morning after his disclosure and has the following exchange with his girlfriend:

"You okay?" Brenda asked.
"Yeah," he lied. He got up and made coffee. *Snow.*
"Whatcha gonna do today?" she asked.
"Check for caribou." *Maybe blow my brains out too.* "You?" (219)

Despite the climactic events of the previous day, things seem to have returned to normal. Sure enough, only a few pages later, James attempts suicide again, and he will try it several more times before the novel ends. The event of the community's "healing," after all, occurs only two-thirds of the way through the book, and rather than arriving at the expected denouement and hopeful, happy ending, we watch the characters continue to struggle, drink, and die. The continuation of the story at this point is radical and strange; Alexie flouts his readers' expectations regarding the preordained progress of a healing journey. Life, he suggests, goes on, and often not in the way we hope for. Despite the characters' powerful attempts to put their pasts behind them, they are unable to find a reliable cure for memory. History, it seems, cannot be so easily dissuaded.

This paper explores the desire for closure that governs not only novels like Alexie's but also national discourses around Aboriginal issues—in particular, the legacy of residential schools. While healing and reconciliation are certainly desirable occurrences, I will argue that these concepts can also entail a fixation upon *resolution* that is not only premature but problematic in its correlation with *forgetting*. The danger is that the discourse of reconciliation—though rhetorically persuasive—can at times be less about the well-being of Aboriginal peoples and communities than about freeing non-Native Canadians and their government from the guilt and continued responsibility of knowing their history. Alexie's *Porcupines and China Dolls*, however, succeeds in derailing these teleological narratives. Although the telling of the survivors' stories is linked to the process of healing, the narrative also works paradoxically to keep wounds open, as the characters continue to stumble under the weight of their history and the readers are required to bear witness. Novels like Alexie's thus work to problematize or resist the amnesia that so often accompanies movements toward reconciliation.

Slaying the National Demons

On 11 June 2008, Prime Minister Stephen Harper told a story much like James Nathan's to the House of Commons, assembled Aboriginal leaders, and other survivors of residential schools. He described the abuse experienced by many former students, and he recognized this trauma as a source of the ongoing suffering and dysfunction in many Aboriginal communities. This high-profile acknowledgement—both of a brutal history and of the state's role in it—was figured as a key factor in the movement "towards healing, reconciliation and resolution of the sad legacy of Indian Residential Schools" (Harper). Several of the Aboriginal leaders present confirmed this point: Mary Simon, President of the Inuit Tapiriit Kanatami, stated that "[T]his apology will help us all mark the end of this dark period in our collective history as a nation." Phil Fontaine, then National Chief of the Assembly of First Nations—and the man whose public testimony of residential school abuse was a major factor in increasing national attention to the issue of reparations—declared that "Canada has come of age today.... The common road of hope will bring us to reconciliation more than any words, laws, or legal claims ever could. We still have to struggle, but now we are in this together. I reach out to all Canadians today in this spirit of reconciliation."

In other words, the event of the apology repeatedly drew attention to its own significance—a performative tactic geared, perhaps, at creating a sense of progress or impending change. Indeed, each of the speakers on that day showed a preference for metaphors of journeying, of stepping forward, and of moving ahead. "You have been working on recovering from this experience for a long time," Harper said, "and in a very real sense, we are now joining you on this journey." Such figures of speech are now customary in the discourse of healing that has developed in response to the disclosure of the abuse prevalent in the residential school system (Episkenew 10–11). As James B. Waldram points out in a 2008 publication of the Aboriginal Healing Foundation, "The dominant metaphor in our research describes healing as a journey, sometimes articulated as following the 'Red Road,' the 'Sweetgrass Trail,' the 'Way of the Pipe'...or the 'Road to Wellness'" (6). Jo-Ann Fiske explains that "Roadways and pathways evoke the sense of journey that compresses the lifelong quest for recovery and personal transformation.... [These] references to pathways offer a sense of the tangible nature of the healing journey" (51). At the official apology, then, this road to recovery became common ground for the assembled speakers, both federal and Aboriginal—and, by extension, for the members of the broader Aboriginal and non-Aboriginal public, who were invited into the process or "journey" of reconciliation. Despite our differences, the speeches suggested, we are all walking the same path; we are all working toward a common goal.

As a sign of his government's commitment to forward movement, the Prime Minister acknowledged the state's ongoing complicity in the harmful legacy of the residential school system, noting that "the absence of an apology has been an impediment to healing and reconciliation." Harper's language here is telling. Absence as an impediment, as a void that forms a barrier: this complex figure of speech hints at the equivocal nature of the apology, as progress is allegedly spurred on by a temporary movement toward the past—a revisiting of past wrongs, or an acknowledgement of things that many would prefer to forget. This is the same contradictory logic that informs psychological talk therapy, Catholic confessionals, and the Truth and Reconciliation Commission of Canada (TRC),[1] now underway. In order to heal, to be forgiven, or to reconcile, we must first re-open wounds, recount sins, and resurrect conflicts. In order to forget, we must remember.

Since the apology, most of the media coverage of the TRC has focused on the disputes and eventual resignations of its former commissioners. But under the new leadership of Justice Murray Sinclair, the TRC held its first ceremony on 15 October 2009, with Governor General Michaëlle Jean as its honorary witness. Its mandate is to provide a forum for survivors to tell their stories and to educate the public about this history ("Our Mandate"). It remains to be seen, however, how Canadians unaffected by the residential school system will respond. Will they act—as the Commission would like them to—as witnesses? Will they attend public events and make use of the educational resources that are being created for them? Or will they react with disinterest or possibly even with frustration that the events are still ongoing? After all, it would have been easy to mistake the high-profile apology as the climax of this particular story. Continuing repercussions and further testimony make for a cumbersome denouement; in the inconvenient way of history, they do not fit tidily into the plot.

As a non-Aboriginal person, I do not have any family members who were victims of the residential school system. Still, many of my relatives and friends tuned in for the apology or caught pieces of it on the news, and many demonstrated a shift in awareness after the fact. "Those schools," one said, "they were worse than I knew." Like me, many Canadians were never taught about federal Indian policy in high school, and as a result they are often unable to contextualize the social problems affecting Aboriginal peoples that they encounter in the media and on the street. As

---

1   The Truth and Reconciliation Commission of Canada (TRC) was a truth and reconciliation commission organized by the parties to the Indian Residential Schools Settlement Agreement. The commission was part of an overall comprehensive response to the Indian residential school legacy. It was officially established on 2 June 2008 and terminated in June 2015.

Roland Chrisjohn (Oneida) argues in his 1997 study *The Circle Game: Shadows and Substance in the Indian Residential School Experience in Canada*, this may well be a strategic omission on the part of the government—designed to bolster the state's legitimacy (1). After all, as I now witness in my own classroom, the discovery of the nation's genocidal history does little for the self-esteem or national pride of mainstream Canadian students; in fact, it often propels them into crisis.

And it is not only the youth who struggle; in the summer of 2009, as I stood in line waiting to buy the new edition of *Porcupines and China Dolls*, a well-meaning elderly woman struck up a conversation. "What's it about?" she asked, indicating the novel. "It's about residential schools," I said, a bit simplistically. "Oh, that," she said, turning away, "I can't even hear about that." Alexie, no doubt familiar with this kind of response, writes a similar scene into the novel, as Brenda, James's erstwhile girlfriend, faces the day following the healing ceremony: "She was surprised by James's disclosure, but she decided not to bring it up. If he wanted, he would talk about it. *Besides, I can't deal with it. Not now 'n maybe never*" (220). For both Aboriginal and non-Aboriginal peoples, the prospect of having to face the past can be terrifying and at times even traumatic. Indeed, the homepage of the TRC contains the following caveat: "This web site deals with subject matter that may cause some readers to trigger (suffer trauma caused by remembering or reliving past abuse)."

The apology, however, despite its candid account of the abuses of the system, was far more palatable than the histories recounted by Chrisjohn, Alexie, and others, as it moved swiftly from atrocity and aftermath to the possibility of reconciliation. This word, "reconciliation," is intoned throughout the official discourse—in speeches, in the titles of reports, in the mandates of organizations—as well as in informal discussions amongst Canadians. With its connotations of peacemaking and of the setting aside of differences, "reconciliation" has become a kind of chant or chorus—an anthem to Canadian identity and ideals. And while this repetition may indeed function to create an impression of the restored peace or friendship denoted by the term, the idea of "reconciliation" is also, I fear, in danger of acquiring the meaninglessness of a refrain. What precisely is required for reconciliation to occur? And what will this happy state look like? In public discourse, the precise details tend to be omitted—perhaps because they are too difficult to determine, too contentious to declare, or because they may detract from the rhetorical power of the performance. While this ambiguity or lack of a firm definition may be the very thing that allows the concept of reconciliation to have such broad appeal, the resulting multiplicity of interpretations may in fact work to prohibit the very commonality that the term tries to evoke.

For example, let us consider the way in which the idea of reconciliation, when articulated in public discourse, is easily, frequently, and perhaps purposefully misunderstood as *resolution*—a term which also evokes the end of conflict but which is less clear about the extent to which it entails an ongoing relationship or responsibility. The commitment to "resolving" issues—whether they be land claims, grievances, or social discord—is a key concept in the federal discourse about Aboriginal peoples. As Indian and Northern Affairs Canada (INAC) declares on its website, the department is "responsible for addressing and resolving issues arising from the legacy of Indian Residential Schools" ("Indian"). The branch responsible for this is known as Indian and Northern Affairs Canada's Resolution Sector, formerly the Department of Indian Residential Schools Resolution Canada. With its dual signification of "putting an end to" and "determination," the term "resolve" works subtly to reassure the public of the government's commitment to solutions and progress. Interestingly, the original sense of the word—from the Latin *resolvere*—refers to loosening, dissolving, or untying. Implicit, perhaps, in the idea of resolution, is the sense of a removal of ties or a separation—a distancing—and even an ending of obligation. And while the term "reconciliation" was predominant on 11 June, it is the idea of resolution that Canadians tend to be very enthusiastic about.

After the apology aired, many were hopeful. "Is it enough now? It is over?" they asked, "Can we finally move on?" Such remarks rarely make it into reputable print sources; however, they are common enough around dinner tables and in the "Comments" sections of internet media sites (where they often take on a less-than-compassionate tone). As residential school survivor Karen Chaboyer testified to the *Toronto Sun*: "You've read them, the hate and the racism being tossed at us.... We're being called whiners. We're being told to 'get over it,' to 'move on.' I'd like for them to walk in our shoes for generations, and then have to read those kind of comments" (quoted in Bonokoski).[1] Indeed, many Canadians, when forced to confront the unpleasant realities of their nation's colonial past and present, express a yearning for the *end* of the story—or for a new chapter in which colonizer and colonized will be able to start over. Again, it seems that they are more interested in reaching a point where the wounds will have healed and the country will have reached that nebulously defined state of having atoned for its sins and reconciled with Aboriginal peoples. The actual work or *process* of reconciliation seems to be less interesting, and less compelling, than that promise of absolution.

Peter Harrison discusses this national desire for closure in his article "Dispelling Ignorance of Residential Schools" (151–60). "Typical comments," he notes, "include

---

1 It is almost impossible to browse the comments following online news stories regarding residential schools without encountering sentiments of the following kind (by one "Amped," a reader of the *Winnipeg Free Press*):

The native people of Canada need to move on with this issue rather than use it as [a] crutch/excuse for all the ills in their lives. Other ethnic groups, i.e., victims of the Holocaust, have experienced worse atrocities and have been able to move on and succeed at life. Also, what is the purpose of the residential school truth and reconciliation commission? Open up wounds and stir the pot? The government acknowledged and apologized for what occurred. Those who were sent to residential schools, mistreated or not, were duly compensated. (quoted in Simard)

While I do not assume this commentator to be representative of all public opinion in Canada, experience tells me that such opinions are far from uncommon.

questions like '*Why can people not just get over it?*' and '*Is it not time to just move on and let bygones be bygones?*'" (154–55, 158). "This opinion," he says,

> is dismissive of the trauma experienced by many Survivors of residential schooling and underestimates the difficulty of coping with the ongoing impact of such trauma. It is the naive view that somehow a page can be turned and all will be well—a matter of pulling oneself together and getting on with things. Anyone who has ever grieved or suffered trauma knows how enormously wrong such statements are and how they reflect a fundamental misunderstanding of the human condition. (158)

This sense of needing to "get over it," I would add, seems to extend beyond the particular history of residential schools to Aboriginal grievances in general. Casual discussions of lands claims and Aboriginal title, for instance, return inevitably to the idea that dispossession happened a very long time ago—or that it was a justified case of the "survival of the fittest"—and that what is really "holding Aboriginal people back" is their insistence upon remembering the past.[1] These kinds of opinions, of course, are based on a very vague or misguided understanding of colonial history and the ways in which it continues to impact some lives and benefit others. "Moving on"—or forgetting—is a luxury not everyone can afford.

Canadians who understood the apology as a solution or an ending to the legacy of residential schools may have been hearing primarily the echo of their own desires rather than the literal sense of the speeches. None of the leaders were so impolitic as to declare the process to be over; while they certainly did posit the end points of "healing, reconciliation, and resolution," they were careful to emphasize that the apology represented an initiation to the process of reconciliation, not an announcement of its conclusion (Harper). As NDP leader Jack Layton put it: "This apology must not be an end; it must be a beginning." Mary Simon agreed: "Let us not be lulled into an impression that when the sun rises tomorrow morning the pain and scars will miraculously be gone. They won't. But a new day has dawned, a new day heralded by a commitment to reconciliation, and building a new relationship with Inuit, Métis, and First Nations."

The Aboriginal Healing Foundation is likewise careful to qualify its definition of the healing process: "[T]here seems to be *no end point to the journey*. No one is ever completely healed. No one speaks of being cured in the same way biomedicine uses this concept. Even those who have been on the healing path for many years and who have become therapists themselves must struggle to remain on the path" (Waldram

---

1 See, for instance, Tom Flanagan's *First Nations? Second Thoughts* or Frances Widdowson and Albert Howard's *Disrobing the Aboriginal Industry: The Deception behind Indigenous Cultural Preservation*.

6, emphasis added). However, when this personal discourse is translated into a national context—when the journey of Aboriginal individuals and communities toward healing is rerouted onto the national expressway toward reconciliation—is this caveat about the lack of an end point still viable? Will the Canadian public and its government agree to remain on this reconciliatory journey in perpetuity? Can they conceptualize a journey without an end or—like the donkey following the carrot—do they require the promise of the achievement of the goal in order to partake in the process? In the context of the Aboriginal healing movement,[1] the metaphor of journeying seems to exist in part to *prevent* the unhealthy focus on the conclusion of the healing process;[2] in the Euro-Western framework, however, "journeying" seems to become tinged with Enlightenment-derived connotations of progress.

Reconciliation and healing are important emotional and political goals, just as they are important narrative devices. Inevitably, they involve stories of advancement, or improvement—teleological narratives, with an often-disproportionate focus on the inevitable end of the story. And while I am certainly not advocating that Canada should not be trying to improve its record, or that attempts to address our colonial legacy should cease, I am concerned about the implications of reconciliation as an unproblematized objective. As Roland Chrisjohn (Oneida) and Tanya Wasacase (Cree) write, reconciliation is a "warm and fuzzy" term which is in need of greater critical analysis—especially because it assumes the pre-existence of a harmonious period in the relationship between Aboriginal peoples and European settlers, which the process of reconciliation will hopefully restore (222).[3] Taiaiake Alfred (Kanien'kehaka) is likewise critical of what he calls the "pacifying discourse of reconciliation" (182):

Without massive restitution made to Indigenous peoples, collectively and as individuals, including land, transfers of federal and provincial funds, and other forms of compensation for past harms and continuing injustices

---

1 I use this phrase to refer generally to the series of diverse healing initiatives—many of which are linked to the Aboriginal Healing Foundation—that exist across the country (or did, before the 2010 termination of the AHF's funding). Marie Wadden, author of *Where the Pavement Ends*, also refers to this assortment of programs as the "Aboriginal recovery movement."

2 Naomi Adelson and Amanda Lipinski quote a (unnamed) traditional healer: "I don't think there is such a thing as being totally healed. I think that you are going to deal with your issues…I think you can function better if you are healing every day, so you are healing for the rest of your life. That is why I call it a journey, because it is a journey" (28).

3 "[B]efore two parties can *reconcile* they must, at some earlier time, have been *conciled*" (Chrisjohn and Wasacase 221). Some might argue, however, that the early days of the fur trade and of treaty-making—the period which the report of the Royal Commission on Aboriginal Peoples refers to as "Contact and Cooperation"—could constitute such a time (*Report*).

committed against the land and Indigenous peoples, reconciliation will permanently absolve colonial injustices and is itself a further injustice. (181)[1]

Alfred identifies an important concern regarding the latent suggestion that "reconciling" has more to do with Indigenous people coming to terms with and accepting their dispossession, rather than with significant changes—or sacrifices—being made by non-Aboriginal Canadians (183).[2]

Roger Epp problematizes the term further by highlighting a troubling aspect of the impact of the discourse of reconciliation on national memory. "Solemn offers of reconciliation," he says,

> however sincere, however eloquent, are still framed within a liberal, settler political culture, fundamentally Lockean in its philosophical fragments: forward-looking, suspicious of history, or, more likely, indifferent to it, and incorporating into its imagined social contract *an almost-willful amnesia about whatever might be divisive.* (126, emphasis added)

In other words, reconciliation inevitably involves an eventual forgetting, even as its processes ask us to remember. Indeed, the "amnesia" that is promised in the discourse of "moving on," or of "putting the past behind us," is, I believe, a major part of what made the idea of reconciliation so appealing to Canadians on 11 June 2008. It seemed to offer the possibility of starting over or of absolution. Arguably, the apology itself demonstrated a kind of therapeutic amnesia; in working to create a sense of its own significance, it down played the occurrence of the 1998 (Liberal) apology or "Statement of Reconciliation," delivered by then-Minister of Indian Affairs Jane Stewart. After all, the remembering of that event—or of the Royal Commission on Aboriginal Peoples (RCAP)—would interfere with the narrative of the 2008 apology, not to mention the current Truth and Reconciliation Commission.

The desire for reconciliation and resolution, as the 1998 apology demonstrates, is not a new arrival on the political scene, even as current initiatives attempt to

---

1 Notably, Phil Fontaine's 11 June 2008 declaration that "The common road of hope will bring us to reconciliation more than any words, laws, or legal claims ever could" seems—problematically—to be making the opposite point: that the details of land claims, rights, and restitution are of lesser importance that the spirit of reconciliation.

2 Sam McKegney, author of the 2007 study *Magic Weapons: Aboriginal Writers Remaking Community after Residential School*, reiterates this critique:

> [I]f these reconciliation and healing strategies neither fundamentally challenge the power imbalance between Euro-Canadian political authorities and Indigenous communities, nor arrest the paternalistic position of non-Native Canada vis-à-vis the First Nations, the programs designed to address the residential school legacy will never facilitate meaningful Indigenous empowerment. (179–80)

convey the impression that Canada is now ripe for reconciliation.[1] No doubt this same sense of readiness or requirement was felt in 1990, when the Oka crisis drew national attention to Aboriginal grievances and soon prompted the establishment of the Royal Commission on Aboriginal Peoples. It was also felt earlier, in 1969, when the Trudeau government released its *Statement of the Government of Canada on Indian Policy*—the infamous "White Paper." In that document—whose proposed amendments were overturned by strong opposition from Aboriginal leaders and organizations—the government declared that it

> believes that its policies must lead to the full, free and non-discriminatory participation of the Indian people in Canadian society. *Such a goal requires a break with the past.* It requires that the Indian people's role of dependence be replaced by a role of equal status, opportunity and responsibility, a role they can share with all other Canadians. (*Statement*, emphasis added)

Via a series of shrewd rhetorical manoeuvres, treaty rights are here transformed into non-equal status, becoming an obstacle rather than a benefit—a mark of discrimination rather than evidence of a series of historical agreements between nations. In an argument still heard today, the past is purported to be a *hindrance* to Aboriginal peoples rather than a source of strength.

The White Paper, however, was undeniably geared toward an idea of reconciliation. In strongly moralistic language borrowed—as Anthony Hall points out—from the American civil rights movement, it declared that "This Government believes in equality. It believes that all men and women have equal rights. It is determined that all shall be treated fairly and that no one shall be shut out of Canadian life, and especially that no one shall be shut out because of his race" (Hall 497; *Statement*). Yet the state's proposed "break with the past" was one of the principles to which Aboriginal leaders objected (*Statement*). The document, with its progressivist model of a continually improving liberal state, located the source of the problem—the "burden of separation"—"deep in Canada's past and in early French and British colonial policy" (*Statement*). Ironically, it was in these "early" policies that Aboriginal sovereignty and land title was arguably acknowledged.[2] Yet the political climate of 1969 allowed these rights and obligations to be conveniently rejected as separatist and discriminatory—ones from which an improved, tolerant, and egalitarian state must turn away.

---

1 As John Ralston Saul writes in his contribution to the Aboriginal Healing Foundation's 2009 publication *Response, Responsibility, and Renewal: Canada's Truth and Reconciliation Journey*, "Travelling around the country over the years, and in particular, over the last two months…I have sensed that people are now ready for reconciliation" (311).

2 For instance, in the 1763 *Royal Proclamation*, "which reserved a large share of these new territories for the Aboriginal populations and placed strict controls on the conveyance of these territories to third parties" (Mainville 11).

Ernest Renan observed in 1882 that "Forgetting, I would even go so far as to say historical error, is a crucial factor in the creation of a nation" (11). Canada in the twenty-first century is no exception to this rule. Prime Minister Harper himself demonstrated it in September of 2009 when, fifteen months after delivering the official apology, he declared to the international community that Canada has "no history of colonialism" (quoted in Barrera). In strategically forgetting, however, we condemn ourselves to rehearsing the same increasingly unconvincing speeches of repentance and hope and to making the same errors. As the state continually attempts to reconcile with Aboriginal peoples by leaving the past behind—as it seeks the comfort and virtue of oblivion—it fails to notice that every new Indian policy risks echoing the one that governed the residential school system itself: the goal of finally "get[ting] rid of the Indian problem."[1] So although "reconciliation" and "healing" may require an eventual distancing from the memory of trauma and abuse, Canada must ask itself whether or not oblivion is something with which it can—or should—be comfortable.

The Failed Pursuit of Oblivion

Porcupines and China Dolls begins by showing us the death of its main character. "Two hours later," the novel begins, "he stood alone beside the highway in the Blue Mountains like he'd done so many times before" (1). We have not yet been told what happened two hours earlier, but it must have been bad, very bad: as James looks to the sky, "hate, rage, anger, and sorrow...burst from his tormented soul, and ripped a hole in his chest and were given a voice. It sounded like a million deaths rolled into one" (1).[2] One death is what this scene swiftly comes to as James, hearing no answer from the heavens, retrieves and loads his gun:

> With no hint of hesitation he got down on one knee, put the barrel in his mouth and pushed the trigger. He watched the hammer fall and closed his eyes. He tensed and waited for the explosion. It came. He heard it: metal on metal. It was the loudest sound he'd ever heard. It shook his entire body and deafened him.
>
> He took a deep breath, dropped the gun and exhaled. He heard it: the peace and the silence.
>
> He waited for his ultimate journey to hell. (2)

---

1 The infamous words of Duncan Campbell Scott, Deputy Superintendent of Indian Affairs (1913–32). Quoted in Stonechild 22.

2 Other readers may understand the unnamed figure in this opening scene to be Michael—the former student who was driven to suicide a few years before the main action of the plot. This is certainly a possibility. However, even if it does depict Michael's (and not James's) death, I believe the scene still functions in more or less the same way, as James bears a striking resemblance to the figure whose (apparent) death opens the book, and the language used to describe James's final suicide attempt is identical.

After this disturbing glimpse of the future, the novel begins, and it proceeds in a more or less linear fashion. Alexie traces the history of the Blue People of Aberdeen—likely based on his own Tetlit Gwich'in community of Fort McPherson, NWT—as they make the transition from life on the land to life in town. Beginning in the early 1920s, we learn, all Blue Indians have been required to hand over their children to the authorities to be educated at the mission school. We see James Nathan and his schoolmates Jake Noland and David William entering the hostel as young children in the early 1960s; we watch their parents grieve. Soon we meet James as an adult, and by his black leather jacket and hell-bent attitude we recognize him as the man we watched die a few pages earlier.

And so the initial death scene haunts James—or his audience—throughout the novel. His ending has already been written, and no matter what he does we know it is only a matter of time before he takes that final drive out to the mountains. As a novel, then, *Porcupines and China Dolls* seems to lean toward its conclusion. It is helped in this by James himself, who likewise is constantly seeking his own ending, as he wonders if today is the day that he will "do it." Suicide attempts are routine for James; almost every other day finds him with a gun pressed under his chin, willing himself to end the nightmares. This death drive, meanwhile, runs parallel to the healing narrative that builds throughout the novel, as James and the other survivors begin to face what happened to them. "When will it end?" James asks, "How long do we carry the hate, the anger, the rage 'n the sorrow?" (181). Readers of *Porcupines and China Dolls* may be asking themselves the same thing; as they bear witness to James's ever-widening downward spiral, they grow to expect—or even to require—a release from this conflict. Narrative conventions demand such a catharsis, and the finite body of the text seems to promise it. Inevitably, the novel will end, and with it must come the liberation and relief of a story concluded. Yet although we might expect the forces of death and healing to work in opposition, their strange concurrence here becomes meaningful; while healing may constitute a triumph over the trauma of the past, and death a failure, both can be read as teleological. As we have seen, particular interpretations of healing assume that the past, once dealt with, will be left behind; the victim will no longer be tormented by unwanted reminders—he or she will achieve the luxury of forgetting. The quest for healing—like the death drive—can equal the pursuit of oblivion.

In Alexie's novel, however, the quest for healing, as we have already seen, is never fully successful; the author does not allow his readers the comfort of watching his characters recover. The forward movement of their small personal victories and temporary relief from the memories of the past are always counteracted by renewed despair, further tragedy, and sometimes simply the inactivity or indifference of everyday life. "What happens now?" Chief David asks aloud at his kitchen table, after the momentary excitement of the healing ceremonies has passed (224). Characters must continue with their lives, which refuse to conform to convenient narrative patterns, as lives often do. In the same way, when at last the terrifying vision of James's ending takes shape before us, his story—surprisingly—continues:

> He took a deep breath, dropped the gun and exhaled. He heard it: the peace and the silence.
>
> He waited for his ultimate journey to hell.
>
> After a few seconds, he wondered if it was over. *Is this it? Is this death?* He opened his eyes and saw the same mountains and the same sky. He looked down at the gun, and then looked for his body. He looked for the blood. He looked at his truck, then at the highway.
>
> "Fuck!" he shouted to the heavens. "Fuck you all!" (304)

The novel ends, then, with the withholding of an ending. James—neither dead nor healed—is forced to face the unpleasant, tedious, and exhausting continuation of a life which, like the plot, everyone expected to end much earlier. Alexie's one concession is to allow James the woman who he loves; together, he and Louise face the burden of carrying on, and the narrator finally releases us: "James's journey had come full circle. The future was unfolding as it should" (306).

The protagonist, in other words, has been unable to author either of the endings that he imagined for himself. Unable to forget, and unable to die, he must submit to the reality of a life path which does not conform to the usual fictional trajectory. Through this eschewing of endings, of resolution, and of conclusions, I would argue, *Porcupines and China Dolls* adds an invaluable contribution—or complication—to current discussions of reconciliation. The end points of healing, or of closure, here remain continually beyond the grasp of readers and characters alike, and denied this state of grace they are forced to continue to grapple with the challenges of the *process* of healing—or simply of continuation. Government rhetoricians and average Canadians alike have much to learn from this inconclusivity; as Alexie demonstrates, this push for closure is in many ways a longing for oblivion—for the luxury of forgetting and for the absolution of amnesia. In the context of the official response to the trauma of residential schools, it seems that by giving voice to our unpleasant history the state hopes to be able to put that history to rest. Reconciliation, it is assumed, cannot be possible when we are surrounded by continual reminders of past atrocities—hence the self-aggrandizing rhetoric of the apology and the cathartic process of the TRC. After these climactic confrontations of our oft-hidden past, our narrative should logically progress into a period of denouement—a tying up of loose ends, a settling of historical dust. The healing narrative, therefore, is invoked on a national scale to permit a sense of closure, and contentment. And this emotional release from the guilt accrued by colonial history, as I have suggested, is privileged above any kind of actual progress toward a functional or just society.

The reading of *Porcupines and China Dolls*, however, forces us to re-examine our expectations of the national healing narrative—and perhaps to align them with the wisdom of the reality of individual healing processes. As Christopher Fletcher and Aaron Denham explain:

> Healing is underpinned by the idea that vigilance over self in relation to others, vigilance over the decisions one makes, and vigilance in one's aware-ness of and ability to empathize with others, are the precursors to a healthy and productive life.... This way of thinking about healing upends the con-cept of an identifiable end point to the healing process (if one is healing, it would be expected that at some point one would be "healed") and substi-tutes *an unbounded process of social interaction centered on mutual caring that can, according to participants, coexist with a great deal of personal pain.* (104, emphasis added)

Rather than searching for the end of this particular story, then, let us turn instead to the messy, quotidian details of the present: the complaints, the confusions, the contradictory claims. Let Canada face itself and its history without the promise of the eventual liberation from this self-critique; let us recognize that with each new apology or federal solution to the problems created by the residential school system, the nation is already exhibiting the painful symptoms of the healing journey, as it staggers, makes headway, and repeatedly falls off the wagon. This humbling state of neverending atonement may be one to which we simply have to grow accustomed; after all, as the history of federal Indian policy demonstrates, the desire for closure—for an end to the problem—has only ever led to further error and injustice.

I am not arguing here that survivors should somehow not be allowed their own healing and even their own forgetting. The decision to forget or to remember, to heal or to continue grieving, is entirely under the jurisdiction of the keepers of these stories. On a national scale, however, I believe that we need to consider carefully the extent to which witnesses are allowed to partake in this relief. If we bracket the frantic desire for closure, or catharsis, which too often accompanies the reading or hearing of Aboriginal stories, we create the possibility that the telling of such stories be about filling in—rather than widening—the gaps in our national history. This is part of the importance of residential school literature, and—ironically—of storytell-ing initiatives like the Truth and Reconciliation Commission. Although ostensibly directed toward healing and closure, they in fact function to ensure that scars remain visible—that historical wounds continue to seep. As Jake Noland declares to the assembled community members—each grappling with the burden of his or her own memories—"Healin' is a journey—there is no end!" (Alexie 201).

Works Cited

Adelson, Naomi, and Amanda Lipinski. "The Community Youth Initiative Project." Waldram 9–30.

Alexie, Robert Arthur. *Porcupines and China Dolls.* Penticton, BC: Theytus, 2009.

Alfred, Gerald Taiaiake. "Restitution is the Real Pathway to Justice for Indigenous Peoples." Younging, Dewar, and DeGagné 181–87.

Barrera, Jorge. "First Nations Leader Demands Meeting with Harper Over 'Colonialism' Comment." *The Gazette.* Montreal Gazette, 1 October 2009. Web. 20 October 2009.

Bonokoski, Mark. "Pope's Apology Too Late." *Toronto Sun.* 30 April 2009. Web. 8 December 2009.

"Canada's Statement of Reconciliation." Younging, Dewar, and DeGagné 353–55.

Chrisjohn, Roland, and Sherri Young, with Michael Maraun. *The Circle Game: Shadows and Substance in the Indian Residential School Experience in Canada.* Penticton, BC: Theytus, 1997.

Chrisjohn, Roland, and Tanya Wasacase. "Half-Truths and Whole Lies: Rhetoric in the 'Apology' and the Truth and Reconciliation Commission." Younging, Dewar, and DeGagné 219–29.

Episkenew, Jo-Ann. *Taking Back Our Spirits: Indigenous Literature, Public Policy, and Healing.* Winnipeg: U of Manitoba P, 2009.

Epp, Roger. *We Are All Treaty People: Prairie Essays.* Edmonton: U of Alberta P, 2008.

Fiske, Jo-Anne. "Making the Intangible Manifest: Healing Practices of the Qul-Ann Trauma Program." Waldram 31–91.

Flanagan, Tom. *First Nations? Second Thoughts.* 2nd ed. Montreal: McGill-Queen's UP, 2008.

Fletcher, Christopher, and Aaron Denham. "Moving Towards Healing: A Nunavut Case Study." Waldram 93–129.

Fontaine, Phil. "Apology Response." *Assembly of First Nations.* Assembly of First Nations, 11 June 2008. Web. 20 October 2009.

Hall, Anthony. *The American Empire and the Fourth World: The Bowl with One Spoon.* Montreal: McGill-Queen's UP, 2003.

Harper, Stephen. "Statement of Apology." *Prime Minister of Canada.* Office of the Prime Minister, 11 June 2008. Web. 20 October 2009.

Harrison, Peter. "Dispelling Ignorance of Residential Schools." Younging, Dewar, and DeGagné 151–60.

"Indian Residential Schools." *Indian and Northern Affairs Canada.* Indian and Northern Affairs Canada, 10 June 2009. Web. 18 March 2010.

Layton, Jack. "Residential Schools Apology—Jack Layton's Response." *NDP.* New Democratic Party of Canada, 11 June 2008. Web. 20 October 2009.

Mainville, Robert. *An Overview of Aboriginal and Treaty Rights and Compensation for Their Breach.* Saskatoon: Purich, 2001.

McKegney, Sam. *Magic Weapons: Aboriginal Writers Remaking Community after Residential School*. Winnipeg: U of Manitoba P, 2007.

"Our Mandate." *Truth and Reconciliation Canada*. Truth and Reconciliation Canada, 6 August 2009. Web. 20 October 2009.

Renan, Ernest. "What Is a Nation?" Trans. Martin Thorn. *Nation and Narration*. Ed. Homi K. Bhabha. New York: Routledge, 1990. 8–22.

Report of the Royal Commission on Aboriginal Peoples. Indian and Northern Affairs Canada. Indian and Northern Affairs Canada, 1996. Web. 21 October 2009.

Saul, John Ralston. "Reconciliation: Four Barriers to Paradigm Shifting." Younging, Dewar, and DeGagné 311–20.

Simard, Colleen. "Too Soon for 'Good' Residential School Stories." *Winnipeg Free Press*. Winnipeg Free Press, 17 October 2009. Web. 9 December 2009.

Simon, Mary. "Speeches in Response to Apology to Residential School Survivors." *Inuit Tapiriit Kanatami*, 31 July 2008. Web. 20 October 2009.

Statement of the Government of Canada on Indian Policy (The White Paper, 1969). Indian and Northern Affairs Canada. Indian and Northern Affairs Canada, 3 December 2008. Web. 20 October 2009.

Stonechild, Blair. *The New Buffalo: The Struggle for Aboriginal Post-Secondary Education in Canada*. Winnipeg: U of Manitoba P, 2006.

Wadden, Marie. *Where the Pavement Ends: Canada's Aboriginal Recovery Movement and the Urgent Need for Reconciliation*. Vancouver: Douglas and McIntyre, 2008.

Waldram, James B., ed. *Aboriginal Healing in Canada: Studies in Therapeutic Meaning and Practice*. Ottawa: Aboriginal Healing Foundation, 2008.

Widdowson, Frances, and Albert Howard. *Disrobing the Aboriginal Industry: The Deception behind Indigenous Cultural Preservation*. Montreal: McGill-Queen's UP, 2008.

Younging, Gregory, Jonathan Dewar, and Mike DeGagné, eds. *Response, Responsibility, and Renewal: Canada's Truth and Reconciliation Journey*. Ottawa: Aboriginal Healing Foundation, 2009.

Kristina (Fagan) Bidwell

"Code-Switching Humour in Aboriginal Literature"

Kristina Bidwell is Labrador Métis (NunatuKavut), and lives in Saskatchewan. She is professor of English and currently Assistant Dean of Aboriginal Affairs at the University of Saskatchewan. A prolific scholar, and an authority on the use of humour as a rhetorical strategy in Indigenous literatures, Bidwell has also worked extensively on Indigenous literary sovereignty in Canada, and on the autobiography and storytelling of the Labrador Métis in particular.

Developing the theme of what poets Joy Harjo and Gloria Bird call "Reinventing the Enemy's Language," as well as picking up the work of ethnographers and linguists such as Keith Basso and Lisa Philips Valentine, Bidwell's 2009 article "Code-Switching Humour in Aboriginal Literature" demonstrates how Indigenous authors writing in English use both English and Indigenous languages as a form of resistance. Code-switching, or language switching, creates humour through word play and through incongruity, and Bidwell deconstructs works by Thomas King, Louise Halfe, Annharte, Tomson Highway, Gregory Schofield, and Maria Campbell in order to demonstrate how their writing destabilizes English as the dominant language.

Fagan, Kristina. "Code-Switching Humour in Aboriginal Literature." *Across Cultures/Across Borders*. Ed. Eigenbrod, DePasquale and LaRocque. Peterborough, ON: Broadview P, 2009. 25–42.

Code-Switching Humour in Aboriginal Literature

Aboriginal people in Canada widely believe that the survival of their ancestral languages is vital to the health of their cultures. However, there has been little critical attention paid to questions of Aboriginal language use in Aboriginal literature in Canada, especially when that literature is in English.[1] Critics seem to assume, when Aboriginal people write in English, that language issues are not relevant. But, on the contrary, even when written primarily in English, Aboriginal literature persistently grapples with the usage or non-usage of Aboriginal languages and English.

One reason that so few literary critics have addressed language issues in Aboriginal literature may be that few of them understand any Aboriginal language. They therefore feel an understandable anxiety when approaching questions that draw attention to those languages. Since I am not fluent in any Aboriginal language, I too felt anxious as I approached this essay on language use in Aboriginal literature. My response to this dilemma is to focus my analysis squarely on the anxiety, confusion, wonder, and humour that occur at the intersection of two or more languages. Such anxiety is not necessarily counter-productive. By acknowledging what we find unfamiliar, strange, and nonsensical, we can become more aware of our own boundaries and of our and the text's positioning. In this essay, I explore how several Aboriginal writers manipulate language to create both anxiety and laughter in their audience. They do this through a technique that linguists call "code-switching," moving back and forth between various languages and styles. Refusing to let readers see language as a transparent mode of communication, the writers remind us of the power politics and miscommunications that mark the interaction of Aboriginal and non-Aboriginal languages.

An Aboriginal writer's use of English is rarely simple and transparent, for his or her choice of language is socially marked and fraught with politics, whether because of the writer's intentions or the readers' expectations. Many writers are torn between the practical appeals of English and the value of Aboriginal languages. While most Aboriginal writers in Canada today either must write or choose to write predominantly in English, this is not necessarily a comfortable position. Despite Craig Womack's

---

1 There has been significant attention devoted to the translation issues involved in working with Aboriginal oral traditions, but this attention has not generally extended to written literature.

claim that English is now an Aboriginal language (120–21), many Aboriginal writers still see Aboriginal languages as the primary carriers of Aboriginal cultures and view English as an "enemy language" (Baker "Borrowing" 59). Language is an important symbol of identity, an issue of sovereignty, power, and group membership. However, for many Aboriginal writers, English is their mother tongue and the means of reaching the most readers, both Aboriginal and non-Aboriginal. Dennis Lee describes "colonial" writers as "gagged" by this dilemma (156). While Lee is referring to Euro-Canadians, his words take on a particular aptness when applied to Aboriginal people who do not speak their ancestral language:[1]

> Try to speak the words of your home and you will discover—if you are a colonial—that you do not know them. . . . To speak unreflectingly in a colony then, is to use words that speak only alien space. To reflect is to fall silent, discovering that your authentic space does not have words. (163)

However, Aboriginal writers have not given in to this apparent stalemate. They do not speak unreflectingly, nor do they fall silent. Rather, many Aboriginal writers are searching for an "authentic space" and distinctive language within English. In this search, they face two important dilemmas. First, how can an Aboriginal person maintain a "language identity" while speaking or writing primarily in English? Second, how can he or she communicate with a wide audience while resisting the power of Standard English? Cree actor and writer Billy Merasty sums up the predicament he faces when deciding whether to write in English or Cree: "[I]t's very hard to give something that a lot of people can't get because it's not their own language. And it's very hard to give something that's very hard to translate because what you're giving can't be fully translated—so there's always something left behind. . . . You can't really strike a balance. You just do the best you can" (40).

As Merasty says, it is difficult for Aboriginal writers to "strike a balance" when faced with this language dilemma. Instead, many have chosen to *emphasize* their and their readers' lack of balance. By code-switching, jumping back and forth between various languages and styles, they challenge the dominance of any one language. By keeping the reader "off balance," the writers bring their language choices to the reader's conscious attention, refuting the transparency of language and reminding us of the powers of language: to disrupt, confuse, exclude as well as to include, inform, and amuse. They remind us of the confusions and miscommunications that can arise between languages and cultures, and they warn us against being too sure of any interpretation. I have seen a number of Aboriginal writers use code-switching

---

1 Most Canadian Aboriginal people do not speak their ancestral language. Of the more than a million people in Canada of Aboriginal descent, only 190,000 have an Aboriginal language as their mother tongue (Abley 41).

to such an effect in their public readings. Before reading their work, which is in English, they will make a few initial remarks in their ancestral language. This gesture has multiple effects. It maintains the writer's resistance to English as the only public language. It reaches out to those in the room who also speak the Aboriginal language, encouraging a sense of community and communicating a respect for the language. And, finally, it creates a moment of discomfort for those listeners who do not speak the language, keeping them on their toes and reminding them that they do not understand everything. Having made this code-switching gesture, the writer then goes ahead and uses English, knowing that he or she has brought forward a challenge to its dominance.

Of course, a code-switch does not always have such a political undercurrent. The collision, translation, and mixing of languages are everyday occurrences for many Aboriginal people (Douaud). But literary code-switching, because it is not necessary for communication, is *marked*. The choice of code frames the content of the words, signalling that they are to be read in a particular way. As sociolinguists have long recognized, code-switches convey specific messages: "the presence or absence of particular linguistic alternates directly reflects significant information about such matters as group membership, values, relative prestige, power relationships, etc." (Scollon and Scollon 9). As readers, we try to understand the meaning of these various linguistic choices. However, depending on what Linda Hutcheon calls our "discursive communities," we may not share the knowledge necessary to understand a particular language or style fully (99). The audience is pulled back and forth between understanding and being reminded that it does not understand. And authors can use this confusion or delayed understanding to create specific aesthetic or political effects. The multiple codes at work in many of these texts assure that few readers, Aboriginal or not, are fully comfortable at all times. If such discomfort is a sign that something has been lost, I would argue that something is also gained—a pressure to reflect on language and on our own position.

Code-switching is widely used by Aboriginal people to negotiate issues of language and identity. While little research exists on code-switching in Aboriginal literature, there have been several linguistic studies of Indigenous people's oral use of multiple languages.[1] These studies can shed light on the literary uses of code-switching. For instance, Basil Sansom's study of the languages of Australian Aborigines who live outside the city of Darwin shows how they have dealt with dilemmas similar to those of Canadian Aboriginal people, trying to maintain a distinctive language while remaining comprehensible. The camps around Darwin are a centre for people from fourteen different ethnic-linguistic groups, most of whom can speak two or three Aboriginal languages. To allow common understanding within this multilingual situation, English has become the common and public language. Sansom found,

---

1   See, for instance, Basso, Valentine, Siegal, and Scollon and Scollon.

however, that linguistic distinctiveness remained important to the Aborigines, since, without it, "issues of identity would be at risk" (31). Thus, although the Aborigine camp-dwellers speak English, their style of speech differs so much from Standard English as to often be nearly incomprehensible to non-Aborigines. Furthermore, they make careful distinctions between forms of English, with certain accents, words, or phrases having strong social associations. The Darwin Aborigines often switch between these various "Englishes," sending strong messages about their identity and activity (38–39). Thus, even within English, the Aborigines find ways of linguistically signalling their identities, in relation both to white society and to each other.

Researchers have also noticed the humour and pleasure with which many Australian Aborigines regard their rampant code-switching, part of their general enjoyment in "putting things to unintended uses" (Cowlishaw 266; see also Hawkins 28). This sense of humour around code-switching is shared by Canadian Aboriginal people. The meeting of two or more languages can create a sense of incongruity, performance, and nonsense, and the potential for many forms of wordplay. As Bakhtin argues, "varied *play with the boundaries of speech types*, languages and belief systems is one of the most fundamental aspects of comic style" (308, italics mine). This kind of play is prevalent in Aboriginal writing. As Nancy Lurie comments, Aboriginal humour "is strong on puns, word play in general, and stunning juxtapositions of seemingly unrelated concepts and contexts" (202). Tom King similarly explains that Aboriginal humour is characterized by

> [v]ery bad puns and lots of them and having to hear the same jokes over and over again. I think the majority of Aboriginals in Canada, if they're not bilingual, they come pretty close to it. Some are even trilingual. It means you can play with language. And because many of the communities still have a strong basis in oral storytelling, play with language, punning, joking is crucial to that thing we call Aboriginal humour. (Interview with Farmer 4)

To understand the humour of Aboriginal code-switching, I find it useful to compare a code-switch to a riddle. Like encountering a riddle, reading a sudden switch into an unfamiliar code is disorienting. In his essay on riddles, Robert Finley calls this experience "the nonsense moment." Finley explains that riddles provoke anxiety by challenging our usual ways of making sense of the world: "[Y]ou enter the country of that which eludes you, and in it you are free from being sure of anything. This moment is brought about by the difficulty of the text, by its nonsense" (4). This seems to me an excellent description, not only of riddles but of coming across, for instance, untranslated Cree words in an English text (if you don't speak Cree, that is). However, a riddle must be more than nonsense. It only becomes funny once we know the answer—which introduces some "sense" to the transaction. On the other hand, if the question is too "sensible" in the first place, then it is not a riddle at all.

Thus, the humour of a riddle arises out of the meeting of nonsense and sense. This conjunction pulls us in, gets us thinking, makes us laugh. Even after we have figured out the riddle, we are still reminded that the boundaries of our knowledge and our language have been stretched. Cree elder Vern Harper explains that this educational function of riddles is a tradition among his people: "The thing too with the Plains Cree is riddles, riddles our people used to do. We've lost a lot of that. The riddles teach you to think, to figure things out for yourself" (qtd. in Ryan 38).

J.E. Chamberlin, applying Finley's riddle theory to the challenges of reading unfamiliar Aboriginal oral texts, reminds us that we must "go into and through that nonsense moment…surrendering to the language, suspending one kind of belief for another" (86). In the same way, we can begin to "make sense" of Aboriginal code-switching by giving over to our impressions of nonsense, our sense of confusion or exclusion. As with riddles, the humour of code-switching works through the simultaneous experience of nonsense and sense. We are accustomed to language operating in particular patterns, systems, or codes. When this system is suddenly disrupted, there is a loss of order or sense. And this kind of disruption and nonsense can create humour. Of course, the code-switching in Aboriginal writing does not lead to the complete dissolution of sense. Even if the code-switching can make reading difficult, most readers can still distinguish some meaning. Furthermore, the ways in which the authors control the switches can send clear messages about the appropriateness of various language forms.

In the remainder of this essay, I explore a number of code-switching techniques that are commonly used by Canadian Aboriginal writers. One common technique is to incorporate words or phrases in an Aboriginal language into a mostly English text. However, this technique requires a careful balance between sense and nonsense, especially if the writer is trying to create humour. If much of the audience cannot understand too much of the work, then readers may lose interest. On the other hand, if the unfamiliar language is too fully explained, then the resistance and distinctiveness may be lost. In negotiating these risks, some Aboriginal writers decide to add glossaries to their code-switching texts while others choose not to translate. This decision is partially a matter of style and partially one of politics.

For instance, the presence or absence of a glossary can affect the humour of a work. Glossing can give access to humour that might otherwise be missed, but it can also remove a playful element of nonsense from the text. As many jokers realize, if you have to explain a joke, then its humour is often ruined. For instance, when Drew Hayden Taylor's play *Baby Blues* was performed in Pennsylvania, he worried that the audience would not understand certain words and would miss the jokes. He therefore provided a glossary in the program. However, he later commented that he would not do this again because it took away from the immediacy of the humour to have people shuffling through their programs ("Native Humour"). Tomson Highway's novel *Kiss of the Fur Queen* (1999) similarly contains a glossary at the back. Without this glossary, many of the jokes would be inaccessible to those not understanding Cree. For example, when the protagonist, Champion, comes across a residential school nun playing the piano, he secretly puts words to the music: "Kimoosom, chimasoo, koogoom tapasao, diddle-ee, diddle-ee, diddle-ee" (56). The translation of Champion's tune, as given in the glossary, is: "Grandpa gets a hard-on, grandma runs away, diddle-ee, etc." (308). Heather Hodgson observes that Highway's glossary paradoxically both reveals and destroys the humour: "While the glossary orients the reader and enables the reader a glimpse of the humour, it also undercuts Highway's linguistic subversion by annihilating precisely the otherness of the other" (par. 37). Hodgson worries that the glossary over-explains, destroying the element of nonsense that keeps readers self-conscious. On the other hand, for Cree-speaking readers, the inadequacy of the glossary may actually add humour; Paul DePasquale has noted, "I've heard several Cree-speaking students talk about the humour that for them is created by the gap between what they perceive as the very rough, approximate English translation provided for 'outsiders' in the glossary and the Cree text's actual meaning."[1]

Other writers share Hodgson's concern that glossaries dull the political edge of code-switching and hence part of its humour. Giving an object or action its Aboriginal name is an act of power; the author asserts the right to define the world in an Aboriginal-centred way. Some writers believe that to gloss Aboriginal words is to remove the power of this naming act and to give the translation the higher status (Ashcroft, Griffiths, and Tiffin 66). Furthermore, for some writers, the audience's incomprehension is part of the joke. For instance, Sto:lo and Cree writer Lee Maracle tells of being at an environmental conference attended by Aboriginal and non-Aboriginal people. For most of the day, various scientists spoke, using a highly technical language that was inaccessible to the non-scientists in the room, including many of the local Aboriginal people. Near the end of the day, an Aboriginal man stood up and said that he would like to give an Indian point of view. As Maracle describes, "The old man spoke in his language for three hours and then sat down. The Natives cracked up" (238).

Thomas King is one writer who, like the Aboriginal people at the conference, finds humour in the way that Aboriginal languages are "nonsensical" for much of his audience. King describes glossaries as "ethnographic" in that they try to "explain" Aboriginal cultures, seeking to cover over any incomprehension. Thus, despite pressures from his publisher, King refused to gloss the Cherokee words in *Green Grass, Running Water*. He felt that this would make the Aboriginal language seem

---

1 Moreover, Highway did not gloss the book's dedication to his brother: "igwani, igoosi, n'seemis." Renate Eigenbrod argues that this untranslated line acts as an "invitation to learn about his people" by pushing those who don't speak Cree to seek Cree help with translation (77). However, I would add that the lack of translation also creates a degree of privacy and intimacy around an emotional and non-fictional moment of communication.

"anthropological" and exotic, rather than playful ("Native Humour"). King also plays with untranslated Aboriginal languages in *The Dead Dog Café Comedy Hour*. In many episodes of the show, Jasper and Gracie have brief conversations in Cree, intentionally excluding Tom. In fact, King has explained, he really is excluded. He does not understand the Cree-speaking actors, along with most of the audience and the CBC administrators, who, he comments, were not happy to hear that King had no control over what his fellow actors were saying. King describes the whole situation as hilarious ("Native Humour"). King refuses to allow the CBC, his publishers, or his audience to entirely "make sense" of his work. But, on the other hand, there is a kind of authorial sense in this nonsense. King intentionally maintains a sense of cultural boundaries and exclusions in his work, subverting any attempt to have power over the words. And this subversion is what King finds so funny.

Rather than using words in Aboriginal languages, some writers choose instead (or also) to code-switch between various forms of English. Even within a single language, there are countless variations and each, as Bakhtin writes, "tastes of the context and contexts in which it has lived its socially charged life" (293). Thus, certain forms of English can be identified as very "Aboriginal" and others as very "white." Aboriginal writers control and play with these various social codes to create particular messages and identifications in their work. Many Aboriginal writers have begun, for instance, to write parts of their work in "Aboriginal English," also known as "Indian English," "Red English," and "Rez English." Aboriginal English, a language spoken by many Aboriginal people, involves frequent combinations of and switches between English and one or more of the Aboriginal languages. The growing popularity of writing in this language is a break away from the shame that has long surrounded its use. Louise Halfe admits that she still worries that people will see her as "making fun" of Aboriginal English ("Interview" 44). But rather than "making fun," these authors are instead "having fun" with the language. Kenneth Lincoln explains that Aboriginal writers take advantage of the expressiveness of what he calls "Red English...its concise dictions, distinctive inflections, loping rhythms, iconic imagery, irregular grammar, reverse turns on standard English, and countless turns of coiling humor" (15).

While Aboriginal English is not, of course, inherently laughable, its frequent and unexpected language combinations do lend themselves to humour. For example, in Maria Campbell's *Stories of the Road Allowance People*, the narrators, who speak Cree English, do not distinguish between he and she or can and can't. A reader not familiar with Cree English would probably be amused and perplexed by the following passage, which occurs very early in the first story of the collection, describing the narrator's seduction by a woman:

> *so I go wit dis woman to hees shack*
> *Hees man was gone trapping so he tole me not to worry*
> *jus get in da bed wit him.* (7)

Campbell recorded the stories from Métis elders who told them in Michif, and she translated them into Standard English and then into Cree English. The multitude of languages involved in this project reflects a multilingualism that is common among Aboriginal people. The stories often emphasize this, giving multiple names for things:

> *Long time ago I knowed dis ole man*
> *hees name was Harry Tistaymow*
> *Dat means tobacco in our language but us*
> *we call him Chi Ka Chee.*
> *He live wit a woman one time and that woman he was a Rou Garou*
> *Josephine Jug of Wine dat woman he was called*
> *Dat not hees real name*
> *Dey call him dat cause he live in da big city for a long time.* (30)

The language's sense of multiple possibilities, of continual renamings, creates a gentle humour throughout these stories.

Some writers use such renamings to make more pointed commentaries. For instance, in "T. For," Métis poet Gregory Scofield describes how his Aunty, a speaker of Aboriginal English, revised country songs to make them more representative of her experience. Her Jimmie Rodgers album was scratched and "even weighted with pennies and promises" the needle would not play beyond these lines:

> *If you don't want me mama,*
> *You sure don't have to stall*
> *'Cause I can get more women*
> *Than a passenger train can haul.* (39)

Scofield refers repeatedly to the skips and scratches on his Aunty's old records (39, 128, 138), gaps that allowed her to compose her own music. She improvised her own ending to the Rodgers tune:

> *If you don't want me daddy*
> *You sure don't have to call*
> *If you don't want me daddy*
> *You sure don't have to call,*
> *Cause I can get more neecheemoosuk*
> *than a sled dog can haul*
>
> *and the needle and Fat Paul [the local bootlegger]*
> *scratched*

and waited, stubborn
as hell,
thinking it was damn funny
till they
both got busted. (40–41)

Aunty reworks the song to reflect her own northern heritage and throws in a little of her Cree mother tongue. Her revision is also a response to the male "drinkin', cheatin', ramblin'" life glorified in most old country songs. Aunty asserts her own right to find many neecheemoosuk (sweethearts), rather than, as Patsy Cline sings, "standing by her man."

Louise Halfe also uses the language crossing of Aboriginal English to create a very pointed humour. For instance, in "Der Poop," the Cree-English speaker is in the outhouse and notices, on the newspaper that serves as toilet paper, an article reporting the Pope's apology to Aboriginal people for the Catholic Church's racist legacy:

der poop
forgive me for writing on dis newspaper
i found it in da outhouse, saw line
dat said you is sorry....
So i was sitting here dinking dat we
maybe dalk
say, I always wanted to dell you stay
out of my pissness

The outhouse situation shows just what the speaker thinks the apology is worth. And Halfe's use of Cree English backs up that judgement. The Pope's business, or "poop's pissness," is associated with the dirty and scatological.

These examples from Campbell, Scofield, and Halfe reveal the ways in which Aboriginal English can mix things up, humorously disrupting standard meanings and forcing us to look at things in new ways. However, by using Aboriginal English forms, the writers are also asserting a linguistic stability. I explained earlier that Aboriginal writers are faced with the challenge of maintaining a distinctive linguistic identity while communicating in English. The use of Aboriginal English, as a sign of a distinctive cultural and linguistic identity, offers a potential solution to this dilemma. While Aboriginal English is decipherable by Standard English speakers, the language slows the reader down. This barrier to easy reading creates a sense of the boundaries between languages, conserving a sense of a distinctively Aboriginal identity. Furthermore, Aboriginal English, even while mostly comprehensible to an exclusively English-reading audience, gives the writer a strong connection to their ancestral Aboriginal language and tribal identity. The various Aboriginal "Englishes" derive distinctive and tribe-specific properties through the crossing over of "rules for ancestral language and discourse," rules governing sound systems, word constructions, sentence forms, and usage strategies (Leap 93).

While Aboriginal English is a distinctively Aboriginal form of English, certain other forms are seen as recognizably "white." In particular, English that is highly formal, formulaic, institutional, or otherwise "fancy" is often viewed as "whiteman's words." To those not used to it, such talk may seem bizarre and hilarious. The perception of this language as nonsense is central to another popular code-switching technique. The writers switch into "whiteman's words" (particularly as that language has been used in Aboriginal-white relations) and then use humour to reveal the absurd gaps in understanding that this language brings about. These gaps, which are often humorous, have existed from the first days of European contact. Upon his arrival in the West Indies, Columbus wrote to Spain that, when he declared his official possession of the land, he was "not contradicted"; therefore the claim was considered to be the "voluntary choice" of the inhabitants (Greenblatt 58). Columbus's tactic was, of course, absurd. Because the Aboriginals did not understand the language of the proclamation, they could not possibly have contradicted it (Greenblatt 58). Stephen Greenblatt perceives a bitter humour in this first contact: "That ritual had at its centre…a defect, an absurdity, a tragicomic invocation of the possibility of a refusal that could not in fact conceivably occur…a hole, that threatens to draw the reader of Columbus's discourse toward laughter or tears and toward a questioning of the legitimacy of the Spanish claim" (80).

It is precisely this politically charged and absurd "hole" between languages that many Aboriginal writers choose to exploit. Saulteaux writer Ian Ross says that he has heard "tons" of jokes in Aboriginal communities revolving around misunderstandings of English (118). In his popular CBC commentary, "Joe from Winnipeg," Ross frequently plays on these kinds of confusions:

> An I turn around and there's my lawyer frien Harvey. I know to some of you
> that's an oxymoron eh? Lawyer frien. But I don't like calling Harvey a moron
> eh? So we talk a bit an then I offer Harvey one of my free tickets. "Boy, thank
> you my frien," he says to me. "Thanks for your largesse," he says to me. "It's
> not that big," I tell him. An then he tries to explain what largesse means. That
> Harvey's always tryin' to use big words eh? An then he tells me he's all agog.
> Imagine this guy thinkin' he's a god? What's up with that? (68)

Ross's character, Joe, combines an Aboriginal English voice with a joking incredulity about the strangeness of "whiteman's words" (the phrase, "What's up with that?" is his constant refrain). By combining Aboriginal-inflected speech with an amused distance from Standard English, Ross can both use English and detach himself from it. Bakhtin commented that comic style is based on such distancing, on "isolating from these strata [of language] one's own intentions, without ever completely merging with them" (308).

Many Aboriginal people from around the world use this same technique of comically distancing themselves from the imperial language. Among the Apache, Ojibway, Fijians, and Australian Aborigines, linguists have documented practices of switching, jokingly and disparagingly, into the language of the colonists (Basso; Siegal; Hawkins; Valentine). These performances send a message that the imperial language is peculiar and inappropriate. However, these linguists also all noted that this was a delicate form of humour that can easily be misinterpreted. These switches must be kept short and obviously exaggerated, otherwise the joke can become inappropriate, with the joker perceived as acting "too white" (or, for the Fijian joker, "too Indian") (Seigel 102; Basso 72; Hawkins 24). In Ontario, linguist Lisa Valentine recorded a situation in which an Ojibway chief switched from Ojibway into "white" bureaucratic language during a radio broadcast. The man wanted a fellow band councillor to join him at the radio station: "Mike, ekwa kekiin pi-ishan. [Mike, come up here too.] I want you to come up here and speak on behalf.... Hm hm heh heh heh.... Ah, amohsha hi. [Well, that's it.]" (321). Valentine argues that the speaker's sudden switch into formal English expresses his authority and his strong desire for Mike to join him. However, he does not complete the English sentence and breaks into laughter, thus distancing himself from the bureaucratic language and ensuring that his request is not seen as rude or threatening.

This technique, making brief code-switches into highly formal English, is popular among Aboriginal writers. Institutional forms of English, such as the tangled language of bureaucracies, as seen in the Ojibway man's speech, or the archaic language of the Catholic Church are particularly common targets for humorous code-switching. These forms of English are, first of all, unusual enough to be clearly "marked." Furthermore, the church and government's use of incomprehensible forms of English is widely seen as a tool with which to have power over Aboriginal people. For instance, the "bureaucratese" of governments and big business is often seen as a way of excluding Aboriginal people from decision making about their land and lives. Lenore Keeshig-Tobias emphasizes the insensitivity and obfuscation of such language by including passages from government documents in her "a found poem." In the poem, Keeshig-Tobias both repeats and critiques Chapter 149 of the Indian Act. That chapter (which was reversed by Bill C-31) decreed that any Aboriginal woman who married a non-Aboriginal man (or a non-status Aboriginal man) lost her own claim to Aboriginal status, as did her children. And yet a white woman who married a man with status "became Aboriginal" in the eyes of the government. This law left many Aboriginal women and their children forbidden to live on their home reserve or to receive any of the benefits that other Aboriginal people received, even if the marriage failed. This act, as Keeshig-Tobias reminds us in her poem, is ironically titled "An Act Respecting Indians." She cites sections 11 and 12 of Chapter 149 of the act. Section 11, as recorded in the poem, reads

Section 11 Subject to section 12.

a person is entitled to
to be registered, if that
that person (f) is the wife
or widow of a person who is
is registered by virtue of paragraph
paragraph (a), (b), (c), (d) or (e); (123)

By repeating the last word of each line, Keeshig-Tobias makes the document even more wordy and difficult to interpret. Its cryptic and impersonal language, which reduces people to letters, cannot reflect the human consequences of the Indian Act. After this citation, the poet introduces her own words with the lines, "(subsequently and/without reservation)"—reservation can, of course, be read two ways. The poem then switches into a very different style, a direct and personal form of speech, addressed to the men who created and upheld the infamous law. The piece ends with bitter black humour:

we have ourselves and our daughters
and you my fathers have
sons and sons and sons

and section 12 (1) (b)
in the Act Respecting Indians. (123)

Other writers have tackled the often equally confusing language of the Catholic Church. For instance, in Tomson Highway's *Kiss of the Fur Queen*, Champion, a young Cree boy in residential school, rattles off the nonsensical prayer: "'Hello, merry, mutter of cod, play for ussinees, now anat tee ower of ower beth, aw, men'" (71). Champion's prayer emphasizes his alienation from the religion that the priests are attempting to instil in him. Again here we can see the riddling interaction of sense and nonsense at work. Highway's joke works because we can make sense of Champion's strange syllables, even though he cannot.

Louise Halfe is also critical of the language of the Church. I described earlier how Halfe uses Cree English to insult the Pope implicitly. In that same series of poems from *Bear Bones and Feathers*, Halfe also switches repeatedly into a language of guilt, apology, and confession, a language that she associates with the Catholic Church. In "I'm So Sorry," Halfe begins by invoking the recent official apologies some churches have offered to Aboriginal people. She plays the kind of devastation that the church has wrought in Aboriginal communities against the small words, "I'm sorry":

> *I'm so sorry, the pope said....*
> *I'm so sorry, I just thought*
> *We could borrow land for a little....*
> *I'm so sorry, I should have told*
> *the settlers to quit their scalping*
> *selling hair at two bits for each Indian*
> *I'm so sorry. I'm so sorry.* (98)

The pathetic insufficiency of the repeated "sorry," juxtaposed with the church's culpability, reveals the insufficiency of the word. Similarly, Halfe plays with biblical language to expose ironic truths:

> *i'm sorry the pope said*
> *i'll write to the priest, the nuns,*
> *make them say, i'm sorry too*
> *for* suffering little children
> coming to me *in the red brick schools.* ("ten" 99)

Thus far, I have emphasized how code-switching works as a practical and political strategy in the face of a language dilemma. However, considering code-switching as a style leads inevitably to questions of aesthetics. As I hope the examples in this essay have shown, reading code-switching texts is pleasurable; we enjoy seeing language in new and challenging ways, in strange and surprising combinations. Part of this aesthetic effect is, of course, the enjoyment of the humour that so often accompanies this technique. This aesthetic is not restricted to Aboriginal literature. For example, Ingrid Monson, in a study of irony in jazz, shows that jazz musicians ironically and often humorously "borrow, quote, transform, and invert music from all kinds of repertories in their musical play" (313). And Wilson Harris makes a similar argument about the mixed nature of Caribbean Creole literature, arguing that language is "better" when it is altered, its power to limit our thoughts exposed, and its words freed to associate in new ways.

Aboriginal people share this aesthetic appreciation of the disruption and mixing of languages. For example, Scollon and Scollon, in their linguistic study of a Chipewyan community, describe the pleasure that the people of that community took in the disruption of language systems. At Fort Chipewyan, where the study was carried out, four languages have had a long history of contact: English, French, Chipewyan, and Cree. The linguists found that, not only do the speakers switch easily between languages, but the four languages have largely converged. The Scollons argue that the community placed a positive value on such switching and convergence because they reduced the "systematicity" of the languages (208). This value, they claim, is just one facet of the community's general preference for "lower-order structures" (181).

As an example of this preference, they discuss the prevalence of practical jokes in the community, in which, they suggest, "the pleasure is derived from the degree of disruption in someone's thoughts, plans, or activities" (181). This parallel between the disruption of jokes and the disruption of language again suggests, as I have been arguing throughout, that there is a strong connection between code-switching and humour. While the Scollons' study is an isolated one, it does offer the possibility that code-switching appeals to a particularly Aboriginal aesthetic. Furthermore, many other writers, Aboriginal and non-Aboriginal, have described Aboriginal people as tending to be especially open to flux and chaos in language (and life).

At this point, it may seem that I am moving towards an argument of linguistic relativity where all languages are constructed and just as easily deconstructed. Overall, my description of code-switching, emphasizing nonsense, gaps in understanding, and fragments of language, may seem characteristically postmodern. However, it is important to remember that the prevalence of code-switching in Aboriginal literature is largely a response to the devastation of Aboriginal languages. Most Aboriginal people believe that their ancestral language is a gift from the Creator, a gift that is in danger of being lost. We should be careful, therefore, not to idealize the disordering of languages. Some postmodern theorists have celebrated and universalized fragmentation as a literary device, losing sight of the actual experience of fragmentation. In contrast, Anishnaabe poet Marie Annharte Baker reminds us that her people have been left "with fragments of history, culture, and land base," describing her own fragmented style as a response to this disintegration ("Borrowing" 59). I will end this essay with a discussion of Baker's poem "Coyote Columbus Café." Baker's elaborate code-switching highlights both the pleasures and the limits of this technique.

Baker speaks English as her first language and is trying to relearn her Aboriginal ancestral tongue, Ojibway. She admits to being comfortable in neither language. Another Métis poet in a similar situation, Marilyn Dumont, has bitterly described herself as stuck between two foreign tongues: "*Cree Language Structures* and *Common Errors in English* book-end my life" (56). For Baker, English is the "enemy's language" ("Borrowing" 60) with "limited foreign meanings" ("Borrowing" 59). She sees English as full of clichés, questionable phrases, buzzwords, and "loose language" ("Borrowing" 65). She worries that, when talking about personal matters, many Aboriginal people use particularly inexpressive forms of English: "Some conversations are laced with words borrowed from AA meetings, government-sponsored conferences, educational workshops, and from a mere glancing through handouts or manuals" ("Borrowing" 59). And yet English is the only language in which she is fluent.

Baker's response to this difficulty is to constantly code-switch, undermining the authority or expressiveness of any language she uses. She writes primarily in English but she is, as she says, "a word slut" ("Borrowing" 61), comically playing with word meanings, sliding from voice to voice, and from language to language. She refers to herself as a borrower of language, using various forms of non-mainstream English in order to "massacre" the language ("Borrowing" 60). She says, like many Aboriginal people, she finds many moments of amusement in speaking English ("Borrowing" 64). In fact, her attitude is so universally parodic that her writing becomes, as Bakhtin wrote of Rabelais's, "a parody of the act of conceptualizing anything in language" (309).

In "Coyote Columbus Café," Baker moves back and forth between a variety of voices, Aboriginal and non-Aboriginal, but they are all presented as deceptive, even meaningless. The poem particularly examines the inability of language to work expressively between Aboriginal and non-Aboriginal people. For instance, Baker presents attempts on the part of non-Aboriginals to learn about Aboriginal culture as an "Indian Act," an insincere effort marked by insufficient language:

> & you must crawl before you
> creep up to rich Indians
> playing casino bingo warriors
> subscribe to Aboriginal news
> & pretend Indian sympathy

> *lo, the po'Indian*
> *Indian Act*
> *Tell Old Indian joke*
> *Like Indian affairs*
> *Act Indian*
> *had an Indian affair lately?*

The non-italicized lines create an image of fraudulent non-Aboriginals who try to "act Indian." Baker, then, in the italicized phrases, switches codes, taking phrases often used by non-Aboriginals in dealing with Aboriginal people (i.e., Indian Act, Indian affairs) and plays with them, highlighting the stagy and secretive connotations of words like "affair" and "act."

However, she does not present this false and clichéd language as exclusively the domain of non-Aboriginals. The first section of the poem is told from the point of view of a 500-year-old Aboriginal woman (or maybe Coyote) who, by "frequenting colonizers," tries to "get discovered again / and again" (192). The speaker's come-on lines, while laced with irony, are clearly indeed "lines":

> *Boozho Dude. Hey, I'm talking*
> *to you, Bozo Dude. My name is*
> *Conquista. Come on adore me.*

suppose my moccasin looms
over your border, mistah,
and you put a teensy toe
on my medicine line.

These lines cross languages (note the play on "Boozho," Anishnaabe for "Hello") and codes, playing on multiple stereotypes. Baker also switches into the voice of a "fakey" elder who is exploiting his or her position:

I said sweat lodge	*I shed shwatch ludge*
makes body clean inside.	*meks buddy kleen insaid.*
Keep it up. Dance pow wow.	*Kip it up. Danz pahwah.*
After this, boy. You me	*Hafter dis, bah. You me,*
go off big West German First	*go hoff big wes churman Furz*
International Wannabe Annual	*Hinter Natchinel Wanbee Annal*
Celebration. Take first, don't	*cel brayshun. Tek furz; don*
need to take plastic money	*need tek plahstik monhee*
visacard. You me same team.	*vissacad. You me sam tim*
Same team. Like hockey team.	*Sam tim. Lak hocky tim.*
Zjoonias, my boy. Think of it.	*Sch - oo - nash, my bah. Tinkobit*
Swiss bank account, hey boy!	*Swish bank a cunt, hey bah!* (194–95)

Unlike some of the writers I've discussed, Baker does not present Aboriginal English as a more expressive alternative to Standard English. Rather, she shows it as yet another voice among many to be copied, exploited, and laughed at. Baker's code-switching style is an aesthetic choice, but it is also a halting and tentative compromise in a painful dilemma. As Albert Memmi writes, "[W]hile the colonial bilinguist is saved from being walled in, he [or she] suffers a cultural catastrophe" (qtd. in Henderson 249). Code-switching gives Baker a way to write, a way not to be gagged by her lack of an appropriate or expressive language. But hers is a voice of voicelessness.

This poem, like many of Baker's, is not easy to read. The constant code-switching is confusing, as is the sense that there is no stable or authentic voice. It seems that Baker creates this confusion deliberately, presenting it as the usual state of affairs in Aboriginal-white relations. She further demands that the audience take a place within the poem by using riddles. The speaker demands, for instance, "*what is paler than stranger?*" and "*how about solving the mystery / did I discover Columbus first?*" (191–92). However, these riddles do not have any clear answer. The poem also administers "random coyote IQ tests," once again switching into a recognizable but seemingly insufficient English code:

> *I warn you multiple answers possible*
> *circle (a) the landlord comes around*
> *first of the month to collect rent*
> *wrong answer but don't pick that one*
> *please follow directions & circle choice*
> *what about (c) a landlord of colour?*
> *right answer is (d) I got my rights*
> *(b) I am the landlord around here*

In this quiz, there is no question, and there are "multiple answers." In an essay, Baker has discussed the danger of "educating the oppressor," worrying that, when Aboriginal people communicate in English, their words may be used by others to seize authority ("Borrowing" 62). Her twisted quizzes and riddles can be seen as a response to this danger, a way of communicating without explaining too much, a way of reminding readers, especially non-Aboriginal readers, that they do not have "the answer." One line, addressed to Columbus, also seems directed towards the reader: "*Don't feel bad bro. / You're lost like the rest of us*" (193).

I began this essay by admitting my own anxiety in approaching Aboriginal code-switching texts. My response to this was to make anxiety and confusion the keys to my analysis. I have argued that Aboriginal writers use code-switching to humorously manipulate the interaction of sense and nonsense in their writing, thereby sending particular messages about language itself—its ability to include and exclude, express and hide, liberate and oppress. I believe that the analysis of code-switching in Aboriginal literature offers the potential for much further study. While my analysis has focussed primarily on how code-switching creates humour, the technique also communicates other important values and ideas. Furthermore, looking at how Aboriginal writers quote, play with, and transform words from numerous social contexts offers a concrete approach to the issue of style in contemporary Aboriginal literature, an issue which has been relatively neglected. Finally, an examination of code-switching in Aboriginal literature is valuable because it raises issues of languages, Aboriginal and non-Aboriginal. Those of us who study Aboriginal literature within the discipline of English are inevitably heavily invested in the use of that language. But we should remember that, for many Aboriginal writers, writing in English may be an uncomfortable compromise. We need to remember the power that English wields and be willing to look outside its boundaries, both to understand and to know that we do not understand.

Works Cited

Abley, Mark. "Outrunning the Sun." *Brick* 58 (Winter 1998): 40–51.

Ashcroft, Bill, Gareth Griffiths, and Helen Tiffin. *The Empire Writes Back: Theory and Practice in Post-Colonial Literature*. London: Routledge, 1989.

Baker, Marie Annharte. "Borrowing Enemy Language: A First Nation Woman's Use of English." *West Coast Line* 27.1 (Spring 1993): 59–66.

———. "Coyote Columbus Café." *An Anthology of Canadian Native Literature in English.* 2nd ed. Ed. Daniel David Moses and Terry Goldie. Oxford: Oxford UP, 1998. 191–95.

Bakhtin, Mikhail Mikhailovich. *The Dialogic Imagination.* Trans. Carol Emerson and Michael Holquist. Ed. Michael Holquist. Austin: U of Texas P, 1981.

Basso, Keith. *Portraits of "The Whiteman": Linguistic Play and Cultural Symbols Among the Western Apache.* Cambridge: Cambridge UP, 1979.

Campbell, Maria, trans. *Stories of the Road Allowance People.* Penticton, BC: Theytus, 1995.

Chamberlin, J.E. "Doing Things with Words: Putting Performance on the Page." *Talking on the Page: Editing Aboriginal Oral Texts.* Papers given at the 32nd Annual Conf. on Editorial Problems, 14–16 November 1996, University of Toronto. Ed. Laura Murray and Keren Rice. Toronto: U of Toronto P, 1999. 69–90.

Cowlishaw, Gillian. *Rednecks, Eggheads, and Blackfellas: A Study of Racial Power and Intimacy in Australia.* Ann Arbor: U of Michigan P, 1999.

DePasquale, Paul. Personal Communication, July 2008.

Douaud, Patrick C. "Métis: A Case of Triadic Linguistic Economy." *Anthropological Linguistics* 22.9 (1980): 392–414.

Dumont, Marilyn. "For Bruce, the Night We Sat Studying Cree." *A Really Good Brown Girl.* London, ON: Brick, 1996. 56.

Eigenbrod, Renate. "Not Just a Text: 'Indigenizing' the Study of Indigenous Literatures." *Creating Community: A Roundtable on Canadian Aboriginal Literatures.* Ed. Renate Eigenbrod and Jo-Ann Episkenew. Penticton, BC: Theytus; Brandon, MB: Bearpaw, 2002. 69–87.

Finley, Robert. "The Riddle's Charm." Unpublished.

Greenblatt, Stephen. *Marvellous Possessions: The Wonder of the New World.* Chicago: U of Chicago P, 1991.

Halfe, Louise. "Der Poop." *Bear Bones and Feathers.* Regina: Coteau, 1994. 102.

———. "I'm So Sorry." *Bear Bones and Feathers.* Regina: Coteau, 1994. 98.

———. Interview with Esta Spalding. "An Interview with Louise Halfe." *Brick: A Literary Journal* 60 (Fall 1998): 43–47.

———. "ten hail mary's." *Bear Bones and Feathers.* Regina: Coteau, 1994. 99.

Harris, Wilson. "A Talk on the Subjective Imagination." *New Letters* 40.1 (October 1973): 37–48.

Hawkins, Jean. *Bridging Two Worlds: Aboriginal English and Crosscultural Understanding.* St. Lucia, Australia: U of Queensland P, 1994.

Henderson, James (Sákéj) Youngblood. "*Ayukpachi*: Empowering Aboriginal Thought." *Reclaiming Indigenous Voice and Vision.* Ed. Marie Battiste. Vancouver: U British Columbia P, 2000. 248–78.

Highway, Tomson. *Kiss of the Fur Queen*. Toronto: Doubleday Canada, 1998.

Hodgson, Heather. "Survival Cree, or Weesakeechak Dances Down Yonge Street: Heather Hodgson Speaks with Tomson Highway." *Books in Canada* 28.1 (Fall 1999): 69 pars. 1 Jan. 2009. <http://www.booksincanada.com/article_view.asp?id=632>

Hutcheon, Linda. *Irony's Edge: The Theory and Politics of Irony*. London: Routledge, 1994.

Keeshig-Tobias, Lenore. "(a found poem)." *Canadian Woman Studies* 11.3 (1991): 68.

King, Thomas. *Dead Dog Café Comedy Hour*. Dir. Kathleen Flaherty. Audio Cassette. Canadian Broadcasting Corporation (CBC Audio), 2000.

———. Interview with Gary Farmer. "Author Thomas King of Medicine River." *The Runner* 1(1): 3–6.

———. "Native Humour." Media Seminar. Aboriginal Voices Festival, Toronto, June 1999.

Lee, Dennis. "Cadence, Country, Silence: Writing in Colonial Space." *Boundary 2* 3.1 (1974): 151–68.

Lincoln, Kenneth. *Indi'n Humor: Bicultural Play in Native America*. New York: Oxford UP, 1993.

Lurie, Nancy Oestrich. "An American Indian Renascence." *The American Indian Today*. Ed. Stewart Levine and Nancy O. Lurie. Deland, FL: Everett and Edward, 1968.

Maracle, Lee. "Oratory: Coming to Theory." *by, for & about: Feminist Cultural Politics*. Ed. Wendy Waring. Toronto: Women's P, 1994. 235–40.

Merasty, Billy. Interview with Monique Mojica. "In the Mother Tongue: Issues of Language and Voice. Excerpts from a Conversation with Billy Merasty." *Canadian Theatre Review* 68 (Fall 1991): 39–43.

Monson, Ingrid. "Doubleness and Jazz Improvisation: Irony, Parody, and Ethnomusicology." *Critical Inquiry* 20 (Winter 1994): 283–313.

Ross, Ian. *Joe from Winnipeg*. Winnipeg: J. Gordon Shillingford, 1998.

Ryan, Allan. *The Trickster Shift: Humour and Irony in Contemporary Native Art*. Vancouver: U British Columbia P, 1999.

Sansom, Basil. *The Camp at Wallaby Cross: Aboriginal Fringe Dwellers in Darwin*. Canberra: Australian Institute of Aboriginal Studies, 1980.

Scofield, Gregory. "T. For." *I Knew Two Métis Women: The Lives of Dorothy Scofield and Georgina Houle Young*. Victoria, BC: Polestar, 1999. 39–41.

Scollon, Ronald, and Suzanne Scollon. *Linguistic Convergence: An Ethnography of Speaking at Fort Chipewyan, Alberta*. New York: Academic P, 1979.

Siegal, Jeff. "How to Get a Laugh in Fijian: Code-Switching and Humor." *Language in Society* 24.1 (March 1995): 95–110.

Taylor, Drew Hayden. "Native Humour." Media Seminar. Aboriginal Voices Festival, Toronto, June 1999.

Valentine, Lisa Philips. "Code Switching and Language Levelling: Use of Multiple Codes in a Severn Ojibwe Community." *International Journal of American Linguistics* 60.4 (1994): 315–41.

Womack, Craig. "The Integrity of American Indian Claims (Or, How I Learned to Stop Worrying and Embrace My Hybridity)." *American Indian Literary Nationalism*. Edited by Jace Weaver, Craig Womack, and Robert Warrior. Albuquerque: U of New Mexico P, 2006. 91–177.

Renate Eigenbrod

"A Necessary Inclusion: Native Literature in Native Studies"

Born in Goettingen, Germany, Renate Eigenbrod (1944–2014) moved to Canada as an adult and became a passionate scholar and educator in the field of Indigenous literatures. Her contributions to the field were numerous, but perhaps most significantly she worked tirelessly as a mentor to students both Indigenous and non-Indigenous, and to promote an ethical approach to the study of Indigenous literatures. As professor of Indigenous literatures and head of Native Studies at the University of Manitoba, Eigenbrod published extensively, addressing questions of sovereignty, ethical criticism, residential schools, and orality, among many other subjects.

Written in 2010, "A Necessary Inclusion" picks up on Basil Johnston's seminal 1991 essay, "Is That All There Is? Tribal Literature" to reinforce the scholarly value of the study of Indigenous literatures. Eigenbrod reframes her argument in the language of literary nationalism, and describes the value of literature as a tool of decolonization, thus reinforcing its inclusion in fields such as Indigenous studies. The existing disciplinary exclusions are dangerous, she argues, because they limit access to grants and funding, and because literature adds meaning and depth to material culture. She also states that in many ways Indigenous studies is better suited to house the study of literature, since it is less dominated by western ideologies than English literature departments, and is instead constructed around decolonization. This can also, of course, be read as a challenge to English departments. Following the publication of this essay, Eigenbrod collaborated to inaugurate ILSA, the Indigenous Literary Studies Association.

Eigenbrod, Renate. "A Necessary Inclusion: Native Literature in Native Studies." *Studies in American Indian Literatures* 22.1 (Spring 2010): 1–19.

A Necessary Inclusion: Native Literature
in Native Studies

I must emphasize that a cross-cultural and interdisciplinary scholarship gained in fields such as Native Studies can only enhance the study of Aboriginal Literatures.
　　　　　　　—Emma LaRocque, "Teaching Aboriginal Literature:
　　　　　　　　　　　The Discourse of Margins and Mainstream"

Native writers of poetry, prose fiction, and nonfiction speak to the living realities of struggle and possibility among Indigenous peoples; they challenge both Natives and non-Natives to surrender stereotypes, committing ourselves instead to untangling colonialism from our minds, spirits, and bodies.
　　　　　　　—Daniel Heath Justice, "Conjuring Marks: Furthering
　　　　　　　　　　　Indigenous Empowerment through Literature"

The two epigraphs to this article highlight two main arguments made in my discussion: teaching and researching Native literatures within the disciplinary context of Native Studies enhances the understanding of these texts; vice versa, Native writers address topics that are intrinsic components in epistemological processes of decolonization promoted in a Native Studies curriculum; therefore, an inclusion of Native literatures in this department strengthens its objectives. Interestingly, the two scholars, whose statements complement each other, speak from different disciplinary perspectives: Emma LaRocque is a Cree-Métis scholar in the Department of Native Studies at the University of Manitoba, and Cherokee scholar Daniel Heath Justice is on faculty with the Department of English at the University of Toronto and only affiliated with Aboriginal studies; he uses a small *s* when he talks about Native Studies as, for him, "empowerment through literature," the subtitle of the special journal issue he edited, may happen in a wide range of approaches crossing departmental boundaries.

In Canada, students who want to study Native literatures mostly enroll in English departments, as it is through them that they will have easy access to presenting their work at conferences; are, as graduate students, in the "right" departmental box for research grants from the social sciences and humanities (which categorizes Native Studies under "other"); and, last but not least, learn theoretical approaches that, generally speaking, adhere to literary analysis more narrowly than taking courses in Native or Indigenous Studies, which requires community-linked scholarship with an ethical orientation.[1] Further, only a few Native Studies departments in Canada include (a few) literature courses in their curriculum, and there is no Association of Canadian Aboriginal Literatures that could promote scholarship on literature. *The Canadian Journal of Native Studies* (*CJNS*) out of Brandon University published one literature issue in 1985 and added only very recently another special issue of this kind. The fact that there is a (hidden) debate about disciplinary contexts for Native literature became more obvious when Gail MacKay organized a panel at the Canadian Indigenous and Native Studies Association (CINSA) conference in 2007 at the University of Saskatchewan on "Indigenous Literature in Native Studies"; with this panel she addressed the marginalization of the field in Canadian Native Studies associations and departments. The paper that I contributed to the panel, titled "What Does Literature Have to Do with This?," constitutes the first draft for the present article. The title goes back to a question by one of our Native Studies students evoking the issue of "relevance" of literature within a Native Studies department. As graduate program chair of the Department of Native Studies at the University of Manitoba, I often encounter in particular Aboriginal students' dilemma—or what they perceive as a dilemma—that they enjoy creative writing and literature but feel the pressure of having to take courses that seem to relate more directly to finding solutions for the myriad social problems in Aboriginal communities. On the other hand, I hear from students interested in literature who prefer to enroll in English departments that do not demand anything "extra" from them. In my own career path I have come to Native literatures as a non-Native scholar (as I outlined in the introduction to my book *Travelling Knowledges: Positioning the Im/Migrant Reader of Aboriginal Literatures in Canada*, 2005) and have gone through a disciplinary shift from teaching this field in English departments to being employed in Native Studies departments. In this article I therefore want to discuss interpretations of Native literatures that speak to their significance as literature and beyond by addressing hermeneutical and pedagogical implications of institutional contexts. I hope to exemplify the richness of Native-authored texts that lend themselves to multiple interpretations in defiance of either/or approaches. At the same time I want to illuminate their special role within a department that works toward decolonization, transformation, and rebuilding. Although Craig Womack pointed to a similar discussion in the United States in an essay in *American Literary Nationalism* (as quoted by Sam McKegney in the collaborative article "Canadian Indian Literary Nationalism?"), my essay will focus on the Canadian context and will privilege Aboriginal authors living in Canada since institutional contexts in *this* country generated the topic for my paper in the first place.

Story constitutes the basis of Native Studies, a discipline defined by Peter Kulchyski as "*a storytelling practice*" that comes "*to resemble forms of narrative knowledge*" (23), inasmuch as it constitutes the basis of Native cultures. So-called creation stories, for example, play a crucial role in spiritually based political and historical identifications of Aboriginal peoples, as highlighted in the *Report of the Royal Commission on Aboriginal Peoples* and, revealingly, in the Native Studies textbook *Expressions in Canadian Native Studies*. It is because of the cultural-political significance of stories, constituting collective identity, that Anishinabe poet Lenore Keeshig-Tobias argued vehemently in her seminal article in Canada's national newspaper, *The Globe and Mail*, in 1990 against the appropriation of stories: "Stories, you see, are not just entertainment. Stories are power. They reflect the deepest, the most intimate perceptions, relationships and attitudes of a people. Stories show how a people, a culture, thinks. Such wonderful offerings are seldom reproduced by outsiders." The stealing of Indigenous stories, she argues, is as damaging as the stealing of spirituality, language, and land.

Aboriginal literatures belong to a whole range of Aboriginal cultural practices, and as such they have been attacked by colonization in the same way as all other aspects of Aboriginal lives. Indigenous peoples of North America share this experience with colonized peoples from other continents. Kikuyu writer and scholar Ngugi Wa Thiong'o, for example, asserts: "Cultural imperialism was an integral part of the thorough system of economic exploitation and political oppression of colonized peoples. Literature as one of the central elements of culture was used in the same way as language and religion" (10). A re-visioning of literature should therefore be part of the process of laying "the foundation for a genuinely postcolonial society" (Huhndorf 32), which is intrinsic to a Native Studies curriculum. According to postcolonial scholar Edward Said, "the power to narrate, or to block other narratives from forming and emerging, is very important to culture and imperialism, and constitutes one of the main connections between them" (113). Indigenous narratives were blocked from forming and emerging in a variety of ways. The resulting "silence" up to the second half of the twentieth century, a period usually cited as the beginning of Native literature in English in this country, should be interpreted with Anishinabe author and publisher Kateri Akiwenzie-Damm: "we were 'silent' not because we had not yet learned how to write 'literature' or to use foreign art forms, but because our own artistic traditions had been banned, denigrated, and even outlawed.... We were prevented from and discouraged from ... telling our own stories" (170). The colonial politics of reading, interpreting, and marketing Aboriginal cultural practices as one example of "cultural imperialism," according to Jeannette Armstrong ("The Disempowerment" 243), goes hand-in-hand with the "linguistic imperialism" (Adams 127) of imposing standard English on Aboriginal verbal media of expression. Both forms of imperialism contributed to the blocking of Indigenous arts, but they eventually generated a resistance response from Indigenous writers "writing back" to dominant society as well as "writing home" to their own communities. However, as the power of the written word has been used as an effective tool by the colonizer

against the colonized, "home" communities still view literature/writing with sus-
picion—one reason why Native Studies (at least in Canada) opens up only slowly
to the integration of literature in its curriculum (and its professional associations)
facing the challenge of unraveling layers of colonization around the very notion of
literature. In her fictionalized residential school narrative, *My Name is Seepeetza*,
Shirley Sterling from the Nlaka'pamux First Nation concludes with "wrapping up"
the journal in which her young character wrote about the school in a buckskin cover
with beaded fire-weed flowers—a symbolic, or ceremonial, gesture trying to undo
the harm caused by the oppressive and brutalizing environment in which writing
in English was taught. The poetic inclusion of the Coyote transformer character in
Sterling's dedication at the outset of the book suggests as well the author's hopes for
the transformative potential of her work, but it will take time until a larger number
of readers from Aboriginal communities faced with the legacy from these schools in
the form of addiction, illness, and violence are able to de-traumatize their associations with books in the English language. (The use of narratives in the work of the
Truth and Reconciliation Committee, which started in Canada just recently, may
aid the process.[2])

So-called creation and trickster stories underlie the meaning of "literature" for
Anishinabe author Basil Johnston when he states, "were you to be asked 'What is
your culture? Would you explain it?' I would expect you to reply, 'Read my literature,
and you will get to know something of my thoughts, my convictions, my aspirations, my feelings, sentiments, expectations, whatever I cherish or abominate'" ("Is
That All There Is?" 100). In the context of his article, *literature* is defined as *tribal
literature*, otherwise called oral literature, orature, or the oral traditions. Johnston
clearly validates this form of literature, if only because those narratives are intricately linked to the use of the respective Aboriginal language that he considers
indispensable for any expression of Indigenousness. Nonetheless, although he sees
orally passed down narratives as central to Anishinabe culture, he does embrace a
whole range of writing in all forms: "words are medicine that can heal or injure,"
he maintains ("One Generation" 95). Also, he uses writing in English as a tool to
educate about tribal literature. He demonstrates how those oral narratives passed
down from one generation to the next for centuries, in spite of being dismissed by
European scholars as "pre-literate," have the same value as the European literary
tradition taught in schools as classics. When he makes the point that the story "The
Weeping Pine" evokes as much the power of love as Elizabeth Barrett Browning's
canonized poem "How Do I Love Thee," he takes the story out of the nonliterary
category of etiological tales (about the origin of pine trees) and reclaims its value as
a story about human sentiments—the material of literature universally ("Is That
All There Is?"). In doing this, he asserts the place of Aboriginal peoples within their
homeland Canada "not only politically and geographically, but artistically as well."
Together with Johnston, Akiwenzie-Damm, also from Cape Croker, claims this to

be necessary (171). Aboriginal literature, then, is more than a teaching tool; it makes a contribution to society in its own right and on its own (aesthetic) terms.

Johnston's use of the term *literature* is inclusive: it does not underscore a rigid divide between orature and literature. By doing this he implicitly argues for a continuation of a literary tradition beginning in precontact times. Other Native authors like Akiwenzie-Damm and Beth Brant also support this idea that Aboriginal literatures are not exclusively rooted in European traditions. Akiwenzie-Damm argues, "Literature is a creative art. The creativity that infuses literature has always been a part of our cultures, and we have always expressed it in various ways. Whether we sing it, speak it, or write it, that creative voice is ever present and unique" (170). Similarly, Mohawk author Beth Brant asserts that "the writing is *not* a reaction to colonialism, it is an active and new way to tell the stories we have always told" (40).[3] The emphasis on a disrupted yet continuous Aboriginal creative/intellectual tradition can be significant for a Native Studies curriculum that aims at reclaiming Aboriginal agency, resilience, and contributions to society all through Native peoples' encounters with Europeans. Some of today's Native writers in Canada, all fluent in English and versed in the European literary genres, like to emphasize the written tradition, but many others highlight "our significant *oral* traditional *literary* contributions" (Baker 61).[4] Anishinabe poet Marie Annharte Baker does not see a contradiction in her wording and adds in a further statement, "to me, a pictograph is a novel" (62). Anishinabe author Louise Erdrich from North Dakota explains the cultural continuum from a different perspective. She points out that in the Ojibway language (Anishinabemowin) "*mazina'iganan* is the word for 'books'... [a]nd *mazinapikiniganan* is the word for 'rock paintings,'" *mazina* being "the root for dozens of words all concerned with made images and with the substances upon which the images are put, mainly paper or screens" (5). It is also the root word for dental pictographs made on birch bark—"perhaps," Erdrich comments, "the first books made in North America.... Books are nothing new at all.... Or painting islands. You could think of the lakes as libraries" (5).[5] Students in my Ojibway Literature course found the revisioning of the concept of literacy as inclusive of so-called pre-literate Anishinabe forms of expression inspiring and empowering. Literacy and the literary represented in the discipline of English taught at all different levels of the Canadian education system strongly influence society's values. After all, according to Daniel Coleman, what has become known as English Canada and its so-called civility is largely "a literary endeavour" (5). Erdrich, the author of many books and the owner of a bookstore, contends that the *concept* of writing, telling stories in images and "books," has always been part of the Anishinabe intellectual tradition and was not only invented by Europeans. Using her writing as "righting," she subverts superficial and stereotypical notions of Native cultures as oral and reinscribes precontact Aboriginal literatures into the mainstream literary discourse. It should be noted here that, although my course context for teaching Erdrich (and other Anishinabe authors) was language based, the students were as interested in *the ideas* conveyed through either Ojibway *or* English as in the language itself. What seems most important in Indigenous writing for Indigenous readers/students is the author's ability "to put a framework around thinking that is good and healthy for our people," as Jeannette Armstrong argues, herself using both English and Okanagan to that effect ("Words" 29). On the other hand, it is precisely in a bilingual class (which I taught together with an Ojibway-language instructor) where students get the opportunity to theorize the depth of culture-specific, instead of homogenized, "Native" intellectual traditions, and Native Studies provides the interdisciplinary context for that.

Aboriginal authors write against the colonial imaginary by telling the story and the history from *their* perspective often with the use of subversive strategies like irony and sarcasm. Armstrong maintains that the "purpose [of Aboriginal literatures] is to tell a better story than the one being told about us" ("Aboriginal Literatures" 186). Among others, they write against what Métis author Marilyn Dumont calls "internalized colonialism" ("Popular Images" 49), which perpetuates colonial categorizations of who belongs and who does not and is often directed against Aboriginal people of mixed ancestry and the urban population. Because any creative writing in all its genres is suggestive and evocative, open-ended, and fluid and does not draw fixed boundaries of right or wrong, it is well suited to engage readers (or, in the classroom context, students and teachers) in a conversation. Marilyn Dumont's prose poem "Circle the Wagons," for example, is a text that provokes critical engagement with the subject matter of "Nativeness," both as a qualifier of identity and as a marker of literature. Is there a prescribed way of life or of creating literature that makes it "Native"? The text speaks to the absurdity of this assumption, but in its circular structure it also exposes the dilemma and the lack of choice and freedom an Aboriginal writer faces due to Indian Act divisions, internalized colonialism, and market expectations.

circle the wagons

There it is again, the circle, that goddamned circle, as if we thought in circles, judged things on the merit of their circularity, as if all we ate was bologna and bannock, drank Tetley tea, so many times "we are" the circle, the medicine wheel, the moon, the womb, and sacred hoops, you'd think we were one big tribe, is there nothing more than the circle in the deep structure of native literature? Are my eyes circles yet? Yet I feel compelled to incorporate something circular into the text, plot, or narrative structure because if it's linear then that proves that I'm a ghost and that native culture really has vanished and what is all this fuss about appropriation anyway? Are my eyes round yet? There are times when I feel that if I don't have a circle or the number four or legend in my poetry, I am lost,

just a fading urban Indian caught in all the trappings of Doc Martens,
cappuccinos and foreign films but there it is again orbiting,
lunar, hoops encompassing your thoughts and canonizing mine,
there it is again, circle the wagons....

In this short text, sentences are structured by commas and question marks but not by periods; yet, their fluidity and open-endedness is interrupted, stopped at the end of each line made to fit the visual arrangement of a square. As well, the thematic circular structure beginning and ending with the phrase *circle the wagons* is also contained within the visual image of a box. Academic institutions are often accused of "squaring the circle" in their scholarship on non-linear Native epistemologies and worldviews and, for that matter, literary expressions. This association with Dumont's text could provide a possible entry point into a discussion with students. Further reading makes it clear, however, that the author takes the idea of the circle into a critique of stereotypes about Native people and Native literature. As the visual arrangement suggests, the speaker of the poem seems to feel confined, boxed in, by preconceived notions of both. While the phrase *circle the wagons* evokes racist stereotyping—protection from "savage Indians"—her deconstructive use of the phrase suggests a need for protection of an individual's freedom of choice. A discussion of Dumont's text may include the author's Métis ancestry as an influencing factor, a query that may in itself be based on preconceived notions of what it means to be Métis. Dumont's prose poem does not espouse a dogma, but it asks, evokes, and provokes important questions and therefore leads toward critical inquiry—in the context of a Native Studies classroom, to a discussion about the challenges of decolonization for both Aboriginal and non-Aboriginal people/students. Because a literary piece like this draws a reader into a questioning process that is ongoing—as suggested by the ellipsis at the end of the poem—it exemplifies how creative writing helps "to *transform* consciousness, not merely to impose consciousness" (37), as Cree scholar and poet Neal McLeod, teaching in a Native Studies department, assesses the significance of literature. Engaging readers or listeners of stories in a way that they draw their own conclusions is an age-old practice in Aboriginal societies based on "an oral aesthetic" (Blaeser) that does not cater to a consumerist reception of stories. Instead, Stó:lo/Métis author Lee Maracle argues, as "listener/reader you become...the architect of great social transformation" (3). It is that kind of transformation that Native Studies aims at as it incorporates an activist strand and is working toward reconciliation, a goal that requires a paradigm shift in *all* of society.

In the text "Circle the Wagons," Dumont undermines simplified notions of the construction of Native identity. Similarly, Anishinabe author Richard Wagamese writes against assumptions of what it means to be "traditional" and what it means to be Anishinabe when he adapts the traditional role of a father introducing his son to his environment (in the old ways, to the natural environment) to writing a book about it. In his autobiography *For Joshua: An Ojibway Father Teaches His Son*, he tells his son that "this book is my way of performing that traditional duty" (9). In Native Studies we often teach Aboriginal students who, alienated from their respective Aboriginal home environment for various reasons, learn about their people's history and culture through books, including novels about displacements through foster care and adoption like the ones that Wagamese himself wrote (*Keeper 'N Me* and *A Quality of Light*). Although books in the Roman alphabet are nontraditional, imaginative writing published as novels, for example, has the potential of playing a particularly significant role for students who have gone through experiences similar to those of a certain story character because a novel, somebody else's story in a fictive setting, is distant enough to be nonthreatening but close enough to leave an impact, to effect change and to heal.[6]

The study and research of literature written by survivors (as, arguably, all Indigenous authors are) forms an important component in the mandate of a department that "represents a working through of historical trauma" (Kulchyski 20). According to Anishinabe poet and critic Armand Garnet Ruffo, Indigenous literatures have two influences or branches: "the mythic/sacred and the historical/secular" or political (119). This duality calls for a form of literary criticism that is both "critical and constructive," echoing the Marxist notion of "a negative and a positive hermeneutic" (Huhndorf 32). Critics have to understand the social and cultural impacts of centuries of colonialism and the cultural continuum that persisted in spite of it all. An approach that applies the seemingly objective notion of "'literary' merit" (Armstrong, "Aboriginal Literatures" 183) denies implicit ideological biases and will not do justice to Aboriginal literature. Ngugi Wa Thiong'o rightly points out that "the whole body of critical appreciation, interpretations, theories, commentaries often carries within itself an entire set of ideological assumptions about society and relations between human beings. Criticism and theories of literature are not themselves neutral entities" (23). Claiming ownership of Aboriginal literatures in Native Studies no longer leaves the politics of interpretation exclusively to English departments, with their strong roots in European traditions and colonial ideology, but asserts an informed position in relation to Aboriginal pre- and post-contact history and cultures. From that position of strength, it may forge "new alliances between English literary studies and Indigenous studies" in a transdisciplinary reading of Aboriginal literature (Len Findlay, qtd. in Huhndorf 32). The use of an appropriate epistemology is central to scholarly debates in Native Studies departments; it is no different with regard to Aboriginal literatures. Métis scholar Emma LaRocque demands that scholars in this field "bring to their teaching and research an Aboriginal epistemological ethos *in addition* to their Western academic training and credentials" ("Teaching" 225). Such an ethos results in a methodology and pedagogy that makes connections with the realities of Aboriginal societies today.

Literature, as commonly understood, is associated with high culture; to a large extent, in the view of dominant society, Aboriginal cultures are associated with popular rather than high culture. However, Native Studies includes all strands of cultural studies in its research and teaching and therefore should also include the "high culture" of literature. According to Peter Kulchyski, high culture, as opposed to elite culture, comprises "the cultural products that gain a venerated status usually because of the strength, vitality, complexity, or richness of the cultural text. Any of these can be of concern to Native Studies" (19). However, in Canadian society both Aboriginal literature and orature are overtly marginalized and too rarely gain a venerated status, and if they do, Howard Adams's note of caution should be remembered: "Enthusiastic reception by white middle class public is not necessarily a measure of literary or artistic success for Aboriginal literary artists. Popularity likely means that the Aboriginal story or creation harmonizes with the archaic racial stereotypes of Eurocentric society" (131). The enthusiastic reception of Joseph Boyden's *Three Day Road*, for example, very quickly catalogued and shelved in bookstores as "literature" and not under "Aboriginal Issues," may be a case in point here. Although the novel is very well written, its theme of "savage" Windigo killings may indeed appeal to archaic racial stereotypes and account at least as much for the book's success in mainstream reception as its literary qualities. Instead of working with assumptions about "Nativeness," as Marilyn Dumont questions in her poem, an uncensored inclusion of Aboriginal verbal arts is needed on all levels. In his article "The Heritage of Storytelling" in the November 1998 issue of *MacLean's*, Canadian author Robert Fulford praises the art of storytelling because it "connects us to our past and to our descendants in the next millennium." "Us" does not include Aboriginal peoples and their stories. Fulford centers his essay on the theme of story deprivation in the canonized children's classic *Peter Pan*, but he fails to mention the real story deprivation suffered by Aboriginal children in residential schools. The children in those schools will have heard stories, but these were European fairy tales, biblical tales and stories about Dick and Jane, not the stories of their cultures, communities, and histories. Native Studies has to draw attention to this particular deprivation—among the many others—and to how it very effectively added to the loss of identity. Anishinabe writer Ruby Slipperjack is one of many Aboriginal writers in Canada who pointed out that she started to write because there were no stories relevant to her background, no stories she could relate to when she grew up (Lutz 213).[7] Fulford perpetuates the sentiment of nineteenth-century settler literature about a land without stories. Catherine Parr Trail wrote in 1836 that "there are no historical associations, no legendary tales of those that come before us" (128). In his exclusionary discourse about the importance of storytelling, Fulford practices a continued story deprivation for Aboriginal people, who rarely see themselves and their literature included in mainstream literary reviews and award ceremonies (and if they do, often for the wrong reasons, as mentioned above). Although Aboriginal authors acknowledge their own communities as their primary audience—and narratives like

Maria Campbell's *Halfbreed* and Beatrice Culleton-Mosionier's *In Search of April Raintree* gained a venerated status with them—they can only thrive and contribute to better cross-cultural communications if "others are willing to listen," as Anishinabe elder Art Solomon states (qtd. in Ruffo 120). The reluctance of mainstream audiences to listen may be a reaction to "the Uncomfortable Mirrors" that Aboriginal writers are holding up to Canadian society at large (LaRocque, "Preface" xxvii). However, departments of Native Studies in Canada were created in order to help lift the denial that this nation was built on stolen land; the inclusion of the nonthreatening, yet eye-opening medium of the verbal arts—both oral and written—will strengthen this educational mandate and grant Aboriginal peoples greater visibility.

The Aboriginal student who, after seeing my Environment, Economy, and Aboriginal Peoples course outline and noting its inclusion of stories and Armstrong's novel *Whispering in Shadows*, asked "What does literature have to do with this?" argued with the understanding that literature is a luxury, an add-on, derived from a social position of privilege. However, in Aboriginal societies the verbal arts have always been multilayered, multipurposed, and intrinsically interdisciplinary. For example, so-called traditional narratives may be read not only for their ecological worldview and their environmental ethics (as in the case of Overholt and Callicott's *Clothed-in-Fur and Other Tales*) but also for their powerful impact as imaginative narratives. As outlined above, Basil Johnston recontextualizes the story of "The Weeping Pine" as literature. This does not mean that the narrative is *not* about the origin of pine trees but that it has more than one layer of meaning. Similarly, in her novel *Whispering in Shadows*, Armstrong addresses issues of poverty, illness, racism, environmental destruction, food issues, and reserve and urban life. She is weaving together the many different strands of being an Indigenous person today in the form of a story that follows the life of a main character. Although Armstrong wrote many nonfiction articles, in particular about environmental issues, here she expresses her anticolonial, anticapitalist, and antiglobalization views through story. A character whom we get to know as lover, a parent, a poorly treated worker, a student, an artist, an activist, and a person dying from cancer touches us as human beings, quite different from the textbook Aboriginal identified by statistics or the media image of the blockade warrior. Creative writing produces for the reader an emotional investment, an intimacy of experience that does not translate into fixed knowledge, categories, or labels—one of the reasons why Dumont may have chosen the poem form for the articulation of her desire to simply be, free from preconceived notions. As social science research tends to dehumanize the "objects" it studies, and as this discourse has been very powerful in Aboriginal contexts generally and in Native Studies specifically, it is time to turn to narratives that reinstate humanity. Emma LaRocque therefore explains, "One of the reasons I like and teach literature is because it may be one of the most effective ways to shed light on Native humanity" ("Teaching" 217).

I attempted to explain and illustrate in this essay that Native literature is an expression of a cultural continuum contributing to Indigenous intellectual traditions and also a form of re-writing, a "dispelling of lies" (Armstrong, "The Disempowerment" 244), and therefore an articulation of empowerment. Adding to both these characteristics, which already make literature a suitable subject in Native Studies, I want to emphasize in my conclusion that, although Aboriginal literature addresses multiple sites of dispossession of Aboriginal peoples and the subsequent tragedies occurring in Aboriginal communities, the stories, written and spoken, as poems or prose or plays, never simply, unproblematically reflect Aboriginal reality. "Literature," theorist Simon Gikandi suggests, "problematizes experiences which might appear to us to be easily accessible and consumable" (qtd. in Brydon 990). Due to the colonial legacy of labeling Aboriginal peoples as primitive and childlike, there is still a perception in dominant society that they and their cultural expressions are simple, easy to understand. Aboriginal verbal arts draw attention to complexities, and it is exactly because of their lack of transparency; their suggestive, allusive, but not prescriptive characteristics; their avoidance of closure and easy solutions; their shifts and gaps and open-endedness that Aboriginal literatures should become an intrinsic component in the discipline of Native Studies, which, with its mandate to further the struggle toward decolonization, continuously engages in critical inquiry.

Notes

1 For the purpose of this article I will use *Native*, *Aboriginal*, and *Indigenous* interchangeably.

2 The Truth and Reconciliation Commission of Canada (TRC), organized by the parties to the Indian Residential Schools Settlement Agreement, was part of an overall comprehensive response to the Indian residential school legacy. It was officially established on 2 June 2008 and terminated in June 2015. Throughout its mandate it listened to the narratives of survivors.

3 Her reasoning echoes Thomas King's often-cited concerns about classifying Native literatures as "postcolonial." One of his arguments against this academic categorization is his contention that they did not only start after the onslaught of colonization but built onto precontact traditions ("Godzilla vs. Post-Colonial").

4 Cree author Tomson Highway, for example, started a project in 2008 with the Negahneewin College at Confederation College in Thunder Bay, which he titles *The Written Tradition: Literature, Literacy and Aboriginal Identity.*

5 "Birchbark Bitings" is the title of a column on Aboriginal literatures that Sinclair writes regularly for the Winnipeg-based newspaper *Urban NDN*; his choice of title alludes to his perception of a continuum between precontact cultures and contemporary Aboriginal, or rather, Anishinabe literature.

6 Just recently Métis scholar Jo-Ann Episkenew published a book-length study of Aboriginal literature in Canada on this particular topic: *Taking Back Our Spirits: Indigenous Literature, Public Policy, and Healing.*

7 In her landmark text on Canadian Literature, *Survival*, Margaret Atwood points out the need for a national literature because it functions as a mirror:

> If a country or a culture lacks such mirrors it has no way of knowing what it looks like; it must travel blind. If…the viewer is given a mirror that reflects not him but someone else, and told at the same time that the reflection he sees is himself, he will get a very distorted idea of what he is really like. (15–16)

Quite ironically, Atwood did not wonder about the mirror effect of the distorted images of Native people in Canadian literature on those people; however, a year after *Survival*, Maria Campbell's *Halfbreed* was published.

Works Cited

Adams, Howard. *A Tortured People*. Penticton, BC: Theytus, 1995.

Akiwenzie-Damm, Kateri. "First Peoples Literature in Canada." *Hidden in Plain Sight: Contributions of Aboriginal Peoples to Canadian Identity and Culture*. Ed. David Newhouse, Cora Voyageur, and Daniel Beavon. Toronto: U of Toronto P, 2005. 169–76.

Armstrong, Jeannette. "Aboriginal Literatures: A Distinctive Genre within Canadian Literature." *Hidden in Plain Sight: Contributions of Aboriginal Peoples to Canadian Identity and Culture*. Ed. David Newhouse, Cora Voyageur, and Daniel Beavon. Toronto: U of Toronto P, 2005. 180–86.

———. "The Disempowerment of First North American Native Peoples and Empowerment through Their Writing." *An Anthology of Canadian Native Literature in English*. Ed. Daniel David Moses and Terry Goldie. Toronto: Oxford UP, 2005. 242–45.

———. *Whispering in Shadows*. Penticton, BC: Theytus, 2000.

———. "Words." *Telling It: Women and Language across Cultures*. Ed. Sky Lee, Lee Maracle, Daphne Marlatt, and Betsy Warland. Vancouver, BC: Press Gang, 1990. 23–29.

Atwood, Margaret. *Survival: A Thematic Guide to Canadian Literature*. Toronto: House of Anansi, 1972.

Baker, Annharte. "Borrowing Enemy Language: A First Nation Woman Use of English." *West Coast Line* 10.27/1 (Spring 1993): 59–66.

Blaeser, Kimberly. "Writing Voices Speaking: Native Authors and an Oral Aesthetic." *Talking on the Page: Editing Aboriginal Oral Texts*. Ed. Laura J. Murray and Keren Rice. Toronto: U of Toronto P, 1999. 53–68.

Boyden, Joseph. *Three Day Road*. Toronto: Viking, 2005.

Brant, Beth. *Writing as Witness*. Toronto: Women's, 1994.

Brydon, Dianna. "Dionne Brand's Global Intimacies: Practising Affective Citizenship." *University of Toronto Quarterly* 76.3 (Summer 2007): 990–1006.

Campbell, Maria. *Halfbreed*. Toronto: McClelland and Stewart, 1973.

Coleman, Daniel. *White Civility: The Literary Project of English Canada*. Toronto: U of Toronto P, 2006.

Culleton-Mosionier, Beatrice. *In Search of April Raintree*. Winnipeg: Pemmican, 1983.

Dumont, Marilyn. *A Really Good Brown Girl*. London, ON: Bricks, 1993.

———. "Popular Images of Nativeness." *Looking at the Words of Our People: First Nations Analysis of Literature*. Ed. Jeannette Armstrong. Penticton, BC: Theytus, 1993. 45–49.

Eigenbrod, Renate. *Travelling Knowledges: Positioning the Im/Migrant Reader of Aboriginal Literatures in Canada*. Winnipeg: U of Manitoba P, 2005.

Episkenew, Jo-Ann. *Taking Back Our Spirits: Indigenous Literature, Public Policy, and Healing*. Winnipeg: U of Manitoba P, 2009.

Erdrich, Louise. *Books and Islands in Ojibwe Country*. Washington, DC: National Geographic, 2003.

Fagan, Kristina, Daniel Heath Justice, Keary Martin, Sam McKegney, Deanna Rider, and Niigonwedom James Sinclair. "Canadian Indian Literary Nationalism? Critical Approaches in Canadian Indigenous Contexts—A Collaborative Interlogue." *The Canadian Journal of Native Studies* 29.1–2 (Fall 2009): 19–44.

Fulford, Robert. "The Heritage of Storytelling." *Maclean's* (2 November 1998). 80–85.

Huhndorf, Shari. "Indigeneity, Colonialism and Literary Studies: A 'Transdisciplinary,' Oppositional Politics of Reading." *ESC* 30.2 (June 2004): 29–38.

Johnston, Basil. "Is That All There Is? Tribal Literature." *An Anthology of Canadian Native Literature in English*. Ed. Daniel David Moses and Terry Goldie. Toronto: Oxford UP, 2005. 98–105.

———. "One Generation from Extinction." *An Anthology of Canadian Native Literature in English*. Ed. Daniel David Moses and Terry Goldie. Toronto: Oxford UP, 2005. 92–97.

Justice, Daniel. "Conjuring Marks: Furthering Indigenous Empowerment through Literature." *Empowerment through Literature*. Special issue of *American Indian Quarterly* 28.1–2 (Spring 2004): 3–11.

Keeshig-Tobias, Lenore. "Stop Stealing Native Stories." *The Globe and Mail*, Jan. 26, 1990.

King, Thomas. "Godzilla vs. Post-Colonial." *New Contexts of Canadian Criticism*. Ed. Ajay Heble, Donna Palmateer Pennee, and J.R. (Tim) Struthers. Peterborough, ON: Broadview P, 1997. 241–48.

Kulchyski, Peter. "What Is Native Studies?" *Expressions in Canadian Native Studies*. Ed. Ron F. Laliberte et al. Saskatoon: University Extension, 2000. 13–26.

LaRocque, Emma. "Teaching Aboriginal Literature: The Discourse of Margins and Mainstreams." *Creating Community: A Roundtable on Canadian Aboriginal Literature*. Ed. Renate Eigenbrod and Jo-Ann Episkenew. Penticton, BC: Theytus; Brandon, MB: Bearpaw, 2002. 209–34.

———. "Preface—or Here Are Our Voices—Who Will Hear?" *Writing the Circle*. Ed. Jeanne Perreault and Sylvia Vance. Edmonton: NeWest, 1990.

Lutz, Hartmut. *Contemporary Challenges: Conversations with Canadian Native Authors.* Saskatoon: Fifth House, 1991.

Maracle, Lee. *Sojourner's Truth and Other Stories.* Vancouver, BC: Press Gang, 1990.

McLeod, Neal. "Indigenous Studies: Negotiating the Space between Tribal Communities and Academia." *Expressions in Canadian Native Studies.* Ed. F. Ron Laliberte et al. Saskatoon: University Extension, 2000. 27–39.

Overholt, Thomas W., and J. Baird Callicott. *Clothed-in-Fur and Other Tales: An Introduction to an Ojibwa World View.* London, England: UP of America, 1982.

Parr Trail, Catherine. *The Backwoods of Canada.* 1836. Toronto: McClelland and Stewart, 1989.

Ruffo, Armand. "Why Native Literature?" *Native North America.* Ed. Renee Hulan. Toronto: *ECW,* 1999. 109–21.

Said, Edward. *Culture and Imperialism.* New York: Knopf, 1993.

Sterling, Shirley. *My Name Is Seepeetza.* Toronto: Douglas and McIntyre, 1992.

Wagamese, Richard. *For Joshua: An Ojibway Father Teaches His Son.* Toronto: Doubleday Canada, 2002.

———. *A Quality of Light.* Toronto: Doubleday, 1997.

———. *Keeper 'N Me.* Toronto: Doubleday, 1994.

Wa Thiong'o, Ngugi. *Writers in Politics: Essays.* Portsmouth, NH: Heinemann, 1981.

Permissions Acknowledgements

Akiwenzie-Damm, Kateri. "Erotica, Indigenous Style," in *(Ad)dressing Our Words: Aboriginal Perspectives on Aboriginal Literatures,* edited by Armand Garnet Ruffo. Theytus Books, 1990, 2001. Reprinted with the permission of Kateri Akiwenzie-Damm.

Armstrong, Jeannette. "Land Speaking," in *Speaking for the Generations: Native Writers on Writing,* edited by Simon Ortiz. University of Arizona Press, 1998: 174–95. Republished with the permission of the University of Arizona Press; permission conveyed through Copyright Clearance Center, Inc.

Assiniwi, Bernard. "Je suis ce que je dis que je suis," in *Le Renouveau de la parole identitaire,* edited by Mireille Calle-Gruber and Jeanne-Marie Clerc. Montpellier, France/Kingston, Ontario: Centre d'Etudes litteraires francaises du XXe siècle, Groupe de recherche sur les expressions francaises, cahier 2, 1993; pp 101–06. Reprinted with the permission of Marina Assiniwi.

Blaeser, Kimberley. "Native Literature: Seeking a Critical Centre," in *Looking at the Words of Our People,* edited by Jeannette Armstrong. Theytus Books, 1993. Reprinted with the permission of Kimberley Blaeser.

Driskill, Qwo-Li. "Stolen from Our Bodies: First Nations Two-Spirits/Queers and the Journey to a Sovereign Erotic," in *Studies in American Indian Literatures,* Volume 16, Number 2, Summer 2004: 50–64. University of Nebraska Press. Republished with the permission of the University of Nebraska Press; permission conveyed through Copyright Clearance Center, Inc.

Eigenbrod, Renate. "A Necessary Inclusion: Native Literature in Native Studies," in *Studies in American Indian Literatures,* Volume 22, Number 1, Spring 2010: 1–19. University of Nebraska Press. Republished with the permission of the University of Nebraska Press; permission conveyed through Copyright Clearance Center, Inc.

Episkenew, Jo-Ann. "Socially Responsible Criticism: Aboriginal Literature, Ideology, and the Literary Canon," in *Creating Community,* edited by Renate Eigenbrod and Jo-Ann Episkenew. Theytus Books, 2002. Reprinted with the permission of Jo-Ann Episkenew.

Ermine, Willie. "Aboriginal Epistemology," in *First Nations Education in Canada: The Circle Unfolds,* edited by Marie Battiste and Jean Barman. Copyright © University of British Columbia Press, 1995. Reprinted with the permission of the publisher. All rights reserved.

Fagan, Kristina. "Codeswitching Humour in Aboriginal Literature," in *Across Cultures/Across Borders,* edited by P. DePasquale, R. Eigenbrod, and E. LaRocque. Copyright © 2010, Broadview Press. Reprinted with the permission of Broadview Press.

Fee, Margery. "Writing Orality: Interpreting Literature in English by Aboriginal Writers in North America, Australia and New Zealand," in *Journal of Intercultural Studies,* Volume 18, No. 1, 1997: 23–39. Reprinted with the permission of Taylor & Francis Ltd (http://www.tandfonline.com); permission conveyed through Copyright Clearance Center, Inc.

Highway, Tomson. "On Native Mythology," in *Theatrum* 6, Spring 1987: 29–31. Reprinted with the permission of Tomson Highway.

Hulan, Renee. Excerpts from "'Everybody likes the Inuit': Inuit Revision and Representations of the North," in *Northern Experience and the Myths of Canadian Culture,* edited by Renee Hulan. McGill-Queen's University Press, 2003. Reprinted with the permission of McGill-Queen's University Press.

Johnson, E. Pauline. "A Strong Race Opinion: on the Indian Girl in Modern Fiction," in *The Sunday Globe*, 22 May 1892.

Johnston, Basil. "One Generation from Extinction," in *Canadian Literature: Native Writers and Canadian Literature* No. 124–125, Spring and Summer 1990: 10–15. Reprinted with the permission of the Beverley Slopen Agency.

Justice, Daniel Heath. "The Necessity of Nationhood: Affirming the Sovereignty of Indigenous National Literatures," in *Moveable Margins*, edited by Chelva Kanaganayakam. Toronto: TSAR Publications, 2005. Reprinted with the permission of Daniel Heath Justice.

Keeshig, Lenore. "Stop Stealing Native Stories," in *The Globe and Mail*, 26 January 1990: A7. Reprinted with the permission of Lenore Keeshig-Tobias.

King, Thomas. "Godzilla vs. Post-Colonial," in *World Literature Written in English*, Volume 30.2, 1990: 10–16. Reprinted with the permission of Taylor & Francis Ltd (http://www.tandfonline.com).

Larocque, Emma. "Preface or Here Are Our Voices—Who Will Hear?" in *Writing the Circle: Native Women of Western Canada*, edited by Jeanne Perreault and Silvia Vance. NeWest Press, 1990. Reprinted with the permission of Emma Larocque.

Maracle, Lee. "Oratory: Coming to Theory," in *Give Back: First Nations Perspectives on Cultural Practice*, edited by Maria Campbell et al. Gallerie Publications, 1992. Reprinted with the permission of Lee Maracle.

Martin, Keavy. "Truth, Reconciliation and Amnesia: Porcupines and China Dolls and the Canadian Conscience," in ESC 35:1, March 2009: 47–65. Reprinted with the permission of Keavy Martin.

McKegney, Sam. "Indigenous Writing and the Residential School Legacy: A Public Interview with Basil Johnston," in Studies in Canadian Literature/Études en littérature canadienne, Volume 34, Issue 2, 2009. Reprinted with permission.

McLeod, Neal. "Coming Home Through Stories," in *(Ad)dressing Our Words: Aboriginal Perspectives on Aboriginal Literatures*, edited by Armand Garnet Ruffo. Theytus Books, 1990. Reprinted with the permission of Neal McLeod.

Momaday, N. Scott. "The Man Made of Words," (1970) from *Nothing But the Truth: An Anthology of Native American Literature*, edited by John L. Purdy and James Ruppert. New Jersey: Prentice Hall, 2001. Copyright © 1970, N. Scott Momaday.

Moses, Daniel David. "The Trickster's Laugh: My Meeting with Tomson and Lenore," in *American Indian Quarterly*, Volume 28, Issue 1 & 2. 2004: 107–11. University of Nebraska Press. Republished with the permission of the University of Nebraska Press; permission conveyed through Copyright Clearance Center, Inc.

Ruffo, Armand. "Why Native Literature?" in *American Indian Quarterly*, Volume 21, Issue 4. 1997: 663–74. University of Nebraska Press. Republished with the permission of the University of Nebraska Press; permission conveyed through Copyright Clearance Center, Inc.

Valaskakis, Gail Guthrie. "Parallel Voices: Indians and Others, Narratives of Cultural Struggle," in *Canadian Journal of Communications*, Volume 18, Issue 3, 1993: 283–96. Reprinted with the permission of the *Canadian Journal of Communications*.